A LITERARY TOUR DE FRANCE

Bibliothèque publique et universitaire de Neuchâtel (BPUN)

A LITERARY
TOUR DE FRANCE

———◦⋗◦⋖◦———

THE WORLD OF BOOKS ON THE EVE
OF THE FRENCH REVOLUTION

ROBERT DARNTON

OXFORD
UNIVERSITY PRESS

OXFORD
UNIVERSITY PRESS

Oxford University Press is a department of the University of Oxford.
It furthers the University's objective of excellence in research, scholarship,
and education by publishing worldwide. Oxford is a registered trade mark of
Oxford University Press in the UK and certain other countries.

Published in the United States of America by Oxford University Press
198 Madison Avenue, New York, NY 10016, United States of America.

© Robert Darnton 2018

Library of Congress Cataloging-in-Publication Data
Names: Darnton, Robert, author.
Title: A literary tour de France : the world of books on the eve of the
French Revolution / Robert Darnton.
Description: Oxford ; New York : Oxford University Press, [2018]
Identifiers: LCCN 2017015375 | ISBN 9780195144512 (hardcover : acid-free paper)
Subjects: LCSH: Book industries and trade-France-History-18th century. |
Booksellers and bookselling-France-History-18th century. | Books and
reading-France-History-18th century. | Book industries and
trade-Europe-History-18th century. | Favarger,
Jean-François-Travel-France. | Traveling sales
personnel-Switzerland-Biography. | Société typographique de
Neuchâtel-History. | Publishers and
publishing-Switzerland- Neuchâtel -History-18th century. | BISAC:
HISTORY / Europe / France. | HISTORY / Social History.
Classification: LCC Z305 .D34 2018 | DDC 070.50944/09033—dc23
LC record available at https://lccn.loc.gov/2017015375

1 3 5 7 9 8 6 4 2
Printed by Edwards Brothers Malloy, United States of America

CONTENTS

INTRODUCTION

The World of Books

THE WORLD OF BOOKS IN PRE-REVOLUTIONARY FRANCE was endlessly varied and rich—rich, that is, in the variety of human beings who inhabited it. As an economic system it remained mired in the corporate structures that had developed in the seventeenth century: a guild of printers and booksellers that monopolized the trade in Paris; a pre-copyright legal system based on the principle of privilege; a royal administration to direct censorship and resolve internecine disputes; inspectors of the book trade charged with enforcing regulations—some three thousand edicts issued during the eighteenth century; and, outside the creaky, baroque institutions of the Bourbon state, a large population of professionals who supported themselves by getting books to readers.

Booksellers existed in all the major towns, and they came in all stripes and colors. A few patriarchs dominated the trade in each provincial center. Around them lesser figures built up businesses, cashing in on the expansion of demand from the mid-century years onward and struggling to survive in the tougher conditions of the 1770s and 1780s. On the outer edges of the legal system, a few dealers scraped together a living as best they could, usually by supplying the capillary system of the trade. In addition to these professionals, all sorts of individuals developed micro-book businesses. They included small shopkeepers who occupied a legal place on the market by purchasing certificates ("*brevets de libraire*") from the royal administration;

private entrepreneurs with no claim to legality; itinerant dealers who manned stalls on market days; binders who sold books on the sly; and peddlers of all varieties, some with a horse and wagon, others who hawked their wares on foot. These scrappy, ragged middlemen (and middlewomen; many of the toughest were wives and widows) functioned as crucial intermediaries in the dissemination of literature. Yet literary history has taken little notice of them. Aside from some rare exceptions, they have disappeared into the past. One purpose of this book is to bring them back to life.

Another is to discover what they sold. The question of what books reached readers and how readers read them opens up larger issues about the nature of communication and ideological ferment. I do not address those problems directly in this work, but I hope to provide a thorough account of how the literary market functioned and how literature penetrated French society on the eve of the Revolution.

In order to do so, I intend to concentrate on the provincial dimension of the book trade. French history tends to be Paris-centric, yet less than 3 percent of France's population lived in Paris during the eighteenth century, and the provincials consumed the great majority of books. They received some of their supplies from Paris, certainly, but more often they filled their shelves with works produced outside France; for as soon as a book began to sell in the capital, it was pirated by publishers who operated outside the kingdom. "Piracy" (the French usually called it "*contrefaçon*" and also referred to *contrefacteurs* by saltier expressions such as "pirates" and "corsairs") is a misleading term, although it was used liberally in the eighteenth century, because the foreign houses operated outside the range of the privileges (*privilèges*) granted by the king of France. Within the kingdom, these privileges functioned as a primitive variety of copyright. Along with less formal authorizations known as "tacit permissions" (*permissions tacites*), they went only to books approved by a censor. The foreign publishers could reprint French books without concern for their privileges, and they could publish works that would never pass the censorship in France. Owing to economic conditions, especially the cost of paper, they also could turn out both kinds of books more economically than their French competitors. As a result, a fertile crescent of publishing houses grew up around France's borders, extending from Amsterdam and Brussels through the Rhineland to Switzerland and down to Avignon, which then was papal territory. These publishers, dozens of them, produced almost all the works of the Enlightenment and, I would say, the greater part of the current literature (books in all fields, except professional manuals, breviaries, devotional tracts, and chapbooks) that circulated in France from 1750 to 1789. They conquered French markets by diffusing their works through an extensive distribution system, some of it underground, especially in border areas, where smuggling was a major industry, but most of it organized along the ordinary arteries of commerce, where the middlemen plied their trade, turning whatever profit they could get.

This vast world, swarming with colorful characters, remained largely hidden from the French authorities in the eighteenth century—and from scholars ever since. Book historians have uncovered corners of it by consulting archives generated by the state authorities in Paris.[1] But the state had a limited perspective. Although the officials in charge of the book trade occupied an important place, known as the *Direction de la librairie*, within the royal administration, they had little knowledge of what really went on outside the city walls of Paris and the "*chambres syndicales*" or headquarters of the book guilds in a few other cities. To enjoy a broad view of the whole system, it is necessary to work through provincial archives and especially the papers of the foreign publishers. The latter, however, have almost entirely disappeared—except in one case: the archives of the Société typographique de Neuchâtel (STN), a Swiss publishing house across France's mountainous eastern border, which did a large wholesale trade everywhere in the kingdom while also producing its own editions.

The papers of the STN, supplemented by the material available in Paris and the provinces, contain thousands of letters from everyone connected with the book industry—authors, publishers, printers, paper millers, type founders, ink manufacturers, smugglers, wagon drivers, warehousemen, traveling salesmen, literary agents, reviewers, readers, and especially booksellers in virtually every town in France. Many of these persons turn up in other sources, such as bankruptcy papers and police records, making it possible to see them from several perspectives and to gain a multidimensional view of their activities. Other kinds of documents in Neuchâtel—account books, shipping records, registers of orders, the pay-book of the foreman in the printing shop—reveal other aspects of the trade. By combining all of them, one can understand how the entire industry functioned as a system—and how the system misfunctioned, broke down, and was repaired by the book professionals as they attempted to make supply meet demand.

The STN's offices were located in the large building to the left, facing the Lac de Neuchâtel.

View of the Basin, by Frédéric-William Moritz, circa 1820. Private collection.

During the period covered by the STN archives, 1769–1789, the legal constraints on the book trade kept shifting in response to changing policies of the French state. The ministries in Versailles, which also were constantly changing, issued a steady stream of decrees, redesigning measures against piracy, creating new guilds, extending the authority of the book police, revamping procedures for inspecting imports, and raising or lowering taxes on paper. The STN followed all these developments closely and adjusted its strategy in accordance with the information it received. Its papers, supplemented by the archives in Paris, therefore reveal the shifting rules of the game in the publishing industry, and, more important, they show how the game was played.

The archives of the STN are so vast, however, that a researcher could drown in them. I began to study them in 1965. Since then, I have spent fourteen summers and one winter reading nearly all of their fifty thousand letters and the complementary material in the STN's account books. It was a long haul but no hardship. Neuchâtel is a beautiful town at the foot of the Jura Mountains overlooking a lovely lake lined with vineyards.

The Neuchâtelois are wonderful, welcoming people. I made many friends among them, spent many happy hours hiking with them from alpage to alpage along the crests of the Jura, enjoyed countless meals in their homes, and watched my children grow up with theirs during constant visits over the course of fifty years. They are thanked in the acknowledgments of this book. But having spent so much time in Neuchâtel and also in Paris searching through related archives, I faced a challenge: how to do justice to the richness of this material. If I recounted all the stories of all the characters I encountered, my book would run to many volumes. Therefore, I have included a large selection of the documents and my earlier publications in an open-access website: www.robertdarnton.org. Readers who want to pursue topics raised in this book can consult the website and find their own paths through the digitized sources. The website relieves me of the need to overload this book with notes, but it does not provide an answer to the problem of ordering my narrative in a way that will get across the somewhat esoteric side of the subject without losing the reader's interest. I have therefore presented my research in an unconventional manner. Instead of composing a systematic treatise, I decided to follow the trail of a sales rep from the STN as he traveled across France and to discuss the most important aspects of the book trade as he encountered them, filling in the picture from the richest dossiers in the archives.

The sales rep or *commis voyageur* (the British prefer the term commercial traveler, and Americans often favor traveling salesman) was a twenty-nine-year-old clerk of the STN named Jean-François Favarger. On July 5, 1778, he climbed on a horse and set out on a five-month journey through France, visiting nearly every bookstore on his route. He sold books, collected bills, arranged shipping, inspected printing shops, sounded markets, sized up businesses, and assessed the character of more than a hundred booksellers. When he arrived back in Neuchâtel in November, Favarger knew more about the book trade than any historian can ever hope to know. Fortunately, he left a paper trail—a detailed diary and meticulous letters—that makes it possible to follow him around France and, by doing so, to investigate the book trade at street level. Moreover, the archives of the STN also contain hundreds of letters by the booksellers Favarger met, along with thousands more by everyone connected with the publishing industry from 1769 to 1789. Favarger's tour de France therefore opens up a vast landscape of literary culture.

Seen from the perspective of a sales rep, literature looks less grand than when studied as a corpus of great books by great writers. I do not mean to disparage that old-fashioned view, described in France by the formula *l'homme et l'oeuvre*, although it no longer commands much respect among literary scholars. On the contrary, I find inspiration in masterpieces like Balzac's *Lost Illusions*, which gives a fictional account of the world I am attempting to reconstruct from archival material, a world that fell apart ten years before Balzac's birth (1799). My purpose is to explore the Ancien Régime of books as it was experienced and understood by book professionals, beginning with a humble traveling salesman. Far from being an exercise in antiquarianism, this approach is meant to lead from minute details to broad conclusions. It will address questions about the practices of publishing, the diffusion of books, the operations of the book market, the role of booksellers as cultural intermediaries, and the demand for literature. In the end, I hope to show what books actually circulated on the literary marketplace during the twenty years before the French Revolution. Despite the imperfections of the data, I will offer retrospective best-seller lists, which illustrate the taste for literature in different parts of the country. Who the readers were and how they made sense of their reading I cannot say, owing to lack of evidence; but I think it possible to reconstruct their patterns of consumption, whatever it may mean to consume a book.

A second purpose is to examine a subject that fascinated Balzac: the tone of life as lived by ordinary people in obscure sectors of society. I want to understand the lives of booksellers and the milieu of the middlemen engaged in getting books to readers. Booksellers appear only as shadows, if at all, in the history of literature. When seen from the viewpoint of a sales rep and studied from the archives of a publisher, they emerge as complex individuals made of flesh and blood. They come in all shapes and sizes, from guild syndics and dynastic patriarchs to *bouquinistes* and underground peddlers.

In the fullest dossiers, one can follow the trajectory of a career. After an apprenticeship, a man finds a woman with a dowry, marries, sets up shop on his own, builds an inventory, takes risks, scores coups, fights off bankruptcy, falls ill, and dies, leaving the business to a son, or in many cases a shrewd and savvy widow. Another dossier contains the story of a village schoolmaster who sells books on the side but rarely earns enough to pay for the shipments he receives. He takes in lodgers, cultivates a tiny vineyard, and dies, while clinging to the hope that the next harvest will bring in the cash required to honor his signature on a pending bill of exchange. A dossier crammed with misspelled and crudely scribbled notes reveals the business of a *marchand forain* or itinerant dealer, who signs his promissory notes from an inn because he has no fixed address. He loads his stock on a wagon and flogs it at country fairs, as long as his horse holds out. If the animal collapses or his purse runs dry, he fails to show up at the inn when the notes become due, and the bailiff writes him off as an adventurer with a *domicile en l'air*. The dossiers document endless varieties of the human comedy as it played out in the world of books more than two centuries ago.

Through them all runs a theme that also fascinated Balzac: the lust for money. Of course, one must allow for a bias inherent in the sources, because most of the dossiers contain business letters, which have to do above all with profits and losses. But the letters also convey the feel and folkways of a particular kind of capitalism—not just the desire to hear the ring of gold coins (*écus bien sonnants*) but the need for trust (*confiance*) in a game fraught with danger, one in which all the players scrambled to avoid being duped by the tricks of the trade: pirating, smuggling, spying, bluffing, staging fraudulent bankruptcies, and conducting operations *sous le manteau* (under the cloak) or *sous le comptoir* (under the counter).

Of course, such practices proliferated in the nineteenth century, when Balzac studied them, and they can be found in other times and places. But there is a peculiar rawness to the eighteenth-century book trade that comes through dramatically in many of the dossiers. A bookseller—or a publisher, a peddler, a smuggler, a shipping agent—fails to redeem a bill of exchange on its date of maturity. Other notes become due. He teeters on the brink of bankruptcy, negotiates a deal with his most relentless creditors, regains a foothold, then slips, falls, and disappears. A letter from a neighbor or a bill collector brings the story to a close: "Left the keys under the door"; "Enrolled in the army"; "Gone to Russia"; "Shipped out to the war in America"; "His wife and children are begging at the door of the church." Not that one can take the letters literally. They always have a slant, always argue for an interest, and never provide an unmediated view of reality. Yet for all their subjectivity, or because of it, they show how reality was construed in a vital subculture of the Ancien Régime.

Moreover, the letters of the booksellers can be read against the testimony of Jean-François Favarger, our sales rep. His mission was to assess the character and business of every bookseller in his path. Favarger's tour de France therefore provides the main thread to which a great many stories are attached. By following him city by city and hamlet by hamlet around the map of France, one can see how numerous lives were woven together in a general effort to make supply meet demand in the realm of literature.

Despite its picaresque character, Favarger's story belongs to economics and sociology as well as literary history. In recounting it, I have tried to bring out its general implications and to avoid the temptation of straying too far into biographical territory. But I have included two dozen biographies on the website, which can serve, in effect, as a portrait gallery of eighteenth-century booksellers. The website also contains transcriptions of Favarger's diary, his correspondence with the STN, the booksellers' letters, and extensive information about the cities they inhabited—population, manufacturing, trade, literacy rates, administrative bodies, cultural institutions, contemporary reports on printing and bookselling, and reference to the secondary literature. Because the website includes so much—digitized versions of all the original manuscripts, documents about policing the book trade, and dozens of articles that I have written over the past forty-five years—I have tried to keep this book relatively short. Readers who want to discover more about particular themes can trace them through the website, using the documentation to develop fresh interpretations and to challenge my conclusions.

This book, in short, tells a story that is meant to hold up on its own yet can be pursued further by consulting an encyclopedic digital database. It can be read in many ways. At the very least, I hope it will bring pleasure to those who want to explore an endlessly interesting subject, the world of books in eighteenth-century France.

I should add a note on terminology. Because the names of institutions from the Ancien Régime do not translate easily into English, I have kept many of them in French. "*Parlement*" refers to the superior or "sovereign" law courts that had some political power but did not remotely resemble the British Parliament. The "Ferme générale" was a private corporation that collected indirect taxes, administered the customs service, and patrolled borders for the French state. "*Livres philosophiques*" was a term used by publishers and booksellers to describe the most forbidden books in their trade. The books might contain philosophically radical ideas, such as attacks on Christian dogma, but they also might be pornographic or seditious or libelous in their references to the private lives of public fig-ures. "*Acquits à caution*" were customs bond notes used by the authorities to keep track of shipments of books. As explained in chapter 2, smugglers and shipping agents had to devise ways of expediting *acquits à caution* in order to prevent shipments from being confiscated. "*Chambres syndicales*" were the headquarters of book guilds in provincial cities where shipments were inspected and "*acquits à caution*" processed ("*déchargés*" or discharged in the parlance of the customs service).

As I do not expect readers to be familiar with the titles that appear in this book or to have a thorough knowledge of French, I have added a translation of the titles in square brackets after they first appear, except in obvious cases such as *Lettre de M. Linguet à M. le comte de Vergennes.*

A Literary Tour de France

I

Neuchâtel

Our Man on Mission

ONE WAY TO GET TO KNOW A SALES REP is to study his expense account. Favarger's expenses, calculated carefully in the French currency of livres, sous, and deniers, appear at the end of his diary.[1] They provide a preview of his journey.[2]

Neuchâtel as it appeared in 1778. The cleft in the mountains, known as the "*trou de Bourgogne*" (hole of Burgundy), indicates the route up the Val de Travers to Pontarlier, the first stop on Favarger's travels.

View of Neuchâtel, from the hill of Crêt, by Goltz, 1826, oil on canvas. Private collection.

Before setting out on his horse, he had his coat repaired: 1 livre, 3 sous disbursed in La Neuveville, his hometown, ten miles north of Neuchâtel, on July 3, 1778, two days before he took to the road. The garment probably was a *redingote* (riding coat), a solid piece of cloth waxed to withstand rain, not at all comparable to the finery that gentlemen wore, with fancy trimming and double rows of well-wrought buttons. Favarger needed protection from the elements. They were kind to him on the first leg of the journey. But in August, when he reached the lower valley of the Rhône, the sun beat down on him relentlessly and the redingote probably was tied across his saddlebags. Favarger encountered very little water, even in riverbeds, until September 6, when he entered Carcassonne. Then it began to pour. From Toulouse to La Rochelle, it hardly stopped. Favarger had to buy a new hat: 10 livres. And he had put up with so much friction in the saddle that he also had to purchase a new pair of breeches: 26 livres, both for the breeches and for a quilt to get him through the chilly nights that set in at the beginning of October. The roads were then so muddy that his horse slipped and fell several times a day. He took to leading it by the bridle and walked so far under such bad conditions that he wore through his boots: 3 livres, 3 sous for resoling. Sweating under the summer sun in Languedoc and shivering through the autumn muck in Poitou, Favarger did not cut much of a figure on the road. He probably smelled when he arrived at country inns. Only twice on the entire circuit did he enter expenses for laundry: 1 livre, 10 sous in Toulouse and 1 livre, 4 sous in Tonneins—the rough equivalent each time of a day's wages for one of the STN's printers. He carried a hunting knife and a brace of pistols, which he had worked over by a gunsmith in Marseilles—10 sous—after being warned about highwaymen on the road to Toulon.

Not that Favarger looked like a highwayman himself, despite the dirt and dust that accumulated on his redingote. He had to be presentable when he walked into a well-appointed bookshop on the high street of a city. After his arrival in Lyon, he bought himself a suit with a waistcoat: 23 livres, 4 sous, 6 deniers for fabric ("voile" or light cotton) and tailoring. That was an important sum for a clerk—5 percent of his annual wages—but not an extravagance. Further along his route he treated himself twice to ribbons (12 sous each) for binding the tress of hair that he wore down the back of his neck. He was not the sort to wear a wig or carry a sword. Like many journeymen, however, he had a watch: repaired in September for 2 livres, 8 sous. And when in company, he exchanged his boots for shoes: he purchased a new pair for 4 livres, 10 sous in Toulouse. Favarger's expense account provides a rare opportunity to picture someone from the lower strata of society two centuries ago. Yet the picture quickly blurs. We do not know the color of his eyes.

It is possible, however, to form some notion of the young man's character. The style of his letters is straightforward and unadorned, the grammar and penmanship excellent, as befitted a clerk. Favarger must have had a good basic education, though he did not attempt the rhetorical flourishes and literary allusions that sometimes decorated the letters of his superiors, the directors of the STN, who were accomplished men of letters. His was a business correspondence, so one should not read too much into it. But insofar as it expressed a turn of mind, it suggests someone serious, eager to please, hard-working, and rather self-effacing. Favarger took the world in at street level, eyeing it squarely and describing it in no-nonsense language: subject, verb, predicate. On rare occasions he showed a touch of humor. He characterized the book inspector of Marseilles as "one of those men who would eat his brother in order to have a meal," and Buchet, a bookseller in Nîmes, as "something of a camera obscura." But he did not go in for figurative language and rarely used the colloquialisms peculiar to the book trade—expressions such as the compliment that he paid to Malherbe, an illegal book dealer in Loudun: "He is very good at selling his shells" [*"Il sait fort bien vendre ses coquilles"*].

Favarger may have been modest but he was no pushover. He negotiated hard with booksellers and did not hesitate to take debtors to court. When Cazaméa, a dealer in Toulouse (the documents often do not give first names), tried to bully him into reducing the fixed prices of the STN's books and then, in a fit of temper, tore up an order, Favarger stood his ground. He was not impressed with Faulcon, syndic of the bookseller's guild in Poitiers, who strode about town "puffed up with his office." Nor did he appreciate the pretentious manner of the patricians in Lyon, who claimed that they could not spare time to negotiate with him and in fact spent more of the day dining than tending their shops. Booksellers farther south, like Chambeau in Avignon and Phéline in Uzès, belonged to a different breed: all talk and no business. The lazy and loquacious did not receive high marks in Favarger's reports to the home office. When he encountered palaver, intrigue, and *dolce farniente*, especially among clients in the Midi, he wrote as if he had come up against a foreign civilization—and indeed he had: he was a good Swiss in a world of inscrutable French.

Despite its commercial character, Favarger's correspondence provides hints about the way he saw that world. It was not entirely businesslike in tone, because he knew his employers well and could confide in them. They were, to be sure, his social superiors—wealthy and learned gentlemen, who commanded a great deal of respect in the small world of Neuchâtel; so he always wrote in a deferential manner. Yet they had invested confidence in him, having hired him as a youth and trained him in their shop. They entrusted him with some delicate negotiations and expected him to send confidential reports on every bookseller that he encountered. His running commentary on the human element in the trade therefore suggests something about his own views as well as the tradesmen themselves. He expressed most sympathy for booksellers in small towns, who bargained in a forthright manner, accepted reasonable terms, took few risks, paid their bills on time, and enjoyed a solid reputation among their neighbors. For example, Pierre le Portier in Castres, received a favorable report: "He seems to do a good business, because his shop is well assorted. He has the look of a decent fellow, and promised me he would soon send an order to the home office." Having taken soundings with local merchants, Favarger rated le Portier's credit as "very good": "You can entrust shipments to him in full confidence. People spoke very favorably of him to me. He is fairly well off, despite the obstacles put in the way of booksellers in small towns who sell pirated works."

Not many booksellers received such high marks, for Favarger had spent enough time sniffing around shops on earlier trips to cure himself of any naiveté about the morals of businessmen. He often encountered rogues and cheats, like Buchet of Nîmes, who was secretly squandering his wife's dowry, and Caldesaigues of Marseilles, who tried to cut a surreptitious deal on his debts after declaring bankruptcy. Although he deplored such behavior, Favarger understood the necessity of dealing with imperfect human beings, especially in the vast illegal sector of the trade. His remarks about booksellers sound realistic but not cynical, critical but not prudish. On rare occasions, he gave vent to indignation. For example, when Vernarel, a bookseller in Bourg-en-Bresse, ordered a shipment of a new book from its publisher in Paris and then sent a copy to the STN for pirating, he exclaimed, "What a character! Didn't he think he would compromise his conscience by sending us the book that I spoke about to you in my last letter?"

In general, however, Favarger reported on business practices, some of them dubious or illegal, without moralizing. He sold plenty of pornographic and irreligious works, treating them and everything off color (*"scabreux"*) in a matter-of-fact manner as articles of trade. The booksellers responded in kind. Only once did Favarger come across a dealer who mixed ideology with business, and that encounter astonished him: "Arles. Gaudion is pure gold, but he is a curious character.... When I spoke to him about the Bible and the *Encyclopédie*, he replied that he was too good a Catholic to try to spread two such impious works, that all the *Encyclopédies* had been offered to him, but that he would certainly not sell any."

The Bible was impious in the eyes of this bookseller because it was a Protestant edition, full of heretical commentary. As a good Swiss Protestant himself, Favarger entered alien territory when he pushed down the Rhône Valley and deep into France's Catholic heartland. Upon arriving in Marseilles, he was disappointed to find all the shops closed, as it was the day before the Assumption of the Virgin: "The cannon in the fort and the ships are booming out wonderfully now in honor of the Virgin Mary." Strange sounds to Protestant ears. Favarger was shocked by the "bigotry" in Toulouse and repulsed by the intolerant attitude of the book inspector there and in Marseilles. Having heard rumors that Louis XVI was about to restore civic rights to Protestants—they had been denied all such rights, including the right to inherit property and be legally married, by the revocation of the Edict of Nantes in 1685—he expected a sympathetic reception in the inspection offices (*chambres syndicales*) of the provincial guilds. In fact, many guild officials promised to look the other way when shipments of Protestant books arrived from Neuchâtel. But Favarger felt he was being eyed suspiciously, as both a heretic and as an agent of a foreign publisher.

Those qualities complemented each other, because the underground channels for diffusing Protestant books in the sixteenth century had opened a way for the Enlightenment two hundred years later. From Pierre Bayle to Jean-Jacques Rousseau, philosophers with a Protestant upbringing had given a particular inflection to radical thought; and from Amsterdam to Geneva, Protestant publishers made use of the Huguenot diaspora in order to market the works of the philosophes along with

Protestant books. Favarger was no intellectual, but he acted as an agent of Enlightenment simply by going about his business. His employers provided him with books to sell, and he sold the Bible along with the *Encyclopédie*, as if they were perfectly compatible. In the context of the eighteenth-century book trade, they were.

Although Favarger may have had his own ideas about philosophical questions, he never expressed them in his business dealings. Nothing in his letters or diary suggests that personal convictions influenced his activities as a book salesman. He simply was born a Protestant and took his Protestantism with him when he traveled. It was a way of being that probably came naturally to him—one that made him feel comfortable in the company of Protestants in France. He could relax among people of his own sort, people who worked hard, talked straight, and paid their bills on time. To be sure, they included a few reprobates, like the pastor Dumont in Tonneins, who sold off his shipment of STN Bibles and then refused to pay for it. But as a rule, Favarger relied on fellow Protestants as people who could be trusted in alien territory, where they still had no civil rights. French Huguenots relied on trust among themselves and had to do so in order to survive centuries of persecution.

Thanks to the long lines of kinship and friendship that bound the French and Swiss Protestants, Favarger could count on help in finding his way around France. He kept a list of Huguenot pastors in his diary, and received hospitality from Huguenots everywhere he went. They also gave him letters of recommendation to others of their religion so that he could draw on reserves of local knowledge and support when he tried to settle accounts and extract orders from Catholic booksellers. In Nîmes he went to hear the great Protestant leader Paul Rabaut preach "in the desert"—that is, outdoors and outside the city limits, because Huguenots were not allowed to worship publicly in churches of their own. Rabaut and his son, the future revolutionary Jean-Paul Rabaut Saint-Etienne, were friends of the STN's principal director, Frédéric-Samuel Ostervald, and they provided Favarger with the addresses of still more Protestant pastors to contact along the rest of his route.

He also received a warm reception from Protestant laymen who had studied in Neuchâtel, often in the boarding school where Ostervald himself gave lessons in arithmetic and geography during the 1750s. Ostervald should not be confused with the humble variety of village schoolmaster, however. He was a wealthy patrician, deeply involved in local politics, but he seems to have been an inspiring teacher as well as statesman. One of his most devoted former students, a merchant named Jean Ranson, provided hospitality for Favarger in La Rochelle and described their time together in a letter. Favarger, he wrote, "has a frankness that is rare among the French and commonplace in your country. I asked him if he had not studied in the *collège* [secondary school] of Neuchâtel. No, Monsieur, he replied. It was at the one in La Favarge, where M. Ostervald took me away from the field I was plowing by asking me to be his clerk, and I became his clerk." Taking measure of Favarger's social graces, Ranson asked him whether he played a musical instrument. "Ah, Monsieur, he said to me. Don't expect to find that I have a talent for anything. I have absolutely none at all." Ranson had not encountered such modesty in the upper ranks of the provincial bourgeoisie, and he was impressed. "There is nothing like good faith of that kind to win my affection."[3] This is the only description of Favarger that exists in the papers of the STN, but it confirms the impression of a self-effacing but self-reliant young man that is conveyed by his letters.

The letters also contain a few hints about his personal relations. When he arrived in Lyon, Favarger sent greetings to his fellow clerks in the STN "whom I embrace" and asked them to pass on a letter to his sister. "*Messieurs les collègues*," as he called them, belonged to the "*comptoir*" or front office, a fairly intimate little world in which three or four clerks busied themselves with accounts, inventory, and shipments, while the STN's directors dictated letters and checked on work in the printing shop, where twenty to thirty workers fed a dozen presses. Favarger seemed to be on friendly terms with the other clerks. In a postscript to a letter from Marmande, he singled out two of them for special greetings: Abram David Mercier, the main bookkeeper, and Schwartz, an apprentice or trainee, who was perfecting his knowledge of the book trade after completing his studies in Colmar. Schwartz had made a note in Favarger's diary, asking him, when he arrived in Colmar, to give "a thousand greetings" to his friends and family, notably M. Billing, his teacher in secondary school, who could provide information about booksellers in Tübingen and Stuttgart. Favarger never got that far, but the note suggests the networks of personal contacts that underlay his commercial dealings.

In another postscript, Favarger sent his respectful regards to the wives of Ostervald and Jean-Elie Bertrand, Ostervald's son-in-law and fellow director. He also inquired about their pet dog: "Is the little doggie (*le petit toutou*) sick? I dreamt last night that he was dead." A clerk who dreamed about the pet of his boss's wife was no alienated worker. Favarger always used the first-person plural when he referred to the affairs of the STN, even in the privacy of his diary: "our Bibles," "our interests," "our house." His remarks about business in his letters to the home office communicated a sense that they were all in it together; and the office—that is, as a rule, Ostervald, who handled the STN's correspondence—showed concern for his welfare. When Favarger left Lyon, which he had visited two years earlier, and headed off into unfamiliar territory, Ostervald wrote encouragingly: "Bon voyage: do good business and have a good time. We will be mindful of the care you take of your health and the efforts you make to fulfill your tasks."

"La Grande Rochette," the family home of Abram Bosset de Luze, who joined the STN as one of its directors in 1777. A wealthy merchant connected with the manufacturing of calicoes and banking, Bosset managed the STN's financial affairs. The grandeur of his house and gardens indicates the patrician character of these publishers who were scorned as pirates in France.

La Grande Rochette seen from the south, by Théophile Steinlen, circa 1805, watercolor. Private collection.

The difficulties faced by solitary travelers on eighteenth-century roads are hard to imagine today. Favarger never had to use his pistols, but he came down with a nasty case of scabies—a rash caused by mites burrowing into the skin—after leaving Avignon: "I will have myself bled one day and purged [presumably by means of an enema] the other. That is the advice of the surgeon I consulted." Once his own health improved, that of his horse began to fail. Having slogged with the animal over hundreds of miles, Favarger seems to have become attached to it. He reported regularly on its condition and wrote worried letters when it began to falter under the storms that pounded down in September. Back in Neuchâtel, Ostervald answered, "We are more concerned about your health than that of your horse."

It would be a mistake to take a sentimental view of the relations between man and beast. Life on the road was rugged. The roads themselves were miserable—dirt trails, potted with holes and clogged with mud, except for a few avenues that led directly to Paris.[4] Inns provided little relief after a hard day on horseback. Their food and filth, equally execrable, was a favorite subject of travelers, especially those who had experienced innkeeping in England like Tobias Smollett, the Scottish novelist: "Throughout the South of France, except in large cities, the inns are cold, humid, dark, sad, full of dust; the innkeepers are both unhelpful and rapacious; the servants are clumsy, dirty, feckless; the postilions are lazy, glutinous, and impertinent." Arthur Young, the English agronomist, whose route in the south was similar to Favarger's, described his inn in Saint-Girons as "a place of the most execrable filth, vermin, impudence and dupery that has ever tried the patience or wounded the sentiments of a traveler."[5]

In later years, after Favarger had left the STN, it hired another *commis voyageur*, Jacob-François Bornand. He had toured France for years and usually traveled by coach, yet he had a harder time than Favarger, both on the road (he was injured when his coach flipped over) and in the bookshops. In 1784 he wrote from Lyon:[6] "I find neither good faith nor delicacy here.... You must know from experience, Messieurs, how difficult it is to settle anything here. I believe I have not done anything to neglect your interests. It would drive me to despair if I thought you could possibly suspect that. But, I repeat, I just want to return home." Paris was even worse:[7] "The long and usually useless errands that you have to do here and the constant postponements that people make on the smallest and most trivial of pretexts cause business to be disgusting and make my stay in this city the most unpleasant that I have ever experienced. You walk around here in muck up to the level of doorsteps. Snow and rain succeed each other alternatively.... The cold is unbearable."

Experiences varied, of course, but all sales reps performed the same functions, and they could be found everywhere in the book trade of France.[8] No important publisher in late-eighteenth-century Europe could do without a sales rep. Every year or two he would select a trustworthy clerk from the home office and send him on a mission, defining his tasks and setting his itinerary according to the exigencies of the moment. The trip might take only a week, to settle a contested account in a nearby city or to scout for fresh supplies of paper from a particular area. Or it could take months, cover vast distances, and involve all aspects of the book business, as was the case with Favarger. Sales reps were constantly crisscrossing the map of Europe. Obscure as they were, they left many traces in the archives of the STN. When the directors of the STN discussed the trade with allied publishers during a trip to Paris in 1777, for example, Clément Plomteux of Liège told them that he was sending a "*commis*" on a "tour de la France" to sell encyclopedias.[9] This was standard practice, which they reported in a matter-of-fact manner to the home office. *Commis voyageurs* of this kind often came through Neuchâtel on business for other publishers, and the agents of the STN frequently crossed paths with them in the field. On an earlier trip, Favarger discovered that a sales rep of the Société typographique de Lausanne was a few towns ahead of him, creaming off the demand for books in Savoy.[10] He also trailed behind a sales rep of Samuel Fauche, a rival publisher in Neuchâtel, who was touring Languedoc in 1778. Fauche's man sold many of the same books as Favarger, often at a lower price, according to the reports that circulated through the bookshops; but he stayed longer at each stop, and his health was said to be failing. Overexposure to the southern sun made him retreat to a sickbed in Montpellier, so Favarger hoped to overtake him. Meanwhile, in Toulon, Favarger met up with Amable Le Roy, the sales rep of Joseph Duplain of Lyon, one of the STN's partners in its speculation on the quarto edition of the *Encyclopédie*. Le Roy was returning to his home office after a swing through the south that had taken him as far as Bordeaux. They spent a happy evening together in an inn, swapping stories about selling encyclopedias.

Encounters of that sort were common, because the sales reps followed similar circuits, checking out the same bookshops and checking in at the same inns. Despite their rivalry, they got to know one another and had a common interest in exchanging information about conditions in the trade. Some could expect to rise through the ranks, because they were sons of master booksellers who were beginning to function as publishers in the modern sense of the word—that is, to speculate on editions of new works, either by jobbing out the printing or by doing it themselves, while concentrating in the wholesale trade. But most sales reps spent their lives in the lower levels of the publishing industry. To break into it as youths, they had to have good penmanship, a solid secondary education (reading, writing, and enough arithmetic to work through accounts in livres, sous, and deniers), and contacts through family or friends. They would sign on with a publisher as a clerk (*commis*), usually, it seems, with a contract for three years. Their normal run of duties—tending to the commercial correspondence, drawing up accounts, supervising shipments from the warehouse—made them familiar with their employers' network of allies among publishers and of customers among booksellers, both in France and, in the case of the big Swiss houses, most of Europe. The clerks would travel as the needs arose, on swings through a few cities or tours across several countries. As they traveled, they accumulated knowledge—the kind of knowledge that was crucial in the eighteenth-century publishing industry. It was concrete and intensely human. An intelligent sales rep learned which booksellers were teetering toward bankruptcy, which syndics dominated *chambres syndicales*, which inspectors had the keenest eye for pirated editions, which shipping agents knew the safest routes, which wagon drivers did not get mired in mud, and above all which customers throughout the entire system would honor bills of exchange. Such a sales rep could make a fortune for a publisher. At times, he might be tempted to move on to another job where the pay was better and the traveling less arduous. If he accumulated enough contacts and capital—the best source being a young woman with a dowry—he might set up shop for himself, either as a bookseller or in another branch of commerce. If he failed, he would take to the road like the journeymen printers on their own tours de France.

Favarger's career seems to have been something of a success story, although it is difficult to follow before and after his employment with the

STN.[11] The first letter in his dossier is dated September 2, 1775. He was then twenty-six years old and reporting to the STN from Geneva, where he was trying to settle its accounts with some local booksellers. His employers probably were pleased with the results, because in August 1776 they sent him on a long tour to sell books and establish relations with retailers in Savoy, Dauphiné, Lyonnais, and Burgundy. He made two short trips into the Franche-Comté and western Switzerland in 1777, mainly to scout for new sources of paper. In 1778 he made his five-month tour de France, which is the subject of this book. And he took two trips for the STN in March 1782 and February 1783. The first was a failed attempt to rescue a speculation on the works of Rousseau in Geneva, the second, an unsuccessful mission to renegotiate the terms for an edition of Raynal's *Histoire philosophique* with another Genevan publisher and then to reconstruct a smuggling route from Besançon. With experience and age, Favarger had taken on heavier responsibilities. Meanwhile, the STN was falling into debt. It suspended payments for a while in 1784 and then was reorganized under new management so that it could continue business on a smaller scale while selling off its stock. By then, two of the STN's three directors, Abram Bosset de Luze and Jean-Elie Bertrand, were dead. Fréderic-Samuel Ostervald continued to participate in its direction, but not as its principal partner. He was seventy, and Favarger, whom he had hired about ten years earlier, had turned thirty-four. While continuing to work for the STN, Favarger had invested in a grocery business founded by his brother Samuel in 1776. Although the documents are not clear, they suggest that he joined Samuel as a full-time partner and left the world of books sometime in 1783.[12]

The only document that actually lays out the terms of Favarger's employment with STN is a contract dated December 18, 1776, but it, too, is disappointingly imprecise. It simply says that he was to serve as a "*commis*" for three years and to be paid 400 Neuchâtel francs (the equivalent of 572 French livres tournois) for 1777, 450 francs (643 livres, 10 sous) for 1778, and 550 francs (786 livres, 10 sous) for 1779 with a bonus of 6 louis d'or (144 livres) if the STN was pleased with his work.[13] Since Favarger joined the firm fresh off the farm—"from the field I was plowing," as he had told Ranson—and received his training on the job, the contract did not need to specify his functions.[14] Fortunately, however, one can get a clearer picture of the relations between a sales rep and a publisher from the dossier of his successor, Jacob-François Bornand.

Bornand first contacted the STN in August 1769, as soon as he had learned of its existence. He wrote from Lausanne and offered his services as a clerk, "for tending to the correspondence as well as shipments, keeping accounts, and providing help in the printing shop."[15] Although the Neuchâtelois could not hire him at that time, it offered him a position, presumably to replace Favarger, in 1783. On August 26 Bornand signed a contract, which stipulated that he would work for three years as a "*commis*" for an annual salary of 840 Neuchâtel francs (1,200 livres tournois) and an increase at the end of the first year, provided there was "mutual satisfaction."[16] The pay came to a great deal more than what Favarger had earned, presumably because Bornand was older and more experienced. He was to work primarily in "the book trade sector, receiving and sending shipments and keeping the relevant accounts while devoting his free time to the ordinary tasks of the office such as correspondence and auxiliary bookkeeping." The contract also specified that he would be expected to travel for the STN's interests, the terms for each trip to be negotiated in the future according to their "reciprocal advantage."

Just what that meant became clear six months after Bornand began work, when he was given formal instructions for a trip that was intended to cover Germany and Italy, although the STN canceled it after he had made a preliminary tour through French Switzerland and eastern France. The STN was then trying to recover from its brush with bankruptcy and to restore order in its affairs by selling off its stock. It gave Bornand formal power of attorney so that he could negotiate freely in its name, and in its instructions it provided him with guidelines for the negotiations. In sales for cash—that is, bills of exchange payable immediately to the bearer—he could reduce the normal price of its books by 30 percent, or, if pushed, even by 35 percent. In other sales, he should take bills of exchange that would become due in eight to twelve months, offering a discount of 1 percent for every month of an earlier maturation date. He was to carry a catalog, which would provide guidelines for the bargaining, because after each title the STN would note the lowest price that it would accept and the number of copies it had in stock. He was also empowered to trade books—that is, to exchange books in the STN's warehouse for those in the stock of other publishers and wholesalers, striking the best possible bargain. Exchanges were crucial in the publishing business, as the instructions explained: "Exchanges cannot be a burden to us; on the contrary, they help us sell off our stock by adding variety to it and thus bring in a profit that we could never expect to make without this kind of transaction. It is a kind, however, that calls for all the sagacity and understanding that sieur Bornand can muster. We therefore leave him entirely free in arranging deals of this sort."

Precisely why and how exchanges were so important to publishers is a subject to be taken up later. At this point it need only be said that anyone who negotiated exchanges had to have a profound knowledge of the book trade. By swapping books that he possessed in large number for books that he thought he could sell, a publisher could vary his stock and accelerate his turnover. But if he misjudged demand or failed to foresee some contingency—the value of the books he procured might be undercut by a new pirated edition or they might be badly printed on cheap paper—he courted disaster. In this as in all his other functions, a sales rep had to be an expert at sizing up people as well as the market. The STN's instructions to Bornand specified that he would provide reports on all the booksellers he encountered, especially those with whom it had not yet done business. It needed information on their moral as well as their financial soundness. In short, a good sales rep had to be something of a psychologist, an economist, and an investigative reporter (as we would say today) in addition to being an expert in the art of selling books.

In Favarger's case, the purposes of his trip were specified in instructions, which the directors of the STN had written into the first pages of his diary. As in the diaries for other trips by commercial travelers, the instructions provided both an itinerary and a strategy for handling the STN's business at each stop. Favarger's tour de France, however, was the most ambitious ever undertaken by a representative of the STN, and the guidelines for it provided a remarkable briefing about the state of the book trade in 1778. They fill thirty-six pages. At first a clerk—young Schwartz, judging by the handwriting—entered the names of the towns along Favarger's route and listed the STN's correspondents in each of them. Then he added a summary of the most important points in the correspondents' dossiers and turned the diary over to Ostervald, who inserted notes in the blank spaces between each entry. The notes concerned the more difficult topics, and they proved to be so extensive that Ostervald appended another whole set of instructions and apparently spliced in remarks from his codirectors, Bosset and Bertrand, on subjects that especially concerned them, such as bills to be collected and provisions to be ordered for the printing shop. In the end, therefore, the instructions looked like a palimpsest: writing piled on writing, phrases added here and crossed out there, references and reminders in several hands squeezed between lines and crowded into margins.

Favarger clearly had his work cut out for him. Most of it was highly specific—settling an account with a client in this town, cultivating an agent of the *chambre syndicale* in that one. It concerned the same tasks that he had performed successfully on earlier, shorter journeys: arrangements

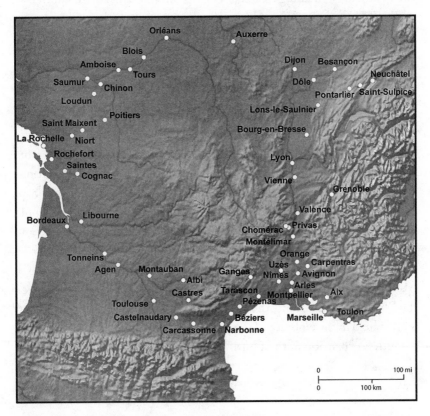

The main stops along Favarger's tour de France.
Scott Walker, Cartography Section of the Harvard Library.

with smugglers, procurement of paper, investigation of the credit of clients as well as the general mission of selling books. But there was a new tone. The STN had expanded its printing shop in order to produce its allotment of volumes in the gigantic quarto editions of the *Encyclopédie*, and it was eager to embark on new speculations. The demand for books seemed to be soaring, especially in fields like travel, novels, history, some natural sciences, and "*livres philosophiques*," the expression used by booksellers to describe the most illegal varieties of literature. Although the STN had established relations with booksellers in all the major cities in France, it wanted to enlarge its distribution network and what is known today as "market share." In the final pages of the instructions, the directors summarized the purposes of Favarger's trip and stressed that he was to "gather information about all booksellers, especially the new ones that you get to know, making clear agreements on the terms for all sales."

The STN expressed its ambition to conquer new markets in the itinerary that it traced for Favarger. He would pass through a fissure in the Jura Mountains known locally as "the Hole of Burgundy," ascend the steep road up the Val de Travers, enter France through Pontarlier, settle some affairs in Bourg-en-Bresse, and then conduct specific tasks during a stay in Lyon. After stopovers in Vienne and Grenoble, he would descend the valley of the Rhône and work through all the bookshops in the south. He would follow the main trade route along the Canal du Midi from Marseilles to Bordeaux, then strike north to La Rochelle and continue westward through Poitiers and the Loire Valley. Next, although as it happened the STN decided to cancel this last leg of the journey, he would head for the rich book country in Lorraine via Montargis, Sens, and Troyes. He could expect to gather a superb harvest of orders in Bar-le-Duc, Verdun, Metz, Nancy, and Lunéville. Then he would return through Alsace to Basel and the Rhine. From their strategic location between the Rhine and the Rhône, the directors of the STN looked out on a vast market held in the embrace of the two great rivers, and they contemplated a limitless expansion of their business.

2

Pontarlier

Smuggling and Border Crossings

AFTER HE ARRIVED IN PONTARLIER, the first town on the French side of the Swiss-French border, Favarger sent an urgent letter to the home office in Neuchâtel. He had not expected to write so soon after his departure, but, while passing into France, he had made an important discovery. He had stopped off in Saint-Sulpice, on the Swiss side of the border, in order to discuss business with Meuron frères, a firm of *commissionnaires*—or shipping agents—often employed by the STN to handle the first leg of its shipments into France. At that time, however, the STN had shifted most of its business to Jean-François Pion, who ran a rival shipping service from Pontarlier.

Les Verrières, engraving on wood, *Le véritable Messager boiteux de Neuchâtel*, 1856.

While talking shop with Favarger, one of the Meuron brothers let slip a crucial item of information: they had recently transported five 500-pound bales of the octavo edition of the *Encyclopédie* across the border.

To understand why Favarger rushed this information to Neuchâtel—and to grasp the nature of smuggling as a major enterprise—it is important to know how books were shipped in the eighteenth century. Although publishers sometimes packed them in barrels or small crates (*ballots*), books usually were shipped unbound and in sheets, which were folded together and combined in large bundles known as bales (*balles*). The sheet was the basic unit in the calculation of publishers when they assessed the costs of composition and printing and sometimes when they set prices. (One sheet of an octavo volume, printed on both sides, contained sixteen pages of text, which would be folded into a gathering and sewn to other gatherings, making a book that normally would be bound by the retailer or his customer.) In order to qualify for cheaper transport costs, the bales had to weigh at least 50 pounds and often weighed 100 pounds or more.[1] They were protected by layers of hay and an outer covering of waste sheets or coarse paper (*maculature*). Once packed, they were wrapped with heavy cords, identified by "*marques*" painted on the outside,[2] and loaded on wagons pulled by teams of horses. Loading required skill, because the wagon driver had to arrange the bales so as to minimize friction from the cords, and he also had to cover the entire load securely with a tarpaulin in order to shield it from rain and snow. Booksellers frequently complained about damage from careless shipping, and they demanded that their suppliers replace spoiled sheets (*défets*) by extra sheets that were kept in stock.[3] To get five 500-pound bales of *Encyclopédies* safely across the border was quite a feat, not merely because of the difficulty of driving heavy wagons up the Val de Travers—a matter of whipping teams of two or four horses up muddy mountain roads, where a slip could bring disaster—but because the books were illegal.

Their illegality had nothing to do with the unorthodox ideas scattered through the text. By 1778 the *Encyclopédie* no longer horrified the French authorities as it had in the 1750s. In fact, the Book Trade Administration (*Direction de la librairie*) had permitted a Parisian publisher, Charles-Joseph Panckoucke, to issue a new edition, and he had formed a consortium, which included the STN, to produce the text, including a four-volume Supplement, in a relatively inexpensive quarto format of thirty-six

This painting by Léonard Defrance shows a bookshop whose facade is covered with posters advertising works of the Enlightenment, which the Hapsburg emperor Joseph II permitted to circulate freely in his territory. Aside from its message promoting the freedom of the press, the picture is notable for its depiction of bales of books, each with its marque or identifying notation, piled up in front of the shop.

Léonard Defrance de Liège, *À l'Égide de Minerve. La Politique de tolérance de Joseph II favorisant les encyclopédistes*, inv 3550-13 ©Musée des Beaux-Arts de Dijon/François Jay.

volumes and three volumes of plates. A rival consortium, comprising publishers in Lausanne and Berne, then reproduced the quarto text in a still cheaper octavo edition. The competition for the French market between the quarto and octavo publishers provoked a fierce commercial war, which broke out at the French-Swiss border near Pontarlier. By discovering that the Meuron brothers had smuggled a load of octavo *Encyclopédies* across the border, Favarger opened the way for a counter-attack. But how had the Meurons turned that trick?[4]

Favarger did his best to wring an answer out of the Meuron brother whom he met in Saint-Sulpice, but all he could get in reply was: "When we have real friends, we know how to give them a hand at a time of need." Elliptical as it was, the response raised the prospect of something more important than getting the police to seize a shipment of enemy *Encyclopédies*. It suggested the possibility of a breakthrough at the French border, which would open up direct access to Paris and other locations in the heartland of France. Until the time of Favarger's arrival in Pontarlier, the border controls and inspections farther inland had forced the STN to ship most of its books through Lyon, taking a detour toward the south instead of striking out directly for Besançon, Dijon, and points north. Despite endless letters and intrigues, it had failed in its prime objective as a shipper: to open up a northwest passage to the great markets of the Parisian basin.

The STN did have many routes at its disposal—down the Rhine and the Rhône, as well as overland itineraries of all sorts; and the Lyon-Paris haul was relatively cheap and efficient. However, the Neuchâtelois still needed a northwest passage, not merely to reduce the time and cost of shipments but above all to improve their smuggling operations. Arrangements to sneak illegal books past the authorities in Lyon were always breaking down. A clandestine route through Pontarlier and Dijon would not merely relieve the pressure on the Lyonnais operation; it could become the main means to reach readers clamoring for illegal works throughout central and northern France.

Although Favarger hardly needed to have this imperative called to his attention, Ostervald had scribbled a reminder on the first page of the instructions in Favarger's diary: upon arriving in Pontarlier, he was to ask Jean-François Pion about the possibility of getting book bales past the authorities in Besançon, and in general "to gather all possible information at the border and elsewhere along the routes." By making his casual remark to Favarger, Meuron had signaled that his firm had pried open a fissure in the barrier to illegal literature at the Swiss-French border. He was vaunting the professionalism of Meurons frères and twitting the STN for having shifted its trade to their arch-rival, on the other side of the border. He could not resist bragging about this coup to Favarger, perhaps with the idea that he might persuade the STN to abandon Pion and shift its business back to them. Of course, Meuron only dropped hints. He refused to reveal the itinerary of the shipment and to explain how they had got it past the border.

As soon as he arrived in Pontarlier, Favarger went to the headquarters of Pion's shipping business. He found only Pion's son, who was tending the shop while his father was on a trip to Besançon. Young Pion reported that he had no direct knowledge of the illegal *Encyclopédie* shipment, but he had noticed several *acquits à caution*, or customs bond notes, that had recently been processed (*"déchargés"*) at Dijon and returned via Pontarlier to the customs station in the border village of Frambourg. *Acquits à caution* were the key implements used to control imports by the Ferme générale, the powerful financial organization that collected France's customs and excise taxes for the Crown and that employed its own militia to enforce its measures. When a wagon driver appeared at a customs station (technically, a *bureau d'entrée*) with a bale of books, the officer from the Ferme issued an *acquit à caution*, which had to accompany the bale and be discharged by an official in a *chambre syndicale*, or headquarters of a booksellers' guild, in a designated provincial capital (*ville d'entrée*) after the bale had been inspected. The shipment could then be forwarded to its final destination while the wagon driver returned the *acquit à caution*, with a discharge certificate (*certificat de décharge*) attached to it, to the customs station where it had been issued.[5]

This procedure may seem to be little more than red tape used by an increasingly bureaucratic French monarchy, but a great deal was at stake in the execution of the formalities. Somehow, Meuron frères had managed to get *acquits à caution* issued for the illegal shipment of the octavo *Encyclopédies*, and the octavo publishers had persuaded Jean-Baptiste Capel, a syndic of the Dijon *chambre syndicale*, to clear them with a discharge certificate, thereby opening the way for the volumes to be distributed legally to the octavo's subscribers. Favarger reported all this to the STN; the STN informed Panckoucke; Panckoucke alerted the government agency in charge of the book trade; and soon the shipment was confiscated. It was a crucial victory in the *Encyclopédie* wars of the 1770s, one worth hundreds of thousands of livres. And it also was a (temporary) breakthrough in the system for controlling books, because the *chambre syndicale* of Dijon had not been authorized to process *acquits à caution*. Capel had done so on the sly, and therefore the STN followed up its victory by contacting him in the hope that "for money, he will provide the same service to us."

The *Encyclopédie* episode illustrates something larger—the frenetic activities of all sorts of middlemen who intervened to get books from one country to another. These *passeurs*—smugglers and a large assortment of their accomplices—inhabited border zones, which deserve special study, not only for their strategic importance in international relations but also because of their peculiar cultures.[6]

When Favarger passed through Frambourg, the tiny border station between Switzerland and France high up in the Jura Mountains, he entered foreign territory, becoming subject to the authority of the king of France, along with codes, customs, and religious practices that made the country alien. Yet it looked the same—granite cliffs above fir-covered slopes and deep, green valleys. The villages also seemed the same—thick-walled houses under steep, shingled roofs strung out along the muddy mountain roads. And the people spoke the same kind of French, slow with a sing-song lilt. Everything was familiarly *jurassien*, yet everything was different.

Borders are ambiguous, no matter how precise they look on maps. To travelers who cross them, the boundary lines blur, and differences between one country and another shade into multifarious nuances, geological, political, economic, and cultural. Regimes have often tried to fence themselves off from their neighbors, but their points of entry take the traveler

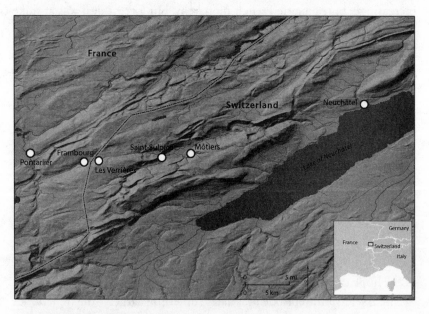

Scott Walker, Cartography Section of the Harvard Library.

through transitional zones—as in the case of international airports, which all look more or less the same, down to the uniforms of the officials checking passports. Transit zones require a great deal of checking, of goods as well as persons, because border crossings involve a shift from one set of rules to another, and a state of suspension exists between them. Most rules can be broken, or at least bent, and therefore border regions favor the development of intermediaries who specialize in negotiating passage. Whether actual *passeurs* or merely guides and money changers, these middlemen lend a human element to geography.

They proliferated at many points along the Swiss border during the eighteenth century, and their population was especially dense in the Val de Travers, where Switzerland shaded into France. All kinds of goods— not just books, but calicoes, watches, and cheeses—passed through Frambourg on their way to French consumers. When Lamoignon de Malesherbes toured the borderlands in 1778, he was told that all the local peasants, French and Swiss alike, dealt in contraband of some kind. It was relatively easy and indeed inevitable, he concluded, owing to the porousness of the border and the profits to be made, especially in the case of books: "Two hundred copies of an illegal brochure do not make up a large packet. It seems to me easy to get them across [the border] in all the wagons that traverse the countryside with all kinds of merchandise."[7]

Books required special attention by the French authorities, because the state, under pressure from the booksellers' guild in Paris, took various measures to block the importation of pirated as well as prohibited works. In order to favor the Parisian publishers, it even imposed a stiff tariff on all book imports. The rate varied, but in 1772, it came to 28 livres (strictly speaking, a duty of 20 livres plus a surtax of 8 sous per livre) per hundredweight or about 18 percent of the value of the merchandise in most cases. Smugglers adapted to the book trade just as they had handled calicoes, which were subjected to a prohibitive tariff designed to protect the domestic silk industry. Of course, book smuggling posed an ideological danger, as it had done since the religious wars of the sixteenth century. But in the period before the Revolution it was basically a business, a service supplied to satisfy demand, and it came in many varieties.

At its most professional, smuggling was known as "insurance."[8] Entrepreneurs signed contracts with publishers, guaranteeing to get shipments across the border for a set fee. They hired teams of porters from among the local peasantry to carry packs from towns on the Swiss side of the border to clandestine warehouses on the French side, where shipping agents combined the packs into large bales and forwarded them to booksellers scattered throughout the kingdom. If the porters were caught by a patrol (*brigade*) of the Ferme générale, the books would be confiscated, and the insurer would reimburse the publisher or its client for their wholesale value as set on the bill of lading. The porters would face punishment, which at its severest could include branding on the shoulder with the letters GAL for "*galérien*" and a sentence to nine years of rowing in the prison galleys of Toulon.

A more common form of smuggling involved techniques of slipping illegal material into legal shipments sent through normal commercial channels. When packing the bales, the STN's employees hid the sheets of prohibited books in the bottom of the packing, covered with hay, or they larded them into sheets of legal works—a technique known as marrying (I have found marriages of Fanny Hill with the Bible and of atheistic tracts with the psalms). The bale was not normally inspected at the border. When the wagon driver pulled up at a border station such as Frambourg, a customs agent—called a *buraliste* or *receveur*—would merely give him an *acquit à caution*, and the inspection would take place in a *chambre syndicale* such as that in Lyon.

This form of smuggling was usually successful—and less dangerous than the "insurance" variety—because inspections often amounted to little more than glancing at a few sheets at the top of the bale, especially if the inspector, an officer of the guild, did business with the STN or was susceptible to bribes. (He might be accompanied, however, by a special *inspecteur de la librairie* of the local police.) To prevent foul play en route, the customs agent at the border tied a rope around the bale and secured the rope with lead seals. These functions were executed in various ways at the border crossing of Frambourg. Sometimes the *buraliste* would only issue the *acquit à caution*, and leave the roping and sealing to be handled by another agent in the nearby town of Pontarlier, where the Ferme générale also had an office—or the second *buraliste* would leave this chore to a shipping agent (hired by the STN or some other foreign publisher) in Pontarlier.

The shipping agent (*commissionnaire*) played a key role in the process. His charges included a fee, 30 sous, for "lead seals, ropes, and *acquit à caution*";[9] and above all he assumed responsibility for the shipment. He usually hired the wagon driver for the next leg of the journey. His name appeared on the bill of lading (*lettre de voiture*), which accompanied the bale, and he was liable for the discharge of the *acquit à caution*. When the wagon driver delivered the bale with its seals intact to the *chambre syndicale* for inspection, he would receive the discharge certificate attached to the *acquit à caution*, and on his return trip he (or the shipping agent acting for him) would deposit those documents with the customs agent in Frambourg. Once the discharged *acquit* was registered by the Frambourg *buraliste*, the legal circuit had been completed. But as all the formalities and paperwork implied, a great deal could go wrong. If a duly discharged *acquit* failed to arrive within an allotted time, usually several months, the shipping agent would have to pay a stiff fee, sometimes as high as 2,000 livres.

A border-crossing of a bale of books, whether legal or illegal, was therefore a complicated affair. It could extend in a formal sense from a *bureau d'entrée* to a *ville d'entrée*—in the case of shipments from Frambourg to Lyon, a distance of nearly 130 miles—because the bale could not be integrated in the French economy until it had passed inspection in a designated *chambre syndicale*.[10] Along the way it passed through several hands, and therefore the STN had to mobilize all sorts of middlemen in the border areas and deep into the interior of the kingdom. Jean-Baptiste Capel was one of them. Favarger had taken his measure during a trip to Dijon in 1776. In a report to the STN, he described Capel as a "solid" bookseller who also functioned as a book inspector for his guild and was more than happy to fail to notice illegal works when he searched through bales.

Writing from Pontarlier on the first stop of his 1778 tour, Favarger thought Dijon looked more promising than ever as an opening to the northern markets. He recommended that the STN write to Dijon immediately, requesting the same service that Capel had provided to its competitors from Lausanne and Bern. The home office—that is, presumably, Ostervald—shot back a letter to Favarger with instructions about how to make the most of "your discovery." While the STN wooed Capel from Neuchâtel, Favarger should adjust his strategy in his negotiations in Lyon. He should say nothing about Capel when he dealt with its new Lyonnais agent, Jacques Revol, because "the more strings we have to our bow, the better it will be."

The dénouement of these intrigues turned out to be disappointing. Capel refused the STN's request to clear its shipments through Dijon. Although willing to help Swiss publishers from time to time, he would not risk opening up a large hole in France's defenses against pirated and prohibited books. The French authorities eventually managed to seize so many octavo *Encyclopédies* that the publishers in Lausanne and Bern sued for peace and abandoned the French market. But the STN never found the much-sought-after northwest passage.

As a chapter in the history of contraband, the little episode at the French-Swiss border in July 1778 is lacking in razzle-dazzle and hugger-mugger. Yet it reveals an important aspect of smuggling: its character as an ordinary and everyday business. Historians have not been able to discover much about this side of smuggling, because they have had to rely on official documents, which mainly concern repression, and the smugglers generally covered their trails well enough to leave few traces in the archives. In the papers of the STN, however, the *passeurs* appear openly as they went about their daily rounds, not as adventurers but as businessmen. Favarger's stop in Pontarlier therefore provides an opportunity to discuss different varieties of book smuggling as they were actually practiced. To understand them as business operations, it is important to consider the two main constraints within which they operated: the geography of the border zones and the character of the individuals available for hire.

The Jura range curves in an arc of 224 miles, thirty-eight miles at its broadest part, stretching from the German territories of the Rhine to the valley of the Rhône in France. Less spectacular than the Alps to its east, it nonetheless forms an impressive wall between France and Switzerland. The twin peaks of the Chasseral and the Chasseron rise abruptly over the Lac de Neuchâtel to a height of 5,272 feet and the Crêt de la Neige, the tallest in the Jura, towers over Geneva at 5,643 feet. To climb them on a sunny summer day is a delightful promenade, but to get past them in winter under a heavy load of books tried all the strength of the underfed and underpaid porters of the eighteenth century. The range consists of accordion-like folds of limestone and marl, pushed up to rugged heights by the thrust of the Alps as they emerged 66 million years ago. The folds run northeast to southwest, separated by valleys. In order to cross them, hiking east to west, it is necessary to find transverse fissures called "cluses," which open passages from one valley to another. But the cluses do not link up easily, and the most manageable of them were the most patrolled by the brigades of the Ferme générale.

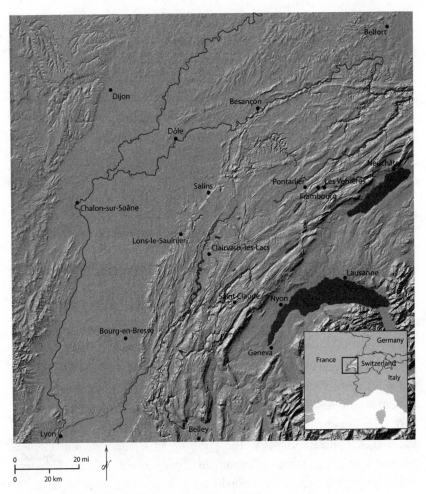

Scott Walker, Cartography Section of the Harvard Library.

Like all the other publishers in French Switzerland, the STN constantly sought new routes into France, shifting its business and spreading it out among different shipping agents as circumstances required. It shipped a great many books to northern markets through Basel, where its reliable agent, Luc Preiswerck, forwarded them down the Rhine. Yet the Rhine was riddled with tolls; and neither Basel nor Strasbourg provided effective entry points into France, because Alsace was cut off from markets deeper inside France by heavy customs barriers. Customs also hurt the trade between the Franche-Comté, at France's eastern border, and "la vieille France," which began in Burgundy and included Paris. But the Comtois duties were less expensive than those in Alsace, and they could be circumvented, once the books had made it into the kingdom, by disguising bales as a domestic shipment labeled as something innocuous such as *mercerie* (haberdashery).[11] To penetrate into the main French markets, however, the STN first had to get its books past the Jura.

Its preferred route led up the Val de Travers past the customs station at Frambourg, where a cluse cut across the high plain of the French Jura, opening the way to Pontarlier. Despite the altitude and the bad roads, the STN shipped thousands of books through this route. They might be inoffensive pirated editions or dangerous *livres philosophiques*, but they had to be handled with care and forwarded on to distribution points within "*vieille France*," especially in Lyon, the most important crossroad in the secondary circuits of smuggling south and west from Switzerland.

When the agents of the Ferme générale at Frambourg refused to cooperate or when snow and mud made the Val de Travers impassable, the STN often shipped its books on wagons bound for Lausanne and Geneva. A wagon driver could turn off the main routes at several points and leave his load with shipping agents, who would store it until they found a wagoner headed westward up a winding mountain road to a pass in the Jura, where a *buraliste* had been bribed or an insurer had found a path around the customs station. The key *bureaux d'entrée* in the southern range of the Jura were Jougne, opposite Yverdon; Morez, opposite Lausanne; and Collonges, opposite Geneva. The publishers of Lausanne and Geneva favored Collonges, which commanded a main route to Lyon, although they, too, kept searching for a northwest passage to Paris. They employed agents in the ports of Lac Léman, from Ouchy to Rolle, Nyon, and Versoix; and the agents cultivated contacts among peasant porters in the foothills and mountains who sometimes opened up new routes through rugged terrain across Mont Tendre, Mont-Rond, and Mont Colomby de Gex.[12]

Shipping agents, warehousemen, innkeepers, wagon drivers, porters, and insurers proliferated everywhere in this high-altitude underground. The STN dealt with dozens of them and played them off against one another, probing constantly for new passages and better prices. Its success as a publisher depended on its ability as a shipper; and to succeed in shipping, whether through legal channels or by contraband, it had to build and maintain a network of people as well as a system of routes. The human factor proved crucial.

Wagon drivers, for example, needed to keep their wits about them and not merely whip their horses over mountain passes. They often had to drop off illegal crates at inns on the outskirts of French towns before proceeding with their main load to the customs barriers and the town centers. This maneuver required cultivating innkeepers and timing arrivals to coincide with the activities of the agents who handled the next stage in the smuggling. Expert wagoners like Jean Heuby and the Martin brothers of Saint-Sulpice, reputedly the ablest in the Val de Travers, could be trusted to keep to their schedule and to follow directions, which often led to a stopover at la Croix Rousse outside Lyon, where they unloaded books under the watchful eye of a certain Tevenet, the innkeeper Aux Trois Flacons. But however much the STN urged its shipping agents to choose such men, it often had its merchandise damaged and misplaced by the likes of Guset, a wagoner notorious for his "unforgivable negligence."[13]

Even Jean-François Pion, who ran the largest shipping business in the Pontarlier area, was famous for his foul-ups. On one occasion, he sent a barrel of sauerkraut to the wrong man in Lyon, and it was eaten before the mistake could be corrected. On another, he forwarded a crate of books to Nantes instead of to Rennes, which was sixty-two miles away. Nonetheless, he had the best stable in the upper Jura. He could provide his own drivers and teams of three to five horses, harnessed to sleighs in the winter. His competitors, the Meuron brothers and Jonas Phillipin from Saint-Sulpice, hired wagoners with horses from the local peasants—mountain men with Old Testament names like Jonas Louis Mathey, Isaac Bovet, and Abram Jenrevetel—but the supply dried up in the spring, when the horses were needed for plowing, and also in the "cheese season" (September–October), when books took second place to more coveted local specialties.[14] At the height of winter the snow could be three feet deep at the mountain passes, and the peasants retired to their fireplaces. If trapped by snow in the Val de Travers, the drivers sometimes abandoned their wagons and struggled home with their horses. The conditions were so difficult and unpredictable that the Meuron brothers could not commit themselves to deliver shipments by a given date. Time limits, backed by penal clauses in contractual agreements, were crucial for some kinds of smuggling, because the forwarding agents had to know when to rendezvous with the wagon drivers at inns outside the cities. Pion sent a wagon to Neuchâtel once a week and contracted to get the books from Neuchâtel to Lyon within fifteen days for 4 livres, 10 sous per hundredweight, which he later raised to 5 livres, while lowering the time limit to twelve days. He may have been slow-witted, but he had the horses. The Meurons, cleverer by far, often lost out to him in the competition for the STN's business, because they had to job out the hauling from their headquarters in Saint-Sulpice. While Pion's wagons shuttled in and out of Lyon, they cursed their lack of a stable and the intractability of the men they hired: "The wagon drivers dictate terms to us."[15]

This kind of competition, compounded by rivalry and feuds, existed everywhere. In the southern range of the Jura, for example, shipping was dominated by the firm of Nicole et Galliard located in Nyon on Lac Léman. Nicole et Galliard handled the trade of Genevan publishers such as Jean-François Bassompierre, and they were willing to help the STN when it ran into difficulties with its insurers. But they themselves would not smuggle, nor would they bid hard for its business: 6 livres per hundredweight to get books from Neuchâtel to Lyons was as low as they would go. They had an enterprising clerk, however, Jean-Jacques Montandon, and in 1771 he left them to set up a shipping agency of his own. In a circular letter to their customers, he explained that after nine years of hard work and poor pay—366 livres a year—he had mastered every aspect of the trade and could provide superior service. True, his former employers considered him disloyal. However, they had refused to give him a share in their business, and he was free to do as he pleased, because he had acquired the rights of a bourgeois. "Only sovereigns have the authority to say, 'I want to impede the industry of an individual and to defy human rights by ordaining that you may not set up business to my detriment anywhere.'" He could not support his family on 366 livres a year, he wrote. He would have been ruined had his wife not helped him out. And as for his former employers, he had "directed their business like a master, not a clerk....Judge for yourselves, Messieurs, whether I am wrong to quit at the age of 40 in order to start my own business."[16]

There spoke the spirit of enterprise. Yet entrepreneurship alone could not overcome the baroque system of tax farming and customs policing along the French border. In response to Montandon's overture, the STN asked him whether he could smuggle books past the *bureaux d'entrée* in the same manner as he had done with calicoes. He took soundings with a *buraliste* named Janet in Morez, "a worthy man, my intimate friend. But still, he is a controller, and I can't press him too hard."[17] Janet would not let the STN's crates pass through his station without at least some inspection. So Montandon tried another friend in Morez, named Charbonnet, who had a way around the inspection and, in addition, a friend of his own in Auxonne, who could forward crates with counterfeit customs seals deep into France. Moreover, a new *buraliste* was soon to arrive in Morez, and Montandon would contact him immediately "in order to know on which foot he dances."[18] Unfortunately a rash of calico confiscations had put the customs officials on the qui vive and had spoiled the amicable arrangements for relaying books. Montandon made a tour of the border stations yet failed to recruit the necessary allies among the *buralistes* and ultimately abandoned his attempt to develop a sideline in smuggling, although he continued to compete successfully with his former employer Nicole et Galliard in the legal trade.

A similar story could be told about Olive, a shipping agent in Ouchy, who, thanks to a local friend, opened a temporary path through Pont-de-Beauvoisin and then closed it, owing to increased vigilance by the customs officials. He cut into the business of Secrétan et De la Serve, the biggest shipping agent in Ouchy, who fought back by reminding the STN that their firm had taken on a new partner whose wife came from Neuchâtel. That kind of argument carried weight (though not as much as price cutting) because trade depended on trust, which worked best among friends and relatives. Hence the constant references to personal contacts in the commercial correspondence. Meuron has a friend in Dijon, a candle maker named Nubla, who knows how to get shipments past the *chambre syndicale*. Bertrand learns that Comte, a bookseller in Bourg-en-Bresse, has a brother in Belfort, who has friends in Besançon, who can sneak books into the city. Another route into Besançon opens up, thanks to a grocer named Millavaux, who helps his bookseller friend Charles-Antoine Charmet to falsify *acquits à caution*, while Charmet befriends the intendant, who has a taste for *livres philosophiques*.

In short, the links among friends offset the competition between rivals, and everyone tried to tip the balance in his favor by cultivating contacts. If ordinary trade depended on connections, clandestine commerce required especially strong ties at all the nodal points of the distribution system. As the Meuron brothers put it in trying to sell their smuggling services to the STN, "With friends, you can do anything."[19] And as the STN remarked in requesting reciprocal favors from its own correspondents, "One hand washes the other."

To maintain a steady flow of forbidden books into France, however, publishers had to rely on something more substantial than goodwill and ad hoc arrangements. "We require a fixed method," the STN explained in discussing shipments with the Meuron brothers.[20] As mentioned above, that method was "insurance," and it became an important element in the STN's business strategy after June 12, 1783, when the comte de Vergennes, France's foreign minister, issued an order requiring that all book imports be inspected in the *chambre syndicale* of Paris before continuing to their final destination. This measure threw the provincial book trade into chaos. Not only did it make shipping costs impossibly expensive, except for books destined for Paris, it also gave the Parisian booksellers' guild the power to search for pirated works in every shipment that arrived from their natural enemies, the pirate publishers outside France.

Faced with this situation, the STN sought information from its correspondents in the border areas about the possibilities of mounting a new insurance operation. François Michaut, a scrappy shipping agent in Les Verrières, recommended Ignace Faivre, a bookseller in Pontarlier, and Faivre eventually dealt so extensively with the STN that his dossier is worth studying in detail, for it provides an extraordinarily rich source of information about the career of a smuggler and about smuggling as an insurance business.

According to Michaut, Faivre had recently hired a porter who had excellent connections with the chief of a border patrol. Given an adequate bribe, the patrol would fail to find anything suspicious, while Faivre's drivers hauled whole wagonloads of books from Les Verrières to Pontarlier. Unfortunately, this service was prohibitively expensive: it cost about three times as much as the normal price of a shipment from Switzerland to Paris. But Faivre could also recruit porters to backpack the books across mountain trails at night; and once he had them safely stocked in his warehouse in Pontarlier, he could send them on as domestic shipments.

The forwarding required a second maneuver. Faivre would combine the packs into bales of 150 pounds or more, mark the bales as "*libri*" (books), and sign the waybill (*lettre de voiture*) attached to them, thereby taking responsibility for their contents and avoiding the danger of inspection en route by ambulatory agents of the Ferme générale. Of course, they would have to be inspected by the officers of the booksellers' guild closest to their final destination, but Faivre had ways of getting around that problem; and as the STN knew from experience, booksellers in provincial guilds were often delighted to cooperate with foreign suppliers at the expense of the Parisians.

The greatest difficulty was the border crossing. The porters would not hesitate to handle contraband goods of any kind, except the most extreme variety of forbidden books—for example, the irreligious tract, *Les trois imposteurs*, and the anti-court libel *Anecdotes sur Mme la comtesse du Barry*—which they considered too dangerous to be worth the risk. If the STN could guarantee that it would ship nothing but counterfeit editions of innocuous works, the porters would get them to Pontarlier for 12 livres per hundredweight—and, a crucial detail, a free drink at an inn in Les Verrières before setting out for the trails across the border. Michaut himself would be glad to help, but he would act only as a shipping agent. To organize the operation, the STN should come to an agreement with Faivre directly. In fact, it should transfer one of its workers to his shop, disguised as his clerk, in order to coordinate the smuggling operation.[21]

The Neuchâtelois did not need an introduction to Faivre. They had been dealing with him for years. In January 1771, they had described him to a Parisian correspondent as "a very scheming, enterprising man, but he has nothing other than his know-how."[22] After some kind of employment in the book trade in Neuchâtel—probably with the Fauche family, who seemed to be close friends of his—Faivre went into business for himself as a bookseller in Pontarlier. His first orders to the STN show a tendency to speculate in *livres philosophiques*, notably d'Holbach's atheistic *Système de la nature*, which he ordered on several occasions, along with other forbidden favorites such as Voltaire's *Questions sur l'Encyclopédie*, Mercier's *L'An deux mille quatre cent quarante* [The Year Two Thousand, Four Hundred and Forty], and *La Fille de joie*, a translation of John Cleland's 1749 novel, *Fanny Hill*. Whether he sold many of these works in Pontarlier seems unlikely. As far as one can tell from a few references in his letters, Faivre's local clientele preferred devotional tracts.[23] Pontarlier had only about three thousand inhabitants and no cultural institutions of much importance. It lived from the French-Swiss trade and a few regional products: paper, wood, cheese, iron, and the sale of the sturdy Comtois horses. Faivre's correspondence indicated that he sold books to other booksellers in Dijon, Besançon, and Nancy, probably because of his ability to provide them with forbidden works. Pontarlier served him primarily as a base for functioning as a middleman between Swiss publishers and the retail trade

501 - FRONTIÈRE FRANCO-SUISSE — Contrebandiers en marche dans la Montagne pour traverser la Ligne française

J. Michaux, édit. Bellegarde (Déposé)

This postcard, probably from the 1930s, shows smugglers carrying packs across the Swiss-French border. Although almost certainly posed, it illustrates an industry that continued unabated for two centuries after the STN used Swiss peasants to backpack its books to secret storehouses in France.

in Eastern France. Not that he did business on a large scale. He frequented country fairs and was often on the road, seizing whatever opportunities arose while his wife tended the shop at home. She handled the correspondence in his absence and seemed to be well informed about the accounts and the trade in general.

Faivre's smuggling operations worked well throughout the 1770s. An innkeeper in Les Verrières named Jannet provided storage on the Swiss side of the border, and Michaut helped to recruit porters and to bribe customs officials. Family connections smoothed the way in Besançon and especially in Pontarlier, where the intendant's subordinate officer (*subdélégué*) agreed to turn a blind eye to everything Faivre brought into the city. By September 1771, Faivre had begun to smuggle on an ad hoc basis for the STN. Although he did not provide a formal insurance service, he promised safe delivery: "Have no fear for these books.... Don't worry about anything." He did not charge much—12 livres per hundredweight— and he paid even less to his porters. They lugged bundles from Jannet's inn to Faivre's secret storerooms in Pontarlier for 25 sous per day, the equivalent of a day's wages for an unskilled Parisian worker, plus the required stiff drink. One of the first bundles weighed 109 pounds, too much, they protested, for a single man to carry. They ultimately persuaded Faivre to reduce the bundles to 60 pounds, so when the trails were covered with snow. As Faivre described them, they frequented the inns in the high valleys of the Jura, and, except for the dependable minority, they were a motley crew. He complained about having to deal with "miserable drunkards," who demanded too much money and talked too loudly about their work when they collected drinks in Jannet's inn.[24] The Ferme générale was said to plant spies at several spots where drinks were served in Switzerland, so Faivre finally shifted his base of operations in Les Verrières to the house of a certain Montaudon. He never got caught.

But he did not make much money, either. The smuggling was a sideline to his legitimate book trade, which kept dragging him into debt. Unable to honor the bills of exchange that he wrote to pay suppliers like the STN, he haggled and quarreled with many of his creditors. In 1771 he became embroiled in a lawsuit with Charles-Antoine Charmet, the most important bookseller in Besançon, and he squabbled with the STN over the balance he owed in his account. It, too, threatened to sue, and to force his hand it refused to send the last two volumes of the nine-volume sets of the *Questions sur l'Encyclopédie* that he had purchased and that he needed to supply to his own customers in order to collect from them.

In January 1772 Faivre declared bankruptcy—that is, he deposited a balance sheet with a bailiff and suspended payments on his debts while cutting deals with his creditors and continuing his business as best he could. The STN engaged a lawyer in Pontarlier to take its case to court, but Faivre wrote defiantly that it would never recover enough to cover its legal fees, even if it won, because he would tie the case up forever in appeals. As he observed in a later letter, "One should not listen to lawyers and legal officials who only try to make money and to drag the parties of lawsuits into labyrinthine procedures of which you will never see the end." More important, he had nothing for the STN to confiscate. Like some other marginal entrepreneurs who overplayed their hands, he had engineered a kind of divorce known as a "separation of bodies and goods" in order to preserve the assets that his wife had brought to their marriage. "The judgment she obtained has shielded me from all prosecution by my creditors," he wrote the STN, "as I don't have enough furniture and stock to pay them. You should be aware of this so that you don't run the risk of losing the entire sum owed to you." In fact, Faivre's wife continued to collaborate actively in their business and even went on sales trips of her own. Having lost a preliminary round in a local court, Faivre did indeed appeal the case; the STN accumulated heavy legal fees, just as he had warned; and after ten years they finally agreed on a settlement.

By mid-1783, five years after Favarger's journey, the STN was ready to resume relations with Faivre, because it needed his services as a smuggler. Vergennes's order of June 12, 1783, had produced such a crisis in the book trade that the STN could no longer count on arrangements patched together here and there with shipping agents in order to reach the French market. It required a professional insurer, even one who had passed in and out of bankruptcy, and therefore began to work with Faivre in the autumn of 1783. After several trial runs, he developed a workable system, and on January 23, 1784, he signed a formal contract with a clerk, who was passing through Pontarlier as the STN's sales rep. The key clause read: "I the undersigned [Ignace Faivre] guarantee to the Société typographique de Neuchâtel in Switzerland that I will pick up all the bales of books that they send to M. François Michaut in Les Verrières and that I will deliver them within two months to Pontarlier at my peril and risk for 15 French livres per hundredweight."

Faivre was to rent a special warehouse in Pontarlier and to store the bales in it until he found an occasion to forward them with his own signature on the waybill, so that he would take responsibility in case they ran into difficulty during the domestic leg of the shipment. The STN was not to send any expressly forbidden books, however, except for its pirated (and expanded) edition of *Description des arts et métiers*, which had run into great difficulty with the French authorities (they had been mobilized by the book's original publisher in Paris, Nicolas-Léger Moutard) and which Faivre agreed to handle for a special rate of 18 livres per hundredweight. It would employ him as an agent for all its normal shipments sent with an *acquit à caution*, so that, when opportunities arose, he could use the legal shipments as a cover for the illegal ones. Should any book be confiscated, he would pay for its full value within a year. Faivre's insurance service corresponded exactly to a contractual arrangement between the STN and an "insurer" named Guillon for smuggling at the border near Clairvaux-les-Lacs in 1772. Judging from the businesslike tone of both agreements, they typified smuggling in general, at least in its most professional form, as a carefully calculated enterprise.

Insurance in 1783 differed from that of 1773 in one respect, however, because Vergennes's 1783 order meant that it was not enough to get books across the French-Swiss border. Faivre also had to take measures for their protection on the second leg of their journey, the one that led from his warehouse in Pontarlier to their destinations in the provinces. As already mentioned, he combined the bundles delivered by his porters into bales marked "*libri*," and filled out a waybill with his signature on it so that they could proceed as a domestic shipment without being forced to make the detour to Paris under an *acquit à caution*. They had to be cleared in the *chambres syndicales* of Lyon or Besançon, but with the STN's help he found allies to handle that formality in both cities. By the end of 1783, he had put together all the parts of his insurance operation. The question then was how it would function once he set it in motion.

At first, he found it difficult to find sober and reliable porters and to convince them that the STN would limit itself to pirated rather than prohibited books. (In fact, despite the provisions of the contract, the STN used Faivre to ship its most dangerous literature.) Eventually, he assured the STN, he recruited a dependable team. He knew several trails around the border station at Frambourg, and in a first essay at a crossing he accompanied the porters himself. Then he began to soften up the local officials of the Ferme générale. After a month of negotiations, he won them over—for a hefty sum: a flat fee of 8 louis d'or (192 livres), in order to look the other way while his porters hauled loads set at a maximum total of 60 bales. Unfortunately for Faivre, the porters also drove a hard bargain. Instead of a flat daily rate of 25 sous, they now demanded 15 livres per hundredweight, plus their drink. "You can send me whatever is most urgent before the snows," Faivre wrote the STN as winter set in late in 1783. All these arrangements cost money: "I must provide wine to these porters and 8 louis d'or to those with whom I made the deal," he explained, referring to his bribes within the Ferme générale. "But with those 8 louis I can bring in 50 to 60 bales and even more."

Faivre therefore insisted on an increase in his own rate, which caused further difficulties with the STN, until they finally agreed on a compromise in February 1784. By this time, Faivre was smuggling for several other publishers, including some houses in Lausanne and Bern. Having greased so many palms at Frambourg, he took charge of several border crossings there himself and worked out a new technique of hiding shipments for the provinces inside bales addressed to Paris.

By April the worst snows had retreated from the passes. Enough of it remained to make the crossings exhausting for his men, but they hauled six shipments across the border one night, six more the next, and another half-dozen before the end of the month. The trails continued to be so difficult that they sent a request for still smaller bundles—40 pounds as a rule, 60 pounds at most. By the end of May, the snow had disappeared and so had some of the porters, because they had to concentrate on the spring plowing. Still, Faivre hired enough of them to maintain a steady flow of shipments destined for Besançon, Lyons, Dijon, Troyes, and Reims. Although difficulties had appeared at nearly every turn, the system worked.

It worked, that is, until disaster struck. In early August 1784, the officials at the Frambourg station seized five bales of *livres philosophiques*, containing among other things the seditious and pornographic tracts of Honoré Gabriel Riqueti, comte de Mirabeau. They came from Fauche fils aîné et Witel, a firm founded in Neuchâtel by Samuel Fauche's son-in-law, Jérémie Witel and his eldest son, Jonas. After quarreling with Fauche père, they had set up shop on their own and followed his example by publishing forbidden books. Mirabeau specialized in the genre. In 1775 while a prisoner in the château de Joux, which dominated the border near Frambourg from a Jura peak 3,024 feet high, he had surreptitiously published his *Essai sur le despotisme* with the elder Fauche. In 1782 and 1783, the younger Fauche and Witel brought out his *Des lettres de cachet et des prisons d'Etat* and *Errotika Biblion*. But their smuggling arrangements went awry, and the capture of the books produced such a scandal that the Frambourg route became impassable. Although he had had nothing to do with it, Faivre lamented, "Many people are grumbling, even against me, innocent as I am of any connection with this affair." He noted that the officers of the Ferme générale were now "on the alert day and night."

There was nothing to do but suspend all operations. Faivre's porters would not venture across the border for anything, and "there are spies and rogues in Les Verrières who betray people for money." He did not think the STN's books safe in Michaut's storerooms on the Swiss side of the border in Les Verrières, so he ordered his men to lug them up to a hiding place on the top of a mountain. There they remained until late October, when things had calmed down and Faivre had come to a new agreement with employees of the Ferme. He had also managed to persuade some of his porters to attempt a crossing, mainly by offering them more drink. Fortified by extra portions of alcohol, the men made it without difficulty; encouraged by additional cash, the agents of the Ferme failed to notice them; and by November the system was functioning smoothly again.

Nonetheless, its collapse during the summer had increased the financial pressure on Faivre. He could no longer fall back on a fraudulent maneuver such as his separation from his wife. In fact, she worked as hard as ever alongside him and even took to the road with their daughter, in order to settle affairs with other booksellers in the Franche-Comté. In response to dunning from the STN, Faivre pleaded for an extension of his debts: "The porters are holding me up for ransom. They have got me to increase their wages by 6 deniers a pound, and I can't clear any profit, considering the other payments I must make to those who lend me a hand," he added, referring to the agents of the Ferme générale.

Some of the bribes went to a *receveur* named Saint André in the customs station in Frambourg and to a colleague of his who oversaw operations from the Ferme's other office nearby in Pontarlier. Faivre knew them well. To ingratiate himself, he asked the STN to send them a translation of Fanny Burney's six-volume novel, *Cecilia, or, Memoirs of an Heiress*. The STN followed up this favor by giving Saint André two free subscriptions to its *Journal helvétique*. As Ostervald wrote in a cover letter, the gifts were a token of gratitude for his services: "We send you a thousand thanks, Monsieur, for the obliging manner that you have employed in relation to the books of our shipments that pass through your office." A few months later, when the new smuggling system was functioning effectively, Faivre requested two copies of *De l'administration des finances* by Jacques Necker, the Swiss banker who had served as Louis XVI's finance minister from 1776 to 1781. Faivre needed an appropriate gift, he explained, because he was soon to have dinner with Saint André. In the small world of Pontarlier-Frambourg, the members of the educated elite all knew one another and read many of the same books, whether they were selling them or confiscating them.

In order to protect himself from undercover agents and to pacify the porters who had quarreled with Michaut, Faivre shifted the Swiss side of his operation from Les Verrières to Saint-Sulpice, engaging Michaut's competitors, the Meuron brothers, as his new agents. And while improving his old system, he devised another one, based on a different route. It was "safe, solid," and suitable for large wagonloads, although the horses had to be strong, since the route went across high mountains. Instead of packing its books into bundles weighing 50 to 60 pounds, therefore, the STN could send them in bales of 200 to 400 pounds. (It had sometimes conveniently forgotten about the necessity of limiting the weight of the bundles. "A man cannot carry 110 pounds on his body," Faivre had protested in November 1784.) Now the STN could revert to the more conventional-sized bales, and Faivre could do without porters. The only problem was snow, more than three feet of it in February 1785, which made the roads impassable. "No wagon driver has dared to attempt them with a sleigh," Faivre wrote. The high-mountain route remained blocked until late April, while the STN's shipments of legal works and pirated books hidden in bales with *acquits à caution* made it into France at lower altitudes.

A coach stuck in the snow high up in the Jura Mountains. Unlike coaches, which were used for passengers, the wagons that carried books often required three, four, or even five horses to make it through mountain passes clogged with snow.

Le courrier de La Chaux-de-Fonds en hiver by Fr. J. Vernay, Indian ink, 1864, Musée des PTT, Switzerland.

The STN sent many of these latter shipments via Pion, who charged less although he still refused to function as an insurer. Faivre had planned to handle all of the STN's trade, assuming a double role as a *commissionnaire-assureur*, and had rented a warehouse to stock the large number of books that he expected to transport across the border. His contract with the STN did indeed commit it to favor him for everything it shipped to France. He especially needed to process bales with *acquits à caution*, because he used them to hide the illegal works that he transported for other publishers. His letters suggest that, like other forwarding agents such as Jacques Revol of Lyon, he slipped packets of forbidden books into large bales of books that the authorities tolerated. Thanks to his connections with the customs agents, Faivre could do the repackaging in Pontarlier before the bales were sealed; and the booksellers who ordered the shipments could find ways to extract the illegal works or have them pass unnoticed during inspections in the *chambres syndicales*.

In response to Faivre's increasingly indignant complaints about its failure to honor the terms of the contract, the STN complained back that his services took too long. He replied that he had served it diligently throughout all of 1784 and had been forced to hold back some shipments in early 1785 only because of the heavy snows. Without a high volume of trade, he argued, his insurance operation would not be worthwhile. He now had no use for the warehouse that he had rented for three years at 33 livres a year. If the STN would pay for the rest of the rent, he wrote on August 15, 1785, he would return their contract, and they could cease to do business together.

At this point, the STN completely stopped sending shipments to Faivre. Faced with financial difficulties of its own, it had begun to cut back drastically in its publishing. It closed his account in January 1786, collecting a small balance of 300 livres. As far as one can tell from the last letters in his dossier, Faivre's business as a bookseller continued to hold up after he ceased smuggling for the STN. Despite their ostensible separation, his wife still worked with him, accompanied by their grown-up daughter in the late 1780s. He probably continued to smuggle books for other publishers until 1789, whether by "insurance" operations or sleight of hand at the customs station.

Just as Favarger typified the functions of a sales rep, Faivre can be taken as an archetypal smuggler. His story shows how an entrepreneur could cobble together a living in the book trade from a small mountain town in the semi-lawless borderland of eastern France. Favarger's tour de France intersected with that story and several others in the upper Jura only for a few days in 1778, while he inspected the STN's supply lines at the French border. He had many other tasks to pursue in his next stops, and they would be embedded in many more stories, each one highly personal yet all of them bound together in the common enterprise of getting books to readers at a particularly difficult period of French history.

3

Lons-le-Saunier

Sizing Up Shops

LONS-LE-SAUNIER, FAVARGER'S FIRST STOP after Pontarlier, yielded no business. After a hard ride across the high Jura plain, he put up in an inn—probably one of the typical, lice-infested lodgings that lured travelers under the sign "*On loge à pied et à cheval*" ("lodging for those on foot and horseback"). Lons was a small market town in a poor, sparsely populated sector of the Franche-Comté, and Favarger wrote it off in his diary as follows: "Lons-le-Saunier has only two booksellers. One is Delhorme [a printer-bookseller], who sells no books aside from those he produces. Gabriel is a decent fellow, but poor. His shop consists of nothing but prayer books, etc. and isn't worth 500 livres. Nevertheless, I left a catalogue and a prospectus of the Description des arts with him. We should only deal with him for cash."

It was a typical Favarger diary entry: concise and matter-of-fact yet also highly revealing, for it referred to an aspect of the book trade that has often escaped attention: the importance of local markets, which catered to the demand for liturgical and devotional works, schoolbooks, almanacs, and ephemera such as public notices.[1] The STN did not handle this kind of material, and therefore Favarger treated many of the booksellers on his route as unworthy of cultivating. When he described what they had for sale in their shops, he normally used the term "*usages,*" meaning prayer books and religious tracts of all kinds, aside from theological works. He usually dismissed these small local booksellers with a phrase or two:

Grenoble: Faure is a printer of the king and produces only public notices [*placards*]. He sold his stock to Brette, who does not deal in trade books [*articles de librairie*].

Orange: Orange has only a certain Jouit, a wigmaker by trade, who sells religious works [*livres d'usage*] and nothing else.

Tarascon: Cordonnecy and widow Tassy are combined in one house, whose business is very limited. They sell only religious works.

Nîmes: Beaume, a printer here, is very good, but he produces and sells only religious works.

Castres: I saw M. Robert, a doctor in theology, printer, and bookseller. But he sells only religious works, which he produces himself; so there is no business to be done with him.

Libourne: Morrin … is good, but he won't do much business. He deals only in religious works and a few other things.

Blois: Charles and Ph. Masson, printers, have formed a single business, and they carry only religious works.

Orléans: Widow Rouzeau is very good; but she deals only in religious works. Perdroux is mediocre, found some items in our catalog that are to his taste but he only wants to deal in exchanges for religious works, which are about all he carries.

Favarger's impressions are confirmed by a survey of all the printers and booksellers in the kingdom, which was conducted by intendants and their *subdélégués* in 1764, over a decade before his trip. When asked a standard question about what sorts of material printers printed and booksellers sold, most noted a certain amount of general fiction and non-fiction, but they stressed the prevalence of religious literature and works of local interest. In the Loire town of Blois, for example, their assessment of Pierre-Paul Charles and Jean-Philbert Masson was very similar to what Favarger would find. They specified that both printer-booksellers dealt in "all sorts of books for schools, liturgical works for the diocese, textbooks, material for offices, posters, placards, burial notices, and from time to time books printed with a royal privilege." In Orléans, the intendant noted, "The booksellers handle only the usual works of their trade, consisting of literature, pious tracts and prayer books."[2]

What the STN sold was *literature*. It was an omnibus term, covering many genres, but generally did not apply to what many small bookshops stocked.[3] Towns the size of Lons-le-Saunier (6,700 inhabitants) usually had one or two printers. They churned out liturgical works for the ecclesiastical authorities, notices for provincial administrators, "factums," or legal briefs for lawyers, bills of exchange for merchants, and all sorts of ephemera. They often sold their products out of their own printing shops, especially if they had qualified as libraires-imprimeurs. The local booksellers dealt in the same kinds of materials—mainly devotional works and tracts related to local affairs. They did not do enough business for the STN to seek them out and did not carry the kind of material that sold best with STN's clients. The STN's trade flowed through France's main commercial channels without branching off into many local markets. It belonged to a current of culture that reached into the farthest corners of the kingdom yet failed to connect local sectors of the book trade in a way that would make *literature* circulate everywhere. Although peddlers distributed general works through the capillary system of the trade, as will be explained in chapter 10, a fully integrated market for books would not appear in France until the late nineteenth century.[4]

Favarger did not indulge in regret over the lack of demand for the STN's books in places like Lons-le-Saunier. He took it for granted and concentrated on towns with bookshops that carried "*articles de librairie*" or general trade books. But he also needed to use some kind of scale by which to take the measure of those bookshops. As indicated in the remarks quoted above, he divided them into three basic categories: the "good" (Beaume, Morrin), the "mediocre" (Perdroux), and the "not good"— that is, those not worth considering as potential clients (Delhorme, Brette, Jouit).[5] The STN used that classification scheme in its accounts and business letters, although it occasionally employed other terms, such as "solid," "mediocre," and "not solid."[6] It seems likely that other European merchants used a tripartite model of this kind for assessing the credit of customers everywhere in the eighteenth century. (By the 1850s sales reps working for British publishers sorted retail booksellers into four categories reminiscent of Favager's: "good," "fair," "doubtful," and "bad."[7]) So crude and subjective a standard of measurement did not take Favarger far when he arrived in an unfamiliar town. What did "good" or "mediocre" mean when it came down to transacting business?

As soon as Favarger arrived at a destination, he consulted the *Almanach de la librairie,* a trade manual first published in 1777 and reissued in an expanded edition in 1778, which listed all of the printers and booksellers in France, town by town.[8] It served as a directory for organizing his visits and as a kind of scorecard for writing his reports about them. When he arrived in Poitiers, for example, the almanac guided him to Félix Faulcon, a bookseller-printer who qualified as "good," although too self-important in his role as syndic of the local guild to order pirated works. A second printer, Braud, also received a grade of "good" in the notes Favarger entered in his diary, but he, too, did not want to order any books. Four booksellers—Bobin, Guilleminot, Giraud, and Joret—went down as "mediocre" in the diary, and all the others listed in the almanac were written off as "not good."

However, the *Almanach* often got things wrong,[9] and in any case Favarger needed more substantial guidelines than it offered before stepping into a shop. Whenever possible, he relied upon the instructions written in the beginning of his diary. In Bourg-en-Bresse, for example, the instructions directed him to "see M. Vernarel and get more information about his solvability." And in Châlons-sur-Marne, he should beware of Sombert: "We have heard many bad things about his character and the state of his fortune." Yet the instructions were limited in scope, because the STN had little knowledge about the integrity of customers located hundreds of miles away. A main purpose of Favarger's tour was to acquire that knowledge, and therefore he had to rely on informants along the way.

Most helpful was Jacques-François d'Arnal, the son-in-law of STN director Abram Bosset de Luze and a partner in Pomaret, Rilliet, d'Arnal & Compagnie, the STN's banker in Lyon. D'Arnal was devoted to Bosset and the interests of the STN. His bank, an important node in the network of Protestant financiers in France and Switzerland, did business throughout the kingdom, especially in the south. Favarger looked up d'Arnal as soon as he arrived in Lyon; and before he left, d'Arnal had helped him refine his itinerary, providing letters of recommendation for contacts along the route—mostly merchants who could be trusted to report on the "solidity" of the local booksellers. Favarger also relied upon the Protestant ministers listed in his diary and upon shipping agents (*"commissionnaires"*), who usually had an intimate knowledge of local businesses.

As he moved across France from place to place and contact to contact, Favarger therefore followed the lines of a human geography. For him,

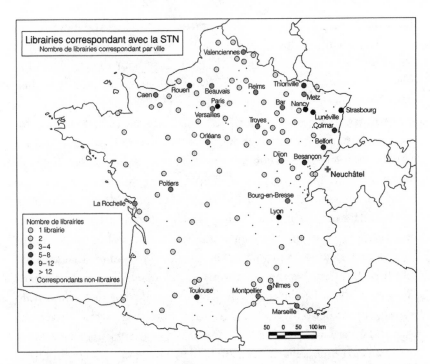

This map shows the density of the STN's correspondents, various individuals as well as booksellers, scattered around France. The STN had contacts nearly everywhere, but in dealing with booksellers it needed to know which ones it could trust as "solid." One purpose of Favarger's trip was to get that information.

BPUN: Map of STN's correspondents in France.

France was a grid of intersecting personal networks. It was also, of course, a succession of landscapes linked by long slogs on hard roads. In fact, he learned that Ostervald, though an expert on geography, had miscalculated the accessibility of towns in the Massif central by sixty to eighty leagues, and therefore he eliminated Le Puy and Mende from his itinerary. But his mental map and the personal contacts that served as its connecting points mattered more than the physical terrain. Then as now, countries exist as mental constructs, not simply as topographical entities set off by clearly demarcated borders.

Thanks to the almanac, his instructions, recommendations, and confidential briefings, Favarger knew how to go about the STN's business when he arrived in an unfamiliar town. Only once during his 1778 trip did he mention the lack of inside contacts—at Rochefort, where he had to fall back on information provided by his innkeeper. He also made good use of his ears and eyes. He picked up rumors about the character and wealth of the booksellers, and he knew how to judge the quality of their affairs from the appearance of their shops, a talent he had acquired on his earlier tours. In 1776, two years before his full-scale tour de France, for example, he had sent a report about the booksellers of Chalon-sur-Saône, which reveals a great deal about his way of assessing businesses: "Laurent is no good at all. M. Royer [a local shipping agent] told me that he would not entrust 12 sous to him for one hour.... Lespinas deals for the most part in old books, but at least his shop is well assorted with them. He does not have a reputation for being solid.... Maudidier was not at home. I gave a catalogue and a prospectus to his son, who told me that they did very little business. Neither he nor his shop look any better than what I said to you about Lespinas, and they, too, are said to be not solid. Livani is solid, according to M. Royer; at least his shop has an attractive appearance and is very well stocked. He has a reading society [*cabinet littéraire*] and seems to be moderate in his habits and to have a good understanding of his trade."[10]

Skill in assessing shops was crucial for commercial travelers like Favarger. They had to know how to grill innkeepers, set the booksellers to gossiping about one another, and judge the degree of a dealer's competence by engaging him in shoptalk. Above all they paid attention to the assortment or stock of books on display. A well-ordered shop, stocked with up-to-date works, was a sign of a potentially important client, whereas slovenliness suggested the likelihood that bills of exchange would be left unpaid at their date of maturity. For example, Favarger did not give a bookseller named Sûre in Aix-en-Provence a high grade, although he enjoyed a fairly good reputation, because his stock had very few works that had been published recently—a sign of weak sales. By contrast, Le Portier in Castres qualified as unambiguously "good." "He seems to have brisk sales, because his shelves are well stocked. He has the look of a decent fellow ["*brave homme*"].... I heard nothing but good things about him."

Wealth was important, of course, because the STN needed to know that its customers could pay their bills. However, other qualities carried considerable weight in Favarger's assessments. A bookseller should be *actif*—that is, hard working, energetic, and enterprising. Thus a bookseller named Delyes in Cognac: "a good selection in stock, seems to be a very energetic [*très actif*] young man." Favarger expressed the same view in a report on the Bouchets of Avignon: "Enterprising people, a very solid house." It did not do to have too many children. Aurel received the highest rating among the booksellers of Valence, although Favarger noted, "He is burdened with a large family and doesn't make much. That is not the way to get ahead." Bonnard in Auxerre looked more promising, because he did not have many mouths to feed: "He is a bachelor, has a good selection of books, and seems to me to be upright [*honnête homme*]."

In his diary and letters, Favarger often used "*honnête homme*" to describe qualities of integrity, decency, and trustworthiness. He used it sparingly, for the book trade was full of scoundrels, particularly in big cities like Lyon and Bordeaux, where he found a dominant tone of duplicity and bad faith. Only two of the many printer-booksellers in Avignon—Fabre and Bonnet—qualified as *honnête*, and some smaller cities like Apt had no *honnêteté* at all: "I met a merchant from Apt who said that the only bookseller in his city was a certain Sorret to whom he would not confide 6 livres without having half of it contested, either from bad faith or from the incapacity to pay." Except for a few *honnêtes gens*, Marseille was worse. Although it had plenty of bookshops, Favarger warned that three of the booksellers could not be trusted with 5 sous and all the rest, except for five, "do not merit the slightest confidence."

"Confidence" (*confiance*) was a key word in Favarger's evaluations. It conveyed the notion of a good credit risk, but it also included a wide range of moral qualities, such as trustworthiness, honesty, reliability, and assiduousness. The STN granted and withdrew confidence in calculated doses, because it had to decide how much value in the form of books it would entrust to a customer and how long it would wait before collecting payment. Most payments came in the form of bills of exchange or another kind of promissory note that normally became due twelve months after the arrival of the merchandise. But booksellers often delayed mailing the notes under various pretexts: the bale contained spoiled sheets, the shipping charges were excessive, delays in the delivery had cost them sales, another edition had appeared at a cheaper price, and so on. Booksellers could find even more excuses to avoid paying the note on its date of maturation. Word about their behavior spread quickly, however, and therefore Favarger sought information not only about the wealth of booksellers but also about their track record in paying bills in a timely fashion. In Auxerre, for example, he warned the STN about dealing with the town's two booksellers (including Bonnare, despite his general up-rightness), because he learned that they were "very difficult in making payments."

Confidence as a form of credit was always rising and falling, except in the case of the most solid booksellers, who never failed to honor their bills of exchange. Should too many notes become due at the same time, a bookseller lacking in solidity might not be able to come up with the funds and therefore would have to suspend all of his payments—a form of bankruptcy (*faillite* as opposed to *banqueroute*, or total collapse), which could ruin him and lead to imprisonment, or that might be finessed by an agreement with the creditors on a schedule of repayments, sometimes with interest, sometimes with write-offs. If he succeeded in striking a deal, the bookseller would then continue in business, struggling to pay off his debts so scrupulously as to regain some confidence in the eyes of all the other players in the system. Favarger had to investigate such cases. In Toulouse, for example, Nicolas-Etienne Sens, a small but reputable book-seller, seemed to be recovering from a *faillite* that had occurred four years earlier, though Favarger was warned by his instructions that it was still too risky to send him books, unless he paid in cash. The prospects of Cazaméa, a bookseller who had declared bankruptcy in Montauban, looked better. Local merchants spoke favorably about him, and other publishers had re-sumed sending him shipments. Favarger left it to his superiors to decide whether to "extend confidence to him." Lair of Blois had missed so many payments that the STN had "removed its confidence from him, as he agrees he deserved." However, he promised to pay cash in advance if it would send him the remaining volumes of its edition of the *Encyclopédie* and the *Description des arts et métiers*, since he needed to complete the sets he had sold to his customers.

Ideally, of course, a publisher-wholesaler would limit its business to sectors of the trade where *honnêteté* reigned and all of its customers mer-ited *confiance*. But such places did not exist; and despite the imperfections of human nature, a favorite topic of the gossips whom Favarger consulted, the STN needed to expand its sales. It had its own bills to pay. Paper re-quired heavy investments, at least half the manufacturing cost of most editions, and it usually had to be purchased long before the books were printed, sold, and paid for. Every Saturday the foreman of the printing shop dispensed wages, in coin, to the compositors and pressmen. From time to time, new fonts of type had to be bought, a heavy expenditure, and there were endless incidental expenses, which added up in the accounts under the rubric *menus frais*. The financial pressure was inexorable, and the only relief came from sales—or rather from payment for sales.

It might seem that pirate publishing would be an easy road to riches. After all, the publisher reprinted books that had already proven their appeal to the market, and then he merely had to get them to retailers. But as we've seen, the nature of the book trade—the prevalence of risks, the uneven distribution of solid customers, the difficulties with debtors, the problems with shipping arrangements, and the vigilance of the French authorities—constantly threatened to tip the STN's balance sheet in the direction of disaster. By the time of his tour in 1778, Favarger had learned to size up bookshops with an expert eye, but the success of his mission ultimately depended on his ability to sell books and to collect bills, and those two tasks looked especially daunting when he left Lons-le-Saunier for his next stop, Bourg-en-Bresse.

4

Bourg-en-Bresse

Selling Books, Collecting Bills

WHEN FAVARGER RODE OUT OF THE JURA MOUNTAINS in July 1778 and into the green pastureland of Bresse, he knew he was headed for trouble. The main bookseller in the province, Robert et Gauthier of Bourg-en-Bresse, had recently declared bankruptcy—that is, the two partners, Jacques Robert and Pierre Gauthier, had suspended all payments, including a bill of exchange for the latest shipment from the STN. Favarger faced the task of collecting that debt and of defending the STN's interest in whatever arrangement Robert et Gauthier might make with their creditors. And how would he sell any of the STN's books in Bourg if its most important client went out of business?

The local market did not look promising. In the government's survey of 1764, Bourg-en-Bresse appeared as little more than a blip on the cultural map. It had two booksellers, both of them considered as "upstanding" (*honnêtes gens*), whose stock consisted primarily of legal and religious works. They had never infringed any of the rules governing the book trade. No forbidden books circulated, and there were no other booksellers in the entire province. The trade almanac of 1777 confirmed that impression, which hardly seems surprising. Even today, the first thing that comes to mind when many people think of Bourg-en-Bresse is chicken—plump capons and hens, the specialty of its cuisine. Chickens were a major product of its economy in the eighteenth century as well, along with grain, horses, and cattle. Bresse was farming country set in gentle hills, swampy in some places but attractive everywhere. Bourg, its capital, had only seven thousand inhabitants. The local bourgeoisie, mainly lawyers and officials attached to its *bailliage* court, attended concerts, plays, and, after 1783, sessions of a small academy devoted to the arts and sciences. The city supported a fairly active cultural life, but it did not seem to offer fertile territory for the sale of books, especially books of the kind that came hot off the presses in Switzerland.

Bourg-en-Bresse was the only city along Favarger's itinerary where the documentation provides a glimpse of the customers who frequented bookshops. Of course, Favarger did not deal directly with them. He sold books to booksellers; and because they knew the trade from the inside, he pitched his sales talk at a professional level. Armed with prospectuses and the latest STN catalog, which contained three hundred titles, he would walk into a shop and ask to speak with its owner. Sometimes he got a chilly reception, as in the case of Arles, where Gaudion, the only bookseller in the city, refused to have anything to do with Swiss publishers and their unorthodox publications. In large cities like Lyon and Bordeaux, the patricians of the trade often gave him a cold shoulder. Judging from their behavior, he concluded they were too self-important to take time out for a discussion with someone else's clerk. If he managed to slip a catalog into their hands, they sometimes set it aside and then asked him to return when they had a leisure moment—but not after they sat down for their midday dinner, which occupied them for much of the afternoon. Ordinary booksellers tended to be polite but demanding. They studied sample copies and prospectuses for the quality of the paper and typography.[1] And they paid particular attention to prices. The STN set a standard wholesale price of 1 sou per sheet for nearly everything it kept in stock. It therefore charged booksellers 20 sous or 1 livre tournois for an octavo volume comprising twenty sheets, which would make 320 pages when folded and cut. Having studied the catalogs of other publishers, a savvy bookseller knew the prices of most current books. In fact, as will be explained later, publisher-wholesalers often competed to sell the same books; so small differences in prices could make a big difference in preferences among the retailers. If a bookseller believed that he could get the same work at a cheaper price from another provider, he might either try to bargain Favarger down or simply show him the door.

Despite the invariability of the STN's pricing, there was a great deal of room for negotiation, because the terms of a sale mattered almost as much as the prices. Booksellers often demanded a free thirteenth copy of a book if they ordered twelve copies at the normal price. Some even held out for a baker's half-dozen. Others tried to pay part of the bill in kind—that is, to give the STN a certain number of books from their own stock—and part in promissory notes, extending the maturation date of the notes as far as possible into the future. Many insisted that the STN cover the transport costs as far as Lyon and even assume the risk of clearing shipments through the Lyon *chambre syndicale*. "*Franco Lyon*"—free shipping to Lyon—was a common refrain in Favarger's reports and also in the letters that the STN received from booksellers in the south. In the west and the Loire Valley, the demand was often "*franco Orléans*." The most "solid" booksellers—meaning the most solvent—drove the hardest bargains. Favarger found it particularly difficult to agree on terms with Gaude in Nîmes, Pavie in La Rochelle, Bergeret in Bordeaux, and Letourmy in Orléans. As to Phéline, a solid bookseller in Uzès, Favarger extracted an order but failed to persuade him to give an inch in the negotiations: "I bargained very unsuccessfully with him. It's final. He won't concede anything."

What then could be expected in Bourg-en-Bresse? Favarger had got to know its booksellers during his earlier tour in 1776. Two of them, Comte and Besson, did not do enough business in "books of literature" to be worth cultivating. A third, Vernarel, seemed quite solid: "has a well assorted stock, is said to be of good conduct [*rangé*] and to pay well." The STN eventually sent Vernarel some shipments, but its main trade was with the firm Robert et Gauthier, which, as mentioned, was the most important bookseller in Bourg, although it never surfaced in official reports and was not even mentioned in the *Almanach de la librairie*. To assess the situation, Favarger took soundings with local informants and discovered that the two partners did not enjoy a favorable reputation: "They are not said to be very good. Although they make a lot of money, they often fail to honor their promissory notes. It is said that the first [Robert] is lacking in good conduct."[2]

The history of Robert et Gauthier is difficult to piece together, although enough of the pieces have survived, scattered in disparate corners of the archives, to provide a general picture of how the firm operated. Among other things, its story suggests that the world of books in a quiet provincial capital and a remote province was less conventional than might be expected. The partnership was stitched together, pulled apart, and patched up at various dates between 1772 and 1785. Although Bourg-en-Bresse served as its headquarters, it operated out of many towns and cities, from Belley, forty-five miles southeast of Bourg, to Belfort, 165 miles away in the northeastern corner of the Franche-Comté.[3] Book businesses with a network of branches were not supposed to exist under the Ancien Régime. Booksellers were authorized to operate in only one location, subject to the jurisdiction of the nearest *chambre syndicale*. Robert et Gauthier set up shop wherever they could find customers, and they found that their customers wanted a large variety of contemporary literature, much of it illegal.

Unfortunately, the correspondence of Robert et Gauthier reveals little about their everyday affairs. Apparently they used Bourg-en-Bresse as a base of operations (they had strong ties to the bourgeoisie of Bourg, including a "Robert" who was—helpfully—an employee of the Ferme générale) and sold books from town to town in the manner of upmarket peddlers (*marchands forains*). They were constantly traveling. They crisscrossed the Franche-Comté and sometimes went as far as Plombières-les-Bains (probably to sell books to the fashionable patrons of its spa) and Strasbourg (in order to do business at the book fair held there, one of the largest in eastern France). A letter from Salins by Jacques Robert said he had been hauling bales of books across the countryside in a wagon. Yet unlike common peddlers, Robert et Gauthier did business on a large scale, larger than they could manage. They went bankrupt shortly before Favarger arrived in 1778, and the papers connected with the adjudication of their case show that their stock was valued at 55,230 livres and that it came from nineteen wholesalers in Paris as well as publishers in Lyon, Geneva, and Neuchâtel.

The character of their business can be followed from their correspondence with the STN. The first letter, written by Robert from Saint-Claude on June 6, 1772, concerned a local affair, a suit against the Abbey of Saint-Claude brought by peasants who complained about the excessive seigneurial dues inflicted on them by the monks. The lawyer for the peasants, Charles-Gabriel-Frédéric Christin, turned the case into a general indictment of the vestiges of feudalism and appealed to public opinion in a tract published by the STN, with the lengthy title, *Dissertation sur l'établissement de l'Abbaye de Saint-Claude, ses chroniques, ses légendes, ses chartes, ses usurpations, et sur les droits des habitans de cette terre*. Robert, who knew Christin, wanted one hundred copies of it; and he hoped that this first transaction could lead to sustained commercial relations, especially if the STN could deliver its books safely across the border. He was eager to order "secret books such as *L'Espion chinois* [The Chinese Spy], *L'Académie des dames* [The Academy of Ladies], *Dom B* [that is, The Story of Dom B....., Gatekeeper of the Carthusians], *Messaline, La Religieuse en chemise* [The Nun in a Nightgown], and others of the same genre." That genre was mainly pornographic. (The term "pornography" did not become widespread until the nineteenth century. Eighteenth-century booksellers used words like *scabreux* or *libre* to describe erotic literature.) The STN did not print such books, but it procured them from other publishers by trading its own editions against theirs. Soon it was exchanging letters with Robert about how it could get this and other varieties of literature to him.

Robert recommended the "insurance" system that the STN was later to adopt with Faivre in Pontarlier, and he had found just the man for the job: Guillon l'aîné—the elder—who operated out of Clairvaux-les-lacs, a village high in the Jura Mountains on the French side of the border near Geneva.[4] Guillon could hire teams of peasants to carry packets of books on their backs to his storerooms in Clairvaux, and then he would forward

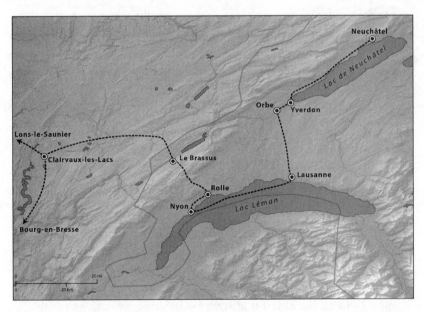

The route of the "insurance" system operated at the Swiss-French border by Guillon l'aîné.

Scott Walker, Cartography Section of the Harvard Library.

them, repackaged as domestic shipments, to destinations in France. Once their supply lines were secure, Robert wrote, they could do a great deal of business. He had already sent a second order, and he asked the STN to supplement it with another lot of "philosophical works and off-color novels." These included a dozen copies of d'Holbach's atheistic treatise *Système de la nature*, a dozen of Louis Sébastien Mercier's utopian novel *L'An deux mille quatre cent quarante* [The Year Two Thousand, Four Hundred and Forty], and a half dozen of the scandalous libel *Le Gazetier cuirassé* [The Iron-Plated Gazeteer].

The first shipments arrived safely. Robert ordered more, concentrating less on *livres philosophiques* than on assortments of legal but pirated works. He sent payment and even offered to transport the STN's shipments to other booksellers from his outpost in Lons-le-Saunier to Chalon-sur-Soâne. But Guillon's operation broke down in 1773. It ran into communication problems (unanswered letters, misplaced shipments), a border patrol arrested a team of smugglers, and the bishop of Saint Claude threatened to have the men sent to the galleys. Robert did not resume ordering books until September 1774. By then the STN had opened up a route through Lyon, and Robert could get small packets smuggled from Meyrin, a village on the outskirts of Geneva, using employees of the Ferme générale itself, who were supposed to patrol the border. Among the wide variety of books desired by his clients, he noted a demand for the apocryphal *Mémoires de Louis XV*, a scandalous account of the reign of the late king, who had died only four months earlier: "Send six of them right away."

The orders and shipments continued for the next three years, accompanied by occasional disputes of the kind that were common in the book trade—about delays in the arrival of bales, spoiled sheets, disagreements over debits in account statements, and arrangements for payment. Despite these complaints, relations seemed quite amicable. Robert and also Gauthier, who usually operated out of Belfort, stopped by Neuchâtel on their travels and the STN continued to supply them with a steady stream of books in Belfort and Lons-le-Saunier as well as in Bourg-en-Bresse until their business collapsed in 1778, the year of Favarger's visit.

The STN first indicated that it was worried about serious trouble in a letter to Robert et Gauthier of November 27, 1777, which complained about a lack of response to earlier letters and an unpaid money order. Several months of silence followed. Then, in March 1778, the STN learned that Robert et Gauthier had suspended all of its payments. Robert submitted the company's balance sheet before a commercial court (*Juges et consuls*) in Paris on July 23, 1778. To the STN and a lawyer it hired in Bourg-en-Bresse, this procedure seemed highly irregular, because the seat of the company was located in Bourg.[5] While the lawyer threatened to take the company to the local *bailliage* court, Robert et Gauthier attempted to appease the STN by offering to repay everything it owed, but with a delay of four years and without interest. Unacceptable, the STN replied: the lack of interest was the equivalent of writing off a fifth of the debt (5 percent over four years). In the face of continued pressure from the lawyer in Bourg, Robert et Gauthier finally paid up. The debt amounted to only 311 livres, and the settlement in Bourg was incidental to the main event, a dénouement that took place in Paris.

On July 29, 1778, the Parisian court heard the case brought against Robert et Gauthier by its creditors. Although the final decision does not appear in the surviving documents, it probably resembled most bankruptcy settlements—that is, the creditors likely agreed to write off some of their debts and to collect the remainder according to a long-term repayment schedule that would permit Robert et Gauthier to continue in business. Fortunately, the documentation includes the company's balance sheet, which provides an unusually detailed view of a provincial bookseller's affairs.[6] It shows that Robert et Gauthier operated on a fairly large scale. Their debts came to 58,618 livres, their assets to 70,905 livres. The balance evidently looked strong enough for the creditors to accept a delay in collecting unpaid bills of exchange rather than to force Robert et Gauthier to sell off everything and abandon their trade. The assets included the company's stock of books, evaluated at 55,230 livres, and debts owed to it by its customers, 15,675 livres—not a solid asset, as uncollected debts often remained unpaid.

The debit side of the balance sheet showed that Robert et Gauthier acquired books from nineteen Parisian publishers, including many of the most important houses in the trade: Desaint, Estienne, Saillant, Moutard, Knapen, Panckoucke, and Didot. The company's remaining sources of supply were three wholesalers in Lyon and three Swiss publishers: Gabriel Cramer and Jean-Samuel Cailler from Geneva and Samuel Fauche from Neuchâtel. (The STN did not appear among the creditors, because it settled its debt in Bourg.) The large number of Parisians may explain why the case took place in the capital, where Jacques Robert was said to have a residence: rue des Fossés St. Germain des Prés. Nevertheless the largest sums were owed to the suppliers in Lyon and Switzerland, who probably furnished the bulk of the company's stock.

The stock, as it appears among the assets on the balance sheet, included forty titles—none of them illegal, presumably because such works could not be mentioned in quasi-public proceedings. The list does not seem to be an inventory of everything in the company's storerooms, as it mentions only works held in large quantities, usually one hundred copies or more. It probably excludes casual *livres d'assortiment* as well as *livres philosophiques*. But it gives a general picture of the kind of books Robert et Gauthier sold. They came from a wide variety of fields:

Literature and belles-lettres ....9 titles
History..7
Religion...6
Law..3
Science and mathematics...3
Medicine..2
Miscellaneous 10

For the most part, these were serious, multivolume works such as *Maximes du droit français* [Maxims of French Law] (six volumes, evaluated at 12 livres a set), *Abrégé de l'histoire ancienne de Monsieur Rollin* [Abridgement of Monsieur Rollin's History of Antiquity] (five volumes, evaluated at 10 livres), and *Théâtre français* (a fourteen-volume anthology evaluated at 48 livres). There was little light literature, and the literary holdings included several large sets: the works of Molière in six volumes, of Rousseau in twelve volumes, and of the popular playwright Alexis Piron in seven volumes.

The list of persons who owed debts to Robert et Gauthier provides an unusual opportunity to identify a retailer's clientele. It consists of thirty-three names. Twelve others were booksellers, mostly small retailers like Faivre of Pontarlier and Considérant of Salins-les-Bains. The rest were individuals who bought books wherever Robert and Gauthier peddled them. Thus "M. Regault, lawyer in Lons-le-Saulnier;" "M. Jacquet, attorney in Trévoux;" "M. l'abbé Paerier à Coligny"; "M. Vauchet, doctor in Pont-le-Saulnier"; and "M. Moreau, town councillor in Macon." Those who appeared without a location after their names probably were customers at Bourg. They were identified by their profession and can be classified as follows:

Law..3
Religion...2
Military officer...3
Medicine...2
Trade ("*marchands*") 4
Administrative official 1
"Bourgeois" 1

The statistics are too small to support general conclusions, but they are suggestive; and they are worth pondering, because they provide a rare opportunity to study distribution not only from the publisher-wholesaler to the bookseller but also from the bookseller to individual consumers. Most of Robert et Gauthier's clients came from the middle ranks of provincial society. The army officers probably were noblemen, as in the case of the only debtor who owed a large sum: "le marquis de Vienne, officer...1,120 livres." The rest belonged to the mixed elite that would be known as the "notables" in the nineteenth century. There were no artisans or workers.

On July 11, 1778, when Favarger arrived in Bourg-en-Bresse, the case was being settled in Paris. The STN had instructed him to look carefully into Robert et Gauthier's affairs, but he had difficulty gathering information. No one except a clerk was present in their office, and he would not reveal anything about the books they kept in stock, would not even give Favarger a copy of their latest catalog. The clerk merely provided a list of ten works that they were willing to send in lieu of payment for their debt. Favarger refused to accept the deal. He also failed to gather much gossip from local merchants, "because," as he wrote the directors, "everything is kept quite hidden here." He heard only that despite the suspension of its payments, the company's business was not altogether bad. Robert, who had left to negotiate terms with the creditors in Paris, was said to offer them full payment, without interest, after a four-year delay or compensation in the form of books from the company's considerable stock.

The exact terms of the settlement do not appear in the proceedings of the bankruptcy court, but Robert et Gauthier were back in business well before the spring of 1781, when their next letters appear in the papers of the STN, some of them from Belfort and some from Bourg. The two main branches of the company do not seem to have collaborated closely. In May 1781, Gauthier in Belfort wanted fifty copies of *Vie privée de Louis XV* [The Private Life of Louis XV]. In June, Robert in Bourg complained that he had ordered the same book much earlier and that it had arrived too late for him to market it. When the STN's shipment failed to arrive, he had ordered copies from another supplier and sold nearly 150 of them. Similar letters—orders mixed with complaints and observations about shipping conditions—continued to arrive for the next three years. Insofar as they discussed demand, Robert (usually from Bourg) and Gauthier (usually from Belfort) showed special interest in *Compte rendu au roi* [Account Given to the King], Jacques Necker's apology for his administration as finance minister published in 1781, which provoked a great deal of polemical pamphleteering (see chapter 12), and in the works of Rousseau. The Rousseau, Gauthier explained, was meant for his customers in the Belfort garrison: "We need these Rousseau urgently. They are for officers who are being transferred [to another garrison] next month." But the STN did not resume trading with Robert et Gauthier on a large scale. Having been burned once, it would not extend much confidence to them. It refused to fill a large order in September 1784 and never sent any shipments thereafter.

Favarger's stop in Bourg-en-Bresse may not have been a success from the point of view of selling books and collecting payment for them. But the information he gathered, seen in the perspective of Robert et Gauthier's correspondence with the STN, reveals a great deal about the book business in a provincial town. And the letters from Bourg-en-Bresse contain enough orders for one to sketch a profile of Robert et Gauthier's trade.[7]

Most in demand according to the orders was Christin's *Dissertation sur l'établissement de l'Abbaye de St. Claude*, because it had such relevance to the local public. It did not sell well elsewhere in France. Necker's *Compte rendu au roi*, *Vie privée de Louis XV*, and Rousseau's works stood out among the books ordered in greatest quantity. What does not appear, at least not in large numbers, is the genre of licentious "livres secrets" mentioned in the first letters. Robert et Gauthier may have stocked many books of that kind, but they probably procured them from specialists in underground publishing, such as Jean-Samuel Cailler of Geneva and Samuel Fauche of Neuchâtel, who had some of the largest uncollected debts mentioned in the balance sheet of the bankruptcy case. Aside from *Vie privée de Louis XV*, the other strictly illegal books among the bestsellers ordered by Robert et Gauthier were works connected with the Enlightenment: d'Holbach's *Système de la nature*, Marmontel's philosophical novel *Bélisaire*, and Mercier's *Tableau de Paris*, a medley of essays, shot through with Rousseauistic observations, about life in the capital. But Robert et Gauthier did not deal primarily in illegal literature. They favored travel books (*Voyages dans les Indes Orientales* by Johann Lukas Niecamp, *Lettres d'un voyageur anglais* by Martin Sherlock), belletristic works (*Essai sur le caractère, les moeurs et l'esprit des femmes dans les différents siècles* [Essay on the Character, Mores, and Wit of Women During Different Centuries] by Antoine-Léonard Thomas, *Les Jardins* by Jacques Delille) and some children's literature (*Annales de la vertu, ou cours d'histoire à l'usage des jeunes personnes* [Annales of Virtue, or a Course of History for the Use of Young People] by C.-S.-F. Ducrest, comtesse de Genlis). They followed a general strategy of ordering a wide variety of books and of restricting the orders to a small number of copies per title, because they tried to keep the supply in their storerooms closely trimmed to the demand of their customers. "We order books according to our ability to sell them," they explained.

That strategy, as Favarger learned on the rest of his tour, was typical of provincial booksellers. He had done his best to market the STN's wares in the first small towns along his itinerary. His next stop was Lyon, a great city and a dynamic center of the publishing industry, where he would confront another set of tasks.

5

Lyon

Entrepreneurs and Buccaneers

BEFORE VENTURING INTO THE BOOKSHOPS OF LYON, Favarger carefully studied the instructions written in his diary by the directors of the STN. He knew that he would have to negotiate with some of the toughest customers in the publishing industry. The second largest city in France and a great center of the book trade since the Middle Ages, Lyon had

Lyon, etching from *Nouveau voyage pittoresque de la France*, Paris, Ostervald, 1817 (Bibliothèque cantonale jurassienne, hereafter BiCJ).

an extensive population of people who lived from the printed word—publishers, printers, booksellers, binders, peddlers, type founders, paper merchants, shipping agents, smugglers, and adventurers of all varieties. Plots and subplots were always simmering among these entrepreneurs, and in July 1778, several were threatening to boil over.

The distinguishing feature of the book trade in Lyon was piracy.[1] The city served as a funnel for the cheap, pirated editions that Swiss publishers aimed at markets everywhere in France. Books had poured through the main route between Geneva and Lyon since the early sixteenth century, and new presses in Lausanne, Yverdon, and Neuchâtel greatly increased the flow during the eighteenth century. Publishers in Bern and Basel usually concentrated on northern routes, and as mentioned the STN also tried, occasionally with success, to open up a route through Besançon and Dijon to Paris. But Lyon remained its most important outlet to the French markets. Not only did Lyon offer excellent communications by roads and rivers, it also provided expert middlemen who facilitated commerce, especially in pirated books.

Piracy flourished as a response to a virtual monopoly of the publishing industry that had been established by the Parisian booksellers' guild at the end of the seventeenth century.[2] Backed by the centralizing policies of the monarchy under Louis XIV, the Parisians bought up most book privileges, collaborated with the state in policing the trade, reduced provincial printing largely to local and ephemeral productions, and dominated much of the national market through networks of client retailers. Unable to compete with the Parisians, the provincial publishers fell back on the trade in *contrefaçons*, sometimes producing their own, more often importing them from abroad. By 1750, cheap pirated books had flooded the markets everywhere in the French provinces, and the booksellers in Lyon had established a network of alliances with the publishers in Switzerland.

In a series of edicts issued on August 30, 1777, the state attempted to reform the regulations governing the book trade (the key decrees went back to 1618, 1643, 1686, and 1723).[3] The reforms redressed the balance somewhat in favor of the provincial booksellers by limiting the Parisians' monopoly of privileges, but above all they announced measures to destroy the trade in pirated books. Piracy had become so widespread, the government acknowledged, that the stock of many booksellers consisted largely of *contrefaçons*. To confiscate all pirated books, even if it were feasible, would be to ruin a vast number of businesses, and therefore the government granted a grace period in which the booksellers could declare their holdings of pirated works, get them stamped in the nearest *chambre syndicale*, and then, having them legalized, sell them off. But after a set date, which varied from place to place, all unstamped pirated books would be hunted down and confiscated. New *chambre syndicales* were to join the old in a nationwide campaign to wipe out piracy. Whether the edicts of 1777 would be implemented effectively remained uncertain, not only because the state often failed to follow through on many of its reforms but also because the book trade administration was deluged with protests from every corner of the kingdom. One purpose of Favarger's trip was to assess the effectiveness of the new measures, and that meant taking the pulse of the market in Lyon.

Lyon's legal market was dominated by a few wealthy houses that produced editions of their own, suitably protected by privileges. But most Lyonnais booksellers lived off the trade in pirated books and many of them also dealt in *livres philosophiques*. They competed fiercely among themselves, made and unmade alliances, and continuously devised tactics to adapt to changing conditions—for they had to cope with shifts in the economy (Lyon was an important center for negotiating bills of exchange) as well as the constant edicts of the government. While sparring with one another at home, the Lyonnais often united against a common enemy outside: the booksellers' guild in Paris backed by the reformers in Versailles.[4]

Yet the history of publishing under the Ancien Régime cannot be reduced to the opposition of the Parisians and the provincials or to the conflict between legal and pirated works. Booksellers took advantage of whatever opportunities came their way. Some Parisian dealers secretly ordered illegal books from the Low Countries and Switzerland. Some provincial firms produced pirated editions of their own, underselling the foreign suppliers. Alliances and alignments were constantly coming apart and coalescing into new patterns. The Lyonnais were especially astute, and, from the point of view of the STN, needed to be watched carefully.

The STN's directors had dealt with Lyon's booksellers for many years, both by trading with them and by visiting them in their shops. As preparation for a business trip in 1773, one of the directors, Jean-Elie Bertrand, described their characters in a series of thumbnail sketches, which he entered in a travel diary very similar to Favarger's.[5] Some of the booksellers were inscrutable, like J. M. Bruysset, "a cold and cunning man." Some were self-important: "The Périsse brothers, clever, with literary pretensions." A few were hostile: "Bruysset-Ponthus will be one of the last to do business with us." Most booksellers seemed sharp, though one or two neglected their business, as in the case of Bernard Flandin: "You have to keep after him, because he is excessively lazy." They might have airs, like J. M. Barret: "He strikes me as blasé"—or they might be masquerading as someone more important than they really were, such as Cellier: "He is nothing but someone who rents out books and passes himself off as a bookseller." Many could not be trusted and were not to be given sensitive information; thus Claude-Marie Jacquenod, père et fils: "Just call on them, don't get involved" ran Bertrand's advice. They abused confidences, hid the true state of their affairs, and canceled debts by staging bankruptcies in the manner of Veuve Réguillat et fils: "Don't say anything to them, other than what is recommended by M. Boy de La Tour [a Lyonnais merchant who represented the STN in the settlement of Réguillat's bankruptcy in 1771]."

Before setting out on his rounds, Favarger read and reread the instructions from the directors of the STN that he had entered at the beginning of his diary. In the first letter that he received from them in Lyon, they emphasized the importance of preparation: "Reread carefully all of your notes for Lyon before making any visits so that you will be ready to return their fire while negotiating, and take as much time as necessary for all the affairs." The instructions provided Favarger with advice about how to handle every aspect of his mission, bookseller by bookseller.[6]

Two tasks stood out among Favarger's many assignments: negotiations related to the STN's part in the publication of the quarto edition of the *Encyclopédie* and arrangements to smuggle books through Lyon's *chambre syndicale*.

The trickiest task concerned the speculation on the *Encyclopédie* and the Lyonnais bookseller who had organized it, Joseph Duplain.[7] As explained in chapter 2, the STN had entered into a partnership to reprint the *Encyclopédie* with Charles-Joseph Panckoucke, a powerful Parisian publisher who had purchased the plates—and therefore, as he construed it, the rights—to the original edition. By this time, the scandal produced by the *Encyclopédie* in the 1750s had died down, and Panckoucke had persuaded the French government to permit a new edition. But Duplain, an

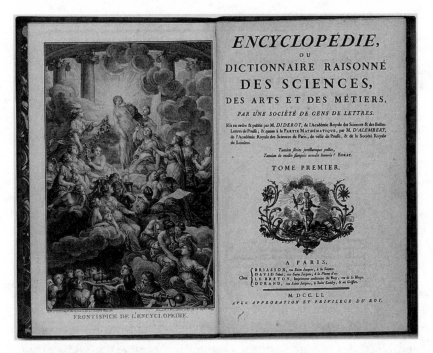

BPUN: title page of *Encyclopédie*.

audacious and unscrupulous entrepreneur, beat Panckoucke to the market by launching a subscription for a cut-rate, pirated edition, which eventually ran to thirty-six volumes of text and three volumes of plates in quarto format. At first, Panckoucke planned to drive the quarto from the French market by mobilizing his protectors in the French government. But the subscription sold so well that instead of fighting Duplain, Panckoucke and the STN ultimately decided to join him.

Between 1777 and 1780, the quarto *Encyclopédie* went through three "editions," as the publishers called them, although their usage did not conform to modern bibliographical terminology, which would distinguish between editions and "states." Duplain began printing at a print run of 4,000 copies (actually 4,400 copies or eight reams and sixteen quires per sheet, allowing for *chaperon* or extra sheets to compensate for *défets* or spoilage). As the subscriptions poured in, he increased the run to 6,000 (actually 6,150, but the publishers used round numbers in their correspondence) and reprinted the sheets that had been completed at the original run: hence, in his language and in the contracts for the printing, two "editions." Even then, subscriptions continued to arrive in large numbers. Therefore, Duplain, Panckoucke, and the STN agreed to publish a "third edition" of 2,000 copies (actually four reams and fifteen quires per sheet, or 2,375 copies). In the end, after allowing for spoilage, the quarto consortium produced 8,011 complete sets. Having begun as a fly-by-night speculation in piracy, the quarto *Encyclopédie* turned into a gigantic, million-livre enterprise—the most lucrative, its backers believed, in the entire history of publishing.

The demand for *Encyclopédies* remained so strong that two Lyonnais publishers, Jean-Marie Barret and Joseph-Sulpice Grabit, who were cut from the same cloth as Duplain, decided to pirate his pirated edition early in 1778. To prove they were in earnest, they printed six sheets (forty-eight pages in-quarto) at a pressrun of 2,000 and told Duplain it would cost 27,000 livres to get them to stop. That was an enormous sum—the equivalent of a lifetime's wages for one of their printers—but after a great deal of agonizing, Duplain agreed to pay it. The three pirates signed a formal non-aggression pact; Barret and Grabit delivered the printed sheets; and Duplain came up with the ransom. It was an extraordinary coup, even by Lyonnais standards; but as Panckoucke later remarked (he and the STN had to approve of the deal in their capacity as Duplain's partners), "When you can't destroy pirates, the best strategy is to cut a deal with them."

At the same time, two pirate publishers from Lausanne and Bern launched a similar attack. They attempted to raid the French market with a cheap reprint of the quarto text in an octavo format—that is, once again, to pirate a pirated edition, although Panckoucke's hold on the rights to the original *Encyclopédie* conveyed a certain legitimacy to the quarto, which the French government openly tolerated. An *Encyclopédie* war broke out between the quarto and octavo groups while Favarger traveled around France. He sold subscriptions to the quarto and did his best to undermine the octavo wherever he went. At his first stop, in Pontarlier, he had discovered how the octavo publishers were smuggling their shipments across the border. As recounted above, that information proved crucial, because as soon as he received it, Panckoucke alerted the French authorities, and they confiscated enough bales to destroy the profit margin of the octavo *Encyclopédie* and to discourage French readers from subscribing to it. The octavo publishers withdrew from the French market in 1779, survived by satisfying the demand for cheap *Encyclopédies* in the rest of Europe, and finally made peace with the quarto group by an agreement signed in January 1780.

While fighting off external enemies, Panckoucke and the STN worried most of all about treason within the ranks of their own consortium, because Duplain's activities looked increasingly suspicious. He ran the entire enterprise, keeping most of it secret and refusing to give full reports of his accounts. His partners began to pick up information and to follow leads that suggested they were being swindled on an enormous scale. After a great deal of detective work and a succession of imbroglios, they came up with proof that he had embezzled at least 48,000 livres. They confronted him with the evidence in January 1780 at a meeting in Lyon that turned into the final settlement of accounts. Duplain put up a fierce resistance, but he ultimately capitulated and agreed to compensate his partners fully— if they would sweep the whole business under the rug, where it remained until it surfaced nearly two centuries later in the archives of the STN.

The dénouement of the speculation on the quarto could not be predicted in July 1778, however, when Favarger called on Duplain. At that time, the plots and counter-plots had not yet come to a crisis, but it was clear that a great deal of money was at stake in every twist and turn of the *Encyclopédie* speculation. Having followed the whole affair as a clerk in the STN's office, Favarger appreciated the importance of remaining on guard against Duplain's duplicity; and at the same time he had to concentrate on the most immediate concern of the STN: its need to win a larger share of the printing operation. It had doubled the size of its printing shop and had hired twenty new workers in order to produce *Encyclopédies* on a large scale, but Duplain had allotted most of the printing to shops in Geneva, Grenoble, Trévoux, and Lyon, whose combined capacity came to fifty-three presses. According to contracts between him and the other quarto partners, he was to draw on the income from the subscriptions in order to job out the printing at specified rates. Duplain raked off the difference between those rates and the payments he actually made to the printers. The STN would not work for such low pay, and therefore he refused to subcontract much of the printing to it. By the time of Favarger's arrival in Lyon, Duplain had given the STN only three volumes to print, and the STN had completed its work on the third. If he refused to give it another volume—a strong possibility considering his profit from the rake-offs—the STN would have to fire its workforce and leave its warehouse full of expensive reams of unprinted paper.

The STN paid for its costs as it accumulated them, expecting to be reimbursed with a profit after it delivered the completed volumes to Lyon. Yet Duplain hinted in his correspondence that he would refuse to honor the bills of exchange that he had sent for the STN's printing of its first two volumes and that soon would become due as it neared completion of the third. As a pretext for refusing, he objected to the quality of the paper used by the STN and delays in its shipping. He haggled and drove bargains at every step, because each volume in the three, thirty-six-volume "editions" raised opportunities for shaving costs and outright speculation. Favarger could not put a stop to Duplain's profiteering. He was only a clerk, not a partner of the STN or an associate in the quarto consortium; but he could help find ways to limit the damage and to increase the profits of his employers.

His first task, according to the instructions in his diary, was to gather information about the general state of the quarto enterprise, for Duplain kept everything so secret that the STN knew little about its actual operation: "Call on M. Joseph Duplain and try to find out, but without seeming to be very curious, where things stand in the printing of the volumes of the quarto *Encyclopédie*; how many presses are being used for it in Lyon and elsewhere; if work has begun on the third edition and what the print run is." The instructions went on in this fashion at great length. Favarger was to listen attentively to every word Duplain said without revealing the STN's anxieties about getting more volumes to print. Yet he should defend the excellence of its printing, the paper it used, its care in correcting the proofs, and the justice of its general claim to have a large share of the work, as it was one of the partners in the enterprise and had expanded its printing shop expressly to produce the *Encyclopédie*.

Geared for battle, Favarger walked into Duplain's headquarters accompanied by Jacques-François d'Arnal, who handled the STN's financial transactions with Duplain. D'Arnal provided critical support, having followed the *Encyclopédie* affair closely. Of course, Favarger also knew it intimately, not only from the instructions he had received but from helping with the STN's commercial correspondence. He had come across letters from Duplain that were openly hostile and nastier in tone than anything it received from its other correspondents. To his surprise, however, he was given a warm reception. Duplain seemed downright affable. He praised the quality of the STN's most recent printing, and without any prompting promised to give it another volume to produce at the increased print run of 6,000 copies. Even better, he said he would allot it three volumes of the third edition, which he had just begun to produce. In fact, he announced that he would market this edition under the STN's name, as if it were the publisher. (The first two "editions" had appeared under the name of Jean-Léonard Pellet of Geneva, while Duplain remained hidden behind the false address on their title pages.) By this ploy, Duplain hoped to boost sales, for word had spread that the Pellet editions were full of faults and inferior paper.

There were two further considerations that, unknown to Favarger, accounted for Duplain's surprising behavior. First, he had made a disastrous mistake in calculating the size of the quarto sets. A printing shop foreman had assured him that the seventeen volumes of text in the original folio edition plus the four folio volumes of the *Supplement* (a separate enterprise published in 1776 and 1777) could be reprinted in twenty-nine quarto volumes. In fact, they barely fit into thirty-six volumes. According to the terms of the subscription, Duplain (hiding behind Pellet as the ostensible publisher) would charge only 344 livres for a set—that is, 10 livres for each of the twenty-nine volumes of text and 18 livres for each of the three volumes of plates. At 10 livres each, the additional seven volumes of text would increase the price of a set to 414 livres, but Duplain could not violate the limit fixed by the contracts with the subscribers. He eventually finessed this problem by charging the subscribers for four of the seven extra volumes without offering any explanations. Then, in the prospectus for the third edition, he announced that the STN would provide thirty-six volumes for a total cost of 384 livres, the same price as in the first two "editions." In this way, he avoided further liability while switching his straw men.

Second, Duplain had run into severe cash-flow problems. He had commissioned so much printing that the completed volumes arrived faster than the payments he received from the subscribers. Most of the subscriptions had been taken out by booksellers, who sold the *Encyclopédies* to their own customers at a retail price. But it took time for the booksellers to collect the payments due to them, and they were in no rush to send those payments, when they arrived, on to Duplain. Therefore he did not have enough cash on hand to redeem the bills of exchange that he had dispatched as payment to the printers. He had sent the STN two notes for a total of 2,019 livres for its work on volumes 6 and 15 of the first two "editions," yet he was not able or willing to pay them on the date of their maturity. He also lacked the cash to pay for the third volume that he had allotted to the STN, volume 24, which it was about to finish. But he offered a strong argument to persuade it to accept a delay in the payments: he would give it more volumes to print—volume 35 of the first two "editions" and the prospect of producing several volumes of the third, which (and this final flourish served nicely as a clincher to his argument) would appear under its name.

Duplain and the STN agreed on this arrangement in letters that they exchanged while Favarger was riding his horse toward Lyon. So everything had been settled before he appeared in Duplain's shop. After Duplain informed him of the increase in the STN's share of the printing and the desirability of a false front for the third "edition," Favarger understood the reason for his surprisingly warm reception. Duplain was not able to redeem the outstanding bills of exchange. The additional printing jobs would serve as compensation for the delay in the payments. The quid pro quo looked quite reasonable, for Duplain stated frankly that he made 1,500 livres in profit for every volume that he had printed in Lyon. Moreover, he argued, the STN, unlike the other printers, was a partner in the enterprise. Partners should share the burden of adjusting payments to the exigencies of production. And the STN could fall back on the support of d'Arnal, who was capable of arranging the bills of exchange in his portfolio in such a way as to cover the extension of Duplain's debt. After all, as Bosset's son-in-law, d'Arnal was connected to the STN by family ties.

Contrary to what he had expected, therefore, Favarger got on well with the person who later turned out to be the supreme villain of the *Encyclopédie* story. Duplain assured him that he had fended off the threat of the pirated quarto edition by Barret and Grabit, and Favarger informed Duplain of his discovery that the pirates from Lausanne and Bern had smuggled the shipments of their octavo edition into France. This news seemed to delight Duplain. "We'll have to shake a leg," he exclaimed. "I'll get on their case, and they will be dumbfounded when they discover that they are the targets of some warrants by the government." In the report that he sent back to Neuchâtel, Favarger confessed that he felt reassured by Duplain's account of his management of the enterprise. But he assured his superiors in the STN headquarters that he had not deviated from their instructions: "Thank God, I conformed at every point to your instructions, which isn't easy when you are with him as long as I was."

Favarger continued to discuss *Encyclopédie* affairs with Duplain every day for the following week. Duplain printed a prospectus for the third edition and a circular letter inviting booksellers to collect subscriptions for it. Both texts looked acceptable to Favarger, who sent them on to Neuchâtel for the STN's approval, which arrived soon afterward. The prospectus made the ostensible STN edition look especially attractive, and it reinforced Favarger's role as an *Encyclopédie* salesman. He put copies of it, along with the STN's catalog and the prospectuses for its editions of the Bible and the *Description des arts et métiers*, in the pack that he loaded on his horse, and he distributed it wherever he went during the next four months. However, he still had a great deal more business to transact in Lyon before he could resume his journey.

An important aspect of Favarger's mission was to engage the booksellers in shop talk so that he could advise the STN about the best prospects for pirating. What books could be pirated most profitably? Like dozens of other publishers on the fringes of France, the STN faced that question every day. Only its directors could make final decisions, relying on their intuition and information gathered from their commercial correspondence. A sales rep could supplement that information by whatever tips he could pick up while chatting with booksellers. The first of many recommendations collected by Favarger came from Vernarel in Bourg-en-Bresse. He encouraged the STN to reprint a work that had just appeared in Paris and that seemed likely to appeal to readers fascinated by the revolution that had erupted two years earlier in America, *Les lois et constitutions de Pennsylvanie, traduit de l'anglais et dédié au docteur Franklin* [The Laws and Constitutions of Pennsylvania, Translated from the English and Dedicated to Doctor Franklin]. A new edition would sell well, Vernarel assured Favarger. If the STN would print one, he promised to commit himself to a large advance order, fifty copies, and even offered to supply the text by sending one of six copies that he had ordered from the original publisher. After passing this news on, Favarger sounded booksellers along the rest of his route. None of them in Lyon had ever heard of the book, and no one expressed the slightest interest in it. When Favarger arrived in Grenoble, he found that Brette, the most important bookseller in the city, had a few copies of it in his shop, but they did not sell. Brette had a low opinion of its quality: "It is nothing but a hotchpotch of laws." Favarger did not hear about *Les lois et constitutions de Pennsylvanie* again until he reached Marseille. There, too, the reaction among the booksellers was negative, and so the project was dropped.

Lyon was the best location to pick up information of this kind, but Favarger found the booksellers tight-lipped. They did a great deal of pirating on their own, and in the summer of 1778 they were obsessed by the sales of the quarto *Encyclopédie*. Nonetheless, Favarger managed to discover that Jean-Marie Barret, one of Lyon's most intrepid pirates, had not been able to sell off his edition of Condillac's sixteen-volume synthesis of Enlightenment thought, *Cours d'étude pour l'instruction du prince de Parme* [Course of Study for the Instruction of the Prince of Parma], and therefore he advised the STN to abandon its plans to reprint Barret's edition. A better prospect would be another edition of the works of Mme Riccoboni: "A copy of the Paris edition would surely sell: this work is always in demand." As he continued his journey, Favarger would collect other tips. The booksellers in Avignon recommended a *Dictionnaire des grands hommes*. In Orléans, Letourmy suggested *Les Lettres d'Eulalie*, a novel by Claude-Joseph Dorat, and Couret de Villeneuve favored *Les Jeux et amusements de la petite Thalie* [Games and Amusements of the Theater for the Young], a book for children "which he says is a very good work—that is, one that sells."

In discussing prospects for bestsellers, the book that stirred up the most enthusiasm among the booksellers was Rousseau's *Confessions*. Rumors about its existence and that of other unpublished works in Rousseau's manuscripts circulated soon after his death on June 2, 1778. In August, when Favarger arrived in Marseille, he reported that everyone was asking him about the *Confessions*. "It is firmly believed that they exist, not in Paris but perhaps in Holland. That would be a book to print at 3,000 copies. If we could get it quickly and announce it by a circular to all of our best correspondents, all of them would take it, even for cash." Although the STN tried hard to get its hands on Rousseau's manuscripts, it eventually had to settle for selling pirated editions put out by other publishers. Meanwhile, it continued to pursue other possibilities, relying on information provided by Favarger and booksellers among its correspondents.

Other objectives of Favarger's mission in Lyon included exploring the possibility of commissioning a new font for the STN's third edition of the *Encyclopédie*, and bargaining with a half-dozen paper merchants in order to line up supplies. He also called on nearly all of Lyon's thirty-eight booksellers, settling accounts and taking new orders. They did not buy large quantities of books from the STN, because they drew a great deal of their stock from Geneva and Lausanne, and they produced many pirated editions of their own. But they were heavily involved in the exchange trade with all the Swiss houses. In his letters to the STN, Favarger included extensive reports about proposed exchanges—that is, offers to swap books from their stock for a corresponding number of sheets from books in the stock of the STN—along with remarks about the booksellers and their businesses. Making such assessments was particularly important in Lyon, as his instructions emphasized: "You will take great care to put into writing everything you learn about the booksellers according to all the information you can pick up." In describing them, Favarger kept his remarks about Lyon booksellers short and unsentimental. Thus his views of Jacquenod: unreliable, "a double-edged sword; I will be careful not to get very involved with him"; Flandin: a hard-bargainer and "a character who has a shrewd sense of the value of books"; and the Périsse brothers: Inscrutable. "They keep their cards close to their chest, these gentlemen, but they agree that there is nothing being printed in all Lyon except some trivia and the quarto *Encyclopédie*." Each bookseller had distinct peculiarities, and most were difficult to deal with: "I've been in this city for a long time, but when you want to talk with these gentlemen, they never have time to listen to you. It's as if they had empires to govern, but in fact they don't do much business at all."

Favarger attributed this slump in part to the boom in *Encyclopédies*, which had diverted resources from speculation on other books: "Anyone who had some money available to invest every month or every year in books has placed it on the quarto *Encyclopédie*." But the main problem was uncertainty about the execution of the government's campaign to destroy the trade in pirated works. The stamping of *contrefaçons* had not yet begun; and when Favarger visited the *chambre syndicale*, he did not detect any enthusiasm for enforcing the edicts of 1777. "I spent yesterday afternoon at the chambre syndicale," he wrote on July 15. "I don't see how this miserable stamping business can be handled without appalling confusion." Although he witnessed the confiscation of a shipment (not from the STN) with a pirated edition of the works of Henri-François d'Aguesseau, France's chancellor under Louis XV, he was gratified by his reception: "While I was at this inquisitorial tribunal I saw nearly all the syndics, who treated me very decently."

Entrepreneurship, Enlightenment, piracy, profiteering—so much converged in Lyon that Favarger extended his stay. He could not leave until he had accomplished the other main purpose of his visit: to find a way to get books past the "inquisitorial tribunal."

6

Lyon

Domestic Contraband

FAVARGER'S VISIT TO THE *CHAMBRE SYNDICALE* WAS CONNECTED to another objective of his trip to Lyon, one nearly as important as the negotiations over the *Encyclopédie*: making arrangements for smuggling. As explained in chapter 2, the Neuchâtelois sent their bales through Frambourg and Pontarlier or other border crossings, where customs agents sealed them and issued the *acquits à caution*. Then shipping agents forwarded them to Lyon for inspection in the *chambre syndicale*. Once they had completed their inspection—with whatever degree of thoroughness they deemed appropriate—the syndics issued a certificate (*certificat de décharge*) that the wagon driver returned with the *acquit à caution* to the border station as attestation that the bale contained no pirated or prohibited books. The shipping agent, often Jean-François Pion in Pontarlier, served as caution—a guarantor—for the return of the discharged *acquit*, and he would have to pay a heavy fine if it failed to arrive before a certain deadline.

Despite all the paperwork that it required, the system functioned fairly effectively as a deterrent to fraud—provided that the inspectors of the *chambre syndicale*, who were sometimes accompanied by an official from the police, did not neglect their job. Of course, their negligence tended to increase in proportion to their trade with foreign suppliers. But complicity and illicit shipping were never straightforward affairs. The bookseller-syndics and their colleagues often quarreled with the Swiss publishers, or favored some publishers over others, or protected their own pirated editions against foreign competition, or marketed the privileged editions that were being pirated, or feared being punished as collaborators in a criminal operation, or (rarely) simply had a distaste for illegal operations.

Although the STN cultivated allies among the provincial booksellers, it could not count on getting shipments through *chambres syndicales* merely by relying on their goodwill or even by bribing them. It needed professional help.

Shortly before Favarger arrived in Lyon, the STN had engaged Jacques Revol to clear its bales through the *chambre syndicale* and forward them to destinations throughout France. It had received a tip from one of its customers in Bordeaux that Revol had ways of avoiding the inspections altogether. Therefore, it sounded him out about his capacity as a smuggler, couching its query in diplomatic language and at the same time dangling before him the prospect of doing a great deal of business.[1] As in its dealings with Faivre and other smugglers at the border, it wanted him to include "insurance" in his service—that is, to guarantee to reimburse it for the value of any books that might be confiscated. In a letter signed "Revol and Company," he replied that the *chambre syndicale* had recently become very severe in policing the trade, because the government expected it to enforce the new edicts against piracy. He had indeed found a "sure means" to circumvent the inspections, but it required a great deal of trouble and expense, and so, "with all possible economizing, it will cost you 4 to 5 livres per hundredweight." He had ties with Duplain and could use shipments of the quarto *Encyclopédie*, which was openly permitted by the government, to hide sheets of clandestine works. The supreme work of the Enlightenment, a book that had been banned after causing a scandal in the 1750s, was therefore being used as a cover for the diffusion of a new wave of illegal literature in the 1770s.

Revol's proposal sounded good, the STN answered, but could he guarantee to get books to its customers everywhere in France? If so, it would pay 4 livres per hundredweight as "insurance." In his reply, Revol avoided the term "insurance," though he committed himself to get the STN's shipments to the booksellers it mentioned, located in Montpellier, Marseille, Bordeaux, Loudun, and Auxerre. The STN sent off these first shipments in June 1778. They got delayed, because they were not sent with bales of the *Encyclopédie*, as Revol had instructed. He promised nonetheless to take care of everything that had been stalled en route and to clear a great deal more through the *chambre syndicale* by means of the STN's shipments to Duplain: "We can apprise you that we have safe storage facilities; and if you want to profit from the opportunity you have with the

Encyclopédie, you can use one bale as cover for four others by camouflaging them at the sides and on the top." Revol assured the STN that with the *Encyclopédies* as cover, he could get its books through "easily." Duplain had hired him to handle all of the incoming shipments of newly printed *Encyclopédies*, and "it is exceedingly rare for them to be inspected in the chambre syndicale; or if they are inspected, no one ever looks inside them but merely examines their sides."

Revol certainly sounded capable and well informed, but how trustworthy was he? Could he provide insurance, and could he handle shipments after the STN had completed printing its volumes for the *Encyclopédie*? Those were the questions Favarger needed to resolve.

The first thing that struck Favarger when he called on "Revol and Company" was that the "Company" consisted only of Revol and his wife. "M. Revol, who has no associate other than his wife, is unknown here. He is a young man, not at all rich, and very daring. To be sure, he seems intelligent, but one should not grant him too much confidence." Self-styled *commissionnaires* often set up businesses on their own, with few assets other than their wits and their connections. Revol apparently had taken up the trade while acting as an expediter for Duplain, who needed help in handling thousands of shipments of his *Encyclopédie*. They had been schoolmates, along with Amable Le Roy, another of Duplain's lieutenants, and Revol wanted to use his contacts as a way to replace the STN's normal shipping agent, Claudet frères et fils.

The Claudets were solid and responsible *commissionnaires* who had successfully handled most of the STN's business in Lyon for the last two years, but they refused to take risks after the French authorities announced the new measures against pirated books. The instructions in Favarger's diary directed him to maintain cordial relations with the Claudets but referred to "Revol and Company" as "our new *commissionnaires*." Favarger was to get information from Revol about how to avoid confiscations in *chambres syndicales* everywhere, not merely in Lyon, and he was to record all the details in writing—even, if necessary, "at their dictation and then send it to us word for word."

When Favarger drew Revol into a discussion of the finer points of contraband, he learned a great deal about a demanding profession. Revol would not accept the formal obligations of an "insurer," and he continued to insist on making the most of the *Encyclopédie* as camouflage for clandestine shipments. But he had an arrangement for handling illegal works when bales of the *Encyclopédie* were not available. The wagon drivers were to drop off shipments for Paris and the north at a designated address in the Croix Rousse suburb of Lyon and shipments for the south at a similar location outside Lyon's Porte de Saint-Clair. Revol would break the seals on the bales, open them, remove the illegal books, replace those books with innocent works, bind up the bales and close them with a counterfeit seal. He kept a supply of legal books in store, and he would be careful to make a selection of them that had the same weight as the books he removed. Bills of lading had to mention the weight of the bales, because as a further measure against fraud, shipments were weighed during their inspection at the *chambre syndicale*. Thanks to this maneuver, the doctored shipments would pass through the *chambre syndicale* without difficulty, while Revol forwarded the illegal works to their destination as domestic shipments, which were rarely inspected en route, especially if they were labeled as *mercerie*. While they might be inspected in *chambres syndicales* located near their final destination, Revol had contacts among the *commissionnaires* in such places who would make sure that the books reached the STN's customers without mishap. It might even be possible for Revol to get some *acquits à caution* discharged without any such maneuvers in Lyon if he could bribe one of the inspectors. In that case, the shipments could wait in Pontarlier until an appropriate time had elapsed, and then they could be forwarded directly to their destinations, while Revol handled the whole transaction through the mail. He never actually managed to execute this feat. Fraudulent repackaging, however, became one of the key items in his bag of tricks.

It took some time for Revol to piece together his system, and the full details of its operation emerged only gradually in the course of his correspondence with the STN, which eventually filled a dossier of 125 letters. The letters produce something of a frisson if read with a romantic notion of smuggling as derring-do, but they do not seem exceptional in the context of the mail that the STN received from other smugglers and middlemen. To eighteenth-century publishers and booksellers, a certain amount of undercover operations went with the business. The STN sought out "insurers" as soon as it began shipping books to France, and it maintained a steady correspondence with several of them. When Jean-Elie Bertrand wrote out instructions in his diary to guide the business trip that he made in 1773, he noted that "insurers are plentiful and unemployed these days," and he made plans to find a "solid insurer" in Saint-Sulpice and also in Les Verrières who could get the STN's books across the border to Pontarlier.

Yet the border crossings were only the first step in a complex process that extended everywhere in the kingdom. If the inspections in the *chambres syndicales* could be finessed, the shipments of pirated and even prohibited books could be grafted onto those of legal works, and the clandestine distribution system would follow the normal trade routes. Therefore, Lyon functioned as the crucial center of communication for the publishing industry that linked Switzerland with France.

Because of Lyon's importance, the STN devoted as much attention to its agents there as it did to its smugglers at the border. Revol was only the most recent in a long line of its Lyonnais *commissionnaires*, one that stretched back from Claudet frères et fils to André Schodelli, Jean Schaub, and several others. Each had special skills. Schaub had ways of falsifying *acquits à caution* and avoiding the *chambre syndicale* by unloading shipments at an inn called Aux Trois Flacons, outside Lyon at La Guillotière. Schodelli cultivated protectors among the syndics. Claudet did, too, and even functioned for a while as an insurer, charging 6 livres per hundredweight, including 30 to 40 sous as his profit. But in each case, the service broke down, owing to a change in the syndics, an unlucky discovery of forbidden books during an inspection, or increased vigilance at a critical juncture. Revol succeeded better and longer than all the other agents employed by the STN, and therefore his dossier contains the richest revelations about smuggling at the most important point in the distribution system.

After describing his service to Favarger and the STN, Revol bargained over its terms. He would not commit himself, he insisted, unless the STN commissioned him to handle all its shipments, not merely those containing illegal books, and that meant cutting Claudet out of its trade. He also demanded that the STN use wagon drivers who could follow his directions exactly. They must drop the bales off at the inn of Boutary, a half-league outside Lyon's faubourg Saint Clair, then deliver the *acquit à caution* and bill of lading to Revol himself, so that he could take care of the fraudulent paperwork. The main danger in his mind was the incompetence of Pion, who dispatched the wagon drivers from Pontarlier and often failed to give them accurate instructions or to notify Revol by mail (the technical term was by a *lettre d'avis*).

The STN agreed to those conditions, and by the end of August Revol had forwarded several bales to its customers after storing them in a secret warehouse outside Lyon. He asked the STN to send him 300 or 400 pounds of legal books so that he had an adequate stock of material to substitute for the illicit works in the bales. He warned that Pion was overcharging for the transport expenses: the haul from Pontarlier to Lyon should cost 3 livres, 15 sous per hundredweight, not the 4 livres, 10 sous demanded by Pion. Revol's own work required more time and money than he had calculated because he had to get the books from his warehouse to the other side of the Saône. "We had to undo bale S66 and to repack it in three packages that are of a decent weight for a man who must carry them on his back for a league along paths where wagons cannot go and then to cross the Saône River in order to reach the road for Roanne or for Paris." Having completed these arrangements, he assured the STN, the shipments wouldn't suffer any further delays.

Of course, such service cost money, more than Revol had anticipated, since getting help from "trustworthy persons" meant paying them. His fee of 5 livres per hundredweight (not 4 livres, as the STN had originally proposed) hardly covered his expenses, he claimed. In fact, he complained that he was making no profit at all and would abandon the whole enterprise if conditions did not improve soon. The STN's directors knew that such talk should not be taken literally. Revol was always looking for a pretext to increase his fees, and his business seemed to be booming. He worked for several other Swiss publishers, including the Société typographique de Berne and Samuel Fauche of Neuchâtel. "All is going well," he assured the STN in January 1779. For the next four years, he got bale after bale past the *chambre syndicale* without a major mishap. His success proved that it was indeed possible to find a way around the measures decreed by the edicts of 1777.

Minor difficulties occurred, of course. Shipments to Marseille were sometimes delayed by flooding of the Rhône. Revol occasionally had trouble counterfeiting the lead seals on the bales. He had to renegotiate his warehousing arrangement when Boutary's inn came under new management. A freak accident took place when some customs agents spotted a wagon loaded with contraband muslins a league and a half outside Lyon. Revol had stashed some illegal books under the muslins; and although he had cleared the books through the *chambre syndicale*, they were confiscated along with the more expensive textiles. It took months of string-pulling to get them released. As business expanded, Revol found it necessary to hire a clerk, who proceeded to run off with a bill of exchange worth 100 livres.

And then there were the constant headaches caused by the incompetence of Pion, who frequently failed to send letters warning Revol about the imminent arrival of a wagonload of books. Sometimes he neglected to instruct the wagon drivers to deposit the books at the designated inns outside Lyon. The drivers took them instead to the Lyon customs and from there to the *chambre syndicale*, where they were in grave danger of being confiscated. Revol managed to extricate one load, because he had ingratiated himself with the syndics while expediting endless shipments of the *Encyclopédie*. On another occasion, he saved a shipment of pirated books because the syndic who was appointed to inspect it "is one of our good friends. Almost all of them are." Revol kept this fund of goodwill in

A loaded wagon crossing a bridge as depicted by Jean-Jacques de Boissieu. Jean-Jacques de Boissieu, *Farrier*. Harvard Art Museum, gift of Belinda L. Randall from the collection of John Witt Randall, R4166. Imaging Department © President and Fellows of Harvard College.

reserve for use during emergencies and maintained it with bribes. But he could not expect the syndics to ignore everything they were supposed to inspect. Instead, he sent them bales repackaged with legal books under counterfeit seals. This operation—his normal mode of business when he was not forwarding illegal works under the cover of the *Encyclopédie*—worked well, as long as he could depend on reliable communication. The mail service between Lyon, Pontarlier, and Neuchâtel was excellent. The STN regularly sent Revol directions along with copies of bills of lading, and its shipping agents alerted him by letter when they forwarded bales from relay stations like Pontarlier. The Pontarlier route was cheaper and four to five days faster than the route through Geneva. However, it also had a disadvantage: Pion.

Although he had the best horses and undersold his competitors among the other *commissionnaires* of the border area, Pion kept bungling operations. His worst error, according to a letter that Revol dashed off on May 19, 1779, concerned twelve bales that he had forwarded to Lyon without notifying Revol and that the wagon driver delivered directly to the customs office for inspection in the *chambre syndicale*. In the dead of the night and with the use of "force," which he did not specify, Revol managed to save them from the "shipwreck." He was furious. "M. Pion is a wretch," he wrote in a later letter, which described the rescue operation as "one of the boldest coups that has ever been pulled off." He claimed that Pion sent a letter after the fact in order to cover up his negligence and that he had not even loaded the wagon correctly, causing many sheets to be damaged by rain. The STN then sent a severe reprimand to Pion along with copies of Revol's letters. Pion answered by denying all the charges and defending his service in a tone of wounded professional pride: "I do not have the honor of knowing MM. Revol and Company, except through correspondence, but the copies of their letters make me think that they are trying to poison things or to exaggerate them so as to inflate their own importance."[2] Unconvinced by his defense, the STN broke relations with Pion—at least for several months: then it had to resume doing business with him because his main competitor, Meuron frères of Saint-Sulpice, failed to find enough horses to haul its shipments on a regular basis.

Revol punished Pion by holding back some discharged *acquits à caution* that he had received from the wagon drivers of other shipments sent by Pion. They had to be returned to the customs bureau in Frambourg by a certain date or Pion, whose name appeared on them, would have to pay a fine of 2,000 livres. As the deadline approached, Pion sent angry letters to the STN as well as to Revol, who was not impressed: "He is an impostor.... He is so lazy with his correspondence that we usually receive his letters about shipments 8 to 15 days after their arrival, which can cause great damage." Eventually Revol returned the *acquits à caution* on time, and the episode blew over. It was a trivial incident, but it illustrates the tensions that were always threatening to pull apart the ties that had to hold together for smuggling to succeed.

Revol's relations with the STN reached a peak of confidence and cordiality during the summer of 1780. By June, he had successfully handled a great many shipments, and his accumulated charges came to 1,991 livres. He got to know the directors of the STN personally during a business trip that took him through Neuchâtel in August. Judging from the tone of his subsequent letters, they hit it off well. They must have discussed the duplicity and embezzlement in Duplain's administration of the *Encyclopédie* enterprise, because after his return to Lyon Revol he wrote that Mme. Duplain had recently died: "It seems to be a chastisement from heaven to punish him for his greed and his hunger for gold, which he satisfies at the expense of everyone else." Revol sent some chocolates for Ostervald, some sample cloth for Ostervald's daughter, and some wine for Bosset. He also sent occasional reports on books the Lyonnais were pirating. In January 1781, for example, he wrote, "*Le Théâtre français* which Grabit is printing, seems to be gaining favor."

By March, however, the STN began to protest about delays and costs. Although Revol did not deviate from the fee he charged the STN, he passed on increasingly heavy charges to its customers, and they responded with angry letters, both to him and to the STN. By 1782, the complaints became so common that Revol complained back: "Constant reproaches, which are so unjustified—that is becoming tiresome." He objected that the STN failed to appreciate the risks he ran and the growing danger of confiscations, not only in Lyon but everywhere in France, where the STN would have suffered serious losses had he not been able to mobilize agents and "secret friends" along all the main routes. He felt so piqued, he claimed (but one must always allow for the overheated rhetoric of his letters), that he was ready to give up the whole business. The STN had no conception of the risks he ran by saving its bales from inspection. "The profits we make are no compensation for the hardship and care that everything requires. A lettre de cachet [an order for imprisonment] may be our reward!"

They patched up this quarrel in July 1782. Thanks to some unspecified "new arrangements," Revol wrote that he could escape the increased vigilance of the French authorities while cutting costs and increasing the speed of deliveries. He reorganized his business under a new name, Revol, Geste et Compagnie, evidently because he had taken on a partner. But the new tactics did not work well. In February 1783 Revol was caught handling a large shipment of prohibited political works, including Mirabeau's radical tract, *Des Lettres de cachet et des prisons d'Etat* [On Lettres de cachet and State Prisons] and two political libels, *Les Fastes de Louis XV* [The Annals of Louis XV] and *L'Espion dévalisé* [The Spy Cleaned Out]. None of them had been sent by the STN, but the crisis was serious enough for it to suspend all shipments to him. He took to bed, suffering from "a very dangerous disease" brought on by the disaster. Favarger, who was on a business trip to Geneva at the time, wrote that Revol's losses were rumored to be as high as 10,000 livres: "It is no small affair for him. It's believed that he may not survive.... We must consider the Lyon route as lost." How and when Revol recovered is not clear, but the Pontarlier-Lyon route remained closed, because on June 12, 1783, the French government issued the order mentioned in chapter 2 requiring that all book imports be inspected by the *chambre syndicale* of Paris, whatever their ultimate destination might be.

Faced with this obstacle, Revol and the STN ceased to do business, and their correspondence turned into a protracted debate over the settlement of their accounts. Revol claimed the STN owed him 2,400 livres for his services; it held out for 1,800 livres; he agreed to cut 300 livres from his version of the balance sheet; and they finally settled for 2,100 livres in July 1784. From that sum Revol deducted 771 livres for some copies of the *Encyclopédie* that he had kept in his warehouse. Therefore, the STN's ultimate payment to Revol came to 1,329 livres, the rough equivalent of four years' wages for a common laborer.

He was not pleased with the outcome, according to a letter he wrote on July 4, 1784, which merits quoting in full:

> You should understand that this sum does not at all compensate us for our trouble, care, and warehousing. It hardly suffices as reimbursement

for what we had to pay to extract ourselves from the mishap that overcame us when we were trying to expedite the transport of your bales. It is absolutely true that—because of our attachment to M. Le Banneret [Ostervald]—we have risked liberty, life, health, money and reputation.

Liberty: In that without the intervention of our friends we would have been locked up by lettre de cachet.

Life: In that we had several encounters with customs agents and have forced them, weapons in hand, to return confiscated crates (at one point they had twelve from your firm which otherwise would have been lost without hope of recovery).

Health: How many nights have we spent, exposed to the most intemperate weather, in snow, fording flooded rivers, sometimes even on ice!

Money: What sums have we not spent, on various occasions, for smoothing the way for shipments and for avoiding prosecution and calming spirits?

Reputation: In that we have come to be known as smugglers.

Revol repeated this refrain in a letter of July 22, 1784, in which he announced his resolve never to work for the STN again. That was the last it heard from him until January 29, 1788, when he answered a query about a report that he had resumed his services. Many booksellers had begged him to do so, he wrote, but he had refused. The wounds, he said, were still too fresh. "You must remember, Monsieur, how much unhappiness we have experienced—health, reputation, a real loss of money, and a great deal of pain." He was also convinced that he was being watched.

And yet...if the STN could get shipments to Macon or Chalon-sur-Saône, Revol told them that he would find a way to clear them through Lyon. It did not bite at the offer, though eight months later he announced that he could send bales to France by disguising them as transit shipments to Avignon. The STN sent him one bale for Avignon in November 1788. It got through without difficulty, and he wrote that he was eager for more. But their correspondence ceased at that point, and the French Revolution broke out soon afterward, freeing the press and destroying an industry that had conveyed books to readers when such freedom seemed unthinkable.

7

Avignon

The Trade in Exchanges

LEAVING LYON, FAVARGER HEADED FOR THE FERTILE MARKETS of the
south. He took a detour to Grenoble and then followed the Rhône Valley,
a major trade route since Roman times. Unlike the calm waterway it is
today, maintained at a steady level by dams and locks, the river remained
untamed during the eighteenth century, flooding and drying up according

Avignon, etching from *Nouveau voyage pittoresque de la France*, Paris, Ostervald,
1817 (BiCJ).

to variations in the seasons. Favarger did not remark on its beauty, nor that of the splendid towns located along its banks, but their names flow through his reports in the order of his itinerary: Vienne, Valence, Montélimar, Orange, Avignon, Arles, Montpellier, Aix-en-Provence (to the east of the Rhône), Nîmes (to the west), all the way down to the Mediterranean at Marseille. To a modern reader who has toured the south, *Guide Michelin* or *Guide Bleu* in hand, the names summon up images of vineyards, châteaux, Roman ruins, Romanesque churches, arcaded streets, and town squares shaded by plane trees. Favarger, always businesslike, restricted his reports to the book trade, although he also mentioned the heat—it was a torrid August—and his horse, which he noted proudly held up well under the punishing sun.

But the book trade gave Favarger a great deal to discuss, and when he arrived in Avignon on August 1, he concentrated on an aspect of it that was crucial for success in publishing during the eighteenth century, although it has been nearly forgotten today.[1] This was the *"commerce d'échanges"* or trade in exchanges, the practice among publishers of swapping books they had printed for a selection of books of equal value from the stock of an allied house. When a publisher printed, say, one thousand copies of a book, he frequently traded one hundred or more of them for works from these other publishers, chosen from their catalogs and commercial correspondence. In this way, he reduced the element of risk—his book might not sell well enough to cover his investment in paper and labor, or its sales might be undercut by a pirated edition that reached the market first—and at the same time he increased the variety of his stock. Thanks to the exchanges, he built up a general inventory of *livres d'assortiment*, or books that he marketed in his capacity as a wholesale distributor, in addition to his *livres de fonds*, or those he had printed himself.

No money changed hands in these transactions—an important consideration, as it was often difficult to procure cash. The publisher would record them in special *"comptes de changes"* in his account books, noting the number of sheets contained in each work. Exchanges were usually reckoned in sheets, although that could cause a problem, because sheets of the same format often varied in value, owing to the density of the type and the quality of the paper. Some publishers preferred to exchange books according to their wholesale prices, but that raised more problems, because publishers sometimes disagreed in their assessments of the market value of a book. As mentioned in chapter 4, the STN set a standard whole-sale price of 1 sou per sheet for nearly all its books, so a typical octavo volume of twenty sheets (320 pages) cost its clients 20 sous or 1 livre tour-nois. It therefore followed a consistent policy, whether trading by price or by sheet, although it preferred the latter, because its trading partners tended to overvalue their own stock.

Exchanges were a vital ingredient in the publishing industry of the eighteenth century. The extent of their use cannot be calculated, owing to the lack of documentation. But the archives of the STN indicate that it was widespread, especially among the publishers of Switzerland and Avignon. Because they exchanged so many of the books they printed, these publishers inevitably evolved into wholesale dealers. They carried large inventories, as indicated by the catalogs that they circulated through the mail. And because the exchanges were so extensive, several publishers often sold the same editions of the same books, whether or not they had printed them. When a client ordered a book that a printer did not have in stock, it sometimes procured it by an ad hoc exchange. The result was a common corpus of literature based on demand and drawn on by houses that traded regularly with one another. The commerce of the STN did not differ greatly from that of the Société typographique de Lausanne and the Société typographique de Berne. These three houses occasionally formed alliances and even pirated books in common, sharing risks, expenses, and profits. Their catalogs, issued at least once a year, were very similar, and they did not undercut one another in their marketing, because each had its own network of customers among the retail booksellers.

Competition was nonetheless so keen, especially in the pirating sector of the publishing industry, that publishers could have more enemies than allies; and the allies could turn into enemies if the trading got too tricky. The tricks were endless. In swapping sheets, for example, one party might provide sheets of inferior paper with worn type and lines set with so much spacing that they required a relatively small investment in labor. Another might eliminate his bestselling books from those he offered to swap, or he might conceal a book that he was printing so that he could cream off the demand before he made it available in an exchange. *Livres philosophiques* involved greater risks and sold for higher prices than pirated editions of books that were not strictly forbidden. Therefore they were swapped at higher rates, usually one sheet of a *livre philosophique* for two sheets of an ordinary book.

Favarger would have picked up the basic information about the exchange trade while learning his way around the stockrooms and administrative offices of the STN. But the STN did not authorize him to negotiate actual exchanges until he had become a veteran sales rep with firsthand knowledge about the operations of other publishers. Negotiations required special skills and judgment: you had to ferret out information about a publisher's stock, to assess the selling power of the books he was willing to swap, and to know whether he could be trusted to execute his part of an agreement in good faith (a publisher could always find ways to quibble over shipping charges, spoiled sheets, and delays). Exchanges called for so much professional savvy that they normally took place only at the highest levels, through the commercial correspondence between publishers. Thanks to letters from booksellers throughout Europe, the directors of the STN had a general sense of supply and demand. But they could not know whether another publisher was suppressing information about books in his warehouse that he wanted to sell rather than swap, or whether he planned to sell books procured from the STN at prices that would undercut its own sales, or whether he would delay shipping his half of an exchange so that he could get to the market first with books that they both planned to sell. To play his hand effectively in these exchanges, a publisher needed inside information about what was going on in the most active centers of the trade—especially in provincial capitals like Lyons and Rouen, where "sociétés typographiques" competed feverishly to supply the demand for cheap, pirated editions of French books. No one was better suited to procure this information than a sales rep, who could make the rounds of the bookshops in a city, picking up gossip and sniffing out secrets about who was printing what.

Reconnoitering of this sort was one of the main purposes of Favarger's tour de France, but he needed to acquire experience before he could be entrusted with such a mission. The shorter tour he had made on the STN's behalf in 1776 provided him with basic training, and therefore it is worth interrupting the account of his grand tour in 1778 in order to see how he had mastered the art of swapping books two years earlier.[2] His first important lesson took place in August 1776 in Lausanne, where he established a good rapport with Jean-Pierre Heubach, a major publisher and ally of the STN. Heubach tipped him off that a Lyonnais bookseller named Jean-Marie Barret was secretly printing a pirated edition of

Condillac's great summa of Enlightenment thought, *Cours d'étude pour l'instruction du prince de Parme* (Paris, 1775, under the false address of Parma). According to the trade gossip—relayed from an Italian book-seller to Jules-Henri Pott, another Lausannois publisher, and from Pott to Heubach—the edition might sell well but it would be flawed, because the original manuscript had been confiscated by the police in Italy. Favarger reported this information to the home office and entered it in his diary so that he would be prepared to negotiate an exchange with Barret in Lyons.

Meanwhile, he picked up the scent of a potential bestseller about a hot topic, the First Partition of Poland in 1772, *Le Partage de la Pologne* ("London," 1775), attributed (wrongly) to Frederick the Great. François Grasset, a crafty (and crabby) Lausannois publisher who often quarreled with the STN, had just finished reprinting it. When Favarger first called on him and asked what he had produced recently, Grasset had replied, "Nothing new." But after he learned of the covert reprint—probably from some workers or fellow clerks, because Grasset was always squabbling with his employees—Favarger returned to the shop and demanded one hundred copies as an exchange. Unable to refuse without alienating the STN, Grasset shipped the copies off to Neuchâtel.

Buoyed by this triumph, Favarger steered for the pirates of Geneva. One of the first he accosted was Grasset's younger brother, Gabriel, a more agreeable but less reliable publisher. The younger Grasset offered *livres philosophiques* at cut-rate prices: two sheets for three from the STN's inventory, and the offer included the philosophical-pornographic *Thérèse philosophe*, which he then was printing. Even more tempting, he told Favarger that soon he would have three new works by Voltaire in press. Voltaire, nearby in Ferney, often sent the anonymous pamphlets that he called his *"petits pâtés"* to marginal publishers like Grasset, while reserving his more substantial works for the other Genevan Gabriel, "angel Gabriel" Cramer. Grasset would not leak any information about these books, not even their titles, but the prospect of an exchange that would bring in more works by the most famous writer in Europe made Favarger's mouth water: "It will certainly sell." Favarger also sent news about what the other specialists in *livres philosophiques* were preparing. Pierre Gallay would soon produce two more pornographic works, and Jacques-Benjamin Téron was about to come out with a new edition of *De l'Esprit*, Helvétius's notoriously irreligious treatise, along with a more openly atheistic tract from d'Holbach's circle, *Essai sur les préjugés*. Favarger did not conclude any exchanges for these books. Instead, perhaps because of beginner's timidity, he relayed the information to the home office and left it to settle the deals.

Favarger continued to take soundings about possible exchanges everywhere he went, especially in Lyon, the other great publishing center that he visited in 1776. As his instructions warned him, however, he had to be on his guard when negotiating with the Lyonnais. They feuded among themselves, played one Swiss house against another, and switched alliances unpredictably. Favarger therefore proceeded with caution. But he could not be too timid either, and to his relief, his first skirmish ended in a victory. Armed with the information supplied by Heubach about the covert edition of Condillac's *Cours d'étude* that was then being printed by Barret, he marched into Barret's shop and demanded a large proportion of the edition as an exchange. Caught by surprise, Barret agreed to trade up to 250 copies for an assortment of the STN's books. Unfortunately, however, when Favarger presented him with the list of books that the STN was willing to swap, Barret noticed a title that did not appear on it and that the STN had just printed, as he knew from his own informants: *Correspondance du pape Ganganelli*, a bestseller that provided revealing glimpses of the life and times of Pope Clement XIV, who had suppressed the Jesuit order in 1773 and died a year later. His letters fascinated the reading public in France, where the suppression of the Jesuits had provoked fierce polemics. The STN had excluded the *Correspondance* from its exchange trade in order to maximize profits by selling it for cash, but Barret demanded one hundred copies as an exchange. Favarger had been caught hiding a desirable book at the very moment when he trapped Barret doing the same thing and thus he could hardly refuse Barret's request. "This item pains me," he wrote to the home office in August 1776. "But he knew that we had printed it, and I could not deny it." Still, it was a mutually beneficial deal, and there was a final twist to it, one that made it even sweeter for the STN. Favarger knew from the STN's correspondence that Hubert-Martin Cazin, a major bookseller in Reims, wanted a large shipment of the Condillac and that he insisted it be delivered to his agent in Lyons—at the STN's risk and free of the shipping charges from Neuchâtel. Favarger therefore dashed off a letter to Cazin, offering the copies he had just procured from Barret without mentioning their provenance. Not only did he conclude a significant sale, he saved the STN a great deal in shipping expenses while demonstrating the excellence of its service to an important customer. The three-cornered deal was typical of the exchange trade and quite a coup for Favarger, who sent the home office a copy of his letter to Cazin so that it would have a record of the affair—and evidence that he was not doing badly as a beginning sales rep.

Two years later, when he arrived in Avignon, Favarger had acquired enough experience to negotiate exchanges directly with the most notorious publishing pirates of the Ancien Régime. Avignon was a pirate's paradise. Although French in culture and surrounded by French territory, it owed allegiance to the papacy. The popes had made Avignon their seat during the political upheavals of the fourteenth century, then withdrew to Rome and left the city's affairs to the lax supervision of an Italian vice legate. Privileges accorded to French books had no legal force in the papal enclave, so the Avignonnais publishers could reprint them to their hearts, content and sell them off to customers everywhere in France at prices far below those of the original editions. By 1769, Avignon had twenty-two booksellers and printers and forty active presses—an enormous number for a city with only 24,000 inhabitants.[3] Its publishers operated on a scale comparable to that of the great houses in Lyon and Rouen, and they competed with the pirates in Switzerland. They also cooperated with them all, depending on where they sensed the best chance to make money. Like the Swiss, they minimized risks and varied their stock by swapping large proportions of their editions against those of allied publishers. Exchanges with Switzerland required long-distance shipping, but shipments up and down the Rhône were relatively cheap: 40–50 sous per hundredweight from Lyon to Avignon and 5 livres (100 sous) going upstream from Avignon to Lyon.[4]

By the time of Favarger's arrival, however, the edicts of 1777 threatened to bring Avignon's golden age of piracy to an end. While worrying about the long-term consequences of the new regulations, the Avignonnais publishers hoped to take advantage of the short-term possibility of marketing their *contrefaçons* in France by getting them stamped in the manner prescribed by the edicts. To do so, they had to persuade the French government that they were actually French, not foreign. Despite the papal legate and his Italian staff ensconced in the Palais des papes, the city did not differ fundamentally from other provincial centers in the south. The common people spoke Provençal and lived from local trade and manufacturing (silk as well as publishing, which occupied five thousand workers). The elite spoke French and participated in a culture shaped by French institutions: a university, an academy, a theater, salons, cafés, and bookshops. The entire city actually became French in 1768, when Louis XV annexed it to exert pressure on the pope during the conflict over Clement XIV's abolition of the Jesuits in France. The change in sovereignty did not interrupt the trade of the printers and booksellers; and they continued with business as usual when Avignon became a papal enclave once again in 1774. But the edicts of 1777 created a new *chambre syndicale* in nearby Nîmes. Although it was not yet operating when Favarger arrived in Avignon a year later, it might soon begin to confiscate the pirated books that flowed out of the city. And if the director of the French book trade decided that the Avignonnais were foreigners, it would refuse to give them temporary relief from the confiscations by stamping their stock. The publishers in Avignon could always fall back on smuggling in the same manner as their counterparts in Neuchâtel, but they all would suffer if the French authorities vigorously enforced their new policy to destroy the trade in *contrefaçons*.

Such was the situation that Favarger confronted when he made the rounds of the booksellers in Avignon in 1778, wondering whether he would be received as a potential ally or an enemy—that is, as a competitor from a rival pirating firm. His first impressions were discouraging. "I have not been able to find out what is being produced here," he wrote to the home office on August 8, "because I've been kept under a tight watch everywhere I go." The city's most important bookseller, Jean Louis Chambeau, received him "very ironically," and the other booksellers also gave him a cool reception. But by now the STN had dealt with the Avignonnais for years, and Favarger came prepared to cut deals. To get his bearings, he asked for advice from Veuve Louis Bouchet et Cie., merchants who dealt in the silk trade and had been recommended by the STN's banker in Lyon, d'Arnal et Cie. As fellow Protestants, they could be trusted, and they gave Favarger a frank appraisal of every bookseller in Avignon. Armed with this information, he called on twelve of them. As he ticked off their names and compiled notes in his diary, he sorted them into the categories that he always used to determine degrees of trustworthiness and solidarity: "good," "mediocre," and "not good." He eliminated the "not goods" and described those who might be willing to make exchanges.[5] Thus a typical note on one of the "mediocre" houses:

> Bonnet frères, mediocre, reputed to be very upstanding, which is quite rare in Avignon. Like the others, they won't place orders for payment in money. They have an edition of the Oeuvres of M. Buffon in 14 volumes, large octavo with many plates; sermons of Massillon in 13 volumes small duodecimo, both of these editions not too badly done, which they will exchange sheet for sheet, the plates for two sheets, against 50 [works of] Molière, 50 [works of] Piron, 50 [works of] Dorat.... This exchange strikes me as possibly worthwhile.

The notes scribbled in Favarger's diary and the fuller reports contained in his letters give a kaleidoscopic overview of the trade in Avignon in 1778, but to see deeper into its operations, one should consult the publishers' dossiers, which cover the entire period 1771–1787, in the STN archives. The most revealing dossier is that of Jacques Garrigan, a fairly prosperous publisher located at the heart of the local industry. Favarger classified Garrigan as "mediocre," but that may have been an under estimate, because Garrigan belonged to a prominent family of bookseller-printers; he was syndic of the local booksellers' guild; and, unlike the correspondence of other Avignonnais (Antoine Guichard, for example), his letters do not reveal the slightest hint of financial instability.

Garrigan had not done business with the STN before Favarger's arrival in Avignon in August 1778. When they discussed establishing relations, they agreed on an initial exchange, which, if satisfactory, would set a pattern for the future. Instead of swapping by sheets, they would calculate exchanges according to wholesale prices, which varied considerably on Garrigan's list. The STN would cover all the risks and costs of its shipments as far as the southern exit of Lyon, and Garrigan would do the same as far as Vienne, just southeast of Lyon. Garrigan offered four reference works that he had printed: *Dictionnaire de l'Académie française*, *Le maître italien*, *Dictionnaire domestique*, and *Mémoires du clergé*. In exchange, he wanted a selection of twenty-four works from the STN's catalog, including multivolume editions of plays (thirty *Oeuvres complètes d'Alexis Piron*, thirty *Oeuvres de Molière*), Protestant works (twenty-five *Psaumes de*

David), some history and travel (twenty-five *Histoire de l'Amérique* by William Robertson, twelve *Voyage à l'Isle de France* by Bernardin de Saint Pierre), and a popular medical tract (twelve *Avis au peuple sur sa santé* [Advice to the Common People on Their Health] by Samuel-Auguste Tissot). The STN was to select the equivalent value from the works he had offered.

It did not pursue this possibility, but in September 1780, two years later, Garrigan—or his son, Jean-Marie, who handled the correspondence and signed the letters "for my father"—proposed a similar exchange with the proviso that each party would deliver its shipment at its own costs and risks to the STN's agent in Lyon, Jacques Revol. The STN agreed and sent 891 livres' worth of books to Revol in exchange for Garrigan's edition of the *Dictionnaire de l'Académie française*. The *Dictionnaires* bore a stamp indicating that they had been cleared through a *chambre syndicale* in accordance with the edicts of 1777. Revol suspected that the stamps were counterfeit. Garrigan assured the STN that they were legitimate, and therefore Revol sent them for inspection in the *chambre syndicale* of Lyon, so that he could forward them to Neuchâtel. But the inspector impounded them on the suspicion of fraud—and counterfeiting a stamp was a far more serious offense than pirating, as Revol informed the STN: "If that is true, Garrigan will be in deep trouble. If such a thing happened to a French bookseller, he would be lucky to get away with a sentence to the galleys." In the end, the stamps were found to be legitimate, and the exchange was completed. Although Revol still considered Garrigan "a difficult customer and a squabbler," the STN remained ready to do more business with him.

In June 1781 Garrigan proposed another exchange. He now found it necessary to stipulate two conditions: the quality of the paper and type must be of the same standard (he would not accept anything printed on paper with a gray hue), and there should be no delays in sending off the shipments (sometimes one partner in an exchange held back its shipment so that it could sell the same book to other clients while the demand was fresh). The STN agreed and asked for thirty-one more copies of the two-volume *Dictionnaire de l'Académie française*, Garrigan's most steady seller, which he supplied at a special price of 18 livres—as opposed to its normal wholesale price of 24 livres. The STN also said it would take a trial shipment of two other reprints from his presses: a handbook on geography, *Dictionnaire géographique portatif* by Jean-Baptiste Ladvocat, known as abbé Vosgien, and an augmented edition of a schoolbook for children, *L'Ami des enfants à l'usage des écoles de la campagne* [The Friend of Children for use in Country Schools] by Friedrich Eberhard von Rochow. Both appeared in the STN's catalog a year later and sold quite well.

Having established relations and completed some successful exchanges, Garrigan began to express an interest in procuring forbidden books, particularly Raynal's radical tract on world history, *Histoire philosophique et politique des établissements et du commerce des Européens dans les deux Indes*, which had recently been condemned and burned by the public executioner in Paris and therefore was in great demand, and two libelous accounts of court life under Louis XV, *Vie privée de Louis XV* [The Private Life of Louis XV] by Barthélemy-François-Joseph Moufle d'Angerville, and *L'Espion anglais ou correspondance secrète entre Milord All'eye et Milord All'ear* [The English Spy or Secret Correspondence between Milord All'Eye and Milord All'Ear] by Mathieu-François Pidansat de Mairobert. He also mentioned that he traded with Samuel Fauche, the former partner of the STN who dealt heavily in *livres philosophiques* while continuing business on his own. Such books may not have constituted a large part of Garrigan's stock, but he seemed eager to acquire them. In a letter of September 20, 1782, he inquired about an unabashedly pornographic work: "Can you procure Foutromanie for me?" It seems in general that the Avignonnais publishers limited their pirating to legal works and frequently exchanged them for the highly illegal ones available from Swiss presses.

The exchanges continued happily until mid-1783, except for an incident in November 1781. Having fallen ill, Revol failed to clear a shipment containing the STN's half of an exchange through the *chambre syndicale* of Lyon. It could have been confiscated, but the syndic of the *chambre*, who was an ally of the STN, rescued it by having it returned to Neuchâtel. The delay, however, looked like foul play to Garrigan, who fired off an angry letter: "I am waiting impatiently for you to order M. Revol to send this bale to me in accordance with our agreement; and if after further delay I do not get satisfaction, I will charge you, Messieurs, for the full cost of what I sent to you. Never in all the time I have done exchanges, have I experienced such a hassle. I had the confidence to send my shipment to you first. Do not make me regret that."

The key expression in this outburst was "confidence." For exchanges to succeed, each party had to send off his half as soon as the agreement was reached. If one party delayed his shipment, he could sell the remaining copies of the books he had exchanged, thereby creaming off the demand before the other party could get to the market with the same books. Wholesalers such as Garrigan and the STN sold their wares in many of the same places, especially the Rhône Valley and southern France. A few regional markets were large enough to absorb many of the same books from different suppliers, but the competition was fierce among pirate publishers, who rushed to be the first to put their cheap reprints up for sale. Although they occasionally cooperated, collusion would not work were it not based on mutual trust—that is, "confidence," a crucial aspect of the book trade in general.

After the STN explained the cause of the mishap, Garrigan resumed swapping and adopted a more cordial tone. "Let us have such confidence in one another as to avoid delays in shipments," he wrote on March 1, 1782. His subsequent letters indicate which books he most wanted from the STN's stock and which he could supply from his own presses. By following the negotiations, one can see the contours of his business. Garrigan also exchanged books with other publishers, notably Samuel Fauche in Neuchâtel and Jean Abram Nouffer in Geneva, and therefore his swaps with the STN give only a partial view of his trade.[6] But a few examples illustrate the general tendency.

On March 27, 1782, Garrigan offered to trade twenty-five of the last remaining copies of his *Dictionnaire de l'Académie française* (a work that he reprinted several times and that seemed always to be in demand), one hundred copies of *L'Ami des enfants*, and one hundred copies of Vosgien's *Dictionnaire géographique portatif,* which he soon would complete printing, against fifty copies of the STN's *L'Espion anglais*, six copies of the works of Molière, six of the works of Claude-Joseph Dorat, and six of the works of Alexis Piron. On May 6, he offered to add, on his side, thirty copies of *Les Trois siècles de la littérature française* [Three Centuries of French Literature] by Antoine Sabatier, and he requested the following additional works from the STN:

> thirty *La Raison par alphabet* by Voltaire;
> twenty *Le Gazetier cuirassé* by Charles Théveneau de Morande;

twenty *Le Bon-sens* by Paul-Henri Dietrich Thiry, baron d'Holbach;

twelve *Consolation de l'âme fidèle* [Consolation of the Faithful Soul] by Charles Drelincourt;

twelve *La Nourriture de l'âme* [Nourishment of the Soul] by Jean-Rodolphe Ostervald;

fifty *Abrégé de l'histoire sainte et du catéchisme* [Abridgment of Holy History and of the Catechism] by Jean-Frédéric Ostervald;

twelve *Prières de piété*;

twelve *Les Commencements et les progrès de la vraie piété* [The Beginnings and Progress of True Piety] by Philip Doddridge;

six *Théologie de l'Ecriture sainte* [Theology of the Holy Word];

twenty-five *Psaumes*; and

six *Sermons nouveaux sur divers textes de l'Ecriture sainte* [New Sermons on Various Texts of the Holy Word] by François-Jacques Durand.

The mixture of Protestant piety and Enlightenment irreligion may look contradictory to the modern reader, but it appears often in orders by booksellers. Another Avignonnais publisher, Pierre Joseph Roberty, imported five hundred copies of *Le Bordel ou le Jean-foutre puni* [The Bordel or the Good-for-Nothing Punished] along with Protestant works from another supplier and explained to the STN, "It is only this genre of Protestant books that will induce me to do an exchange for the works that I offered to you. You know how dangerous it is to print these kinds of books and the expenses that they require."[7] Evidently Garrigan sold religious works to the Huguenots of southern France while supplying other customers with some downright atheism.

The exchange took place without incident, and the two parties agreed to settle their mutual exchange accounts in August 1782. Then, after the accounts were squared, they began negotiating again. Garrigan announced that he had a "good new work in press": *Les Liaisons dangereuses*, one of the few novels among the exchanges that is still widely read today and that, despite its emphasis on scandalous love intrigue, was not strictly forbidden in the eighteenth century. He also offered *Les Jardins* [The Gardens], a volume of sentimental poetry about the beauties of nature by Jacques Delille, and *Description abrégée de la Jamaïque* [Abridged Description of

Jamaica], a short geographical tract by Jean-Claude Pingeron. From the STN he requested twelve copies of a twenty-five-volume edition of Rousseau's works, twenty-four copies of the *Confessions*, twelve *Nouvelles découvertes des Russes entre l'Asie et l'Amérique* [New Discoveries of the Russians between Asia and America], an account of the expansion of Russia, by William Coxe, and one hundred more *L'Espion anglais*. After the completion of that exchange, Garrigan wrote that he was especially eager to get a new edition of Raynal's *Histoire philosophique* along with a further supply of *Vie privée de Louis XV* and *L'Espion anglais*. Although it was to collaborate with Jean Abram Nouffer in an edition of the Raynal in 1783–1784, the STN informed Garrigan in 1782 that it would not produce its own edition. He replied on October 4: "I am sorry that you cannot provide the Histoire philosophique. Why pass up the opportunity for a work like that? You should print it, along with the Vie privée! I would take 100 copies of each." He even offered to put money into an STN edition of the *Histoire philosophique*: "I would invest in 500 copies at the production cost." He withdrew the offer three weeks later, having procured one hundred copies as an exchange with another Swiss publisher.

Meanwhile, Garrigan was turning out another edition of the *Dictionnaire de l'Académie*, and in March 1783 he concluded a new exchange with the STN, this one valued at 543 livres. Garrigan provided 181 copies of his *Dictionnaire géographique portative*, and the STN sent the following:

six *Oeuvres complètes d'Alexis Piron*;

thirteen volume 8 of Piron's *Oeuvres* (a separate volume of "*Poésies libres*");

twelve *Oeuvres posthumes de Jean-Jacques Rousseau*;

twelve *Les Confessions de Jean-Jacques Rousseau*;

twenty-four *Nouvelles découvertes des Russes* by William Coxe;

twelve *Le Droit des gens* [Law of Nations] by Emer de Vattel;

twelve *Eléments de l'histoire de France* by Claude François Xavier Millot;

twelve *Eléments de l'histoire d'Angleterre* by Claude François Xavier Millot;

fifty "*Trois pièces de Mercier*" (probably *Les Tombeaux de Vérone* [The Tombs of Verona], *La Destruction de la Ligue* [The Destruction of the Catholic League], and *L'Habitant de Guadeloupe*); and twenty-four *Les Liaisons dangereuses* by Pierre-Ambroise-François Choderlos de Laclos. [Evidently Garrigan needed more copies of this work because he had sold out his own edition.]

This exchange took place successfully, although Garrigan complained about "the hassle of dealing with shipping agents, notably sieur Revol, who made me undergo a great deal of unpleasantness."

After several years of mutually beneficial swapping, the two publishers had established a strong degree of mutual confidence. Garrigan kept the STN informed about what books he was printing, and he continued to make occasional recommendations about what it should pirate. In March 1783 he urged it to reprint James Cook's *Voyage au Pôle austral et autour du monde* [Voyage to the South Pole and Around the World], "an excellent book." "I won't hide from you my intention, if you don't do it, to print it myself in 7 volumes duodecimo. But I won't decide to do that without your agreement."

The exchanges came to an abrupt end in June 1783, when Vergennes issued his order requiring that all book imports be sent to Paris for inspection instead of being cleared in provincial *chambres syndicales*. A shipment from Neuchâtel to Avignon therefore had to make an impossibly expensive detour to Paris, and the Parisian inspectors, who were arch-enemies of foreign pirates, were certain to confiscate anything illegal.

All shipments between the STN and Garrigan—and all its other contacts in Avignon—ceased in the summer of 1783. Two years later, Garrigan wrote that he was eager to revive their exchanges. The STN replied that it, too, wanted to resume trading, but it knew of no way to circumvent Vergennes's order, the "fatal cause" of the interruption in their relations. At Garrigan's suggestion, it looked into the possibility of using the Genevan house of Barde, Manget et Cie. to slip bales past the French officials. Barde, however, reported that, like the Neuchâtelois, the Genevan publishers could not penetrate the French market.

At the same time, the Avignonnais ran into an insurmountable barrier on their own border. In 1778 they had petitioned Le Camus de Néville, the director of the book trade in Paris, to treat them as if they were French, and Favarger had reported that they expected their lobbying to succeed: "They flatter themselves that their pirated books will be stamped just the same as in the cities of France. They made their case to M. de Néville, who, according to their reports, listened to them favorably." Still, Favarger could tell that things had come to a crisis. "Since Avignon is surrounded by France [they argued], they would no longer be able to sell anything, and this branch of trade would completely collapse and ruin all of them. Meanwhile, they are rushing to pirate while they can."

But Néville knew full well that Avignon produced a large proportion of the pirated works that had flooded France. He ruled that it was foreign territory, whose exports would be subjected to severe surveillance. An edict of March 1785 required the new *chambre syndicale* in Nîmes to inspect every bale of books that was exported from Avignon. Confiscations mounted. One publishing firm after another went bankrupt or closed. In 1786, Avignon had only twenty-five active presses—fewer than half the sixty that had churned out *contrefaçons* at the height of its activity in 1760.[8] By the time of the Revolution, its pirating industry was dead.

8

Nîmes, Montpellier, Marseille
The Struggle for Survival in the South

Nîmes

Things went well for Favarger after he left Avignon. He held up under the August heat, and his horse seemed as fresh as on the day it left Neuchâtel. His only problem was his nasty case of scabies. The itching, usually

Nîmes, etching from *Nouveau voyage pittoresque de la France*, Paris, Ostervald, 1817 (BiCJ).

accompanied by a red rash and even blisters, can cause extreme discomfort. Today it is easily cured by the application of permethrin cream, an insecticide that kills the mites that cause it, within twelve hours, although the itching can continue for two or three weeks. Favarger had to rely on the medical science of his era. After consulting a surgeon in Nîmes, he decided to follow the standard treatment: "I will have myself bled one day and purged [given an enema] the next."

He did not know how he had contracted the disease. Modern dermatologists usually attribute it to infection from mites hidden in bedding, towels, or upholstery. Unlike the clean and tidy inns of Switzerland, French inns were notoriously filthy in the eighteenth century. At the time of Favarger's journey, one French traveler described them as "real cesspools. Everything one eats there is disgusting. The house, landlord, landlady, staircase, room, furniture, down to the servant girls, everything is in the same style. Add to that the hardest possible beds, the most filthy and badly washed sheets, walls or fireplaces nearly always covered with the most stupid and obscene graffiti.... Filth is a national vice."[1] Favarger did not complain about the conditions in French inns, but he probably picked up the scabies from their bedding. Scabies mites normally die within 3 days; so the infection must have disappeared (likely after a great deal of scratching). At any rate, he did not refer to it in his subsequent letters.

Nor, true to form, did he mention anything about the cities he passed through, except their bookshops—or, more often, the lack of them. After Avignon, the density of bookstores in the Rhône Valley and the southern coast of France looked surprisingly thin, judging by Favarger's reports and the *Almanach de la librairie*, which he carried with him.[2] Although he sought out bookshops everywhere, he found none at all in towns that look fairly prominent on today's maps: Chomérac, Privas, Viviers, and Carpentras. He turned up only one bookseller in Montélimar, one in Apt, one in Orange (whose local "bookseller" was actually a wig maker who sold liturgical works as a sideline), one in Uzès, and one in Tarascon. None did enough business to order books from Neuchâtel. In fact, they sold little except religious books and ephemera. On the other hand, Arles had two booksellers, Valence had three, and Aix-en-Provence had four. But when Favarger looked over the stock in these stores, he found no recent publications (*nouveautés*), except in the shop of David frères, the largest of the four in Aix. Favarger gave the Davids high marks for their solidity, though they told him that their retail business was "so mediocre that they sell only one or two copies of each new work."

When Favarger reached the Mediterranean and explored commercial routes along its basin, he did not find much evidence of a booming book trade. Toulon had only three booksellers, and they assured him that their sales consisted of little more than works on seafaring. Pézenas and Béziers also had three, of whom Fuzier in Pézenas seemed to Favarger to be the most promising. He had taken out several subscriptions for the *Encyclopédie*, wanted three copies of a forty-eight-volume edition of Voltaire's works, and pledged to supplement them with enough additional books to make up a bale of 300–400 pounds. In Béziers, Veuve Odezenes et fils qualified as "fairly good" and had subscribed to six copies of the *Encyclopédie*, though Favarger did not expect them to place any orders. Carcassonne's one bookseller, Raymond Hérisson, enjoyed a reputation as "very good," although his trade did not amount to much, and Favarger could not wring a single order out of him. The other important towns—Ganges, Agde, Narbonne, Lodève—did not have a single bookstore.

All these places offered wonderful sights—medieval fortresses, gothic churches, Renaissance *hôtels*—but, again, Favarger's diary registered nothing aside from his disappointment at the poor prospects for selling books. There were three notable exceptions, however: Nîmes, Montpellier, and Marseille. The demand for current literature was concentrated in those cities, and their top booksellers dominated the trade throughout the region. The STN did a great deal of business with all of them, and all pursued the same goal: to grab the largest possible share of the market and to undercut the others. The result was a general struggle for survival, which can be followed closely from Favarger's reports and the booksellers' correspondence with the STN throughout the 1770s and 1780s.

Favarger stopped first in Nîmes. It had a thriving book market, owing to two basic factors: silk and Protestants. The manufacture of silk and other textiles had driven the expansion of the local economy in the mid-eighteenth century, and the city's numerous population of Protestants, composing probably a third of its 39,000 inhabitants in 1778, consumed large quantities of books, primarily Bibles and liturgical works but also Enlightenment tracts. Protestantism, a religion of the book, created fertile territory for the reception of philosophic ideas. The correspondence of Nîmes's booksellers indicates the way those cultural currents converged.

Nonetheless, as in most provincial centers, only a few booksellers operated on a scale large enough to order supplies from foreign publishers on a regular basis. Two of them, Michel Gaude and Buchet (the documents don't give his first name), overshadowed the others. Although it would be anachronistic to speak of "business plans," they operated in opposite ways: Gaude adhered to a conservative strategy in placing orders and paying bills, and Buchet played for high stakes, taking many risks.

When Favarger entered Gaude's shop in the *grande rue* at the heart of Nîmes, he found himself in friendly territory. Protestant books were everywhere. Gaude probably was a Huguenot himself and he catered to a Huguenot clientele. His letters, which had arrived regularly in Neuchâtel since 1771, indicate that he was sober, strict, and a hard bargainer, but scrupulously honest about paying bills and settling accounts. After receiving shipments, customers of the STN paid with money orders (bills of exchange or other kinds of drafts), which usually became due in twelve months. The STN kept track of the accumulated debts for each customer in open accounts and then from time to time closed an account by reaching a settlement with him: It would send him a statement with its version of his debits and credits and he would draw up his own statement (a "*contrecompte*"). If there was any discrepancy between his version and the STN's, they would come to an agreement, and then he would send a note to cover the outstanding debt. Before opening a new account, however, the two sides often became embroiled in arguments over the discrepancies, and the arguments reveal a great deal about the character of a bookseller and his business. In settling his account in 1772, for example, Gaude corrected several mistakes made by the STN, including one to its own disadvantage. In 1774 the STN thought it had caught him in an error. It sent him an indignant letter, and after a frosty exchange even threatened to sue. But Gaude would not back down, invoking "our probity, which matters more to us than all the threats in the world." It turned out, as the STN later conceded, that he had been right all along. This sort of rectitude impressed Favarger more than the palaver that he encountered in many other bookshops. After taking soundings with local merchants, he reported that Gaude père et fils continued to enjoy an impeccable reputation, and he recommended opening a new account with them. Tough as they were about negotiating terms, he preferred them to all the other booksellers in the city: "I would be delighted to renew contact with them. They are amiable people."

This personal affinity may have been reinforced by a sense of solidarity among Calvinists. Soon after arriving in Nîmes, Favarger went to hear Paul Rabaut, the most prominent leader of the Huguenot community, preach a sermon in *le desert*. By the time of Favarger's visit in 1778, Protestants were no longer persecuted, but they had vivid memories of the atrocities they had suffered after the Revocation of the Edict of Nantes in 1685, which had deprived them of all civil rights and led to the Camisard uprising and civil war of 1702–1715. During a revival of repressive measures enacted between 1745 and 1753, Rabaut had been forced to go into hiding, with a price on his head. The STN's principal partner, Frédéric-Samuel Ostervald, knew him personally, and Rabaut, along with his son, Jean-Paul Rabaut de Saint-Etienne, who would become a prominent member of the National Assembly in 1789, promised Favarger to promote the sales of the STN's Bibles and also gave him additional addresses of Huguenot ministers who would furnish help and customers throughout the rest of his route.

The first order that appears in Gaude's correspondence was for 105 copies of the Bible—that is, the Calvinist edition of the Bible augmented with a commentary by Jean-Frédéric Ostervald (a relative of Frédéric-Samuel), which was forbidden in France. It was too dangerous to be shipped via Lyon, and therefore Gaude directed the STN to use the overland route to Turin and then to Nice and Marseille, where he had a trustworthy agent. Undeterred by the extra cost, he soon asked for 100 more Bibles, along with a large assortment of secular works, notably a six-volume edition of Raynal's *Histoire philosophique et politique des établissements et du commerce des Européens dans les deux Indes*. The *Histoire philosophique* sold very well, he wrote. He would take fifty copies of it, if the STN could produce a pirated edition at top speed. It failed to seize this opportunity—one of its biggest mistakes, as later became clear—and therefore Gaude drew his stock from a more enterprising pirate in Lyon. Five months later he was providing large quantities of it as an exchange to the STN, which had been unable to satisfy the demand from its other clients.

Gaude did not hesitate to order fifty or one hundred copies of a work that he thought would sell well. Few provincial booksellers could operate on such a scale, and Gaude's business continued to expand throughout the 1770s. According to one contemporary source, its annual turnover amounted to 600,000 livres.[3] It was a family affair: "Gaude père et fils," which was reorganized in 1773 as "Gaude père, fils et A. Gaude" and in 1774 as "Gaude, père, fils & Cie." While keeping to the anonymous *nous* of commercial correspondence, Gaude père (Michel) revealed some personal details. In a letter of October 18, 1774, he mentioned the recent marriage of his son Jacques, and in a letter of August 22, 1781, referred to "Sens, our brother-in-law"—Nicolas-Etienne Sens, a major bookseller in Toulouse with whom he cooperated in ordering books. Other letters mentioned buying a new house and setting up a new warehouse. They convey an air of prosperity, although they include plenty of complaints about the general state of the economy after 1775.

Gaude published books of his own, mainly serious works, all of them perfectly legal, such as *La Science parfaite des notaires, Dictionnaire de physique*, and *Histoire de l'Eglise gallicane*. He also developed a large wholesale trade, taking advantage of the fair in nearby Beaucaire, which attracted publishers and booksellers throughout France and much of Europe. Therefore, like the publisher-wholesalers in Avignon and Switzerland, he traded a large portion of the books that he produced for the equivalent value in works from other publishers, including many of the Swiss houses. In this way, while increasing the variety of the literature available in his bookshop, he built up a set of alliances. He favored his allies—in addition to the STN, Bardin of Geneva, Heubach of Lausanne, Grasset of Lausanne, and the Société typographique de Berne—when he placed orders. Typically, he would pay for half of the total value of an order in exchanges and half in bills of exchange, which he redeemed faithfully in cash at their date of maturity. Because the Swiss publishers also exchanged their editions among themselves, Gaude could procure virtually everything he wanted from the publishers he favored, and he could shift his orders to the suppliers who offered the best terms without cutting himself off from the general body of available literature. In fact, he sometimes ordered the same book from several Swiss houses so that he could diminish the risk of confiscations or delays in the shipments.

The STN learned to appreciate Gaude's bargaining position as soon as it began to negotiate over the terms of its sales and shipments. Unwilling to assume any risks on his end, he insisted that it ship its illegal works (mostly Protestant books) through the safe but slow and expensive Turin-Nice route. After several shipments, the STN offered to get his books to him through Lyon by smuggling them across the border at an "insurance" rate of 16 percent of their value. Gaude bargained them down to 12 percent.

Then the insurance system ran into difficulties, and the STN fell back on seeking a reliable shipping agent to get its books past inspection in the Lyonnais *chambre syndicale*. In July 1773 it announced that it had solved the problem, and Gaude, who had recently requested twenty-five Bibles and fifty Psalms, doubled his order. Unfortunately, however, that shipment got stalled at the Swiss-French border and finally had to go via Turin. Gaude complained about the delay, reiterated his refusal to assume any risks, and warned the STN that the French authorities treated Protestant books as harshly as the most immoral, seditious, and irreligious works. If it wanted to do business with him, he insisted, it would have to get its shipments safely through Lyon at its own expense.

For the next four years and until Favarger's visit, the STN kept readjusting its operations in Lyon, and Gaude kept ordering books, although some shipments went awry. The path seemed to be cleared for an expansion of their trade in 1778, after the STN had settled on Jacques Revol as its Lyonnais agent. Therefore, Favarger entered Gaude's shop with high hopes for concluding an important deal. Gaude was eager to order the works of Molière, Alexis Piron, and Claude-Joseph Dorat, which the STN had in stock. He had just published an edition of the *Dictionnaire de l'Académie française*, a steady seller, which he had had printed by Pierre Beaume, one of the two printers in Nîmes. He proposed covering half the cost of his order by a swap for his *Dictionnaires* and half by the normal mode of payment. But Gaude, like Garrigan, swapped books according to the prices he set for individual works rather than by the sheet, the STN's preferred manner. When Favarger calculated the relative value of the books to be exchanged, he realized that the STN would lose from Gaude's proposition. On his end, Gaude argued that he could get most of the books that the STN had to offer from other Swiss houses with whom he swapped frequently. No swaps, no sales—that was the argument Favarger had to confront in negotiating with Gaude. He could not find any way around it and therefore left Gaude's shop on that August day without a deal. Although it continued to correspond with Gaude for the next five years, the STN never won him back as a regular customer. Gaude got the books he wanted, including the STN's editions, from his other Swiss suppliers, and long before he ceased to send it large orders the STN had transferred most of its business to Buchet, the other major bookseller in Nîmes.

Looking over all of Gaude's orders (they can be studied in detail, along with the orders of the other booksellers Favarger visited, on the website accompanying this book), it is clear that Protestant books formed the core of his business. The top-four works in the list of books that he ordered most often were editions of the psalms and the Bible along with *Histoire du Vieux et du Nouveau Testament* [History of the Old and New Testament] by Claude de Langes and *Le Vrai Communiant* [The True Communicant] by Daniel de Superville. Gaude also ordered a great many books of sermons, along with Condorcet's tract in favor of religious toleration, *Réflexions d'un Catholique sur les lois de France relatives aux Protestants* [Reflections of a Catholic on the Laws of France Relative to Protestants]. Enlightenment treatises supplemented the religious literature favored by Gaude, who, from the beginning of his relations with the STN, requested Rousseau's works and Raynal's *Histoire philosophique* along with the Genevan Bible. His orders included several tracts by Voltaire, along with three forty-eight-volume sets of Voltaire's complete works, Mercier's *Tableau de Paris*, *Les Liaisons dangereuses*, and a variety of other kinds of literature. Gaude never asked for atheistic treatises or illegal political tracts, and only one anti-court libel (*Mémoires authentiques de Mme la comtesse du Barry*) appeared in his orders. Insofar as one can detect a pattern in the highly diverse corpus of books he ordered, it shows a preference for Protestant literature supplemented by works from the moderate, Voltairean strain of the Enlightenment.[4]

From the STN's viewpoint, Buchet looked similar to Gaude. He did a large business, both wholesale and retail; ordered books from many suppliers, especially in Avignon and Switzerland; published a few books of his own; varied his stock by means of exchanges; and dealt in the same kind of literature—above all, Protestant works. He seemed to offer an opening to a promising market. But the STN was too careless in extending its confidence to Buchet; and after five years of trading, it discovered that he had built his house out of straw. His business collapsed in 1778, and his subsequent efforts to stave off bankruptcy illustrate the vulnerability of a seemingly eminent bookseller who had overreached.

Buchet first contacted the STN in 1773 at the recommendation of Guillon l'aîné, the smuggler-insurer who had been lining up customers among booksellers at the fair of Beaucaire. An introduction from such a source did not bode well for business with the up-market sector of the trade, but

Buchet soon was sending orders for Protestant books, and the STN welcomed the opportunity to make some sales. Had it done due diligence before sending off shipments, it would have learned that Buchet had been suspended from the trade ten years earlier for dealing in forbidden books. He had lost 600 livres' worth of works confiscated by the authorities.[5] Somehow, however, he had managed to resume activity as a full-fledged member of the local booksellers' guild, and his business seemed to expand in the early 1770s. When Favarger arrived in Nîmes in August 1778, he learned that Buchet possessed a house worth 20,000 livres and that having been widowed some time ago, he had recently made an advantageous marriage.

Unlike Gaude, Buchet did not bargain hard when he negotiated with the STN over the terms of its shipments. His first orders, which included a few volumes of Voltaire and Molière along with the Protestant works, were quite substantial. They reached him without difficulty until January 1775, when a shipment was seized near Avignon. Buchet blamed the STN for this mishap, on the grounds that it had sent the bale to an incompetent shipping agent instead of to his own man in Lyon, Gabriel Regnault. But by pretending that he had merely been involved in forwarding the books, not in ordering them, Buchet persuaded the authorities to send them back to Neuchâtel—all of them except a few strictly forbidden works such as *Anecdotes sur Mme la comtesse du Barry*.

Buchet's interest in forbidden literature became clear soon after this incident when he proposed that the STN publish its own edition of *Anecdotes sur Mme la comtesse du Barry* and offered to purchase five hundred copies as an advance order. The STN did not take the bait. It rarely printed such disreputable works, preferring to acquire them by exchanges with the publishers who did—marginal entrepreneurs such as Jean-Samuel Cailler, Gabriel Grasset, and Jacques-Benjamin Téron of Geneva. It therefore could furnish plenty of illegal literature, which made up a fairly large proportion of Buchet's orders from mid-1774 until the spring of 1778. On September 5, 1776, for example, he ordered thirteen copies of the atheistic *Le Christianisme dévoilé* [Christianity Unveiled] and twenty-six copies of the *Nouveau Testament*. Along with a constant demand for Protestant works, his orders included many tracts by Voltaire, a large number of subscriptions to the quarto edition of the *Encyclopédie*, and a few political libels, such as *Mémoires de Louis XV* and *Mémoires de l'abbé*

Terray. By 1778 the pattern of his orders suggested that he was taking more chances and having more difficulty in paying his bills. In December 1777 the STN had refused to accept one of his notes, which he had written on Boisserand, an underground dealer in Roanne who had recently fled to avoid debtors' prison. And in squaring accounts in May 1777, it found that Buchet had credited himself twice for the same transaction. Accounting mistakes occasionally occurred in the book trade but never among the most solid booksellers, such as Gaude, père, fils & Cie.

In a letter from Buchet dated May 4, 1778, a few months before Favarger's visit, the STN learned that he had suspended all payments. His debts amounted to 30,012 livres. He evaluated his assets at 53,026 livres, but that sum included his own, unsubstantiated assessment of the value of his stock (42,258 livres) and 10,767 in debts owed to him. The possibility of collecting those debts looked unlikely, especially in light of another item in his report on his financial situation: 12,412 livres that he had written off as losses from unpaid debts accumulated since he began operating in 1763. In self-defense, he attributed those losses to "the bad faith of those whom I have treated with too much decency." He also blamed the poor state of the local economy. But he promised that he could restore his affairs should the STN, like his other creditors, accept a proposal for the long-term redemption of its debt: he would pay off everything with 5 percent interest in installments spread out over four years. "To demand more than what I have the honor to propose would be to demand the impossible or my total ruin and the loss of what I owe."

Having received many such propositions from desperate debtors, the STN had learned to be tough. It did not want to open up new lines of credit to tradesmen who might go under at any time, and it feared the kind of deals that could take place behind its back and favor some creditors at the expense of others. It therefore replied to Buchet that it would agree to his proposal only if he could find someone trustworthy to act as a backer, guaranteeing payment of the installments. Buchet answered that other creditors had accepted his terms. Should the STN take him to court, it could ruin him, and that would not produce the payment of his debt. On the other hand, it could collect everything he owed, with interest, if it gave him the four-year extension. While the STN continued to sound implacable in its letters to Buchet, it entrusted Favarger to negotiate in its name as soon as he could size up the situation in Nîmes. He was to find out whether Buchet could be trusted, discover the true state of his affairs, and determine whether anyone reliable would provide security for the repayment of the debt.

Favarger made the rounds of merchants and pastors, using the letters of recommendation that he had accumulated along his route. His report provides a good example of the bill-collecting function of the *commis voyageur* and of the importance of reputation. Montaud et compagnie, the most reliable firm that Favarger consulted, informed him that it would be difficult to make a clear judgment about Buchet, although there was much to be said in his favor. He was very enterprising, had built up a large business, and until the current crisis had usually paid his bills on time. His second marriage was bound to bring him a new infusion of wealth. All things considered, in Montaud's view, he probably would honor his obligations. A leader of the Protestant community, Rabaut de Saint-Etienne, gave Favarger precisely the opposite advice: the STN should not let Buchet inveigle it into accepting a long-term repayment scheme; instead, it should collect all the cash it could as soon as it could, even if it had to write off some of the debt.

Armed with this contradictory information, Favarger bearded Buchet in his shop in the rue des Greffes. He learned immediately that there was no cash to be had and no guarantor to stand security for future payments. Yet the situation did not look impossible. When Buchet opened up his accounts, as debtors often did when they had their backs to the wall, Favarger noted that the balance sheet seemed to be in good order. And Buchet's correspondence showed that many of his creditors—in Paris, Lyon, Avignon, and Switzerland—had accepted the four-year repayment plan. Favarger was convinced that he had not made secret deals with any of them. In the course of a long debate about all the possibilities of acquitting the debt, Buchet argued that it was in the STN's interest to let him continue his business while collecting the debts owed to him and making enough through sales to repay everything he owed to it: 1,120 livres plus 5 percent interest. He had already committed himself to redeem 20,000 livres to his other creditors. "That's rather a lot for a provincial bookseller," Favarger observed. And more worrisome were rumors that Buchet was an inveterate liar and had apparently not told his new wife about the critical state of his finances.

Instead of attempting to settle things on the spot, Favarger left the decision to his superiors in Neuchâtel. They tried without success to extract better terms from Buchet and finally agreed in September 1778 to a schedule of payments that would clear his debt by the end of 1780. Buchet resumed ordering books from the STN in February 1779. He asked for twenty-six Bibles and arranged to pay for them in advance. Although he acknowledged that he would have to win back their "confidence," he boasted to the STN about his behavior in the past: "Whatever your confidence in relation to me, your house will never be the dupe of any favors or advantages that it could extend. Frankness and probity is the path that I have always followed and will never abandon."

Buchet did indeed honor all the notes that he had written to clear his debt. He supplemented his bookselling with a *cabinet littéraire*, or commercial book club, using his stock as a lending library; and by May 1782 he was again publishing books of his own—notably a *Traité d'orthographie* [Treatise on Spelling] that he offered to the STN in exchange for its publications. Although the STN refused to engage in swapping, it filled some large orders for Buchet during the next two years. In February 1785, however, he failed to pay three of his notes for a debt of 355 livres. He had suspended his payments once again and again asked his creditors to accept a repayment plan, this time extending it for two years. In fact, he used the same phrasing, word for word, as in his appeal for clemency in 1778: "To demand more than what I have the honor to propose would be to demand the impossible or my total ruin and the loss of what I owe."

Although this was a familiar refrain—and one that it had heard in various formulations from other debtors—the STN grudgingly accepted the proposal. It had little choice, given that Buchet could not come up with cash; his creditors had nothing to gain by forcing him into outright bankruptcy. That at any rate was the advice of a merchant in Nîmes who considered the repayment plan a "ruse" but found it impossible to collect the debt for the STN.[6] Three years later, Buchet still owed money to the STN. He finally cleared his account in April 1788 by means of a promissory note for 240 livres and another exchange arrangement, swapping his edition of the *Dictionnaire de l'Académie française* against the STN's Psalms and a Protestant tract, *La Nourriture de l'âme* [The Nourishment of the Soul]. When the STN last heard from him, in October 1788, he was still operating out of his bookshop, managing his *cabinet littéraire*, and publishing the occasional volume.

By then, however, Buchet had sunk into the second rank of booksellers. His signature on bills of exchange no longer commanded respect. A merchant-banker who specialized in collecting debts from booksellers had written him off and warned the STN to do the same: "Buchet is a poor devil who can barely earn enough to live. He is being prosecuted on all sides, and no one ever extracts anything from him."[7]

The contrast between Gaude and Buchet illustrates two tendencies among booksellers in the upscale sector of the trade. Some avoided risks, especially if their financial base was solid enough to protect them from unforeseen contingencies, while others pursued profits beyond the limits of their capacity, writing more bills of exchange than they could cover from sales at their counter. The former tended to avoid the most dangerous works, although they stocked their shops with plenty of Enlightenment tracts and relied heavily on pirated works. The latter sold those books, too, but supplemented them with the kind that had to be hidden under the counter—atheistic treatises and scandalous libels.

Montpellier

By the time Favarger reached Montpellier, he had stopped complaining about his scabies and started worrying about his horse. It kept tripping over its front legs. Favarger tried to remedy this tendency by having it shod in different ways, but the poor animal's feet became so swollen that he resorted to the same treatment that he had applied to himself: bleeding (10 sous to the veterinarian). "You will understand that we are more interested in your health than in that of your horse," read a letter from the STN waiting for Favarger in Montpellier. Still, Montpellier was an easy ride from Nîmes; and once there, man and beast got some rest, for Favarger had enough business in the bookstores to keep himself busy for several days.

Like Nîmes, Montpellier was excellent book territory. In fact, the two cities, located only thirty-five miles apart, had much in common. In 1780, Nîmes had 49,000 inhabitants, eight booksellers, and two printers. Montpellier had 31,000 inhabitants, nine booksellers, and two printers. Each had a large population of Protestants, and each enjoyed a period of commercial prosperity during the mid-century years. Although smaller than

Montpellier, etching from *Nouveau voyage pittoresque de la France*, Paris, Ostervald, 1817 (BiCJ).

Nîmes, Montpellier was the administrative capital of all Languedoc. As the seat of an intendancy, a university with a famous medical faculty, and several high courts (but not the provincial *parlement*, which was located in Toulouse), it had a high percentage of officials, lawyers, professors, and students, along with clergymen connected with its archbishopric, and soldiers stationed in its garrison. By the time of Favarger's visit, an urban elite patronized its concerts and theater, attended meetings of its academy, subscribed to its local newspaper, and frequented its bookshops.

When Favarger inspected the shops, he immediately wrote off two booksellers, Bascou and Tournel, as insignificant. A third, J. B. Faure, who managed the business inherited by widow Gonthier, had a good reputation but would not place any orders. A fourth, Abraham Fontanel, dealt mainly in prints and sold books only as a sideline. Cézary, the fifth, was considered honest but poor. Two printers, Martel and Picot, limited their trade to religious tracts and ephemera. That left Isaac-Pierre Rigaud, or Rigaud, Pons & Compagnie as the firm was known, because Rigaud had absorbed the small business of Albert Pons, who was little more than a secondhand dealer (*brocanteur*). Rigaud gave a fairly large order to Favarger, who confirmed what the STN had known from many years of experience: Rigaud was as solid as they came in the book trade.

Rigaud's correspondence in the STN archives—ninety-nine letters spread out over seventeen years—illustrates a pattern that runs through many of the dossiers. It shows how a veteran bookseller could dominate the trade in a provincial capital by squeezing out competitors. Like Gaude in Nîmes, Rigaud bargained hard, avoided risk, and kept his eye on the bottom line. Although he did everything possible to crush the competition, he never resorted to the duplicity and cheating common among less respectable dealers, who could always find a pretext to avoid paying off their debts. He protested every malfunction in the service of his suppliers and pushed hard whenever he saw an opportunity to cut costs, but he always paid his bills on time. He epitomized the characteristics most valued in the book industry: *honnêteté* and *solidité*.

The best description of Rigaud appears some years before Favarger's visit, in the government's survey of the book trade in 1764. He stood out as the most important bookseller in Montpellier, according to the report for Languedoc, though no one could estimate his wealth. Some put it at 50,000 or 60,000 livres, others at more than 150,000. It was hard to judge, because his assets were tied up in his business rather than in real estate, and "he is very secret in his affairs." Above all, the report noted, he commanded a great deal of respect: "This bookseller runs his business with great intelligence. He is a Protestant and has a reputation for being very upright, although he is accused of carrying many books of his religion and other prohibited works. He produced a certificate of Catholicism at the time of his reception [into the booksellers' guild] and since then has performed some functions of a Catholic."[8]

That diagnosis was confirmed by reports that the STN received about Rigaud's relations with two of the other booksellers in Montpellier, Cézary and Fontanel. After sounding local opinion, Favarger assessed Cézary as "very upright" (*fort honnête homme*) and sent on an order from him to the STN. It contained twenty-three titles, many of them medical treatises in Latin, which must have been intended for the doctors and students in the university's faculty of medicine. Most of the others were Protestant works and history books.

But before he could further develop his trade with the STN, Cézary ran into disaster. He drew much of his stock from the printers in nearby Avignon and had ordered more books than he could sell—that is, the bills of exchange that he sent for the accumulated shipments became due before he had acquired enough cash to honor them. Three Avignonnais publishers pressed him hard for payment, and he persuaded one of them, J.-J. Niel, to take a selection of books from his stock in exchange for writing off a debt of 1,400 livres. Niel chose the bestselling books, an assortment worth 3,000 livres, according to a letter that Cézary sent to the STN in an attempt to persuade it to accept a delay in the payment of its own bills. Then things spiraled downward: Cézary refused to give up the books, Niel had them seized and carted off in seven crates by Montpellier's bailiffs, and Cézary went into hiding to escape debtors' prison. His mother got a court to seal off the bookshop in order to prevent more raids on the stock, and from his hiding place Cézary attempted to negotiate a settlement with all of his creditors. He had enough assets to pay them all if given adequate time, he assured the STN. However, first he needed to get a safe conduct from the authorities so that he could deliver installments of the *Encyclopédie* to customers who had subscribed to it through him.

To decide how to respond to Cézary's plea, the STN contacted an attorney in Montpellier and also a local merchant named Vialars, of Vialars, père, fils et Thouron, a Protestant and a friend of Ostervald's. The attorney confirmed that although Cézary remained in hiding, he should eventually be able to pay back his debts. He had declared himself insolvent by submitting a balance sheet, which showed that his debts came to 64,410 livres and his stock was worth 42,668 livres. He also owned two houses worth a total of 30,000 livres. It would be better, the attorney advised, to grant him enough time to resume business and sell off his stock at reasonable prices than to force an immediate sale, which would ruin him and produce relatively little in the way of repayment.

Cézary's creditors or their representatives met on June 24, 1781, to discuss a possible settlement. Cézary himself reported the result in a letter to the STN on the following day. Rigaud had done the evaluation of his stock, he explained, and now was attempting to persuade the other creditors to force him out of business. His only hope of survival was to get the creditors to write off half of his debts and to give him six months to pay the other half. "I am upright [*honnête homme*] and of rigorous probity," he insisted. "All my desire in this world is to work night and day in order to pay off my account with you." In Rigaud, however, Cézary faced a formidable enemy: "It is very painful for me to have learned that a certain Monsieur of this city [later he mentioned Rigaud by name], impelled by cupidity and determined to wipe me out in order to decrease the number of booksellers in Montpellier and to have my books for nothing, has written to some of my creditors to dissuade them from accepting this arrangement."

That was the last the STN heard from him. Vialars later reported that the creditors had decided to sacrifice half of the debt and to sell off Cézary's entire stock in order to cover the other half. They had appointed an agent named Luc Biron to dispose of the stock and to pay off its assessed value over a period of three years. Vialars suspected that Biron was a proxy ("*homme de paille*") for Rigaud, but there was nothing the STN could do to prevent this arrangement. In March 1784, it received 142 livres, half the money owed to it. By then, Rigaud probably had acquired most of Cézary's inventory at a bargain price, thanks to his own assessment of it, and Cézary had disappeared from the book trade.[9]

There was nothing personal about this feud. Rigaud merely sought to eliminate a competitor, and as explained below, did the same with the other bookseller whom Favarger recommended to the STN, Abraham Fontanel. Rigaud did not allude to this commercial warfare in his correspondence with the STN, which remained strictly professional, although in his first letter he sent a personal greeting to Ostervald. In fact, the relentlessly businesslike character of Rigaud's letters is what makes them interesting. They show how a successful bookseller managed his affairs, mediating between supply and demand. A typical Rigaud order contained between a dozen and two dozen titles but only a small number of copies per title so that he minimized the risk of failing to sell all the copies of a particular work while ensuring that the shipment would be heavy enough for him to pay for it at the cheaper, bulk rates. Shipping costs were such an important factor that they outweighed another key consideration, one that he also stressed in his letters: speed. Like all booksellers, Rigaud wanted to receive his books, especially topical works or *nouveautés*, in time to beat his competitors to the market. Nonetheless, he instructed the STN to delay filling an order if it did not have some of those books in stock rather than to send others in a small package that would incur heavy shipping charges: "Don't send any small packages to us. The transport costs are ruinous. Wait until you have accumulated enough to make up a shipment of a certain weight."

The order that Rigaud gave to Favarger in August 1778 typified the way he built up his stock. It included eighteen titles, and 291 books in all.[10] Of them, he ordered between two and four copies of eleven works, six copies of seven works, and a dozen copies of only one: *Les Plans et les statuts des différents établissements ordonnés par S.M.Impériale Cathérine II pour l'éducation de la jeunesse et l'utilité générale de son empire* [The Plans and Statutes of Various Establishments Created by Her Imperial Majesty Catherine II for the Education of Youth and the General Utility of Her Empire]. By restricting the number of copies per title, he avoided clogging up his warehouse with unsold books. And if his customers kept asking for a particular title, he could always order more, adjusting supply to demand.

The pattern of repeated orders shows sustained demand for certain works and, at the same time, Rigaud's conservatism in stocking them. For example, when the STN published a pirated edition of Baculard d'Arnaud's popular, sentimental novel *Epreuves du sentiment* [The Trials of Sentiment] in 1773, he ordered six copies; and then he renewed his orders as follows:

July 21, 1773 (initial order) ....6 copies
September 20, 1773 ....12 copies
March 19, 1777...2 copies
September 26, 1777..3 copies
November 22, 1779 ....4 copies

A similar pattern of moderate but continuous demand for light fiction can be seen in his orders for the works of Mme Riccoboni, Mme de Genlis, and Claude-Joseph Dorat. The book that he ordered most repeatedly was the one that topped the list of his "bestsellers" or most frequently ordered books (listed in the website, along with the "bestseller" lists of the other booksellers): Louis-Sébastien Mercier's utopian fantasy, *L'An deux mille quatre cent quarante*. The sequence went as follows:

September 21, 1772...12 copies
September 29, 1773 ....50 copies
March 23, 1774...12 copies

October 14, 1774.. 60 copies
August 16, 1775... 25 copies
June 2, 1777... 20 copies
November 22, 1779.. 12 copies
September 8, 1780.. 13 copies
September 13, 1780.. 12 copies
January 17, 1781.. 12 copies
November 7, 1783.. 26 copies
Total... 254 copies

Had Rigaud ordered one hundred or more copies all at once, as occasionally happened when booksellers took chances on making a *coup*, as they called it—that is, timing large orders to profit from a spike in demand—his speculation might be considered something of a gamble. But the repeated orders over a period of eleven years demonstrates that *L'An deux mille quatre cent quarante* was a great favorite of the reading public in Montpellier—as it was, in fact, everywhere else in France.

To some extent, as measured in Rigaud's orders, demand reflected the supply of what the STN had to offer. In some of his letters, Rigaud noted that he selected books from the STN's catalogs and its prospectuses for new editions. But on several occasions, he asked the STN to procure works that it did not have in stock. The references in his letters indicate that he had many suppliers and that they often offered to provide him with the same books—a consequence of the trade in exchanges, as explained in chapter 7. Rigaud understood the operations of the exchange system perfectly and dealt in it himself, using medical works that he had printed in Montpellier. Therefore, he instructed the STN not to ship him any books that it had procured in Lyon, Avignon, and Rouen, where he already did much of his own exchanging. When the STN could not provide a particular book on time, Rigaud went elsewhere, usually to another Swiss wholesaler-publisher. He did not play them off against each other, because, as he put it, he did not care to "haggle." But he sometimes ordered the same work from several suppliers so that he would be sure of receiving it on time. He also drove hard bargains. Occasionally he asked not merely for a baker's dozen but for a free seventh copy if he bought a half dozen. He also requested free copies for his personal library. He was always looking for the bestselling books at the lowest prices and the quickest, cheapest delivery.

The endless quest for bargains did not exclude a concern for quality—of the physical aspects of books as well as their contents. Whenever he found fault in the STN's editions, Rigaud sent stern criticism. He abhorred inferior paper, not simply because it offended his professional eye but because it hurt sales. In the age of handmade paper, consumers were conscious about the qualities that Rigaud stressed in his letters: degrees of whiteness, evenness in hue, strength, and weight. The STN had difficulty in producing well-made books when it first set up its printing shop in 1769–1770, and Rigaud shot off complaints about the use of worn-out type, typographical errors, clumsy corrections, mistakes in the assemblage of sheets, unseemly margins, and inappropriate formats (the Bible, he insisted, should be printed in quarto rather than folio).

Whenever possible, Rigaud wanted to inspect books for their physical qualities: "It is not prudent to buy without having seen." He often asked the STN to send him one or two copies of a work "as a trial" (pour essai). These trial shipments served above all as a way for him to test demand; if the copies did not sell, he would not order more. Although he seems to have been especially astute in assessing demand, he sometimes got things wrong. L'Anarchie médicale, for example, a polemical tract about the ill effects of common medical practices, seemed certain to sell well in Montpellier, where the faculty of medicine played such an important part in the city's intellectual life. Rigaud (who published the dissertations defended in the faculty and specialized in medical literature) sent a trial order as soon as he learned that it had been published: "We will take three or four copies of L'Anarchie médicale in order to make this work known and to prepare for a large order later if one is justified." However, the book did not take, He sent in only one more order, for a mere two copies.

The only case in which Rigaud seemed to go out on a limb concerned a frothy book about theater life in Paris, Supplément au Roman comique ou mémoire pour servir à la vie de Jean Monnet [Supplement to the Roman Comique, or Memoir to Serve for the Life of Jean Monnet]. He sent an initial order for two dozen copies. They evidently sold well enough for him to ask for one hundred more four months later. When this unusually large order finally reached him after a delay of two months, he seemed to regret his decision: "At last we have received the Mémoires de Jean Monnet, a work that was so much desired but is hardly desirable, because it is a real rhapsody. We cannot understand how such a work created a sensation among people with taste." He never ordered any more copies—nor did other customers of the STN.

Rigaud asked the STN to supplement the main fare of his orders with "some spicy new works" (*quelques nouveautés piquantes*). But when it began to insert short, topical books into his shipments, he objected that they were "only good for peddlers." He preferred solid works, including several that ran to many volumes, such as *Histoire de France depuis l'établissement de la monarchie jusqu'au règne de Louis XIV* [History of France from the Establishment of the Monarchy until the Reign of Louis XIV] by Paul-François Velly: "We will take as a trial two copies of *L'Histoire de France* by Velly, 20 volumes in-12, and we will decide about ordering a larger number if the execution of the work satisfies the public." Two years later, he ordered two more sets; and three years after that, he ordered four. Eight copies of a twenty-volume work, though in a small, duodecimo edition, represented more of an investment than one hundred copies of the *Supplément au Roman comique*.

In assessing demand as refracted through Rigaud's orders, it is therefore important to consider factors such as format and the number of volumes in addition to the number of copies ordered. In the "bestseller" list compiled from his orders, the *Supplément au roman comique* stands out as second on the list, although it does not really deserve to be considered a bestseller; and the *Histoire de France* does not appear at all, although it eventually filled a great deal of shelf space among some of Rigaud's customers. Allowing for such peculiarities, two main tendencies can be detected in the orders: first, a demand for sentimental fiction, as exemplified by the novels of Mme de Genlis, Mme Riccoboni, and Baculard d'Arnaud; second, a demand for works of the Enlightenment, especially those by Mercier, Condorcet, and Voltaire.

The Enlightenment strain in Rigaud's business stands out even more clearly in his correspondence. He ordered twenty-five copies of the STN's edition of the atheistic *Système de la nature* and said that he would have asked for one hundred had it been able to get them to him safely and on time: "It is a lost opportunity" (*un coup manqué*), he wrote regretfully. He collected a great many subscriptions, eighty-four in all, to the quarto edition of the *Encyclopédie*; and in November 1779 when he learned that Rousseau's *Confessions* were being printed somewhere in Switzerland, he urged the STN to send him a sizable shipment. In the end, he received his supply from another publisher, probably the Société typographique de Genève, which published the first posthumous edition of Rousseau's complete works, including the first part of the *Confessions*, in 1782. During the previous ten years, Rigaud had ordered twenty-one sets of Rousseau's works in editions that varied from eleven volumes in-octavo to twenty-one volumes in-duodecimo. Some individual titles, such as *Rousseau juge de Jean-Jacques* [Rousseau Judge of Jean-Jacques], did not sell well, he observed, and so much Rousseau had appeared by July 1782 that the market was flooded.

Rigaud was equally interested in everything by Voltaire, also because of its sales potential. In 1770, the STN informed him that Voltaire was writing an ambitious new work, *Questions sur l'Encyclopédie*, which eventually ran to nine volumes, and that the STN would publish it by a special arrangement with Voltaire. As already explained, the STN edition was actually a pirated version of the original produced by Gabriel Cramer, Voltaire's publisher in Geneva. Voltaire, who cared more about diffusing his works than making money from them, cooperated with the STN edition behind Cramer's back—that is, he pirated himself, tinkering with the text that he forwarded to Neuchâtel. But the secret arrangement led to endless imbroglios and delays. Rigaud jumped at the chance to get advance copies as soon as he heard from the STN. He ordered thirty in August 1770 and fifty more in September. Then, when the STN failed to get them to him on time, he complained bitterly—about Voltaire as well as the STN: "It is astonishing that at the end of his career M. de Voltaire cannot give up his habit of duping booksellers. It would not matter if all these little ruses, frauds, and hoaxes were attributed only to their author. But unfortunately, the accusations normally fall on the printers and, even more, on the retail booksellers."

Rigaud continued to complain until the STN's final volume arrived in June 1772. The differences between the STN and the Cramer editions were so unimportant that they meant little to his customers, he objected, and he had lost sales because of the delays. He may have been less unhappy than he sounded, however, because he ordered another dozen copies in June 1772, an additional copy in June 1773, and two more in November 1774, making a total of ninety-five copies—an impressive number for a nine-volume work.

Nothing in Rigaud's correspondence suggests that he felt committed to the Enlightenment as a cause or that he subscribed to its ideals. Perhaps

like many Protestants he sympathized with the Voltairean values of toler-
ance and reason, but one cannot tell by reading his letters. Their main
theme was money. On the rare occasions when he inserted personal comments into his discussion of business, he sounded disabused. The book
trade, he noted, "is quite similar to that of jewelers—that is, once a fashion has passed, one cannot make a sale at any price." Books were luxury
goods, "a merchandise that is slow in consumption.... Books are not like
meat and bread." Yet Rigaud remained respectful about a few classics,
such as those by Molière, whose works "will always sell, in all places and at
all times." He also expressed interest in the fate of contemporary authors,
especially those whose works sold best: Mercier, Linguet, and above all
Raynal. Raynal inspired more commentary in the correspondence of booksellers than any other author after the death of both Rousseau and Voltaire
in 1778. Was it true as rumored, Rigaud asked the STN in 1781, that the
old Abbé, having been driven out of France after the condemnation of his
*Histoire philosophique et politique des établissements et du commerce des
Européens dans les deux Indes*, planned to settle in Switzerland and to
marry "a young and amiable Swiss girl"? "You must understand that
everyone in general and booksellers in particular have to be interested in
the fate of such a famous man."

Political issues did not come up in Rigaud's correspondence, except in
relation to government policies on the book trade. He did, however, order
some of the radical attacks against the Maupeou ministry of 1771–1774.
During these years Chancellor René Nicolas Charles Augustin de Maupeou
reformed the judicial system in a way that destroyed the political power of
the *parlements* and that provoked a wave of anti-government protests.
These were political libels published after Louis XVI ascended the throne
in May 1774 and the fall of Maupeou in August. As soon as he learned
about the publication of *Maupeouana ou correspondance secrète et familière du chancelier Maupeou avec son coeur Sorhouet* [Maupeouana or Secret
and Familiar Correspondence between the Chancellor Maupeou and His
Favorite, Sorhouet] in April 1775, Rigaud asked the STN to rush one
hundred copies to him. This two-volume satire was such a hot seller that
the STN was unable at first to procure it from other publishers, and
therefore Rigaud sent his order elsewhere. But he successfully placed an
order with the STN for twenty-eight copies of a similar and equally popular work, *Journal historique de la révolution opérée dans la constitution de*

la monarchie française par M. de Maupeou [Historical Journal of the
Revolution Produced in the Constitution of the French Monarchy by M.
de Maupeou]. Although this hard-hitting political literature was aimed at
a government that no longer existed, it was treated as highly seditious by
the authorities under Louis XVI—and understandably so, because in re-
galing readers with anecdotes and scandals, it conveyed the idea that the
Bourbon monarchy had degenerated into a despotism. Rigaud ordered it
under the proviso that the STN would assume all risks. "No risk" was a
constant refrain in his letters. Unlike marginal booksellers, he never dealt
heavily in forbidden books. He sold some of them, as the intendant noted
in the report of 1764, but he refused to expose himself to any danger.
Whatever his personal views, which he kept to himself, his business practices were profoundly conservative.

For some reason, Rigaud's letters from 1776 are missing from his dossier. (The STN's account books indicate that he continued to do business
with the STN throughout that year.) His correspondence during the next
decade shows the same preoccupations as those in his early letters. He
bargained hard, complained about delays, and insisted on avoiding risks.
After the 1777 edicts went into effect, he worried that the campaign
against piracy would create a new barrier between him and his Swiss suppliers. But the edicts were not applied until well into 1779, and they don't
seem to have constrained his trade. His orders with the STN declined
after 1783, when its financial crisis forced it to cut back on its publishing.
But he, too, faced increasingly difficult conditions in the late 1780s. He
paid his last bill to the STN in February 1786—as always, without raising
the slightest difficulty. His final letter, dated July 27, 1787, indicates that
times were hard everywhere: "It's not my fault if I don't send frequent
orders to you. It's the fault of the public, which seems to be in no hurry to
buy books." By this time, the interests of the reading public had shifted to
newspapers and pamphlets, and judging by Rigaud's experience, the book
trade had gone into a severe decline on the eve of the French Revolution.

Abraham Fontanel, the STN's other important client in Montpellier, did
business in the shadow of Rigaud, but he did enough of it to build up a
considerable dossier in the STN archives, and his correspondence is interesting primarily as an account of how a small retailer managed to scratch
out a living at the margin of a local market.

The STN first heard from Fontanel in August 1772, when he was planning to establish a *cabinet littéraire* or commercial lending library in Mende, in the remote upper Lot Valley at the edge of the Cévennes Mountains in Languedoc-Roussillon. That was Protestant territory, and Fontanel had received a copy of the STN's catalog from one of its Huguenot contacts, Jean-François Malherbe, a bookseller in Loudun. Fontanel had no experience in the book trade. He had been trained as an artist and engraver. But he thought he could set up a bookshop that would double as a *cabinet littéraire* stocked by cheap, Swiss, pirated editions. He offered to buy two copies of every book in the STN's catalog, so that he could sell one and rent out the other. After studying the catalog, he sent an order in September for twenty-three works, mostly on medicine, agronomy, and natural history. A month later, he informed the STN that he had moved to Montpellier, where he expected to obtain a license (*brevet de libraire*), which would permit him to operate as a bookseller. The shipment of his first order reached him there at the end of November. Although he found the transport costs heavy, he was satisfied enough to order more, and he especially asked for books on medicine and surgery, which as noted sold well in Montpellier, thanks to the city's medical school.

By May 1773, Fontanel had established a small bookshop and had learned that ordering books from Switzerland was not a simple affair. He had thought that the STN could send its shipments to him most effectively by including them in the bales it sent to Rigaud. But Rigaud held on to Fontanel's books for several weeks, delaying their sale; and before releasing them, he removed the STN's catalogs in order to make it difficult for Fontanel to send more orders. Once he cut his ties with Rigaud, Fontanel encountered the usual difficulties in the long-distance book trade: the shipments took too long, the middlemen charged too much, and the merchandise frequently arrived in damaged condition. Moreover, the bookbinders in Montpellier, under pressure from Rigaud, refused to fold and stitch the books that Fontanel received in the bales of loose sheets from Neuchâtel. Therefore, Fontanel asked the STN to take the unusual step of sending him copies already stitched, and to avoid any arrangement that might let his shipments fall into Rigaud's hands. Having watched Rigaud destroy Cézary and marginalize the other booksellers, he worried about his own survival. Yet he still remained hopeful that he could develop a large business and was eager to order a thousand livres' worth of books, so as to take full advantage of the market in Montpellier, "where new works [*nouveautés*] and especially philosophical works sell pretty well." The latter, as he specified in one of his first orders, included "6 *Système de la nature*, 6 *Colporteur* par Chevrier, 6 *De l'Esprit* par Helvétius, and also two or three copies of every work in this genre."

The STN could not accept Fontanel's conditions, but in May 1773 it had subscribed to an "insurance" service, which, as explained in chapter 2, guaranteed to get its shipments across the border for 16 percent of their value and to provide compensation if any were confiscated. It offered to pay 4 percent of that charge and to cover shipping as far as Chalon-sur-Saône or Bourg-en-Bresse. Fontanel countered with a demand that the STN assume all costs and risks to Lyon. The negotiations stalled at that point and did not resume until January 1775, when Fontanel completed payment for his first orders and the STN agreed to pay half the shipping costs to Lyon. He sent a large order in March, noting that he especially wanted "books that you call philosophical and that ordinarily are those that sell best." He later decided to procure those forbidden books from François Grasset, the publisher-wholesaler in Lausanne who sometimes undersold the STN. Fontanel nonetheless drew a good deal of his stock from Neuchâtel, judging from a large order that he sent in December 1775. It included a wide variety of books, from history and travel literature to fiction and belles-lettres. "I recently opened a *cabinet littéraire* based on subscriptions, which will give me the opportunity to order from you a certain number of good novels and other works of literature," he explained.

Fontanel's *cabinet littéraire* seems to have been the heart of his business. It attracted customers to his shop, and he used his stock for renting out books as well as selling them. He also developed a sideline in prints and drawings. When Favarger assessed the shop during his 1778 tour, he noted, "Fontanel is mediocre. His trade is more in portraits and prints than in books." Fontanel relied on these supplementary activities in order to survive in the early 1780s, when his business held up, despite a decline in the local book trade. Having acquired a *brevet de libraire*, he now figured as an official bookseller in the *Almanach de la librairie* and felt confident about the future, as he noted in a letter to the STN: "My book business is going to expand, since the other [booksellers] seem not to be continuing, and I am now alone with M. Rigaud. That makes Rigaud, who wants to be the only one, furiously jealous. He expresses his hatred for me every day."

In August 1781, however, Fontanel failed to acquit a money order for 660 livres, and he still could not come up with any cash in November, when he fell severely ill during a business trip to Bordeaux. His wife, who had been minding the shop in Montpellier, came to nurse him, and the STN agreed to extend his debt while he recovered. Once he was back on his feet in Montpellier, he regained control of his finances and continued ordering books. In May 1782 he reported that his situation looked promising. He had helped create an academy of painting and sculpture, and the province had rewarded him with a pension and the "title of honorary associate and keeper of drawings, which makes things somewhat easier for me." His orders show that he was stocking his shop with a wide variety of literature, including new editions of Rousseau's works, which he was especially eager to procure. By the end of 1782, he had honored all the payments that had become due in his account with the STN.

Then, again, the wheel of fortune turned against him. It is difficult to determine what went wrong, because none of Fontanel's letters from 1783 have survived. Like many marginal retailers, he probably ordered more books than he could sell. In June 1784, the STN sought help once again from the firm of Vialars, père, fils et Thouron, to collect the debt that Fontanel had accumulated: 1,216 livres, a hefty sum for a small bookseller. Vialars negotiated a repayment scheme, but Fontanel could not keep up with it. The problem, according to Vialars, was that Fontanel had overextended himself: "I believe that he undertakes more than he can bear." For the next two years, "by means of threats and dunning," Vialars extracted a succession of small payments. There was no point in taking him to court, Vialars wrote, because nothing would be gained by forcing him into bankruptcy. "I see that there is nothing to do, except to continue demanding installments and to make a great many threats."[11] When the last payment arrived, in September 1786, Fontanel still owed 218 livres, and the STN had stopped sending him books.

By that time, Fontanel had done enough business with the STN for one to form a general picture of his trade. His orders show a strong demand for the writings of Rousseau, both early editions of the complete works and the posthumous supplements to them, including the *Confessions*.

His stock contained many works by Voltaire and probably all sorts of "philosophical books," but as he explained in his correspondence, he preferred to purchase that genre of literature from other suppliers, who charged less than the STN. As he also noted in his letters, he especially wanted medical books, the treatises of Albrecht van Haller and Herman Boerhaave as well as the popular tracts of Samuel-Auguste Tissot: *Traité d'épilepsie, De la santé des gens de lettres, L'Onanisme,* and *Avis au peuple sur sa santé* [Treatise on Epilepsy, On the Health of Men of Letters, Onanism, and Advice to the Common People on Their Health]. The most unusual book among those Fontanel ordered was a historical drama by Barnabé-Firmian du Rosoi, *Henri IV, drame lyrique,* which did not appeal to other booksellers. Like many others, Fontanel favored works by classic authors such as Erasmus, Cervantes, La Fontaine, and Molière. And he asked for a large variety of Protestant works, pedagogical tracts, histories, and novels such as *Les Malheurs de l'inconstance* [The Misfortunes of Inconstancy] by Claude-Joseph Dorat and *Epreuves du sentiment* by Baculard d'Arnaud.

Those books probably circulated widely in Montpellier, thanks to Fontanel's *cabinet littéraire.* Unfortunately, he did not describe the way this lending library functioned and the kind of people who frequented it. One can imagine officers from the local garrison, administrators from the intendancy, and abbés from the cathedral perusing the shelves of Fontanel's shop, leafing through his portfolios of engravings, and exchanging remarks about the latest editions of Voltaire and Rousseau. Favarger might have mixed with such company when he called on Fontanel, though he said nothing about the atmosphere of the shop. Fontanel himself said little; and when he ventured some general observations, they came out as truisms, typical of the shop talk among nearly all the minor booksellers. "The times are hard," he emphasized in one letter; and "I work to make money, not to lose it," in another.

Favarger encountered many variations on those themes, notably in his next stop, Marseille, where he witnessed a conflict similar to that between Rigaud and Fontanel in Montpellier. A pattern was beginning to become visible in the large provincial centers: nearly everywhere Favarger went, he encountered one or two powerful booksellers at the center of the trade and desperate dealers struggling to survive at the margins.

Marseille

With the Protestants behind him and the Mediterranean in front of him, Favarger knew that he was in another world as soon as he arrived in Marseille. He sent a long report to the STN on August 15, a holiday to celebrate the Assumption of the Virgin Mary. The streets were full, the shops closed, and cannons from the fort and the ships in the harbor were booming out in honor of the Virgin. Marseille (population 85,000 in 1780) was France's third-largest city and its most important port. People from around the Mediterranean, many of them in native costumes, swarmed through its streets, pursuing pleasure with an abandon unthinkable in Switzerland. A contemporary described the Marseillais as "gay, lively, carried away in their pleasures as in their anger. Their spirit is brilliant, their temperament quick to take fire, their blood to boil." And he noted a general lack of inhibition: "Debauchery takes place openly."[12] To be sure, that description conforms to the genre of "mores" (*moeurs*), a common rubric in eighteenth-century

Marseille, etching from *Nouveau voyage pittoresque de la France*, Paris, Ostervald, 1817 (BiCJ).

travel literature, and it deals in stereotypes, some of which are still alive today. It should not be entirely dismissed, however, for despite its exaggeration, it has some relevance to the marketplace for literature.

When the intendant wrote up Marseille for the national survey of booksellers and printers in 1764, he stressed the prevalence of illegal books and pamphlets, "which are equally pernicious to religion and morality and which produce an unbridled license in opinions of a sort that could have very dangerous consequences." Marseille had a booksellers' guild with a *chambre syndicale* that was supposed to inspect all imports, but the intendant noted that all sorts of shipments slipped past the inspectors, especially if they were shipped via Nice. He advocated better policing.[13] The government eventually responded by sending an unusually tough inspector of the book trade, Pierre Durand—the one described by Favarger as capable of eating his brother in order to have meat on his plate.[14]

In light of those conditions, Favarger made a special effort to enlist the service of Jean Isnard, a bookseller who was helping shipments from Geneva and Lausanne to get through the *chambre syndicale* and agreed to do the same for the STN. Isnard received a good rating from Favarger when he made the rounds of Marseilles's corps of nineteen booksellers. Though numerous, most of them fell into the category of the "mediocre" or the downright "bad." Favarger went down the list rapid-fire in his report to the STN:

> Allemand: a young man who inherited his father's stock of books but made poor use of it. Bad reputation. Best not to deal with him.
> Boyer: disappeared, gone to America.
> Abert, Chambon, Paris: all untrustworthy.
> Roulet: mediocre, acceptable to deal with him for cash.
> Taine: good, but orders only an occasional assortment of books to keep up his *cabinet littéraire*, which is the basis of his business.
> Isnard: very good, but is selling off his stock so as to retire.
> Sube et Laporte: very good and sympathetic; will send an order soon.
> Caldesaigues: a disaster (see below).

None of the others warranted a comment, to say nothing of confidence.

In fact, the STN limited nearly all of its trade in Marseille to Jean Mossy, the city's most important bookseller, who also ran a printing and publishing business. His dossier of forty-eight letters in the STN's archives makes for very good reading. Instead of limiting himself to immediate items of business, Mossy dropped remarks about all sorts of subjects, and adopted a personal tone. He comes across as garrulous, witty, crafty, cautious, and tough—very different from the STN's correspondents in northern France. And because Mossy often held forth about recent publications, authors, and economic conditions, his letters serve as a running commentary on the book trade as well as on the hard times that beset Marseille during the last two decades of the Ancien Régime.

In one of his first and most loquacious letters, dated December 25, 1771, Mossy parried a proposal by the STN to establish commercial relations. It had claimed that it could undersell his French suppliers, because it charged a standard price of only 1 sou per sheet, and therefore, as the French government had just levied a tax on paper of 20 sous per ream (five hundred sheets), the STN's books, which were printed on paper manufactured outside France, were an unbeatable bargain. In reply, Mossy noted that to offset the unfair advantage in the cost of paper, the government had also begun to tax the imports of foreign books at a very expensive rate: 60 livres per hundredweight. In any case, he pronounced rather grandly, he would not enter into a discussion about such fiscal considerations, because he was, first and foremost, a patriot: "I will not hide from you the fact that I am a good Frenchman and that I love my fatherland, that I do not at all like to favor enterprises that can harm my fellow countrymen."[15]

This was sheer palaver. Mossy went on to congratulate the STN for its astute decision to pirate a French edition of Bougainville's *Voyage autour du monde* [Voyage Around the World], and in later letters he revealed that he traded extensively with foreign pirates, including Swiss houses in Geneva, Yverdon, and Bern. The real difficulty, he explained, was that he based his relations with other publishers on exchanges. By swapping sheets with them, he acquired what he needed for the general stock of his shop while avoiding the danger of overstocking his own publications. He did not have a huge retail trade, and he did not like to part with cash; so if the STN insisted on selling him its works instead of trading a portion of them in exchange for his, he could not deal with them. He admitted that the book duty threatened to cut off all trade between French booksellers and their foreign suppliers, and adopted a tone of resignation: "What can I do about it? I can only sigh…. In great illnesses, it is sometimes necessary to use remedies that disrupt the body but save the patient." This pose, however, reinforced a bargaining position: Mossy would trade with the STN, but only on his terms, which combined swapping with the purchase of "*nouveautés*." Like other well-established booksellers, he asked only for a few copies of each work and included a large enough number of different works to make up a considerable bale, thereby saving on the shipping charges. In some cases, he arranged in advance to sell the books to his clients before ordering them. Above all, he avoided risks: "As to new articles, I go slowly. They don't all succeed; and unless I know them, I cannot order them in large numbers. I feel my way tentatively, and so I am holding up pretty well. Besides, these are quite rough times, especially in this city, and one must of necessity proceed with caution."

This strategy was typical of the dealers that Favarger put down in his diary as "good" and "solid." Yet Marseilles enjoyed an enormous trade in all kinds of commodities, and Mossy, the largest bookseller in the city, could have ordered books in great quantity. He had established his own printing shop in 1768, despite the efforts of the other printers to prevent him from breaking into their ranks. There were only three of them, and Mossy pointed out to the authorities that Marseille was entitled to six masterships, according to an edict of 1704. By 1771 he employed sixty persons in the combined bookshop and printing shop that he had established in Marseille's arsenal.[16] Unlike the other printers, who, according to the survey of 1764, limited their production to religious works and administrative ephemera, he produced trade books and a commercial journal, the *Affiches de Marseille*, which he replaced in 1781 with a more ambitious periodical, *Journal de Provence*. Mossy also ran a *bureau de recette* where customers could subscribe to other journals, and he acted as a wholesaler, providing supplies to the smaller bookshops in Marseille and the surrounding area. By combining roles as a printer, publisher, wholesaler, and retailer, he had become the wealthiest and most powerful figure in the book trade throughout the entire province.[17]

Judging purely from the two surviving professional directories, the trade might seem to be flourishing. The *Almanach de la librairie* for 1777 listed the full nineteen booksellers in Marseille, and the almanac for 1781 listed fourteen. But as the fluctuation of the numbers suggests, most of those retailers ran marginal businesses. According to the survey of 1764, "Their reputation is fairly good, but they are lacking in resources" and publishing in Marseille remained underdeveloped.[18]

Why was Marseille such a relatively weak market for books—much weaker, for example, than Besançon and Rouen, which had much smaller populations? The crucial factor was the city's rather thin infrastructure of administrative and legal institutions. Provincial capitals like Besançon and Rouen had *parlements*, intendancies, and all sorts of official bodies, which supported the well-educated professional classes. Unlike nearby Aix-en-Provence, whose *parlement* and administrative offices attracted much of the province's legal business, Marseille remained a commercial center attached above all to its port. Of course, the merchants and manufacturers of Marseille were perfectly literate, but were they avid book buyers? Unfortunately, booksellers throughout France rarely identified their customers in their letters. When they did—in exceptional cases such as references to subscribers of the *Encyclopédie*[19]—they mention far more lawyers, doctors, administrative officials, and priests than businessmen. Still the evidence is too thin to support general conclusions about the demand for literature in the commercial and industrial bourgeoisie. Moreover, the dossier of Caldesaigues, the other bookseller in Marseille who dealt extensively with the STN, includes a few remarks that suggest that at least some merchants in Marseille spent sums, sometimes significant sums, on books. Before he abandoned his business, Caldesaigues collected many subscriptions to the *Encyclopédie*, and he identified twelve of the subscribers in his letters to the STN. They included an infantry captain, a broker (*courtier*), a tradesman (*marchand*), and eight merchants (*négociants*).

Although Mossy did not identify the professions of his customers, he did remark on their general character: "As you must know, the public is extraordinarily impatient, and that is especially true of the Provençal, who is all fire." Mossy's customers demanded quick service and spicy *nouveautés*. One might expect, therefore, that he did a large trade in forbidden books. They sold well in Marseille, as the book-trade survey of 1764 had mentioned, and marginal booksellers such as Caldesaigues speculated heavily in this sector of the trade.

Mossy, however, did not. To be sure, when he saw an opportunity to sell some hot items from the underground trade he seized it, but only if he did not run the slightest risk. In 1774, when the works about the political crisis during the last years of Louis XV's reign began to appear, he ordered a certain number, insisting that the STN clear them through the *chambre syndicale* of Lyon, where the danger was greatest. *Espion anglais, ou Correspondance secrète entre mylord All'eye et milord All'ear* figured near the top of the list of the books he most often ordered. So did Mercier's *Tableau de Paris.* Mossy ordered forty copies of it as soon as he heard that it had been confiscated in a raid on a Parisian bookshop: "That will make it sell pretty well in these parts." When *nouveautés* hit the market, he snapped them up, but only if he felt certain that he could sell them rapidly. He would not order them if they could not be supplied right away, not even if they came from the pen of Voltaire. In fact, like Gaude in Nîmes, Mossy deplored the profusion of Voltaire's works, which were constantly pirated and cobbled together in ways to make them seem newer than they actually were. "The science of our trade is not to acquire too much inventory and to get rid of it quickly.... The new works of M. de Voltaire, except at the moment when they first appear, don't sell, because they are constantly reworked into edition after edition. One adds two or three [old] pieces to them, and the once new work remains in a corner."

In short, Mossy conducted his trade according to a strategy based on two principles: adhere as closely as possible to demand and avoid risks. He never ordered more books than he expected to sell: "I must calculate according to my sales," as he put it. Instead of taking chances with a large order, he would ask for a few copies of a book and then, if it sold well, order more. "When one knows the value of an item and one has a rough idea of its success, then one can go after it full throttle." Above all, he practiced caution: "If prudence does not guide us in our operations, we will soon be wiped out."

Remarks of this sort might seem obvious, since commerce consists in the effort to match supply with demand. But few booksellers observed this principle as assiduously as Mossy, for they often overestimated potential sales, and their miscalculations led to requests for deferring payments of bills of exchange. Mossy always paid his bills on time. He also expanded and contracted his orders according to circumstances, both economic and political. And because he accompanied the orders with so much shop talk—unlike most booksellers, who kept their correspondence terse—his letters to the STN provide a rich vein of information about the changing conditions of the trade.

The first series of letters emphasized the problems of coping with the import duty on books and the need to set up effective supply lines. By mid-1775, the duty had been rescinded, and the STN had succeeded in getting its bales cleared through the *chambre syndicale* of Lyon. In 1777 Mossy hired an agent of his own, Roubert frères, to get them to his shop in Marseille without running into difficulties with the authorities. The main route, which went from Neuchâtel to Pontarlier, Lyon, and Marseille, then functioned reasonably well, although shipments sometimes took more than two months and cost more than 15 percent of the value of the merchandise. At the end of 1776, however, Pierre Durand, the police official described by Favarger as fiercely repressive, assumed the position of *inspecteur de la librairie*. Mossy later attributed this repression as the first step in the government's campaign, which came to a head in the edicts of 1777, to stamp out piracy. As Favarger had learned in Lyon and Avignon, everyone in the trade worried about how the government would enforce its policy of permitting booksellers to sell off their stock of pirated books after the volumes had been stamped in a *chambre syndicale* and how it would continue its war against piracy.

The new regulations did not go into effect in Marseille and most other cities until the spring of 1778. Mossy suspended all orders from his foreign suppliers in March and warned the STN that they could not renew trade for the foreseeable future, owing to the severity of Durand, whom he describes as one of the most rigid inspectors in all of France. "The bales are so thoroughly searched that I have resolved to suspend all orders until this first fire has burned out. I have agreed to have all my pirated books stamped and now am in the midst of that operation. The inspector is in my shop every day. As you can imagine, this is hardly a propitious time for our trade."

Despite strenuous efforts to rebuild its contraband routes, the STN did not resume shipments to Mossy for a year—and even then he reduced his orders, because the book trade suffered badly from the economic downturn produced by the American war. Mossy reported that his customers among the small retailers of the region were unable to pay their bills on time, and he worried about his own exposure to events far away. He had 40,000 livres invested in the Caribbean.

The campaign against piracy continued with such rigor in Marseille that Mossy feared his correspondence was being intercepted or might be confiscated in a raid on his shop. In February 1782 he resorted to a trick used fairly often in the book trade: he sent a *lettre ostensible*, or fake letter, ordering the STN to cease all shipments of works that could not pass openly through the *chambre syndicale*. He kept a copy of it in his files as evidence of his respect for government regulations and explained the maneuver in a confidential letter sent by a safe route. He also instructed the STN to say in its next letter that it would use him only as a shipping agent to forward books to its Italian customers, and sent the names and addresses of several Italian booksellers that the STN should mention in order to make its own *lettre ostensible* convincing.

Mossy relied on this subterfuge for more than a year. He insisted that the STN take great care in the phrasing of its letters and that it send its shipments to him as if they were meant for Gravier of Genoa or Bouchard of Rome. As he relied on Roubert to get the bales to him from the port in Marseille, his main concern was Lyon. The STN had agreed to cover the risks in that stage of the distribution system. It relied mainly on its most professional smuggler, Jacques Revol, who earned Mossy's respect, although he worried that confiscations of several bales in the Lyon *chambre syndicale* had made Revol look suspicious to the Lyonnais authorities.

As these arrangements finally began to function smoothly and the bales arrived safely, the tone of Mossy's letters became more confidential. He ordered only books that he felt sure his customers would buy, but he also had tastes of his own and did not hesitate to pronounce on the quality of the works that appeared on the market, especially if he disliked them. He felt nothing but scorn for an edition of the works of Alexis Piron: "I think that the name of the author has made more of a sensation than the book itself, which is full of twaddle." He dismissed a botched edition of Pierre Bayle's encyclopedic *Dictionnaire historique et critique* as a "tedious rhapsody." And although he bought a fair number of the libels against Louis XV and his mistresses, he had a low opinion of some of them. The *Mémoires authentiques de Mme la comtesse du Barry*, he proclaimed, "is a work that certainly was not worth the trouble of printing."

The authors who interested Mossy were those most in the public eye on the eve of the Revolution, largely because they had been persecuted by the authorities. He may have collected information about them for the sheer love of gossip, but gathering information through the professional grapevine was an important aspect of the bookseller's business. Mossy often asked the STN for reports about Raynal, Mercier, and "the too notorious Linguet"—a reference to Simon-Nicolas-Henri Linguet, the polemical journalist, whose defiance of the French authorities had led to imprisonment in the Bastille in 1780 and then to his best-selling account of that experience, *Mémoires sur la Bastille* (1783). After Rousseau's death in 1778, the talk in the trade was all about the possible existence of the *Confessions*. Mossy wanted to be among the first to get his hands on them: "We hear a great deal about the posthumous works of J.J. Rousseau.... It is the memoirs of his life that are being talked about. Rumor has it that they are even being printed right now in Switzerland. One could certainly order a large number of them."

In the end, Mossy succeeded in stocking his shop with the *Confessions* and new editions of Rousseau's works, which he probably procured from the Société typographique de Genève. For that reason, the list of the books that he ordered most frequently does not include Rousseau, but it highlights many books by the other authors that he mentioned: Raynal (*Histoire philosophique et politique des établissements et du commerce des Européens dans les deux Indes*), Linguet (*Mémoires sur la Bastille*), and Mercier (*Tableau de Paris, L'An deux mille quatre cent quarante*, and *Mon Bonnet de nuit—My Nightcap*). The list also contains some utilitarian works: a Latin-French dictionary, a textbook on German, and *Traité des maladies vénériennes* [Treatise on Venereal Diseases], along with a few classics (*Fables de la Fontaine, Lettres de Mme de Sévigné*), and several sentimental novels (*Cécilia ou Mémoires d'une héritière* [Cécilia, or Memoirs of an Heiress] by Fanny Burney, *Les Aventures de l'infortuné Napolitain* [Adventures of an Unfortunate Neapolitan] by the abbé Olivier, and Sterne's *Voyage sentimental*). Mossy trimmed his orders to suit what the public wanted. Of course, he procured other works from other publishers, although he noted that he sometimes ordered the same books from several Swiss houses in order to be sure of receiving an adequate supply on time. All in all, everything one can learn about his way of doing business indicates that his orders provide a fairly reliable index to literary demand in Marseille.

Literature, however, was overshadowed by current events, especially the American war, according to Mossy's remarks about the temper of the public in Marseille: "One thinks of nothing but politics." When at last the war came to an end in 1783, he expected business to pick up, but he was disappointed. Throughout the 1780s he continued to complain about hard times. He tried to take advantage of the public's increased interest in America by publishing a *Traité général du commerce de l'Amérique* [General Treatise on the American Trade] and arranged to exchange fifty copies of it for a selection of works from the STN's stock. But when the STN began selling it to its own customers, it received complaints that the book had already appeared under a different title, *Essai sur le commerce de l'Amérique*. Publishing old works under new titles was a well-known trick of the trade among eighteenth-century publishers. After receiving an angry letter from the STN, Mossy prevaricated, protested about worse "foul play" among Swiss houses, and finally admitted that his product might not have been "one hundred percent new." He reduced the value of his share of the exchange in the hope that he and STN would remain "good friends."

By the time they had patched up this quarrel, Mossy and the STN had to cope with another difficulty, which ultimately led to the end of their commercial relations. The French government's order of June 12, 1783, requiring that all imports of books be sent for inspection to the *chambre syndicale* in Paris, threatened to burden shipments from Neuchâtel to Marseille with impossible transport costs along with the hostile examination of the bales. As soon as he learned of this measure, Mossy warned the STN about the new danger and noted its perplexing character. Regulations of the book trade normally came from the *Direction de la librairie* and were enforced in *chambres syndicales*, but the order of June 12 was issued by the ministry of foreign affairs and directed to the Ferme générale. Because Mossy had an extensive correspondence and worked hard to keep himself informed about the innermost operations of the industry, he eventually determined that the government meant to stamp out the trade in highly illegal works, not merely pirated books, and that it did not trust the provincial *chambres syndicales* to do the job. The order from the foreign ministry threatened to close off the STN's route to Marseille via Lyon and to cripple its shipments everywhere in France.

Faced with this catastrophe, the STN fell back on the more expensive route via Turin and Nice, and it agreed to cover the costs as far as Turin, where Mossy had a trustworthy agent. He was especially eager to receive the forbidden books that then were selling best, as mentioned above—Raynal's *Histoire philosophique*, Linguet's *Mémoires sur la Bastille*, Mercier's *Tableau de Paris*, and the anonymous libel titled *Espion anglais*. The STN managed to get a few bales to him in 1784, but the Turin route took too long and cost too much. In December 1785 he reported that agents of the Ferme générale were confiscating all shipments of books that came through Nice. If the STN wanted to continue their trade, it would have to get its goods through Lyon, from which point they could be sent safely as domestic shipments, provided they had made it past the Lyonnais *chambre syndicale*. But the STN failed to make the necessary smuggling arrangements, having by then given up on the services of Revol; and it ceased corresponding with Mossy after February 1786. His last letters showed that he was still king of the roost in Marseille and still buying books from other foreign suppliers, but had become pessimistic about the future of the trade: "We are only too aware that the trade is being hindered to an extraordinary degree, and we have no doubt that in ten years all of the retail booksellers will be ruined."

In the spectrum of booksellers in Marseille, Caldesaigues and Mossy occupied opposite extremes, somewhat as Cézary and Rigaud did in Montpellier and Buchet and Gaude did in Nîmes, except that Caldesaigues occupied a particularly low rung in the social hierarchy. He started from nothing, built a small business, gambled recklessly, and lost everything. Although his dossier is relatively thin, it can be supplemented by enough material from other sources to illustrate the precarious character of life at the bottom of the retail trade.

Caldesaigues did not even appear among the booksellers listed in the trade almanac of 1777, when he began to correspond with the STN. Having received a copy of its catalog, he asked it to send a small assortment of books. Then, at the end of his letter, he indicated the kind of literature that interested him the most: "I would need philosophical books. I don't know whether you can procure them for me." If the STN could fill his order, he wanted fourteen of the most notorious forbidden books then on the market, including pornography (for example, *Histoire de Dom B . . . . . , portier des Chartreux* [The Story of *Dom B . . . . .* [Bugger], Porter of the Carthusians]), irreligion (*imposteurs* [Treatise on the Three Imposters], that is, Moses, Jesus, and Mohammed), and political libel (*Anecdotes sur Mme la comtesse du Barry*).

The titles suggested that Caldesaigues had built his business around the illegal trade. Unlike Mossy, who used *livres philosophiques* as a kind of spice, to be sprinkled lightly through his orders, Caldesaigues treated them as a main dish. He ordered other kinds of literature, too: story books for children, light novels, the popular judicial memoirs of Beaumarchais, even political theory by standard authors like Pufendorf, Burlamaqui, Vattel, and Mably. But he never drew a large supply from the STN, which began to harbor doubts about his solidity soon after it sent its first shipment.

The shipment arrived on May 14, 1777, after nearly four months of snags in the underground route through the Franche-Comté and the Rhône Valley. First it got stuck in Pontarlier—owing to the incompetence of the STN's shipping agent rather than difficulties at the border—and then it was stalled in Lyon. Claudet, the Lyonnais agent of the STN at that time, had great difficulty getting it past the inspector of the *chambre syndicale*, who was going through a distressingly rigorous phase in the performance of his duties. Claudet found it necessary to scramble the sheets in order to disguise the contents of the bale and to wait several weeks before finding the right moment to slip it past inspection. When he sent his bill to Caldesaigues—6 livres per hundredweight in "insurance"—he thought he had earned every penny of it. Caldesaigues, however, complained bitterly to the STN. The smuggling service in Lyon was dreadful, he wrote—too sloppy, too slow, and too expensive. But he was delighted with the books themselves. He wanted more of them, and he had nothing but praise for the STN: "Your letters are so obliging that, to tell the truth, it would be desirable that you were the only top people in the book trade."

To an experienced ear, that might have sounded suspiciously ingratiating, especially as Caldesaigues failed to send the customary promissory note (*billet à ordre* or *lettre de change*) upon receipt of the goods. He had an excuse. Booksellers often delayed payment until they had "verified" the state of a shipment by collating sheets. That job would take time, Caldesaigues explained, owing to the disorder in the bale. Couldn't the STN accept two years instead of one as the maturation date of his note? The STN turned this request down flat. A solid bookseller might bargain for an extended period of payment before making a purchase, but he would not try to change the terms afterward. Caldesaigues seemed to accept the refusal with equanimity. His reply suggested that he fully appreciated the importance of sound finances. For that reason he was doing everything possible to avoid straining his credit, he reassured the STN, and therefore he would cancel an order that he was about to mail to Neuchâtel. As to the promissory note, he would dispatch it as soon as he received the books back from the binder, who had taken over the collating job. On September 1, four months after the arrival of the shipment, Caldesaigues finally sent a note for 468 livres and declared his account clear.

At that point, the STN began to worry about whether he would honor the note when it came due, because while Caldesaigues was sending reassurances from Marseille, Claudet was issuing warnings from Lyon. The most worrisome message came from one of Claudet's contacts in Marseille, who described Caldesaigues as "a rotten piece of work; we would not advise anyone to place any trust in him."[20]

Claudet knew how to assess danger signals. As a seasoned smuggler, he dealt regularly with marginal booksellers who left publishers holding unredeemed notes for considerable sums. The STN extended credit too lightly, he warned, and to drive the point home, he transcribed a second letter from his friend in Marseille. It provided a full character sketch of Caldesaigues, which is worth quoting at length:[21]

M. Caldesaigues was a clerk in the bookshop of M. Jayne for four or five years. He put on the airs of a gentleman, cultivating friends by small gifts and showing up at all pleasurable gatherings. M. Jayne, knowing that he had no funds of his own, kept a close watch over him and then accused him point-blank of infidelity… but did nothing more than fire him. At that point, M. Caldesaigues decided to go into business for himself, and he began asking all his friends to open their purses—for six louis from some, four from others, and in the end for everything he could get. We ourselves were taken in for 450 livres, and after all the trouble in the world, we were not reimbursed until the middle of last February, which is to say a few days after his marriage with the daughter of a cabinet maker whose dowry of 6,000 livres is already pretty well shot. The father-in-law, without being opulent, is very obliging, but in a crunch he will not come to [Caldesaigues's] aid. He has sworn that, because the marriage was made against his will. In light of all this, we would not grant him a credit of six livres.

By the end of the year, the STN knew what kind of customer it had on its hands. It stopped shipping books and concentrated on collecting bills, for it had received nothing but promises and promissory notes, all unredeemed. When Favarger arrived in Marseille in August 1778, he did everything possible to convert the notes to cash. They had matured long ago, but Caldesaigues found all kinds of pretexts to avoid payment and even managed to be absent from his shop whenever Favarger called. Tired of sparring with "the most open liar" in all Marseille, Favarger finally enlisted an attorney and a local bill collector. Even then, he extracted only a down payment of 150 livres, and he had to leave town with yet another promissory note, this one for 400 livres, left hanging. After venting his frustrations in his journal, he concluded, "This Caldesaigues is a true scoundrel, and we should have nothing more to do with him."

The STN never collected the 400 livres. In February 1779, it learned that Caldesaigues had disappeared, leaving behind his wife and a mountain of debt. A letter from one of his friends arrived in July with the beginning of an explanation: Caldesaigues had run off to Cadix, but now he wanted to return and resume his business. If his creditors would write off 85 percent of his debts, he would work hard to pay back the rest. He was young, industrious, and eager to start over again if given half a chance.[22]

Caldesaigues himself took up this theme in a letter to the STN written from an unnamed hiding place in September. He had panicked, he explained, as he watched his debts mount up. A loss of a 10,000-livre speculation made debtor's prison look like an inevitable fate. Therefore, he decided to flee, taking two suits, twelve shirts, and four crates of books, which he planned to sell in Cadix. He had hoped his wife could continue the business, because he had left behind a storehouse with 19,000 livres' worth of books, and he thought their creditors might write off half the accumulated debts. But upon his arrival in Cadix, he had received a letter from a friend saying that his wife had gone back to her father, who had had all their property seized in order to save what was left of her dowry. If Caldesaigues wanted to prevent all the goods from being auctioned off, the friend warned, he had better return by the first boat. He did so, but when he arrived the sale had taken place, and his father-in-law accused him of absconding with three-quarters of the estate. He could not dispute that accusation in the courts, "since I am no longer free." But he could start all over again with the remnants of his old business. He asked only for some help in his distress—that is, the sacrifice of 85 percent of the STN's debt. He knew it had received some unflattering reports about him, but they were bound to be exaggerated: "It is not so much dissipation and libertinism that have caused my misfortune as ambition.... I am young; I will work hard to pay all my creditors and rehabilitate myself some day, unless you force me to leave the country and to go die in the Antilles."

There might be a remote possibility that this appeal came straight from the heart, but Caldesaigues was careful not to attach a return address to it. He did not want to risk arrest for unpaid debts and a fraudulent bankruptcy. He therefore proposed that the STN subscribe to the repayment plan through a friend named Isoard, who meanwhile had sent several letters testifying to Caldesaigues's sincerity and to the fact that most of the other creditors had agreed to settle for the 15 percent. That, after all, was better than nothing. Caldesaigues returned to this theme in another letter, written two months later. Although he already had collected many agreements to his proposal, he claimed, he would offer the STN 25 percent, instead of 15 percent, "in the greatest secrecy."

Debtors with their back to the wall sometimes struck a secret bargain with some creditors in order to get signatures on a refunding proposal that would win the agreement of others, who received less favorable terms. The STN knew better than to be taken in by that maneuver. It had asked a merchant in Marseille to investigate, and he reported that Isoard could not produce a single signature on the proposed settlement. Caldesaigues's plan therefore looked like "a new way to trap his creditors, as all of his conduct until now has proven beyond doubt his lack of honesty."[23]

This information did not make the STN inclined to give a favorable reception to Caldesaigues's final letter, which arrived in January 1780. He needed an answer desperately, he wrote. He could hold out no longer. A yes or a no from the STN would determine his fate, because if he failed to win enough support from his creditors, he would have to flee, whatever the damage to his honor. "I prefer my liberty to all the honors in the world, because if I take that step, I will be able to say that I was forced into it by my implacable creditors." The STN did not write back and never heard from him again.

9

Toulouse, Bordeaux, La Rochelle, Poitiers

Hardscrabble in the Southwest

Toulouse

After leaving the Rhône delta, Favarger made his way through a string of lovely towns and a series of disappointments. Few towns had bookshops, and those bookshops did too little trade to justify ordering books from as

Toulouse, etching from *Nouveau voyage pittoresque de la France*, Paris, Ostervald, 1817 (BiCJ).

far away as Neuchâtel. The *Encyclopédie* had sold quite well in some places (Ganges, Pézenas, Béziers, Carcassonne); a few booksellers received grades of "good" and promised to mail orders to the home office (Fuzier in Pézenas, Le Portier in Castres); but the names that appear in the *Almanach de la librairie* give a misleading impression of a fairly dense network of dealers. The two listed under Castelnaudary, for example, were small shopkeepers who merely sold a few books, mostly liturgical works, on the side, and poor Jean Besse of Carcassonne had to give up his trade after succumbing to dumbness, presumably from a stroke. So the towns went by quite quickly: Pézenas, with its gorgeous ancient mansions; Béziers, its fourteenth-century cathedral visible from a great distance on the road to Narbonne; Carcassonne, the fortified city bristling with fifty-three imposing-looking towers. Favarger may have tasted the delicious *petits pâtés* of Pézenas (he would not have ordered the famous cassoulet in Castelnaudary, since it was out of season), but tastes and sights did not figure in his diary. The only personal observation that he noted during the journey between Marseille and Toulouse concerned the weather: rain. It began to pour in buckets before he reached Carcassonne, and he was delighted, because the sun had beaten down on him for so long that he and his horse were parched. Then at last, on September 11 or 12, he arrived at a promising market place for books: Toulouse.

To all appearances, Toulouse (54,000 inhabitants) had everything needed for a flourishing book trade—a strategic location along routes that linked the Mediterranean to the Atlantic and that spread throughout southwestern France; its function as a commercial hub at the heart of a fertile grain region; a *parlement*, a large university, two academies, and a good number of administrative and ecclesiastical institutions. Yet the trade was not as prosperous as one might expect. The general survey of 1764 described the city's two dozen booksellers as highly respectable but not very prosperous: "None of them has built up a large fortune, since the trade is rather limited in this city."[1]

After inspecting Toulouse's bookshops, Favarger attributed their relative lack of prosperity to two factors: excessive severity in enforcing regulations by the local *chambre syndicale* and cutthroat practices: "Nothing is more rigid than this chambre syndicale, and it is the booksellers themselves who have made it that way by betraying one another and by the unparalleled discord and jealousy that prevails among them." He cited the example of a bookbinder who had collected eighty to eighty-five subscriptions to the *Encyclopédie* only to have them appropriated by some booksellers on the grounds that he had stepped over the boundary that separated his trade from theirs. The booksellers generally relied on the sales of cheap, pirated editions yet denounced one another as soon as they found evidence of piracy. Moreover, the denunciations seemed likely to increase as soon as the *chambre syndicale* began to apply the measures against pirated books promulgated in the 1777 edicts: "They are all afraid of being caught or betrayed." And they would not tolerate the sale of Protestant works, though Toulouse had a large population of Huguenots. "It must be said that this city is the center of bigotry," Favarger concluded.

Favarger reached these conclusions after interviewing nearly all of the city's twenty-three booksellers and discussing their business with a local merchant named Chaurou, who agreed to represent the STN if it ran into difficulties. In his report to the home office, Favarger summarized his evaluation of each bookseller according to his usual manner of grading. His top grade went to Antoine Laporte, "the cock of the booksellers in Toulouse and as good as gold." He also recommended François Resplandy, who cooperated with Laporte in shipping arrangements: "They are good friends, and neither of them belongs to the lot who betray one another."

In the end, after a great deal of inspecting bookshops and bargaining with booksellers, Favarger found the results disappointing: "For a city like Toulouse, I should be sending you orders worth thousands of francs instead of hundreds." He sent in orders from Laporte and Resplandy, which provide a brief glimpse of their trade in 1778. Laporte wanted standard works: history (William Robertson's *Histoire de l'Amérique*, Claude François Xavier Millot's *Eléments d'histoire générale ancienne et moderne*), two novels (*Jezennemours, roman dramatique* by Louis Sébastien Mercier and Voltaire's *L'Ingénu*), and some current nonfiction (*L'Adoption ou la maçonnerie des femmes* [The Adoption or the Masonry of Women] by Guillemain de Saint-Victor and *Le Thévenon ou les journées de la montagne* [The Thevenon or Days of the Mountain] by Elie Bertrand). None of those books would cause much trouble if the bale fell into the hands of Toulouse's book-trade inspector, a tough lawyer, or the syndics who also inspected shipments in the *chambre syndicale*. But Laporte was taking no chances. The STN was to send his bale to Revol in Lyon, with instructions to repack it and forward it to Chaurou disguised as a domestic shipment of textiles—that is, in a square-shaped bale of the kind used for draperies. Chaurou had agreed to serve as the STN's agent in Toulouse, where he could get its shipments to the booksellers without passing through the *chambre syndicale*.

Resplandy's order was very different and far more risky. Although it contained a few standard works (La Fontaine's *Fables*, Robertson's *Histoire de l'Amérique*), it consisted primarily of irreligious Enlightenment tracts (Voltaire's *La Bible enfin expliquée* [The Bible Explained at Last], d'Holbach's *Système de la nature*), and a great deal of pornography, much of it anticlerical (*Vénus dans le cloître* [Venus in the Cloister], *Vie voluptueuse des Capucins* [The Voluptuous Life of the Capuchins], *Le Monialisme, histoire galante* [About Nuns, A Gallant Tale]). It was to be shipped through the same underground route. In fact, Resplandy and Laporte negotiated together with Favarger and planned to have their books sent in the same bale. That proved to be impractical, however, because the orders were too large; but the two clearly operated as allies—a prominent dealer, who kept to the legal or quasi-legal trade, and a smaller retailer, who did business in his shadow, selling the most dangerous works. When a customer appeared in Laporte's well-appointed shop and dropped remarks about certain kinds of books—*curiosa, livres philosophiques*—Laporte knew how to supply him.

The shipments arranged by Favarger made it safely to Toulouse, but getting them there took time and money. Resplandy complained about the delay—three months, most of them spent with the bales gathering dust in Revol's secret stockrooms—and especially the cost: 69 livres in shipping charges for merchandise that cost 656 livres. Yet in a letter of January 2, 1779—six months after Favarger's visit—he expressed eagerness to do more business with the STN. He found its catalog full of "very good articles" and felt optimistic about overcoming the hostility of the other booksellers. His friend Laporte had been chosen as syndic when the local guild was reorganized in accordance with the 1777 edicts. But Resplandy had difficulties in paying promissory notes, owing to the lack of specie among the money changers of Lyon and Paris. Therefore, he proposed to the STN doing some of their trade in exchanges and offered to supply the following titles, according to the prices he set:

La Raison par alphabet de Voltaire, 2 vol.............................3 livres.
D. B...., portier des Chartreux, 2 vol., figures.............................5 l.

Thérèse philosophe, 2 vol., figures ....4 l.

Vie et lettres de Ninon de Lenclos, 3 parties...............................24 sous

Voix de la nature, 5 parties...30 s.

Lettres de Mme de Pompadour, 2 vol ....20 s.

Anecdotes de Mme du Barry, 2 vol. avec le portrait........................40 s.

Mémoires de l'abbé Terray, 2 vol...40 s.

However, the STN had no interest in exchanging books with a marginal dealer located so far away that the shipping costs would be prohibitive. Moreover, it already had in stock the books that Resplandy proposed, thanks to its exchanges with publishers in Geneva and Lausanne. Resplandy's correspondence confirmed what the STN already knew: the demand for this kind of forbidden literature was widespread, but it was not strong enough to sustain trade with a provincial bookseller unless his orders contained a large proportion of legal works—that is, books in all sorts of genres that gave no offense, except for the fact that they were pirated.

The STN faced similar difficulties in dealing with the other Toulouse booksellers. Laporte never followed up his first order with Favarger with another one, presumably because he found the shipment too slow and expensive. Dupleix, another bookseller, refused to trade unless the STN agreed to supplement sales with exchanges. And two others, Sacarau and Moulas, also wanted to do some swapping. In a letter of September 2, 1777, they explained that they had recently merged their businesses and that they disposed of a large stock. The catalog that accompanied their letter contained 125 titles, many of them works by the Enlightenment philosophes—Montesquieu, Helvétius, Rousseau, and especially Voltaire—and a wide variety of others, including some Protestant and Jansenist books. But the STN wanted to sell books, not to exchange them. Forest, another major dealer with a large stock, had tried without success to establish relations in 1772. He drove a hard bargain, insisting that the STN pay for all shipping costs and accept as payment bills of exchange that would not mature for eighteen months or even two years. The STN would not accept those terms, and Forest would not modify them. He claimed that he could get some of the books offered by the STN at the same price from his suppliers in Brussels; so he never developed a supply line from Neuchâtel. Manavit (whom Favarger had described as "very good," but in "difficult conditions") bought a dozen copies of Raynal's *Histoire philosophique et politique des établissements et du commerce des Européens dans les deux Indes* from the STN in 1781, but he did not send any payment for four years, and even then he refused to pay for two copies on the pretext that they were lacking some sheets.

The only bookseller from Toulouse who did extensive business with the STN was Nicolas-Etienne Sens. Favarger did not give him a very good rating in September 1778, because the firm that presented itself as "Sens et compagnie" in its business letters did not look impressive when seen up close. "The only company that Sens has is his wife." Sens had succumbed to a partial bankruptcy in 1774—that is, he had suspended all payments of his bills while persuading his creditors to give him enough time to redeem his debts. According to Favarger's informants, he had made a fairly successful recovery, but their advice was that the STN should not sell him anything unless it received payment in cash.

Sens had first contacted the STN in October 1776. For testimony as to his soundness, he recommended they contact several booksellers in Lyon and his brother-in-law, Michel Gaude, the most important bookseller in Nîmes. The book trade had gone into such a slump recently, he added, that he had supplemented his normal business with a sideline in second-hand books, which he purchased at sales of private libraries. Yet he foresaw promising opportunities for trading with the STN, if it could cover all expenses and risks for its shipments as far as Lyon. After receiving a favorable reply, he wrote that he was especially eager to purchase "all of the philosophical and gallant books that you can supply." He also wanted to exchange books, and as an example of what he kept in stock offered one hundred to two hundred copies of Voltaire's *Lettres philosophiques* and one hundred to two hundred of the pornographic bestseller, *Thérèse philosophe*.

The STN replied that it would not be drawn into exchanges over such a great distance and sent a list of *livres philosophiques* that it could sell. As a consequence, Sens's first order contained a large proportion of highly illegal works. He also asked to stagger his payments in promissory notes that would become due over a period of eighteen to twenty-one months—which he justified by explaining that he had to extend long-term credit to his own customers, "as this town isn't rich." Having experienced great difficulties in collecting bills from small, provincial dealers who specialized in forbidden books, the STN had learned to be cautious when it received letters with that kind of language. It replied that Sens would have to have his notes (ordinary *billets à ordre*, carrying his signature and made payable to the bearer) guaranteed by the counter-signature of a well-established bookseller, such as Gaude.

In that case, Sens answered, adopting a miffed tone, he would cancel his order. "We have reflected about the hazards of selling certain philosophical books and others of that nature, and therefore we have changed our opinion and won't carry them, particularly as they are repugnant to our way of thinking." Furthermore, he added, he could procure nearly all of the STN's books from other suppliers. But the books had been shipped five weeks before he threatened to cancel the deal. In the end, therefore, he agreed to honor his order, and he assuaged the STN's worries by offering to pay for it in cash—with a 6 percent discount, as was usual in cash transactions.

This response mollified the STN, which continued to supply Sens, who, in turn, continued to try to persuade it to enter into exchanges. He was particularly eager to get rid of his excessive supply of *Thérèse philosophe* and the *Lettres philosophiques*. In a letter from Lyon dated November 4, 1777, he told the STN that he had just arrived from Paris and soon would leave for Avignon on a trip to replenish his stock. While in Paris, he learned that the government's edicts would go into effect sometime in the near future. Therefore, he suggested that the STN rush a large number of its pirated editions to him so that he could get them stamped, taking advantage of the window of opportunity before it closed.

Although this arrangement never worked out, the STN fell back on its smuggling operation in Lyon, and Sens relied on protection by his ally, Laporte, after Laporte took up his duties as the syndic of the reorganized *chambre syndicale*. By September 1778, Favarger calculated that conditions were favorable enough for the STN to continue its trade with Sens. But shipping remained difficult. A bale that the STN sent off in June 1777 did not arrive until December, and in 1779 Sens finally abandoned his attempts to draw supplies from Neuchâtel.

Because they extended over only a brief period of time and did not involve a large number of books, Sens's orders give only a limited picture of his trade. He certainly dealt heavily in illegal literature—the works of Voltaire, erotic libertine novels like *Thérèse philosophe*, and the polemical tracts of Simon-Nicolas-Henri Linguet (*Essai philosophique sur le monialisme, Lettre de M. Linguet à M. le comte de Vergennes*). The books he ordered in large number also included some novels (*Jezennemours* by Louis-Sébastien Mercier and *Les Sacrifices de l'amour* by Claude-Joseph Dorat), along with some travel literature (*Voyage en Sicile et en Malte* by Patrick Brydone) and works for Protestants (editions of the psalms).

The relations of the STN with Sens and the other booksellers in Toulouse leave an impression of missed opportunities. There was plenty of demand for a wide variety of books, especially cheap, pirated editions, but it was stifled by quarrels among the booksellers and, above all, by the difficulties of doing business over a large distance. Aside from the hazards of smuggling, the bottleneck in Lyon, and the shipping costs, the publisher-wholesaler had to develop confidence in its clients. It relied on contacts among local merchants and the occasional visit by a sales rep such as Favarger, yet it often had to make judgments based on the scanty information that came through the mail.

A final dossier from Toulouse, that of "Bergès et Cie.," illustrates this dilemma. In a letter to the STN dated May 26, 1781, Bergès said that he had not heard from the STN in a long time. He was pleased to inform it that he had just acquired the stock of theatrical works of Veuve Calamy in Bordeaux. As an enclosed sample half-page demonstrated, the quality of the printing and paper was splendid. Bergès would part with these books at a lump price of 30 livres per hundredweight in bales delivered free of charges as far as Lyon. He also offered to exchange books and sent a catalog of those he could make available: medical works, schoolbooks, science treatises, and a great deal of forbidden literature such as *La Raison par alphabet* [Reason by Alphabetical Order] by Voltaire and *Dom B ....., portier des Chartreux.* If the STN preferred to purchase them, he would give it a discount of 5 percent on the prices listed after the titles and a year's credit for making the payment.

The STN indicated a willingness to enter into negotiations and sent a copy of its own catalog. Bergès replied with a large order: thirty titles of works by popular authors worth a total of 864 livres. He also demonstrated a great deal of professional savvy about what was selling and what was available from other suppliers. For example, he noted that Jean-Abram Nouffer of Geneva was selling his edition of Raynal's *Histoire philosophique* for only 24 livres, the atlas included, with a 25 percent discount and a free copy for every dozen ordered. Bergès had ordered fifty copies of it—and he would not take any of the STN's edition of Necker's *Mémoire au Roi sur l'établissement des administrations provinciales* [Memoir to the King on the Establishment of Provincial Administrations] because "it has been printed near here, and Toulouse is flooded with it." He did a large business in Bordeaux as well as Toulouse, he explained in a letter of July 23, 1781, and he was ready to open up a supply line from the STN so long as it could be "flexible in your terms." "We have just reprinted our catalogue, and we have inserted some of your books in it, as you will see from the copy that our sales rep—who will be traveling in your cantons next month and is currently in Paris—will give to you."

In acknowledging Bergès's order, the STN asked him to excuse a delay, because it took time to assemble everything. Meanwhile, it wrote to Chaurou, the merchant in Toulouse who provided information about the solvency of the local booksellers, asking him whether the STN should extend its "confidence" to Bergès and if so, up to what sum of money. Chaurou replied that the business did not exist. Bergès had been a clerk of Sacarau et Moulas, where he had learned the tricks of the trade. Then he had tried to lure publishers into sending him books, which he intended to sell on the sly. He had been discovered and was currently in hiding: "This young man possesses nothing in the world, and if he gets caught, it's likely that you will not get a penny from anything you entrust to him."

It was a good try. Bergès had mastered the style of business letters, down to the all-important "signature" of the owner of the business (always different from the formal handwriting of the clerk who drafted the letter) at the end. He had accurate information about the current prices of books. He knew how to negotiate for favorable terms and to entice a publisher-wholesaler who was anxious about selling its stock. But everything about him was a bluff: the catalog, the sales rep, the correspondence with other firms, and the firm itself. Similar swindles appear elsewhere in the STN archives, some of them successful. Selling books was a tough business in the eighteenth century—at every level, from publishers and their journeyman printers down to booksellers and their clerks.

The main theme of Favarger's letters as he made his way along the Garonne from Toulouse to Bordeaux was not the book trade. He mentioned only five booksellers in that stretch of the journey: four in Montauban and one in Agen, and of them only Crosilhes of Montauban looked like a promising client of the STN. His horse occupied nearly all of Favarger's attention.

It collapsed four or five times a day on the muddy road between Toulouse and Montauban, a distance of thirty miles. When he prepared to leave Montauban, Favarger realized that the horse was seriously ill. It had a swollen gland in its neck, enflamed nostrils, and a strong cough. A local blacksmith who functioned as a veterinarian thought something had probably got caught in its windpipe. Determined to press on to Tonneins, where he had an assignment to collect a bill, Favarger set off on foot, leading the horse by its bridle. He got as far as Marmande, eighty-five miles away. Apparently he spent several nights en route (the diary does not say where he slept, perhaps in a blanket by the side of the road), because the horse was too weak to travel long distances and refused to eat. His contact in Marmande, a certain Ballier, accompanied him to another blacksmith, who gave the horse a long and expensive (24 livres) examination and treatment. The diagnosis was "gourme" (known as "strangles," a disease in horses characterized by an inflamed swelling of the throat), which the blacksmith attributed to overheating. After a day of unspecified "remedies," the horse ate a good meal of bran with some hay. Favarger was delighted to see that it had even recovered some of its "vivacity." But it spent the night vomiting up everything it had consumed and was clearly too weak to continue. Therefore, Favarger left it in the care of the blacksmith and rented a horse for the journey to Tonneins, a distance of ten miles.[2]

Once there, Favarger faced the problem of extracting 646 livres from a pastor named Dubois, who had ordered a large quantity of religious literature from the STN, sold it to his fellow Huguenots, and refused to pay the bill, despite endless dunning letters. Favarger learned that everyone in town knew Dubois as an incorrigible "bad subject." He therefore resorted to the system of protections that sometimes worked as a way to resolve imbroglios under the Ancien Régime. The STN had a contact in Marmande who had a friend, who in turn had a relative in the house of Baillas, the most powerful aristocratic family in the region. When presented with evidence of Dubois's duplicity, Baillas de Soubvent, the patriarch of the family, offered his "high protection" and summoned Dubois to give an account of his behavior. According to Favarger, Dubois, "trembling all over," abandoned every attempt to defend himself, and wrote two promissory notes to be paid under the supervision of Baillas, which finally resolved the affair. Noblesse oblige.

Back in Marmande on September 28, Favarger found that far from having recovered during his absence, the horse had developed a second swollen gland next to the earlier one. Therefore, he subjected it to a standard treatment of veterinary science, which was no more advanced than other branches of medicine in the eighteenth century. The blacksmith drove a red-hot iron into both glands and charged 1 livre, 10 sous for the operation. By now the STN had written to Favarger, urging him to make better time. He was needed back at the office and should abridge his itinerary, avoiding small towns and hurrying to get back before snow set in. But how could he hurry with a horse that could barely walk? He tried to sell it and found it would fetch only 2 louis (48 livres), whereas a new mount would cost 12 louis (288 livres). Also, he seems to have become attached to it: "I know it is of good quality" (*Je le connais bon*). In the hope that the horse would regain its health under the care of the blacksmith, Favarger decided to take a coach to Bordeaux, then to return to Marmande, fetch the horse, and ride it directly to his next major stop, La Rochelle.

Bordeaux

When Favarger arrived in Bordeaux at the beginning of October 1778, he would have taken in an impressive urban scene: a port flanked by the magnificent crescent of Ange-Jacques Gabriel's Place de la Bourse, completed only three years earlier; Victor Louis's Grand Théâtre still under construction; large quais lined with palaces; avenues, squares, and townhouses, about five thousand of them erected since 1700—all proclaiming the new wealth of the fourth-largest city (population 83,000) in the kingdom. But Favarger had no eye for architecture. He immediately set to work, trying to extract orders from the most solid of the city's twenty-five booksellers.

To his chagrin, however, Favarger discovered that their way of doing business did not suit his. They were even more casual about keeping appointments than the Lyonnais and they spent even more time at the dinner table, making it nearly impossible to meet with them in the afternoon. Favarger would stop by a bookshop and ask to see the owner. The owner would be out or busy or unwilling to do anything more than accept

Bordeaux, etching from *Nouveau voyage pittoresque de la France*, Paris, Ostervald, 1817 (BiCJ).

a copy of the STN's catalog, promising vaguely to discuss affairs once he had found the time to study it. Favarger would return two, three, four times, only to be told to come back later. When at last he buttonholed his man, he rarely closed a deal, for nearly all the booksellers refused to order shipments until they knew how the 1777 edicts would be applied. In his report to the STN, he complained that he had run from one end of the city to the other for several days and had accomplished very little.

After sorting the potential customers into the usual three categories, Favarger eliminated four "not good" booksellers along with a binder and a paper merchant who should not have been listed in the *Almanach de la librairie*. The remainder merited varying degrees of confidence, but they worried too much about the imminent crackdown on pirated books to buy supplies from Switzerland at that time. Only one, Guillaume Bergeret, agreed to place an order. Favarger copied it into his letter to the STN: nineteen titles, including the plays of Molière, the novels of Claude-Joseph Dorat, the *Histoire de l'Amérique* of William Robertson, and a variety of nonfiction works, none of them illegal. But Bergeret insisted on receiving one free copy for every six that he purchased instead of one for every dozen, and therefore Favarger doubted that the directors of the STN would agree to the deal. The only other prospect he turned up was a perfume merchant named Roques, who was willing to sell Protestant works on the sly. So there was no getting around it: Bordeaux was a disappointment; the American war had disrupted its trade; and "everything in general is in a miserable state of inactivity."

In fact, the hard times had begun several years before the outbreak of the American Revolution. In January 1774, Chappuis frères, one of the "mediocre" booksellers, informed the STN that they needed an extra two years to pay for a shipment. The market was glutted, they explained, and they complained bitterly about "the hard times at present and the consequent lack of consumption. In fact, we don't know any branch of commerce that is more disagreeable or unrewarding than the book trade."[3] They declared bankruptcy nine months later, although they eventually resumed business by negotiating an agreement with their creditors.

Despite appearances, therefore, Bordeaux—with a *parlement*, an intendancy, a university, an academy, a garrison, and the largest port on the Atlantic—did not become a major outlet for the STN. Nevertheless, for twelve years the Neuchâtelois maintained commercial relations with Bergeret, one of the largest booksellers in the city, and his correspondence provides an indication of the local demand for books.

Bergeret's letters show that he was a veteran of the trade.[4] He drew supplies from many publisher-wholesalers and played them off against one another, because, as he noted, the same books could be procured from many different sources. In dealing with the STN, he bargained for the cheapest possible prices, but the savings were offset by the shipping costs. In fact, shipping—routes, arrangements, delays, and expenses—was the main theme that ran through his letters and the replies from the STN.

Bergeret tested the STN's services with a small order that he sent "as a trial" on June 22, 1773. He made a selection of titles from the STN's current catalog, noting to his regret that it was lacking in "philosophical articles." The French government had just imposed its duty of 28 livres per hundredweight on all imports of books. Bergeret was willing to pay an "insurance" charge of 12 percent in order to avoid the duty by having the books smuggled across the border. But the STN had run into difficulties with its main smuggler, Guillon l'aîné, and therefore recommended the

Geneva-Turin-Nice route, which would work well, at a charge of 16 livres per hundredweight, it assured Bergeret, provided he had a reliable agent in Nice. It included in its reply a manuscript catalog of the *livres philosophiques* that it kept in stock.

Although Bergeret did not specialize in forbidden books, the catalog whetted his appetite for them; and he asked the STN to add several copies of *Théologie portative*, *Thérèse philosophe*, and similar works to the bale it was preparing. He would pay for the shipping but not the smuggling. The STN answered that it had recently opened up a route through Lyon, where it had hired a new agent to get its books past inspection in the *chambre syndicale*. Prospects therefore looked promising, provided they could reach an agreement on prices. Bergeret was not willing to pay what the STN charged for illegal literature, but the STN in turn refused to reduce its prices for reasons it explained: "We notice that among the articles you order there are several in the genre that one calls philosophical and which we do not keep in stock but can supply with the help of our correspondents. In this respect, we must warn you that these books sell for more than others for reasons that are easy to imagine.... We cannot sell them to you at the same price as the others in our catalogue, because we must buy them ourselves at a higher price. Nonetheless, we will try to procure them for you at the best possible price. Books of this kind are multiplying all around us."

Bergeret finally agreed on the prices that the STN set for his order. It sent off the shipment in September 1773, and the bale arrived successfully via the Lyon route. Bergeret paid for it on time and without squabbling—unlike the less solid dealers, who, as we've seen, often found pretexts to avoid paying the full cost of their bills. In February 1775, he sent another large order: sixty titles of which eleven were *livres philsophiques*. He placed an *x* next to the titles of the latter, all of them bestsellers in the underground trade, and explained: "You will please marry the articles marked by an x with the others." As explained in chapter 2, "marrying" was a technique of larding the sheets of illegal works inside those of innocent ones so that nothing would be confiscated when the bales were inspected in *chambres syndicales*. Most inspections for shipments to Bordeaux occurred in Lyon, where the STN's agents made sure that they were done with a suitable degree of superficiality.

This shipment made it safely, although with a delay of more than two months. Bergeret grumbled about the slow service and some of the STN's prices, but he appreciated the quality of its printing. In fact, he commissioned it to print a pirated edition of a manual about spelling and reading that he planned to sell as a speculation of his own. But relations began to sour during the summer of 1775. In April, Bergeret ordered thirty copies of a radical political tract, *Journal historique de la révolution opérée dans la constitution de la monarchie française par M. de Maupeou, chancelier de France*, volumes 1–3. The STN did not get them to him until late June, and it took even longer to provide him with its continuation, volumes 4–5, because, unknown to Bergeret, it got its own stock from a dealer in Lyon who favored his French clients. Bergeret complained that his competitors, who were supplied directly from Lyon, received those volumes three months before he did. The delays could cost him customers, he warned the STN in October, and he might have to take his own custom elsewhere: "It will be necessary, much against my will, for me to completely give up ordering your articles. There still is no sign of the shipment you announced nearly three months ago. You must realize that I cannot do business in this manner."

The STN apologized and patched up its Lyon operation as well as it could, but it never regained a large share of Bergeret's trade. It sent him a few shipments in 1776 and 1777; then in 1778, the year of Favarger's visit, it failed to supply him on time with fifty copies of William Robertson's four-volume *Histoire de l'Amérique*, a bestseller, owing in large part to the interest in the American Revolution. Editions from Paris and Rouen reached Bordeaux long before the STN could get its relatively cheap *contrefaçon* as far as Lyon. Therefore, Bergeret canceled the purchase and sent another scolding letter: "You know full well that if one does not receive new works while they are fresh, they usually remain in the warehouse." Nonetheless, he ordered a dozen of Robertson's history when Favarger called on him in October. Interest in America had not declined, although the war had had a disastrous general effect on Bordeaux's commerce: "Business is so slow and bad because of the war that all kinds of commerce have gone into a decline in this city. Accordingly, I am limiting my orders to small assortments."

For the next six years Bergeret continued to place orders whenever he sensed that new works offered by the STN would appeal to his customers.

In 1781, he ordered twenty-five copies of Mercier's *Tableau de Paris*. In 1782, he wanted one hundred copies of Mercier's *Portraits des rois de France* but canceled the order when the STN ran into problems getting its bales across the border. In 1784, he ordered a dozen copies of the STN's ten-volume edition of Raynal's *Histoire philosophique*. But the trade that had looked so promising in 1773 never developed to the extent that both sides desired. Supply and demand were separated by too much distance and too many obstacles.

Still, Bergeret's orders provide an indication of the literature most in demand in what probably was the largest bookshop in Bordeaux. Despite his interest in highly illegal books, Bergeret favored pedagogical and utilitarian works, such as Restaut's *Abrégé des principes de la grammaire française* [Primer on the Principles of French Grammar], Tissot's *Avis au people sur sa santé*, and (not surprisingly for Bordeaux) *L'Art de faire le vin* [The Art of Making Wine] by Maupin, a prolific writer on viticulture. Bergeret ordered a great many books for children: *Les Hochets moraux, ou contes pour la première enfance* [Moral Baubles, or Tales for Very Young Children] by M. Monget and an anonymous anthology, *Lectures pour les enfants, ou choix de petits contes également propres à les amuser et à leur faire aimer la vertu* [Readings for Children, or Choice of Short Stories Suited Equally to Amuse Them and to Make Them Love Virtue]. His orders also included a large number of history and travel books along with popular works that pretended to reveal secrets about freemasonry (*Abrégé de l'histoire de la franche-maçonnerie* [Short History of Free Masonry] by J. J. le François de Lalande) and magic (*L'Albert moderne, ou recueil de secrets éprouvés et licites* [The Modern Albert, or Collection of Tried and Lawful Secrets] by P.-A. Alletz). Although his letters showed interest in the works of Voltaire and Raynal, Bergeret did not order many treatises by Enlightenment philosophers. The author who stands out above all others in his orders is Louis-Sébastien Mercier, a great favorite among French readers, although his prominence in the orders received by the STN can be explained, at least in part, by the fact that it featured his works in its catalogs and printed many of them on its own presses. The statistics drawn from the orders also show a large demand for the libels and tracts related to the political crisis during the last years of Louis XV's reign, notably the *Anecdotes sur Mme la comtesse du Barry*. Taken as a whole, Bergeret's orders suggest a demand for a wide variety of literature—some of it spicy but most of it similar to the ordinary fare in "assortments" that filled the shelves of other large provincial bookshops.

La Rochelle

Having taken the coach back to Marmande, Favarger was relieved to find his horse much recovered. But it had rained incessantly for the previous two weeks, and he could not make more than seven leagues (about fifteen miles) a day, because of the miserable, muddy trails. Even worse, "the poor beast is still so weak that she constantly wants to throw herself to the ground." The route from Libourne to Cognac was so slippery that the horse's shoes came loose, and it took 4 days to cover that stretch of the journey, a distance of seventy-two miles—which now takes an hour and a half by car. Favarger's expense account shows that he stopped several times at blacksmith shops to have the horse re-shod (the cost varied from 1 livre, 10 sous to 2 livres). He also bought a whip (1 livre, 10 sous), which may indicate that he had to use some force to keep the horse going. Another expenditure, 4 livres

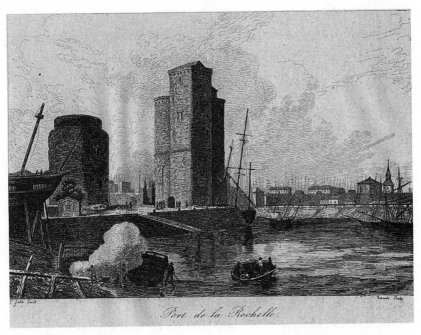

La Rochelle, etching from *Nouveau voyage pittoresque de la France*, Paris, Ostervald, 1817 (BiCJ).

A humble blacksmith's shop as depicted by Jean-Jacques de Boissieu.
Jean-Jacques de Boissieu, *Farrier*. Harvard Art Museum, gift of Belinda L. Randall
from the collection of John Witt Randall, R4105. Imaging Department © President
and Fellows of Harvard College.

for repairs to his boots, suggests that he probably walked much of the way.
Although he never complained in his letters, it clearly was a hard slog.

Some of the bookshops along the way looked promising, although
none of them had a large clientele. Fontaine, a dealer in Libourne recommended for his exactitude in honoring bills of exchange, said that he had
long wanted to trade with the STN and soon would send an order. Louis
Delyes, an energetic young man with a well-assorted shop in Saintes,
promised to do the same. The shop of Faye in Rochefort looked fairly well
stocked, and he made a substantial order for a wide variety of books. Then
at last Favarger arrived in La Rochelle, where he received a warm welcome
from Jean Ranson, a wealthy merchant and former student of Ostervald's,
who was delighted to offer hospitality to an unpretentious man of the
people from the far-off Calvinist stronghold in the Jura. Favarger then
trudged through the rain from bookshop to bookshop, while leaving his
horse to recover in a stable.

La Rochelle, famous for its port and its Protestants, might seem to
have been a promising market for books in mid-October, when Favarger
arrived. Its merchants had prospered from the Atlantic trade: exports of
paper, textiles, and wine; imports of sugar from Saint Domingue and furs

from Canada; and profitable stopovers in Africa to pick up slaves for the plantations in the Caribbean. But La Rochelle never went through a boom comparable to that of Bordeaux and Nantes. In fact, its population grew slowly. It contained only 16,200 inhabitants in 1780, ranking fiftieth among all the cities in France. The government's book-trade survey of 1764 noted that La Rochelle had merely two booksellers and two printers— not enough to warrant the establishment of a *chambre syndicale*. The local intendant was responsible for overseeing their activities, and that did not require much effort: "They are all decent people," he noted, "very sagacious and well behaved. Their wealth consists only in the fruit of their work, and it is not considerable."[5]

When Favarger surveyed the trade, he, too, found that it did not amount to much. The number of booksellers had expanded to three since 1764. One, Pentinelle, belonged to the lowest category, "not good." A second, Chaboceau, qualified as "good" but did not want to order books from suppliers located as far away as Switzerland. That left Pavie, also "good" but a tough customer, as the STN had learned from dealing with him since 1772.

The firm was formally known as Pavie père et fils. Pavie second fils wrote most of its letters, using correct but somewhat awkward turns of phrase in correspondence scattered with mistakes in spelling. His first letter, dated February 8, 1772, suggested that the shop catered to La Rochelle's large Huguenot community—and perhaps, too, that Protestantism led to sympathy for the Enlightenment. He inquired about the STN's ability to provide Protestant Bibles and sermons, and he also showed interest in "philosophical books like *Système de la nature*." The duty on book imports of 68 livres per hundredweight had recently been reduced to 28 livres: "That is still plenty expensive but at least it's more civilized and just." Pavie expected the STN, like his other foreign suppliers, to split the cost of the duty, but wondered what the best route would be. Shipments via Nice and Marseille were very expensive, so he hoped the STN could get its bales cleared through Lyon at a reasonable price.

If they did, Pavie indicated in his next letter, he would take two Protestant liturgical works, a dozen copies of Mercier's *L'An deux mille quatre cent quarante*, and ten copies of *Système de la nature*, provided the quality was adequate. He knew of four editions of the *Système*, the recently published atheistic treatise that was enjoying a *succès de scandale*: a magnificent Dutch printing, two acceptable editions, and one on such "detestable" paper that he would not take it. (As already mentioned, the quality of paper was crucial in satisfying the eighteenth-century reading public.) In a letter of April 25, Pavie asked the STN to add an assortment of other titles to the shipment, if it could be sent safely and at a reasonable cost. They included Bayle's *Dictionnaire historique et critique*, some political tracts, and "the *Lettres de Mme de Pompadour*, which have just appeared, as well as other items that you may have in this genre." Evidently, Pavie was well informed about the latest works to appear on the market and did not hesitate to order the most illegal among them.

For the next two years Pavie continued to sound out the STN on its ability to provide him with books, mostly Protestant works along with several on history and travel and various *livres philosophiques*. But it was not until March 1776 that he sent a firm order, which was to be shipped through Lyon to Orléans, where he had an agent who could forward it safely to La Rochelle. The order contained twenty-three titles, some from the STN's catalog and some that he expected it to procure for him from other Swiss publisher-wholesalers. In a subsequent order, he indicated that his choice of books depended, at least partly, on what his customers asked him to provide: "I am asked for the following items, which you will please send to me if you have them." The orders arrived regularly for the next twelve months, and the STN filled them without mishap, assuming costs and risks as far as Lyon.

By that time, the STN also sent some small shipments to private individuals in La Rochelle. They were merchants, including Jean Ranson, who maintained cordial relations with Ostervald and ordered several books for himself and his friends. Pavie objected to this informal trade, because it might cut into his market: "These friends put in requests for other friends, so that from friends to friends the whole city will be supplied, and the booksellers will be stuck with unsold copies. I ask you to pay attention to this, for otherwise we will have a quarrel." In fact, this small-scale trade among amateurs never amounted to much, but Pavie's reaction illustrates a widespread concern of the established booksellers, who were often eager to deal in forbidden books (provided they did not run serious risks) but hated competition from interlopers—peddlers, binders, and individual entrepreneurs.

What most hampered Pavie's relations with the STN was the increased severity of the government's attempts to repress the trade in pirated and forbidden books. Already in the summer of 1776, Pavie reported a new threat of rigorous inspection in the *chambre syndicale* of Orléans. Four shipments to him made it past that dangerous forwarding station in 1777, though he advised the STN to switch to a safer route. It favored the relatively cheap inland waterways, which led down the Saône to Lyon, across to Roanne, and then down the Loire to Orléans and various points in western France. Pavie recommended the more direct route to Limoges, which was safer yet much more expensive, because the books had to travel along mountainous trails on the backs of mules in packs that could not weigh more than 150 pounds.

Faced with a decline in Pavie's business in 1778, the STN offered to cover costs and risks as far as Orléans, where he had a reliable agent. This proposal, it emphasized, represented a large concession on its part, "because we have to make hefty payments to the persons we employ, and that cuts into a large part of our profit." Pavie's orders then resumed, mainly in Protestant and erotic works, which formed a large part of his business. He also ordered the same books from other suppliers and demonstrated considerable expertise about conditions in the underground trade. In August 1776 he bargained down the STN's price for *La fille de joie* (a translation of John Cleland's *Fanny Hill: Memoirs of a Woman of Pleasure*) from 36 to 30 sous and for *La Contagion sacrée* [The Holy Contagion] from 40 to 30 sous. In July 1779, however, the STN informed him that it no longer would procure *livres philosophiques* for its customers. It had run into too many difficulties, both on the supply side (quarrels with marginal Genevan publishers who had the books printed) and among its customers (refusals to pay bills and to share the cost of confiscations).

Pavie's reply sounded almost too pious to be true. "I strongly praise you for having eliminated certain articles from my order. In fact, I was going to write to you about this subject, as I want to stock only things that are good, things that will revive on the market while measures are being taken to wipe out works that tend to trouble the social order, especially when they are read by people who don't have enough education to make allowances for their vicious ingredients." As in its correspondence with Mossy, the STN sometimes received "ostensible letters," full of pious sentiments, from booksellers who wanted to be able to produce evidence of their respect for the law if they got into trouble with the authorities. By this time, however, the main attention of the book police had shifted to the

confiscation of pirated works, which formed the bulk of Pavie's trade with
the STN. The edicts of 1777 were strictly enforced in his area, he wrote on
July 31, 1779. All bills of lading on the bales had to specify that the goods
had been inspected and repackaged with lead seals at a *chambre syndicale*.
Of course, the STN's agents had ways of coping with this problem in
Lyon, and so did Pavie's other Swiss suppliers, including Samuel Fauche
and the independent firm of his son, Fauche fils aîné et Cie. But the shipping costs continued to mount. In December 1779, Pavie complained that
he had just received a bale whose transport came to 36 livres for books
worth 169 livres. In August 1780, he settled his account for 515 livres,
5 sous, and he did not order any more books for nearly four years.

The other administrative measure that disrupted the trade was the government's 1783 order requiring all foreign shipments to be inspected in
the *chambre syndicale* of Paris no matter what their ultimate destination.
Pavie informed the STN on February 21, 1784, that he had stopped ordering books from Switzerland: "The current difficulties of receiving supplies from abroad must have badly damaged your sales. The rigidity with
which this order is being executed has made me suspend all correspondence with your cantons." A month later, he wrote that the STN should be
able to overcome this obstacle by hiring a Parisian bookseller to get its
shipments through the Parisian *chambre syndicale*. He dealt with everyone in the book trade of Paris, he said, but he could not handle the arrangements himself. He would pay 10 livres per hundredweight for the
undercover service and the transport costs from Neuchâtel to Paris, provided the STN assumed all risks. He was particularly eager to get fifty
copies of the *Vie privée ou apologie de Mgr. le duc de Chartres* [The Private
Life or Vindication of Mgr. the duc de Chartres], a libelous work that was
much in demand.

By September 1784, Pavie had abandoned hope that the 1783 order
would be revoked, and the STN had given up on the attempt to recruit an
agent to arrange smuggling through the *chambre syndicale* of Paris. It
raised the possibility of sending its bales to Lyon, where its agents could
repackage them and forwarded them to La Rochelle disguised as domestic
shipments. But that service would cost 15 livres per hundredweight. Pavie
now wanted to get a new edition of Mercier's *L'An deux mille quatre cent
quarante*. When he calculated the expenses, however—15 livres for smuggling and 25 livres for transport, totaling 40 livres per hundredweight—he

concluded that each book would cost him 6 to 8 sous more than its whole-sale price, which he pronounced "revolting." The Lyonnais managed to get Swiss books to him, he insisted; so the STN should be able to do so as well, while paying half of the 15 livres' smuggling charge.

On October 24, 1784, the STN replied that no such arrangement was feasible: "The passage through Lyon is dangerous; inspections there are rigorous. One must evade them and Orléans, too, by going through Auvergne and Limousin, where, however, the trails are bad." Although Pavie and the STN continued for a year to discuss various possibilities—smuggling through Lyon, boats along the Rhine to Holland, mule trains in Auvergne and the Limousin—nothing worked out. They settled accounts in December 1785 and never restored their trade.

As Pavie made clear in his letters, he wanted a great many Protestant works and *livres philosophiques*. His orders were somewhat less varied than those of other provincial booksellers, perhaps because he concentrated, at least at first, on the forbidden books that the STN kept in stock or procured by exchanges with publishers who specialized in the underground trade. On the list of the fifteen titles that he ordered most, the top three were editions of the Bible, the psalms, and a catechism. Two others were collections of sermons—two of nine books of sermons that he ordered on different occasions. To the modern reader, they look out of place on a list next to works that would be considered pornographic today: *Histoire galante de la tourière des Carmélites, ouvrage fait pour servir de pendant au Portier des Chartreux* [The Gallant History of the Tourière Nun of the Carmelites, a Work Made to Serve as a Sequel to the Porter of the Carthusians], *La Putain errante* [The Wandering Whore], and *La Nouvelle Académie des dames* [The New Academy of Ladies]. But to eighteenth-century booksellers, literature aimed at Huguenots was as risky as works that were merely salacious, even those that laced sex with anticlericalism.

Among the other works that Pavie ordered most often were many that figured prominently in the trade of other booksellers, notably Mercier's *L'An deux mille quatre cent quarante* and *Anecdotes sur Mme la comtesse du Barry*. *L'Adoption, ou la Maçonnerie des femmes*, fifth on his list of most-ordered books, illustrates the widespread fascination with freemasonry among French readers. Judging from the pattern of Pavie's orders, the demand for it remained strong among his customers. He sent for twelve copies on March 16, 1776; thirty-nine on July 27, 1776; twelve on January

19, 1779; and six on September 18, 1779. He also ordered a dozen copies of *Les Devoirs, statuts, ou règlements généraux des francs maçons* [The Duties, Statutes, or General Regulations of the Free Masons] on March 16, 1776. Among other tendencies, the orders suggested a strong demand for political tracts such as *Catéchisme du citoyen* [Catechism of the Citizen] by Joseph Saige and *Essai sur le despotisme* [Essay on Despotism] by the comte de Mirabeau. And they included a sizable proportion of Enlightenment works, from Voltaire's *Lettres philosophiques*, which had lost much of their shock value by 1770, to d'Holbach's *Système de la nature*. Pavie ordered up a spicy diet of literature for his customers, and like many established booksellers he would have provided them with more spice had he been able to count on stable supply lines.

Poitiers

Having completed his business in La Rochelle, Favarger had to resolve his horse problem. It continued to rain; the road to Poitiers, eighty-three miles

Poitiers etching from *Nouveau voyage pittoresque de la France*, Paris, Ostervald, 1817 (BiCJ).

away, was very muddy; and he had to hurry, because the last letter from the STN, which he collected in La Rochelle, urged him to come home without delay by the most direct route. Despite the unfavorable circumstances, he decided to give the horse another try. On October 23 or 24, they made it to Niort, a distance of thirty-five miles, where he turned up one good bookseller (by the name of Elies) who promised to send an order, then to Saint-Maixent (sixteen more miles through constant rain), where he found another (Brunet). But from that point on the horse could barely walk. When at last it hobbled into Poitiers (thirty-two more miles), its legs had swollen so badly that the swellings burst, leaving deep wounds.

Much to his regret, Favarger resolved to sell it and to buy a sturdier animal, though he was unsure about how to bargain over horseflesh among unknown traders in a foreign country. There were endless ways to be swindled. Fortunately, he ran into a fellow Swiss, a merchant from La Chaux-de-Fonds who had come to Poitiers on business, and he also received help from Michel-Vincent Chevrier, the STN's main customer among the booksellers in Poitiers. In the end, Favarger got a better deal than what he had been offered in Marmande. He sold the horse for 4 louis (96 livres) and bought another—nearly a hand (4 inches) taller, much stronger, six years old, and "well reputed"—for 9 louis (216 livres). "I regret this loss very much," he wrote to the STN. Presumably he was referring to the financial loss in having to buy a new horse, but he may also have felt a tug on his emotions at abandoning an animal that had accompanied him for nearly four months and over many hundreds of miles. Even today, traveling salesmen are said to develop a fondness for their cars.

Having braved Poitiers's horse market, Favarger explored the rest of the city. Although Poitiers offers great charms to the modern visitor, it received poor reviews from travelers in the eighteenth century. They deplored its narrow, badly paved streets, dilapidated houses, and general backwardness. Its population remained stagnant throughout the century at about 18,000 souls, "poor from the lack of trade and their natural laziness."[6] Poitiers was indeed a provincial capital with an intendancy and some important judicial and administrative bodies. It had a dozen booksellers in 1778, and they could count on customers from among the wealthier inhabitants—described shortly before the Revolution as "gentle, witty, inactive, and unsuited for commerce"[7]—the law courts, the local garrison, and the university, which had two hundred students enrolled in its faculty of law.

When Favarger surveyed the booksellers, he wrote off most as "not good." Four qualified as "mediocre," but they did not do enough business to support the cost of shipments from Switzerland. One, Jacques Bobin, had sent a large order in December 1776. However, the STN refused to supply him, because it did not trust his ability to pay his bills. Bobin kept a stall inside Poitiers's Palais de justice and catered to a clientele of lawyers. According to the book-trade survey of 1764, he was a peddler who could neither read nor write. His letters to the STN are perfectly legible, though they probably were drafted by his son, who had entered the clergy— against his father's will—and then left it to work in the family business. In one letter, Bobin (or his son, writing in his name), admitted frankly, "My intention is not to dazzle anyone by an extensive display, and I will never blush to say that I do not have a large fortune." He eventually agreed to pay in cash, and in 1782 the STN sent him a shipment with a wide variety of books (none of them illegal), but it took so long and cost so much that he never ordered any more.

Only two booksellers had the capacity to enter into sustained relations with the STN, according to Favarger's estimate. One was Félix Faulcon, the wealthy syndic of the local *chambre syndicale*. Favarger found him to be "a strange character," and so committed to his role as syndic that he would not purchase any pirated books. Michel-Vincent Chevrier was another story. He promised to help the STN get its bales past Faulcon when they were inspected in the *chambre syndicale*, and he wanted to expand his trade with the STN if they could agree on terms. Indeed the effort to arrive at mutually advantageous terms was the main theme of the letters that the STN had exchanged with Chevrier starting in June 1772. To get its shipments to Poitiers, the STN first had to cope with the tariff on book imports, then the irregularities of the smuggling/insurance system, and finally the snags in the route that led from Lyon through Orléans. Chevrier seemed undaunted by the difficulties of drawing supplies from a long distance—he mentioned ordering books from the Société typographique de Bouillon—but the prices had to be right.

Chevrier wanted a little of everything that the STN had to offer, including works in its manuscript catalog of *livres philosophiques*. Though forbidden books made up only a small proportion of his trade, he had an expert's knowledge of them. In fact, he sent the STN a "catalog" of his own *livres philosophiques*. It featured sixty-seven titles—more by far than the STN offered—arranged alphabetically, except for four popular pornographic works, which he added at the end: *Thérèse philosophe*, *L'Académie des dames*, *La Religieuse en chemise,* and *Margot la ravaudeuse* [Margot, the Seamstress]. Aside from this erotic element, Chevrier's list covered the full gamut of irreligious literature that was then available in print. A great deal of it derived from the corpus of clandestine manuscripts that had circulated widely during the first half of the century, including translations of works by English deists and freethinkers—John Toland, Anthony Collins, Henry St. John, viscount Bolingbroke, and Thomas Woolston—along with French tracts that, as in the orders from Pavie, extended from Voltairean anticlericalism to the atheistic writings of the d'Holbach circle. Only a few of the books mentioned in Chevrier's first letters ever made it to Poitiers, because he would not commit himself to large-scale purchases until the STN set up a safe route to his bookshop.

A trial shipment, sent through Lyon, made it without mishap in December 1772, but it took five months en route. If the STN could solve the shipping problem, Chevrier promised, he would give it a great deal of business. In fact, he would take a baker's dozen of everything it printed along with books from its general stock in exchange for a monopoly of its trade within 100 miles of his shop. The STN would have to cover all costs and risks as far as Lyon, but as compensation for this service he would pay 4 percent more than the sales price—or 5 percent if it could get the bales to Orléans, where he had an agent, widow Fleury, who could handle them safely. The STN replied with a counterproposal, offering slightly different conditions at a somewhat higher price. Chevrier parried with a counter-counterproposal, and the negotiations continued for three months, each side adjusting its terms in response to the other and calculating costs down to a third of a percentage point.[8] Meanwhile, Chevrier sent another order; the STN shipped it off and soon afterward wrote a note (*billet à présentation*) on him for his accumulated debt: 474 livres, 15 sous, payable within ten days of its presentation.

Chevrier refused to accept the note. The shipment had not even arrived, he objected, before the STN demanded payment. When and if the bale made it to widow Fleury's warehouse in Orléans (her husband had recently died, and she had taken over the family business), he would pay for it in a note of his own, due to mature in a year, allowing an extra 10 percent to cover transport and risks. He warned the STN that he could easily do without their trade, as he could procure all of the books it sold from suppliers in Bouillon and Holland with whom he did a great deal of business. "I would regret it if we ceased to do business together, but I prefer to do nothing at all rather than to trade at my disadvantage."

A great deal of money hung on every detail of these negotiations, because Chevrier and the STN expected to do business on a large scale. While addressing Chevrier's objections, the STN apologized for having written a note on him without adequate warning, although it also insisted that it could not modify its terms—not from any lack of respect, but because it had worked through every aspect of the proposed deals according to "calculation, a demonstrative science." In reply, Chevrier said that he, too, was sorry, but he would not modify his terms. "You will lose a good customer, who would have marketed many of your products and would have paid you well." Furthermore, he complained, he still had not received two of the STN's shipments.

They had been delayed, it turned out, by the inability of the STN's "insurer," Guillon l'aîné, to smuggle them across the border near Clairvaux-les-lacs. Therefore, the STN had been forced to send the two shipments by mule along a safe but circuitous mountain route that led through Limoges. They did not reach Chevrier until December 1773, eleven and nine months, respectively, after their departure from Neuchâtel. The transport cost 160 livres, 15 sous for merchandise valued at 626 livres, 19 sous, and 9 deniers.

Chevrier paid 10 percent above the list price of the books in notes with six-month maturity, and he offered to continue paying at that rate if the STN could get its shipments free of transport charges and risks to Orléans. That arrangement looked feasible in 1774, because the French government reduced and then revoked the duty that had made all book imports prohibitively expensive. As it no longer had to deal with tax inspectors, the STN could now ship its books through Lyon, using its own agents to avoid confiscations in the Lyonnais *chambre syndicale*. Its trade with Chevrier resumed and continued for eighteen months, although he continued to complain about delays and also about damages: the STN's warehouse workers did not pack the bales tightly enough and therefore the sheets were sometimes torn by rubbing against the ropes.

A more serious problem arose in mid-1775. Chevrier discovered that Jean-François Malherbe, a dealer in Loudun, twenty-eight miles away, was underselling him with STN books. Malherbe had no right to engage in the book trade, because he had neither been received in a *chambre syndicale* nor purchased a license (*brevet de libraire*). He had nonetheless ordered large shipments from Neuchâtel and sold them off at reduced prices for cash, mainly to peddlers who hawked them throughout Poitou and the Loire Valley. Like Pavie in La Rochelle, Couret de Villeneuve in Orléans, and other major booksellers from the region, Chevrier was indignant at competition coming from such an outsider. "If M. Malherbe were a bookseller, I would not be so angry. But you must admit that it is unconscionable that a man who has no notion of the book trade can make it known everywhere in Poitiers that any individual who desires books can rely on him and get them at a price of one sou per sheet." Chevrier was still seething when he discussed the trade with Favarger in October 1778. Although he placed an order with Favarger, the STN still found his terms—delivery free of risks and costs to Orléans—unacceptable. By the end of 1778 it had stopped doing business with him.

Despite all these difficulties, Chevrier ordered enough books for one to assess the general pattern of his trade. Also, as he mentioned in several letters, he could obtain the books offered by the STN from other publisher-wholesalers, such as the Société typographique de Bouillon with whom he regularly did business. His correspondence confirmed what Favarger knew from discussions in Lyon and Avignon: the widespread exchanges among publishers meant that the same works could be procured from many different suppliers. There was nothing peculiar about the orders Chevrier placed with the STN; and as he was one of the two most important booksellers in Poitou, the statistics drawn from his orders provide an indication of the demand for literature throughout the province in the pre-revolutionary era.

Like Pavie in La Rochelle, Chevrier catered to the Huguenots in the area. He sold many Protestant editions of the Bible and the psalms. Mercier's *L'An deux mille quatre cent quarante* stood second on the list of books he ordered most, and it was followed by the works of Rousseau. Chevrier also ordered a great deal of Voltaire, Raynal, and several Holbachean works, though none of them in large number. The Enlightenment certainly occupied a large place in his trade. History was also important, as suggested by his orders for Paul-François Velly's *Histoire de France*, Jacques Tailhe's *Abrégé de l'histoire ancienne de Monsieur Rollin* [Abridgement of Monsieur

Rollin's ancient history], and William Robertson's *Histoire de l'Amérique*. Chevrier spiced up his orders with some erotic *livres philosophiques*, such as the aforementioned *Margot la ravaudeuse*. But he showed relatively little interest in light fiction, despite an order for Mme Riccoboni's sentimental novels. On the whole, he favored tried-and-true works such as Molière's plays and the popular *Dictionnaire raisonné universel d'histoire naturelle* [Analytical and Universal Dictionary of Natural History] by Jacques-Christophe Valmont de Bomare.

Judging from his success, Chevrier understood the book market very well. His shop, located in Poitiers's principal street, the rue de l'intendance, made the main currents of contemporary literature available throughout the city and much of the surrounding area. The same can be said of all the principal booksellers that Favarger encountered from Toulouse to Poitiers. They wanted the latest *nouveautés* along with standard books in fields like history and travel and some strong doses of *livres philosophiques*. Having passed the halfway point in his tour de France, Favarger had found a great deal of homogeneity in the markets he encountered. Not only did the booksellers want the same kind of books, they also procured them from several publisher-wholesalers who offered the same basic fare. At his next stop, however, Favarger confronted a completely different aspect of the book business: diffusion by obscure dealers who operated far outside the established channels of the trade.

10

Loudun

Peddling and the Capillary System

FAVARGER MADE IT EASILY FROM POITIERS TO LOUDUN (twenty-five miles) in less than a day. He was happy with his new horse, which made much better time than the old one. Yet Loudun, on the face of it, hardly merited a half day's stop. It had nothing to recommend itself as a market for books, or indeed for anything else. Its population remained stagnant at a low level, about four thousand. Its economy depended on local farming supplemented by some small-scale production of woolens and leather goods. It had no important educational and administrative institutions— nothing more than the office of an intendant's unpaid *subdélégué*, a minor court, and a small college. Its connections with commercial routes amounted to little more than a few small roads leading to Tours in the northeast and Poitiers in the southeast. And it had no booksellers or printers.

Between 1770 and 1786, however, Loudun became the hub of an extensive business that linked Swiss publisher-wholesalers with French peddlers or *marchands forains*, who sold books throughout the Loire Valley and the surrounding provinces. Its out-of-the-way location was actually an advantage for this sort of trade, because the French authorities did not trouble themselves with overseeing commerce in such an unimportant town. Loudun therefore provides an ideal site for studying the capillary system of the book trade.

The entrepreneur at the heart of this network was Jean-François Malherbe l'aîné. He had no right to deal in books, as he had no connection with a *chambre syndicale* and no *brevet de libraire*. Officially, Malherbe was a *commissionnaire*, one who dealt in all sorts of goods. He was listed in a trade almanac in 1779 as an expediter, especially of agricultural products and also "diverse works of literature," for a 2 percent commission.[1] Strictly speaking, therefore, he did not hide his ancillary trade in books, although he appeared only fleetingly in the almanac as a dispatcher rather than a bookseller.

References scattered through the first letters in Malherbe's dossier indicate that he was a Huguenot who had relatives in Switzerland and knew all four of the STN's founding partners. He probably had studied in Neuchâtel, boarding with Samuel Fauche, at a time when Ostervald, Bertrand, and Berthoud ran the local college. His first letter, written to Fauche on March 10, 1770, includes many intimate details, suggesting close relations with the entire Fauche family. Among other things—greetings to the children and mutual friends—he asked Fauche to sell a watch that he had left behind after a visit to Neuchâtel. By then, Malherbe had made a first attempt to set up business as a *commissionnaire*, but it had not gone well, and he needed money badly. In fact, he sent the letter from a secret address in Saint Maixent, where he was hiding in order to escape debtors' prison after going bankrupt in 1767.

While his lawyer tried to negotiate a settlement with his creditors, Malherbe toyed with starting some kind of business with a friend in Cadix or perhaps in Switzerland, provided that Fauche could help him acquire a crucial asset: "Procure for me an amiable girlfriend with a dowry of 20 to 25 thousand. I hope to come in for more but can't expect anything above 10 to 12 thousand during the lifetime of my father, who is too attached to his pleasures." His father was a hard man, he added, so he could not expect to revive his bankrupt business with the help of a family loan. The most feasible plan was to put together assets that he had dispersed in various places—no doubt without the knowledge of his creditors—and begin again collecting commissions on sales of imports and exports. Books figured prominently among the articles he had in mind. "Your New Testaments and Psalms would do well with our peasants in Poitou." By the end of 1772, a court in Poitiers had finally disposed of the suit connected with his bankruptcy and he was back in business in Loudun.

Malherbe's shaky financial past did not make him look like a promising client. Yet he managed to ingratiate himself with his Neuchâtelois contacts by a stream of letters that mentioned all sorts of helpful-sounding activities. He announced that he would attend Huguenot services outdoors in "the desert," where he would sell religious works to ministers and their flocks. He offered to collect subscriptions for the STN's *Journal helvétique*. He knew booksellers in Poitiers, Saumur, Tours, Angers, and Nantes; and he was trying to win them as customers for the STN. He also had contact with individual entrepreneurs like a schoolmaster in Blois named Lair; Desbordes, a merchant in La Rochelle; and Boisserand, a shipping agent in Roanne, all of whom were eager to speculate on books. To drum up orders he circulated the STN's catalogs among his correspondents and placed advertisements for its books in commercial news-sheets (*affiches* and *feuilles d'avis*) published throughout the Loire Valley. Malherbe clearly knew his way around the book trade. In fact, he had marketed books for Samuel Fauche and Gabriel Cramer of Geneva before he went bankrupt.

But books were incidental to his main business, which consisted of forwarding shipments for suppliers of all kinds of goods, collecting payment for sales that he arranged for them, and marketing local products. He was eager to supply Swiss correspondents with "nut oil, flax, hemp . . . our coriander seeds, anise, fennel, pumpkins, goose feathers, duck, poultry, our lamb skins, parchments, shagreens, etc." Through all their verbosity, Malherbe's letters pointed to the same conclusion: he did a little of everything and was ready to do anything. He lived by his wits—and by gathering information from an extensive network of correspondents.

Thanks to Malherbe's experience as a shipping agent, the information that he provided the STN concerned the best routes for its shipments and the best ways to prevent them from being confiscated, both at the French border and at *chambres syndicales* inside the kingdom. He sent reports about the "insurance" operations of smugglers and advised the STN about their rates. He dispatched warnings when segments of the shipping lanes became clogged or excessively expensive. And in letter after letter, he demonstrated his usefulness in opening up new markets for the STN's books. By the end of 1773, Malherbe had set up some storerooms in an inn at Saumur, and he had hired a local worker to forward shipments that arrived there from various locations along the Loire, all the way up to Roanne, the main port for goods shipped from Lyon.

After a succession of letters attesting to the promise of his new business, Malherbe asked whether the STN would send him an assortment of books that he could keep in stock, selling them off at a commission as occasions arose. The STN refused. Like most publisher-wholesalers, it did not engage in *à commission* speculations of that sort. Undaunted, Malherbe came back with a more attractive proposition. He had just arranged for advance sales of several books of Protestant sermons, which the STN could ship to him while crediting him with a small payment for his role as an intermediary. They agreed on the price and route in March 1773, but the shipment got stalled at the border and then was sent over the Massif Central by mule from Lyon to Limoges, in two packets weighing 190 pounds each. When they finally arrived in Loudun, ten months after leaving Neuchâtel, they had accumulated 118 livres, 10 sous in charges for goods worth 250 livres, 10 sous—at least 30 livres more than they would have cost, Malherbe complained, had the STN's agent in Lyon followed his instructions to send them down the Loire.

The nature of the business that Malherbe had in mind began to show through his letters early in 1774. On January 17 he wrote that a "merchant peddler" had come to see him with a long list of books he wanted to order. Peddlers (*colporteurs*) came in many varieties.[2] In large cities, they walked the streets, hawking their wares from trays suspended from their necks (hence *col-porteurs*). They had to be authorized to do so by the police and to wear a copper badge as certification of their legitimacy—at least in principle. In practice, they frequently operated outside the law and sold forbidden books *sous le manteau* (under the cloak). The peddlers encountered by Malherbe were a cut above the shoe-leather *colporteurs*, for they belonged to the variety of itinerant tradesmen known as *marchands forains* (yet also as *colporteurs*) who traveled from town to town on horse-drawn wagons loaded with large assortments of books, which they purchased from wholesalers, including publishing houses in Switzerland and the Low Countries. They set up stalls during market days and annual fairs, and served customers scattered around the countryside. Many came from Normandy, especially Coutances, where entire families lived from peddling, generation after generation. But they often had no *domicile fixe* or permanent address to which bailiffs could be sent to collect unpaid money orders. Wholesalers mistrusted them, as they were notorious for failing to pay their bills. In order to persuade a supplier to provide them with a shipment, they usually paid for a portion of it in cash and left a promissory note (normally a *billet à ordre*), binding them to come up with the balance at a certain date and place—often an inn, which supposedly served them as headquarters but sometimes turned out to be what creditors called a *domicile en l'air*.

Malherbe knew that peddling was a risky business, but the peddler who approached him seemed to represent a promising opportunity: "If this man is exact, he could procure a lot of business for you, as he travels from city to city." He included a letter from the peddler, J. Blaisot, inside the one he sent to the STN. Blaisot had wanted a dozen copies of each of nineteen books that he chose from the STN's catalog, but Malherbe persuaded him to limit his order to three or four copies of each so as not to expose the STN to the risk of a large transaction. Blaisot's selection was similar to those of established booksellers—an assortment including some history, travel books, Mercier's *L'An deux mille quatre cent quarante*, and an edition of Rousseau's works. The shipment had to be delivered at the STN's expense and risk to Orléans, where Blaisot would pick it up in the storeroom of Pisseau et Cagnyé, a well-known shipping agency. As a reference, he suggested the STN contact Couret de Villeneuve, a reputable bookseller in Orléans with whom he did a good deal of business.

In February 1774, Malherbe wrote that Couret and Pisseau had both reported that they knew Blaisot as someone who made occasional purchases of books and always paid for them on time. Therefore, he recommended that the STN fill Blaisot's order. It sent the books through its smugglers in the Jura Mountains, and Blaisot picked them up safely in Orléans about six weeks later. He made no difficulty about paying for the transport and "insurance," although those expenses came to a third of the books' wholesale price: 30 livres for a shipment worth 91 livres. Four months later, he reappeared in Loudun and paid Malherbe for the books themselves. Everything seemed to suggest that Malherbe had opened up a rich new market for the STN.

The demand in that market, as Malherbe assessed it, favored the works of the Enlightenment: "The taste for books connected with the views propagated by the new philosophers is the only one in vogue, and those are the only books that sell well." The STN had high hopes of satisfying the demand in 1774, because it had then succeeded in getting its shipments through Lyon. Malherbe assisted it with expert (if unsolicited) advice on the shipping costs. In fact, he drew up a general model to guide its calculations. It usually sold its *livres philosophiques* at a wholesale price of 2 sous per sheet (twice its normal price for pirated versions of legal books), which came to 1 livre (20 sous) for ten sheets. Ten sheets weighed slightly less than 5 pounds (in units known as *poids de marc*). So a bale with a hundredweight of sheets, packing included, was worth about 200 livres tournois. The costs for a shipment of a hundredweight of books from Neuchâtel to Lyon could be calculated as follows:

Transport Neuchâtel-Lyon via Geneva.. 10 livres
Supplementary payment to the driver at Geneva and Lyon 1
Commission to smuggling agent in Lyon 2
Various other charges 1
Total...14 livres

Fourteen livres for a hundredweight worth 200 livres was 7 percent of the value of the merchandise. The STN should therefore be able to make its shipments available, free of costs and risks, to its customers as far as Lyon at a reasonable percentage of the wholesale price. If the STN followed this model in arrangements with its wagon drivers and shipping agents in Geneva and Lyon, Malherbe argued, it could avoid arbitrary surcharges and put an end to complaints about poor service from its customers in France.

Whatever one makes of the arithmetic, the calculations illustrate the way the book professionals thought about their business. The underground distribution system, as they saw it, was economically feasible. Its main problem was poor coordination and dysfunction at the human level—in particular, the unreliability of the peddlers.

While the STN rebuilt its route through Lyon, word spread among the peddlers that Malherbe represented a breakthrough on the supply side. He provided them with copies of the STN's catalogs, including the hand-written lists of forbidden works (at one point he hired a scribe to make multiple copies), and they added Loudun to their itineraries in the hope of tapping into the flow from Neuchâtel. In March 1774, Malherbe again proposed that the STN supply him with enough books to create a "deposit" so that he could parcel them out in small amounts to the peddlers, collecting down payments in cash. Every six months he would send the STN a bill of exchange to cover the sales, minus a small commission for his services. He had seen the *Mémoires de Mme de Pompadour*, *Dieu et les hommes* [God and Men], and *L'Arétin moderne* [The Modern Aretino] sold in his region for the extravagant price of 6 livres a volume. They could charge less and still make a killing for that kind of illegal literature.

A characteristic road scene, in this case near Fontainebleau, as depicted by Jean-Jacques de Boissieu.

Jean-Jacques de Boissieu, *Entrance to the Forest of Fontainebleau on the Road of Lyon.*
Harvard Art Museums/Fogg Museum, gift of Miss Elizabeth R. Simmons, M554,
Imaging Department © President and Fellows of Harvard College.

   The directors of the STN knew better than to supply Malherbe with a whole warehouse of *livres philosophiques*. But they kept filling his orders, which began arriving with greater frequency and higher proportions of illegal books. Soon Malherbe was buying the books on his own account. By ordering them from the STN and selling them to the peddlers, he turned a nice profit. From his vantage point in Loudun, unlike the Swiss in Neuchâtel, he could assess the peddlers' reliability, accept promissory notes from those he trusted, and demand heavy down payments in cash from those he did not know. In some cases, as in his dealings with Blaisot, he passed their orders directly on to Neuchâtel, and therefore one can catch glimpses of the peddlers' trade.

   For example, in June 1774 Malherbe recommended a peddler from Saint Maixent named Planquais, who had gone off three months earlier with one of the STN's manuscript catalogs and returned with an order for fifty-nine works, most of them in units of two to four copies. Having sounded out his customers, Planquais evidently decided that he could order enough books from the STN to fill half his wagon. His order included a few legal works (Marmontel's *Contes moraux* and the novels of *Mme Riccoboni*), a good deal of Rousseau (two copies of *Emile*, four *Contrat social*, two fifteen-volume editions of the collected works), some Voltaire and Diderot, and an assortment of scabrous works (four *Thérèse philosophe*, four *Lauriers ecclésiastiques* [Ecclesiastical Laurels, meaning sexual adventures among the clergy], and three *Chandelle d'Arras* [The Candle of Arras, secular sex]). He even ordered a copy of *Le Colporteur*, a scandalous satire by François-Antoine Chevrier. What he thought of it, as a *colporteur* himself, is impossible to say, as the order was little more than a list of titles drawn up without commentary in Malherbe's hand, perhaps because Planquais could not write.

Two months later, Malherbe reported that more peddlers were coming to his house and that he needed more catalogs of *livres philosophiques*: "The peddlers are very eager to get this kind of books. They make more from them than from others, because they can set whatever price on them that they like, depending on what they gauge to be the desire for works of this sort." By September, the catalogs had arrived, and Blaisot and Planquais had returned for fresh supplies accompanied by a third peddler whom Malherbe did not name. All three placed large orders composed entirely of forbidden books that Malherbe passed on with a request for a 2 percent commission and some additional remuneration for his success in procuring customers.

Instead of rewarding him, however, the STN demanded that he collect its bills before it would fill any more orders for the peddlers. Malherbe replied that he would settle with them when they resumed their rounds in the spring of 1775. Blaisot had inquired about his shipment in letters written from Confolens and Angoulême. It would be a pity to disappoint him, and Planquais, too, Malherbe added—although he probably could satisfy both peddlers by ordering from the STN's rival and former partner, Samuel Fauche, who had left the firm after a quarrel in 1763 and continued on his own, selling a great many *livres philosophiques*. This argument brought the STN around. But when its bales arrived in June 1775, Malherbe wrote that he had not seen Blaisot or Planquais since the autumn. Rumor had it that they were running away from bankruptcies. Indeed, if the other peddlers were to be believed, Planquais had abandoned his circuit and disappeared somewhere into his native Normandy, while Blaisot had vanished in Languedoc. Still, Malherbe could find replacements for them; and his own position now looked better, because his father had ceded him some property worth 10,000–12,000 livres. He could buy Planquais's shipment himself and sell it off to his most recent acquaintances among the itinerant dealers.

One acquaintance who looked especially promising was Noël Gille, a *marchand forain* based in Montargis. Gille set up a stall and hawked his wares in Loudun for a week in August 1775. Malherbe gave him a clean bill of health and sold him a thousand livres' worth of books, most of them "philosophical." But as recounted below, Gille declared bankruptcy a year later. Meanwhile, the STN was chasing after payment for a note of 237 livres that Planquais had sent for a shipment. When it made inquiries in Saint Maixent, it learned that he had no home address. Malherbe came up with even more distressing information: Planquais had defaulted on a debt of 1,000 livres owed to Pavie in La Rochelle, and Pavie was trying to get him arrested, but no one could pin him down. "It is suspected that he turned in his balance sheet [that is, effectively declared bankruptcy] at Cognac.... A tradesman in Tours who deals in prints and who recently bought some books from me, said he knew him and had nothing good to say about him."

Blaisot, Planquais, and Gille belonged to the same species, and Malherbe stood to lose a great deal by trading with them. The question was how he could avoid entanglement in their affairs, a web of debts strung out between obscure nodal points in market places, country fairs, and wayside inns. He had no purchase in the merchant houses of high street. Therefore, he remained stuck in the role of a middleman, mediating between the international and the rag-and-bone elements of the book trade. "How to cope with peddlers who pay so badly?" he lamented. "I sell little to them but even so cannot avoid being their dupe. Now Noël Gille has gone bankrupt. Nearly all of them are rotten, and the established, domiciled booksellers demand such impossible prices that one cannot deal with them."

From this point on, November 1776, Malherbe had nothing good to say about peddlers, although he still felt tempted to do business with them and occasionally gave in to the temptation: "One could make some money from the most far-flung peddlers, but they are such down-trodden characters, without a home or domicile, that one is duped by three-quarters of them." In January 1777, he wrote the STN that he had sold some of their books to "a certain Quesne, nicknamed the Englishman, from the outskirts of Meaux," who had disappeared. So had another peddler, "a certain Denis Bouillard." By October the list of defaulted debtors had grown so long that Malherbe hired a bailiff to track them down in the diocese of Coutances, Normandy, where many of the peddlers were born, though he did not expect to find "people without a domicile" installed at addresses in their hometowns. There seemed to be no solution, except to resolve once more to do without them, or at least to sell to them only for cash.

Although he continued to operate as a *commissionnaire*, Malherbe had become a bookseller operating on a fairly large scale. There was no way out of it, for he had accumulated a large stock, which he kept hidden in a warehouse in Loudun. Therefore, while the peddling sector of his trade collapsed, he tried to find another outlet. In the spring of 1777, his thoughts turned to "a new market that will be much safer than the peddlers"—the one located in the one-year-old American republic. "If this nation succeeds in gaining its independence, as everything seems to indicate, we will acquire a beautiful branch of commerce." His imagination warmed as the Americans' prospects improved: "The English look with envy on the advantages for our trade that result from our willingness to permit American ships to enter our ports and from the shipments we are sending directly to Boston and other destinations. General Waginsthon [*sic*] seems to have gained the upper hand against the Howe brothers and general Cornwallis. If that turns out to be true, the campaign will be won by the Americans and the English will be crushed.... This conflict is a sign of a favorable revolution in political affairs."

But "Waginsthon" and world politics did not offer an immediate escape from the problems of the book trade in Loudun. Boat captains who docked in Nantes sometimes picked up a few goods (*pacotilles*) and sold them as a private speculation in other ports of call. Thanks to the good offices of a friend, Malherbe unloaded 1,200 livres' worth of books in this way. Then he imagined he could expand from the Loire to the coastal trade while waiting for the New World to open up; for at the very least, *pacotilleurs* were better than peddlers. "If this outlet produces still more customers, it will be more solid than anything involving peddlers, who have neither hearth nor home and are often swindlers."

These prospects turned out to be fantasies. Malherbe was trapped in the smallest circuit of the retail trade, where there was plenty of demand and little cash or credit. The established booksellers would have nothing to do with him. They protested in their correspondence with the STN that he was undercutting their own trade by selling the STN's books at reduced prices.

When Favarger traveled through the area in 1778, he heard the same thing from many of the important booksellers: Pavie in La Rochelle, Elie in Niort, and Chevrier in Poitiers. In Orléans, Couret de Villeneuve warned the STN to steer clear of Malherbe. Interlopers like him were illegal in themselves, and also specialized in illegal books, courting disaster: "As they sell many books that are hostile to morals, religion, and the government, people of this sort rarely escape being denounced and ruined."

Yet Malherbe never got caught, and after conferring with him in Loudun at length, Favarger sent a favorable report: "Having gathered information about the present state of affairs of this man, I was told that there is nothing to fear from him; that he is very ordered and active in his conduct; that the death of his father has left him quite well off, although his mother is collecting an annuity of 1,200 livres per year; and that in general he is very clever at selling his wares. It seems to me that he is very sharp." A few months earlier, however, the STN had received a warning about Malherbe from Batilliot l'aîné, a banker and bill collector in Paris who specialized in affairs of the book trade: "I know that Malherbe is not worth anything at all. Beware of him."[3]

How "solid" was Malherbe, really? Information scattered through his letters indicates that he came from a well-educated and fairly well-off family with agricultural holdings around Loudun and connections with the trans-Atlantic trade from Nantes. When asking the STN for an extension of "confidence" in a letter of June 28, 1777, he said that his parents had permitted him to sell one of the houses they owned for 11,500 livres in order to prop up his business. He also possessed two *métairies* (sharecropping farms) and tried to raise funds by selling them. That effort failed, he wrote, because the collapse of overseas trade during the American war had damaged the regional economy so badly that land prices had fallen below an acceptable level. He had invested in the coffee and sugar trade himself, he explained, but could not collect on debts owed to him in Port-au-Prince, Capetown, and Cadiz. Unable to raise cash, he tried to pay off some of his own debts by shipping coffee to the STN. It refused to write off a substantial amount from his account, however, because it found the coffee undrinkable. As one prospect after another failed to produce much income, Malherbe relied increasingly on his parents. Writing before the death of his father in 1778, he explained, "M. Ostervald knows very well that I am not rich, my best hopes remaining subject to the power of my father and mother."

The ups and downs of Malherbe's business after Favarger's visit in late October 1778 can be followed in detail through his subsequent letters. They make for dreary reading, owing in large part to their verbosity and poor handwriting. Indeed, the STN asked him to keep to the terms on which they had agreed for each of his orders "without fatiguing us with long and undecipherable verbiage." Yet the wordiness of Malherbe's letters actually adds to their value, because they show how the contingencies of the book trade were experienced by a marginal dealer; and as Malherbe knew the directors of the STN personally, he talked about his situation in a familiar manner unlike that of the established booksellers.

Malherbe paid his bills on time for four years until 1777, when he ran up a deficit for the sizable sum of 1,494 livres. In June 1777, the STN warned him that it would not send any more books until it had received payment, because it would extend its "confidence" only so far. Malherbe answered reassuringly with the information that he would come into a considerable inheritance after his father's death, which then seemed to be imminent. That happy event occurred on April 21, 1778.[4] Malherbe then managed to redeem one unpaid note and wrote hopefully about the prospects of reviving his business, thanks to the assets inherited from his father and some new arrangements for getting shipments past the authorities.

Early in 1779, a few months after Favarger's visit, Malherbe agreed to purchase a large portion of the STN's stock of *livres philosophiques* at a 35 percent reduction. The books went off in seven huge bales in May and arrived safely in September. The bill came to 3,356 livres, a large sum for a book-trade transaction at that time. Malherbe had made a commitment to discharge the debt by notes that would mature at successive dates over a period of less than three years. When the first note, for 848 livres, became due in March 1780, his banker in Paris refused to honor it.

For the next six years, most of Malherbe's letters represented attempts to dodge, delay, and write off his debts. He strung out endless excuses: the general disruption of commerce owing to the American war; the lack of specie and difficulties in negotiating bills of exchange; increased costs of shipments, especially after the 1777 edicts; and the decline in his own sales accompanied by an increase in the difficulty of collecting payment for them. Of course, the STN suffered from the same problems. As pressure mounted on its own finances, it had less sympathy for Malherbe's predicament. In May 1780, it refused to let him reschedule some of his payments. In November, his Paris banker refused another note, this time for 408 livres. Malherbe claimed that it should have been covered by funds deposited for him by Prudhomme, a bookseller in Meaux—one of many booksellers who owed him nearly 1,500 livres in unpaid bills. To compound his difficulties, he could not raise money by selling any of the land he had inherited, because it had fallen dramatically in value, and potential buyers could not find enough cash to purchase agricultural property even at bargain rates.

The STN warned Malherbe in December 1780 that it had unleashed Batilliot to do everything necessary, including legal action, to force him to pay. Batilliot was known in the trade as a bulldog, pitiless about his measures to extract funds from indebted booksellers. He charged a great deal for his services, and that expense was added to the growing deficit in Malherbe's account, along with the heavy cost of *protêts*, the legal formalities that took place when a creditor presented a money order for payment on its date of maturity and the debtor or his agent (often a merchant banker with whom he had supposedly deposited funds) refused to honor it. In February 1781, the STN warned Malherbe that a note for 1,318 livres would be due soon and that it had better be paid.

On March 3, 1781, Malherbe sent a circular letter to his creditors, announcing that he had suspended all payments and was facing bankruptcy. He had deposited his balance sheet with Veuve Boutet, Daillé et Dupuis, a merchant house in Saumur, and pleaded his case for an *arrangement à l'amiable* in personal letters to his main creditors that he sent with the circular. According to the circular, his debts came to 58,000 livres, an amount offset, at least in principle, by 73,002 livres in assets. The latter included 36,000 livres in real estate (three *métairies*, a vineyard, and a house in Loudun) and 400 livres' worth of furniture "in the room that I occupy, as I do not have a house or family of my own and take my meals with my mother, which should assuage any fears you might have that I have been ruined by luxury." The other assets consisted of debts owed to Malherbe, though many of them were "doubtful," and he had written off still more—25,785 livres, as "unpaid debts, some owed by persons incapable of paying." The balance sheet covered all of his transactions as a *commissionnaire*, not just his activities as a bookseller. He estimated the debts that might still be collected from his sales of books at 800–1,000 livres. But in a special letter to the STN begging for mercy, he held out little hope of payment in the near future. "I no longer know whom I can trust, as I have had such bad experience with booksellers. Those who are established pay badly or not at all. The peddlers steal from me. They have carried off 10,000 livres." The collapse in the value of land made it impossible for him to sell his farms. The only way he could reduce his debt to the STN was to send it some coffee by an arrangement with friends in Nantes—or goods produced in the area around Loudun: nut oil, wax, and honey. As explained in the circular, he proposed to pay off his debt in annual installments, each for one-third of the total, extending from 1782 to 1784. Meanwhile, he would continue his business, doing everything possible to force his own debtors to pay up. "That is the only way to prevent my ruin and to avoid a loss for you, despite all my hard and unrelenting work for the last ten years."

The STN answered on May 8, 1784, that it had made inquiries about his situation and had gathered enough information to feel justified in demanding full payment right away. But it would agree to a delay if he paid the first of the money orders he owed them, the one for 1,318 livres that he had failed to honor a few months earlier. Impossible, Malherbe replied. He could not come up with the cash. He owed more money to Fauche than to the STN, yet Fauche was being flexible. If the STN resorted to litigation, it would crush him, and it would fail to collect much in repayment. He was honest and upright, a victim of circumstances. He would work day and night to pay off everything, down to the last penny. And he would continue to deprive himself of any indulgences, as he had always done. "I work assiduously, spend nothing on luxuries or anything superfluous, I am not married, my mother provides my meals.... My liberty, my affairs, are at the mercy of my friends. All I want is to continue working for them."

In June, a bailiff sent by Batilliot knocked on Malherbe's door and demanded payment of a new order written on him for the 1,318 livres plus expenses. Malherbe could not pay it. All he could say to the STN by way of explanation was that he had no access to cash. "It is cruel to be assailed by tribulations in this way when one is full of good will." He followed this lament two weeks later in a letter that sounded truly desperate. Batilliot had impounded three bales of books from the STN that had remained unpacked in Malherbe's storeroom. They had cost 1,559 livres, and Batilliot was threatening to auction them off for whatever price he could get. "Those 1,559 livres, 10 sous won't fetch 300 livres in Loudun, and you know very well that the nature of the merchandise is such that it cannot be exposed in public. I will therefore be subject to crippling legal fees…perhaps to have the police intervene to confiscate my books and to search through my house—how much pain are you prepared to inflict on me?"

It is difficult to know how Ostervald and the other directors of the STN read this appeal. Having received many overwrought missives from Malherbe over the years, they may have come to distrust his letters. He might, after all, be bluffing. Other indebted booksellers also sounded desperate; and then, when faced with bankruptcy, they sometimes (as in the case of Caldesaigues of Marseille) tried to play some creditors off against others, offering secretly to pay a few of them in exchange for favorable terms, while putting off the rest. Batilliot's threat could have been a way of calling a bluff. But there was no denying Malherbe's argument about the counter-effectiveness of a public auction. In the end, therefore, the STN sent a warning that it would not permit him to favor any other creditor (presumably Fauche) at its expense and granted the three-year delay. Malherbe replied in July 1781 that he was relieved and grateful, and he sent four new money orders to repay the debt, with 3 percent interest, over three years.

Even then the haggling continued. The STN refused to accept the money orders, insisting on receiving three larger notes at 5 percent interest, which would be due, respectively, in 1782, 1783, and 1784. Malherbe complied, but extended the maturation dates by a year to 1785. In October 1782 he failed to acquit a note related to another transaction worth 490 livres and parried the STN's objections by sending a substitute note with a later date of maturation. Things continued to get worse as the due dates of the three big notes got nearer. By 1783, Batilliot himself had gone bankrupt; and the STN was having trouble meeting its own payments, mainly because it suffered on a larger scale from the same problem that crippled Malherbe: unpaid debts from besieged booksellers.

In April 1783, when the first of the three notes had come due, Malherbe failed to pay once again, and again sent a substitute note due at a later date. In May 1784, he could not pay the second note. This time, he attempted to fend off the STN's threats by writing a note on a certain Caboche in Bailleul, far off in Flanders, for 500 livres. Caboche refused to honor it and then disappeared—to Gothenburg, Sweden, according to some rumors, although Malherbe had heard he would probably return to Bailleul in order to collect an inheritance from his mother and an uncle, who had just died. Malherbe's third note went unpaid in 1785. By then, he no longer pretended to have correspondents who could redeem his old notes.

He continued his book business, however. Having failed to extract any more goods from the STN, he received shipments from Brussels and Avignon. He may have taken to peddling them himself, because in his last letters to the STN he mentioned trips to sell merchandise in Poitou and Saintonge. The final letters repeated the same complaints: unpaid debts, unavailable cash, underpriced land. Although the STN continued to threaten him with litigation, it had little leverage to force payment. It could hardly persuade a French court to award payment for books that the French authorities should have confiscated. "We are tired of such a disagreeable correspondence," the STN wrote in July 1785. By then Malherbe had failed to pay yet another note that he had written to replace the unpaid note for 500 livres on Caboche. As a token of his good faith, he sent some more bad coffee and some inferior textiles, which the STN said it would sell for whatever small sum they would fetch. He never came up with cash and never ceased sending testimony to his own uprightness: "I am not afraid of being talked about by anyone. I live frugally in the house of my mother, who has offered to share her table with me since my father's death. I have no household expenses, living as a bachelor. My upkeep is minimal. I spend money only for what is necessary for my business— postage and some trips."

Malherbe died in January 1787. The STN tried to collect something from his estate, but its agent, a merchant in Poitiers, reported that there was little hope,[5] and a correspondent in Loudun confirmed that Malherbe's assets were buried under a mountain of debts. Three attorneys spent twenty-three days taking an inventory of his papers and effects. His books were disposed of for 5,202 livres, apparently without any objection from the *subdélégué* of the intendant. His furniture and other property might bring in 20,000 livres, the Loudun correspondent reported, but that would be offset by 60,000 in debts.[6] The STN eventually wrote off Malherbe in its account of "bad debtors" for a loss of 1,368 livres, 15 sous, and 3 deniers.

Malherbe's orders reveal the kind of literature that circulated in the capillary system, and the comments that accompanied them show how he assessed the demand for such books. He seemed to know the market very well, and he also had informants in Paris, including a relative, Jacques-Henri Meister, a friend and collaborator of Diderot. Before their falling out, the STN even solicited Malherbe's advice about what books to pirate. He recommended works of the philosophes and libertine literature: "There is talk of a new tract by M. de Condorcet. And there is an edition of bawdy plays in two volumes octavo which is much better than the one I had from you. The *Tableaux des saints mystères ou Christianisme dévoilé* [Pictures of the Holy Mysteries or Christianity Unveiled] is sought after."

Although Malherbe's early letters suggested that he concentrated on the market for Protestant books, he changed his tune by 1775, noting that while Voltaire's new works "will certainly be much in demand" there was a surplus of devotional works and "religiosity has cooled off a great deal." Many of his letters registered strong demand for the political libels that attacked Louis XV and his ministers. On November 4, 1775, Malherbe wrote that a new edition of *Journal historique de la révolution opérée dans la constitution de la monarchie française par M. de Maupeou, chancelier de France* was sure to sell well. His customers frequently asked for similar works, which combined political protest with scandalous reportage, notably *Maupeouana, ou correspondance secrète et familière du chancelier de Maupeou* and *Le Gazetier cuirassé, ou anecdotes scandaleuses de la cour de France*.

Aside from assessing the demand for individual titles, Malherbe developed a keen sense of what genres were most popular. In December 1776, he wanted "some good works on political economy written during the last eight to ten years." In November 1779, he noted that the demand for books by the philosophes had continued to hold up, accompanied incongruously with works on black magic: "Would you have *Politique naturelle* [an anonymous tract from the circle of d'Holbach], the works of Fréret, Boulanger, Helvétius, Shaftesbury (the Dutch edition), *Véritable secret du Petit Albert éprouvé dans plusieurs villes et villlages avec appellation et conjuration* [The True Secret of the Petit Albert as Tested in Several Cities and Villages with the Appellation and Conjuration], *Le Dragon rouge* [The Red Dragon], *Grand grimoire* [The Large Book of Spells], *Agrippa, Enchéridion*? The latter are stupid but much in demand." By the end of 1781, when he started to get into serious financial trouble, Malherbe detected a decline in the sale of books by Voltaire and found it difficult to sell off the large stock of the cut-rate *livres philosophiques* that he had bought from the STN in 1779: "This genre no longer is much in vogue." Consolation was only to be had in the continued demand for sex books: "Gallantry is still doing pretty well."

Although Malherbe's comments on literary demand are not very different from those of established booksellers, they show a distinct emphasis on forbidden books—the kind favored by the peddlers who used him as an intermediary. The statistics based on his orders with the STN are quite exhaustive, because until 1785, as Malherbe emphasized in his letters, he acquired all of his supplies from the STN and from its former partner, Samuel Fauche. (To reflect his trade more accurately, the statistics cover only Malherbe's own orders, not those that he passed on to the STN for peddlers like Blaisot, Planquais, and Gille; nor do they included his large order of February 1779, which did not express current demand but rather was a one-off deal done at a discount when the STN was trying to clear old stock from its warehouse.)

Aside from Protestant editions of the Bible, the psalms, and liturgical works, the top "best sellers" among the books Malherbe ordered most often were the political libels aimed at the most prominent personages from the last years of Louis XV's reign. Further down the list came works of materialistic philosophy (d'Holbach's *Système de la nature*, Helvétius's *De l'homme*), some anticlerical fiction (*La Pucelle d'Orléans* by Voltaire, *Le Compère Mathieu* [Brother Matthew] by Henri-Joseph du Laurens), some bawdy poetry (*Recueil de comédies et de quelques chansons gaillardes* [Collection of Comedies and Some Bawdy Songs], an anonymous anthology), and the erotic novel by Nicolas-Edme Restif de la Bretonne, *Le Paysan perverti ou les dangers de la ville* [The Perverted Peasant or the Dangers of the City].

Malherbe's proclivity for the varieties of illegal literature sold under the rubric *livres philosophiques* should not obscure the fact that he also ordered many perfectly legal books, although they came in pirated editions.

Among works in light fiction, he favored the frothy plays and poetry of Claude-Joseph Dorat and the sentimental, bucolic writings of Salomon Gessner, translated into French. He requested a total of 127 copies of Claude-François-Xavier Millot's *Eléments d'histoire générale ancienne et moderne* [Elements of General History, Ancient and Modern], a fifteen-volume survey of Western history, and he ordered it repeatedly—eight times between 1775 and 1785. The reorders are especially revealing, because they indicate sustained demand. Malherbe sent in five separate orders for the twenty-volume *Histoire de France* by Paul-François Velly. He ordered Jacques-Christophe Valmont de Bomare's twelve-volume *Dictionnaire raisonné universel d'histoire naturelle* eight times. And he sent four orders for a six-volume edition of Montesquieu's works.

The overall pattern suggests that the public served by Malherbe and his peddlers wanted substantial, serious literature along with a spicy assortment of scandalous and irreligious books, and it demonstrates that radical works penetrated the smallest channels of the book trade.

Because Malherbe dealt so extensively with peddlers, his dossier serves as a point of entry into an investigation of peddling, the shadiest and least known sector of the book trade under the Ancien Régime. Peddlers show up often in the archives of the police but only for an instant—at best, for as long as an interrogation in the Bastille—and then they disappear. As mentioned, the most substantial, known as *marchands forains* (sometimes "*foirins*," evoking fairs—*foires*—where they sold books), crisscrossed the country with a horse and cart, sometimes following regular routes, sometimes straying far from beaten paths. They appear so fleetingly in the "floating population" of eighteenth-century France that when one of them shows up in several sources, his trail is worth following. The peddler I encountered most often was the *marchand forain* who drew some of his stock from Malherbe in Loudun: Noël Gille, known as "La Pistole" (a pistole was a foreign coin or an expression for a sum of money worth 10 livres, but it also could denote a kind of incarceration in which a prisoner paid extra for better conditions).

Gille first surfaces in the archives of the police.[7] On July 23, 1774, Joseph d'Hémery, the veteran inspector of the Parisian book trade, found him selling books at a stall behind the Eglise de la Madeleine in Montargis, a minor provincial center forty-three miles east of Orléans. D'Hémery had been assigned to investigate suspicious activity at the fair of the Madeleine in Montargis, and immediately fastened on Gille. He examined eight hundred to nine hundred volumes displayed at the stall, discovered several forbidden works, and summoned four officers of the local constabulary to confiscate the books and to escort Gille to his residence in the home of his father-in-law, rue du Puits de l'Encan. After combing through every armoire in the house, d'Hémery found some more books, none of much interest, aside from a copy of Diderot's *Bijoux indiscrets*. He climbed to the second floor, where Gille and his wife, who also worked in his business, occupied a small bedroom overlooking the street. D'Hémery ordered both of them to empty their pockets and collected a few letters and receipts. Then he demanded to see their account books and correspondence. According to d'Hémery's report on the interrogation that then took place, Gille replied "that he did not know how to write and that it was his wife and his brother-in-law, a cobbler by trade, who wrote for him, ... that he did not have any papers, not even any pens or a writing desk." That sounded suspicious, d'Hémery noted, though he also observed that Gille had difficulty in signing his name at the end of the interrogation, and in fact the signature does look primitive. D'Hémery turned up enough letters from booksellers and suppliers to justify a full investigation. He then sent Gille off to the local jail and retired to his inn for supper and sleep, having put in a productive day's work.

After studying the confiscated papers, d'Hémery arrived at the jail at nine o'clock the next morning in order to conduct a full-scale interrogation. The account of it, carefully recorded by a scribe, reads like most interrogations: a dialogue of questions and answers, recorded in the past tense, which constituted a cat-and-mouse game. In putting the questions, d'Hémery tried to trap Gille into revealing compromising information; and in answering them, Gille attempted to avoid self-incrimination. The dialogue can be paraphrased as follows.

Age? Thirty. Place of birth? Montsurvent, near Coutances in Normandy, son of a cobbler. Residence? At the house of his father-in-law, also a cobbler, but Gille was almost always absent. As a *colporteur* or *marchand forain*, he traveled from fair to fair and from marketplace to marketplace. When did he begin to sell books? At the age of twelve, hawking almanacs and popular prints. Six or seven years later, he started selling ordinary books, following the example of his two brothers, who were peddlers. One of them had lost an arm in the war and collected a pension of 1 pistole a month: hence the nickname "La Pistole," which young Noël inherited. What was his residence during this time? He had none. He lived on the road and traveled everywhere—in Normandy, Ile-de-France, Champagne, Anjou—with a horse and cart. What right did he have to be a bookseller? "He assumed the status of a bookseller because he sold books."

That was an insolent reply, as Gille knew full well; one had to belong to a booksellers' guild or at least to have an official license (*brevet de libraire*) in order to exercise the trade. But d'Hémery let it pass in order to concentrate on the crucial question of Gille's sources of supply. Gille said that he acquired books in Paris and also from widow Machuel in Rouen, always avoiding everything illegal.

Didn't he have other suppliers? Not at all. Did he not recollect the name of a certain Adam? Well...yes, there was an Adam who once had been a clerk of widow Machuel, but Gille had not heard from him for a year. That was a lie! In going through Gille's papers, d'Hémery had found a letter from Adam written only a few weeks ago. It must have come from his wife's pocket, Gille replied rather feebly, because he knew nothing about it. How could he explain that in the letter Adam had confidentially offered to supply him with immoral books? Well...Gille had acquired a few copies of *Académie des dames* (a work that today would be considered hardcore pornography). To whom did he sell them? "To village priests in the places where he traveled and also to various individuals."

At this point, Gille's defenses were crumbling, and the questions began to hit hard. The following paraphrase, in dialogue form, remains close to the original.

D'HÉMERY: Don't you do business with other booksellers whose names you are hiding from me?

GILLE: No, except Buisson in Lyon.

D'HÉMERY: Why then have I found so many letters from booksellers in your papers? This catalog, for example, where does it come from?

GILLE: Perhaps it's from Benoît Duplain or from Benoît Ponthus Bruysset in Lyon.

D'HÉMERY: No: it's certainly from a confidential contact, because at the top it says, "Keep my catalog secret." Who is this supplier?

GILLE: Maybe I knew some time ago, but I don't remember any more.

D'HÉMERY: Do you mean to persist in affirming to me that you do not do any business with other booksellers, neither as their client, nor as their supplier?

GILLE: I informed you about my relations in Paris, Rouen, and Lyon. Aside from a few trips to Lille and Orléans, I limit my trade to that region.

D'HÉMERY: You are lying. Your papers prove that you do business with Geneva, Bouillon, Bourges, Tournai, Liège, and other places as well.

GILLE: I admit that I received some almanacs and the Bijoux indiscrets from the Société typographique de Bouillon. As to the rest, I only deal with binders.

D'HÉMERY: What? You have your books bound in Bourges and Fontainebleau, whereas you could have that done near your home, thereby saving on the transport costs? Don't you have other so-called binders?

GILLE: No.

D'HÉMERY: Think hard. At Orléans, for example?

GILLE: I remember having had some Coutûmes de Montargis bound in Orléans.

D'HÉMERY: How do you explain this note where Letourmy, a bookseller in Orléans, asks you to send him bound copies of a work that looks very suspicious, since he indicates the title only by a few letters?

GILLE: It's only a matter of the *Imitations des journées chrétiennes*.

D'HÉMERY: And this other book that Letourmy says he requested from you in a separate note enclosed in his letter?

GILLE: It's only an arithmetic book and the *Journées chrétiennes*.

D'HÉMERY: You are lying. It's not possible that someone would ask in a separate note for anything other than a forbidden book. And what are these works that Manoury orders by designating them as "three Ciel" and "four Christ," referring to the separate note for an explanation?

GILLE: I have no idea.

D'Hémery knew very well that the reference was to two irreligious works, *Le Ciel ouvert à tous les hommes* [Heaven Opened to All Men] and *Histoire critique de Jésus Christ* [A Critical History of Jesus Christ], and as the context indicates, Gille knew that he knew. But they continued to spar in this fashion until d'Hémery realized that he could not extract any more information. Then he ended the interrogation, sent Gille back to his cell, and wrote a report to the lieutenant general of police in Paris:

> Noël Gille, who acts as a bookseller without having any authorization and who travels about from place to place, has the most suspicious relations.... The late widow Machuel and sieur Ferrand in Rouen supply him from afar with forbidden and dangerous books. There is also a certain Adam in Rouen who supplies him with all sorts of bad books and who also seems to be a most dangerous character. Noël Gille has connections, proven by his correspondence, with very suspicious sources in Geneva, Orléans, Bourges, etc.
>
> I will put aside the matter of pirated books, and I will discuss only books against morality and religion, which are one of the main elements in his trade. He seems to be at the heart of all the maneuvers and subterfuges that they require. I am quite sure that he is involved with books that have no respect for anything.
>
> I had Gille initial all the papers, and I subjected him to an interrogation that could have been pushed much further. He was so embarrassed about the letter from his friend in Orléans that he pretended to have forgotten it even though it has a very recent date and it cannot be misconstrued.
>
> You will see, Monsieur, that I have done everything that was possible. This man seems to me to be very interesting.

Gille spent two months in prison. Once released, he went back to his horse, his cart, and his trade in forbidden books. A year later, he appeared in the correspondence of the STN, first as one of the peddlers supplied by Malherbe in Loudun, then as a customer of the STN who ordered supplies directly from Neuchâtel. As Malherbe explained to the STN, peddlers dealt heavily in the illegal sector of the book trade, despite the risks, because that was where the profits were greatest. Of course, they often failed to pay their bills, and one had to be careful about accepting their promissory notes. But Gille was married and had a *domicile fixe* in Montargis. He impressed Malherbe when he stopped by Loudun for a week in August 1775, hawking his books from a stall in the marketplace. After he rode off on his wagon, Malherbe took soundings about his reliability and received "a favorable report."

Three months later, when Gille asked him to procure supplies from the STN, Malherbe agreed to act as a middleman. He requested the STN to send two invoices, one with its normal prices, which he would keep for himself, and one for those prices plus an additional 5 percent, which he would present for payment to Gille. In this way he could collect his commission surreptitiously from his customer. He needn't have taken the trouble to disguise it, however, because two weeks earlier Gille had written to the STN from Fontainebleau asking it to deal directly with him on the grounds that Malherbe charged "an exorbitant commission." The STN refused, having learned to beware of peddlers. But under the assumption that Malherbe would act as its bill collector, it agreed to fill the order, which contained twenty-one titles. All but two were highly illegal, and Gille wanted them in large numbers: fifty *Système de la nature*, fifty *Système social*, fifty *Pucelle d'Orléans*, fifty *Bon sens*, twenty-four *Politique naturelle*, twenty-four *Oeuvres d'Helvétius*, twenty-six *Journal historique de la révolution opérée dans la constitution de la monarchie française par M. de Maupeou*, twenty-four *Compère Matthieu*, twenty-four *Parnasse libertin*, twelve *Questions sur l'Encyclopédie*, twelve *Maupeouana*, twelve *L'An deux mille quatre cent quarante*, twelve *Gazetier cuirassé*, twelve *De la nature*, twelve *Les Loisirs du chevalier d'Eon*, twelve *L'Evangile du jour*, twelve *Miracles de Jésus Christ*, and six *Espion chinois*.

The shipment arrived safely in Loudun. Gille picked it up in April 1776. He made a down payment in cash of 12 louis (288 livres) and drove off, leaving a positive impression behind. "Sieur Gille spent three or four days here," Malherbe wrote to the STN on April 24, 1776. "He had a heavily loaded wagon and a clerk with him. He seemed to have a good assortment. He paid me a dozen louis and took books worth 300–400 livres more.... He seems responsible. Unless he gets drawn into some bad affairs from the many forbidden works that he sells, I don't believe that he will cause any losses." Four months later, Gille went bankrupt.

In Gille's case, bankruptcy took the form of suspending all payments on debts and depositing a balance sheet with a commercial court (*juridiction consulaire*) empowered to make an arrangement with his creditors.[8] The balance sheet showed that Gille's debits came to 28,874 livres and his credits to 37,097 livres, though the latter included 24,097 in debts owed to him, mainly by "bad debtors" who could not pay. In the face of an unmanageable deficit, Gille went into hiding. He engaged a certain Eustache Briant, who identified himself as "Porter of the King's Ponds in Versailles," to argue his case in a memoir addressed to the court. The memoir pleaded for a delay in the payment of Gille's debts so that he could resume business and ultimately reimburse the creditors. It also requested the court to issue an order (*lettre de cession*) that would prevent the creditors from having him thrown into debtors' prison: "The prospect of physical arrest has filled him with fear and has forced him, to his deep chagrin, to leave his trade, to abandon his wife and children, and to seek refuge in order to escape imprisonment."[9]

How desperate was Gille's situation? The information in the balance sheet indicates that he stood to lose everything he owned if the creditors had his assets confiscated. He possessed a wagon, two horses, harnesses, and other equipment that he valued at 1,000 livres. He estimated his stock of books to be worth 10,000 livres—not much compared with the holdings of established provincial booksellers. And his wife's possessions, "in beds with bedding, furniture, linen, clothing, silverware, mirrors, and other objects," came to an estimated 1,000 livres. The couple and their children made up a modest household with a few luxuries but no home of their own, as they boarded with Gille's father-in-law.

In listing Gille's debtors, the balance sheet shows that he operated within a network of other peddlers and unofficial dealers who bought and sold books among themselves while retailing them to customers. It mentions twenty-seven debtors of whom ten are described as *marchands forains*. The rest appear as *marchands libraires*, meaning booksellers with small shops, although they probably peddled a great deal as well. None of them appear in the *Almanach de la librairie*; so most of them probably operated outside the legal restrictions on the book trade. The peddlers are identified only vaguely, and mainly by their debts. Thus Morelle, who owed 725 livres, "peddler in Normandy"; Pillait, who owed 933 livres, "from Lorraine"; and two who may have been among the peddlers who supplied themselves with Malherbe and then disappeared without paying: André Le Planquer (probably one of many peddlers from the Planquais family in Coutances; he owed 836 livres); and François Quenelle (debt of 475 livres).

The balance sheet also gives glimpses of Gille's customers, those who owed small sums for the books they purchased. For example: Dantais, "seigneur de campagne in Artois"; Courtais, "country curate in Boulonnais"; and seven other country curates. Although the evidence is spotty, priests and notables (wealthy bourgeois and some aristocrats) seemed to make up most of the clientele. A notebook on debtors that was deposited with the balance sheet mentions de La Brûlerie, lord of the Château de Joigny, for the purchase of *Lettres et mémoires de Mme de Maintenon*; Dusailly, "city mayor" living in Nemours, for *Révolution romaine*; Marian, councilor in the Châtelet court of Melun, for *Journal des audiences*; a vicar in Châteaurenard for *Apologie de la religion*; and an attorney in Châteaurenard for a *Dictionnaire de droit* and a *Parfait notaire*. Some of Gille's customers were professional men who purchased books that would be useful for their work, but the evidence is too thin to support general conclusions. Gille may have extended credit only to members of the elite and sold books for cash to humbler folk who frequented fairs and markets. Unsurprisingly, the papers he deposited with the commercial court do not mention any of the forbidden books that he received from the STN. After his arrest in Montargis, he probably had learned not to preserve evidence of his activity in the illegal trade.

Finally, the debits in the balance sheet reveal the names of his suppliers: several Parisian publishers and many provincial booksellers who dealt heavily in forbidden works and appear often in the archives of the STN. He owed 4,000 livres to Machuel of Rouen, 742 livres to Henry of Lille, 336 livres to Boubers of Dunkerque, 750 livres to Blaisot of Versailles, 1,080 livres to Couret de Villeneuve of Orléans, and 1,085 livres to Malherbe.

How Gille extricated himself from his burden of debt is impossible to say, but he certainly escaped. He appeared in the *Almanach de la librairie* of 1781 as a "bookseller" established in Montargis. (It also mentions a "Noël Gille" in Aire, presumably Aire-sur-la-Lys in Flanders.) And he reappeared in the papers of the STN. In a letter dated July 30, 1779, he sent a large order, almost entirely for *livres philosophiques*, offering to pay for them in cash or with a bill of exchange on a house in Paris. At the time of his arrest, Gille had told d'Hémery that he could not write. In fact, he was able to scribble this letter, though his handwriting and spelling were so primitive that it deserves to be quoted in full and in French (a translation of the main text follows), because it demonstrates the extent to which a peddler of books had mastered the written word:

Monsieur

jeresus lhoneur delavotre an dat du courant je vous suit tres oblige de voux ofe de credit que vous aves biens voulut mefaire mais entansions ne sent pons dajete des merchandise accredit pour an peier des jroenteres jeme beaucoup mieux a jete au contans pour le peu que jajete contant onmefai la remis de 12 a 15 pour sant de fasons que jevoi monbien efis de dime sit vous voulet trete avec moi vous pouve manvoier votre cathalo sur tout les livre [« filo » crossed out] philosophique duquelle je poures vous faires eun debis au condisions que vous meranderrer les marchandise fran de porre jusqualion voicit monnadres est ches monsieur pierre tair alions roulier faubour de resse a lions ala quelle persone vous pouve anvoier mes balle e tire anranbourcemans il vous an refuserapons pour vous surte vous pouve luiecrire sitvous voulet manvoier dans la premier ball

[Gille then listed twenty-three titles of forbidden books, all of them badly misspelled, which he wanted the STN to ship.[10]]

Sit vous juge aprepau demepedier mademan je vous cert aublije demandanet avis evous oservere que cest au contant cit vous ne trouve pas la comodite a tire a vu sur le roulier vous pouve tire aus sur moi au je vous anverret une lette de change sur paris

Vous obligeres monsieur celui qui a lhoneur destre tres parfetmans votre serviteur noel gille

Demontargis le 30 juillet 1779

Vous manverret vouz propetus dant la bale

Monsieur,

I received the honor of yours of the current date I am much obliged to you for your offer of credit which you have kindly made to me my intentions are not at all to buy merchandise on credit in order to pay after I return I much prefer to buy for cash for the small amount that I buy for cash one gives me a discount of 12 to 15 percent in such a way that I can see my benefit and make a profit if you want to deal with me you can send me your catalogue especially the philosophical books of which I could make sales for you according to the condition that you will deliver the merchandise free of transport costs as far as Lyon here is my address it is chez Monsieur Pierre Tair at Lyon wagon driver at the faubourg de resse [?] at Lyon to the said person you can send my bales and collect reimbursement he will not refuse you for your security you can write to him if you want to send to me in the first bale... [the list of titles follows as above and the letter ends with this conclusion:]

If you decide it is fitting to ship my order to me I would be obliged
if you sent me a notice and point out that it is for cash if you do not
find it convenient to write a note on the wagon driver you also can
write a note on me and I will send you a bill of exchange on Paris

You will oblige, Monsieur, him who has the honor to be most
perfectly your servant Noël Gille

From Montargis 30 July 1779

You will send me your prospectuses in the bale

The best way to decipher this letter is to read it aloud and listen to the
sounds evoked by the scribbling on the page. The STN did not reply.
A clerk wrote on the back of it, "Order not filled." Nonetheless, it is a
valuable document. Taken with the other material in his bankruptcy dossier, it shows that Gille sold a little of everything. As occasions arose, he
provided a curate with a breviary and a lawyer with a tract on jurisprudence. But above all, he sold "philosophical books." The disparity between
his spelling and the texts he peddled provides a measure of the culture
among the distributors in the capillary sector of the book trade, where the
"heuvre de janjacle rousau" (works of Jean-Jacques Rousseau) jostled
"tereaise philosf" (*Thérèse philosophe*) on the carts of peddlers.

It is impossible to say how typical Gille was, considering the paucity of
information about such obscure characters. A considerable gap separated
the impecunious street peddlers from the *marchands forains*, described by
the police as driving about France (*roulant par la France*) on horse-drawn
carts. Gille actually owned two horses, at least for a while in 1776.
Although he lived with his cobbler father-in-law, he had a home base,
unlike many *marchands forains*. His wife owned a mirror and some silver
cutlery. Yet Gille was always on the road and, as far as one can tell, nearly
always in debt. The precarious and marginal nature of his life made him
resemble the other peddlers who show up in the police archives, owing to
their trade in forbidden books. Two examples:

Lelong: In the country for a month with a cart and a horse. Normally
stays in Meaux, where he has some kind of a storeroom with a certain
le Breton, innkeeper at the large marketplace... Lelong is fat and short,
walking with a solid tread; brown, curly hair, which circles his head; a
whitish overcoat.[11]

Picaud: Picaud is five foot two inches tall, blond hair, blue eyes, a filled-out face with a somewhat fat nose, broad shoulders, a short neck, speaking the Norman dialect a little bit through the nose, walks heavily.... Picaud also travels near Villers-Cotterets and Soissons and usually lives in Charleville in the house of a stocking maker. He has a horse and a wagon. He also keeps many rifles and pistols.[12]

When they appear in the bankruptcy papers, the *marchands forains* are mentioned only in passing, but they have a common characteristic: they are always on the move, and in lieu of a *domicile fixe*, they often had, as mentioned earlier, *domiciles en l'air*. To win over a supplier like Malherbe, they would make a down payment in coin, preferably a few gold louis, presented as cash on the barrel head (*espèces sonnantes et trébuchantes*); write a promissory note with the address of an inn; and disappear before it became due. They also sold books among themselves and therefore ran up debts within their own circles. The peddlers who owed Gille money made up a long list of names attached to unstable addresses: François Quesnel, "aux Trois Rois" in Orléans; Joseph St. Denis, "chez M. Viardain, aubergiste, rue Ste. Croix à Provins en Brie"; Jean St. Denis, "chez Brouillez, aubergiste, au Dauphin à Clermont en Beauvaisis"; J. B. le Gendre, "chez Mme Hachette, à l'Ecu de France à Vertu près de Châlons-sur-Marne"; Robert Planquais, "chez M. Mangin, aubergiste au Grand Turc à Melun"; Jean Planquais, "chez M. Viardain à Provins"; J. B. Thezard, "chez M. Viardain, rue Ste. Croix à Provins"; Bigot, "chez M. Godard, au Lion d'or à Vernon sur Seine"; Joseph Le Lièvre, "chez M. Perrin, aubergiste au Signe de la Croix à Sézanne en Brie"; Guillaume Dubost, "aux Trois Rois, aux Andelis en Normandie"; Michel Galonde, "chez M. Doucet aubergiste à la Croix Blanche à L'Aigle"; and Pierre le Petit, "chez M. Maréchal, aubergiste au Grand Cerf à La Fere [*sic*] en Picardie." [13] Such men left behind few traces of their existence, yet they played important parts in the world of books. Like red corpuscles in the blood stream, they carried literature throughout the book trade's capillary system.

One final piece of evidence also warrants being quoted at length. It is the memoir submitted to the commercial tribunal in Paris by the aforementioned Eustache Briant, the "Porter of the King's Ponds," who seems to have functioned as a scrivener in addition to his duties in Versailles.[14]

Its purpose was to win sympathy for Gille by describing the hard life of a *marchand forain* (the following translation does not correct the scrivener's faulty grammar):

> Sieur Noël Gille, marchand foirin [*sic*] bookseller, traveling across France [« roulant par la France »], at present lodged at the Grand Montreuil near Versailles: considering the losses, misfortunes, illnesses, and expenses that he has experienced and thus the difficulty he has in collecting money that is firmly and legitimately owed to him, which means that at present he does not have the capacity to pay back the sums he owes to the collectivity of his creditors, that is why there will be drawn up two statements relative to his assets and his debits, the latter showing the losses, misfortunes, illnesses and expenses he has experienced, which two statements are to be deposited both in the clerk's office of Messieurs the juges consuls of Paris and that of the Châtelet court…

The memoir then listed the « misères » suffered by Gille:

First, poor health:

> The said sieur Gille has suffered six illnesses, which illnesses drove him nearly to his death, one having forced him to keep to his bed for almost six months…

Then commercial setbacks:

> The said sieur Gille having undertaken the trade of a bookseller traveling throughout France, as is the usage among peddlers, this trade can only be done with considerable costs. In view of the weight of the merchandise and the need to transport them from city to city across the kingdom in order to sell them, it was important for him to have wagons and horses. Therefore, he resolved to buy a wagon and some horses, loaded his wagon with merchandise, and set off. He traveled from city to city to sell the said merchandise. He was forced to make long journeys in order to sell his merchandise, since the wholesale merchants had sold them to him at excessive prices…

Bad weather:

The said Gille being on the road under rain and bad weather, had his wagon broken. He had to search for help. He was forced on different occasions to unpack and repack the merchandise on the road and under rain. He experienced considerable damages. The rains spoiled a large quantity of the merchandise. He still has some of it that was spoiled at fairs and marketplaces....

Extortionate suppliers:

The wholesalers sold their merchandise to him for exorbitant sums, and in order to make sales he had to take losses by cutting prices....

Poor horseflesh:

The illnesses and losses of the horses caused big delays in his business. His trade was interrupted, sales were lost, and he could not come up with funds to pay Messieurs his creditors, which forced him to take out large loans, to renegotiate money orders, all of it at high interest charges...

Prison:

The said Gille had the misfortune to be suspected of selling forbidden books, for which he was physically seized and made a prisoner. He remained in prison for nearly two months. Then, in view of his justification, he was given his liberty....

The lamentations went on and on: disastrous delays in supplies, bloated shipping costs, ruinous charges for postage.... Every aspect of the peddling business had gone wrong, none of it through any fault of Gille.

It seems unlikely that the court found that argument convincing. Seven months later, it received a memo for another bankrupt peddler written by the same scrivener from the same address and in the same terms, almost word for word.[15] None of the documents can be taken literally. None provides a clear view of book peddling. The peddlers appear only fleetingly—in police reports, bankruptcy papers, business correspondence, and, very rarely, in their own words, crudely scrawled across a sheet of paper. Yet in the years leading up to the Revolution they were the agents who connected supply with demand in the remotest regions of the book trade.

II

Blois, Orléans, Dijon
Upmarket and Downmarket in France's Heartland

Blois

Still happy with his horse and in a hurry to get home, Favarger headed east through central France and some of its most beautiful country. From Loudun to Saumur, Chinon, Tours, Amboise, Blois, Orléans, and Dijon, his itinerary took him past vineyards, pastures, and riverbanks crowned with châteaux. But it was November and chilly. The vines had been

Blois, etching from *Nouveau voyage pittoresque de la France*, Paris, Ostervald, 1817 (BiCJ).

stripped of grapes, many of the châteaux were falling into ruin, and the roads remained abominable. Favarger passed by sights that evoked the glories of the sixteenth century, a time when the Loire Valley was the center of the kingdom and sovereigns with their courts migrated from palace to palace, spreading a way of life that eventually became identified with French civilization itself—courtesy, gallantry, refinement, an appreciation of good food and drink, and a mastery of language that owed much to the Loire's greatest writer, François Rabelais.[1] Yet this social code did not extend far below the elite, and it probably was alien to Favarger, who had informed Jean Ranson in La Rochelle that he possessed no artistic talents whatsoever, certainly none that would shine in a bourgeois drawing room. Judging from his letters, his main concern was to make it back to Neuchâtel before the snow set in.[2]

Although the STN had instructed him to avoid detours and to skip unpromising addresses, Favarger still had plenty of bookshops to inspect. Along the Loire as along the Rhône he found printers who sold only the ephemera they produced and booksellers who carried little more than schoolbooks, breviaries, and religious tracts. Saumur had one printer and two booksellers, neither of any importance, "as this city does not amount to much." Chinon was "still worse than Saumur," although it had one solid bookseller. Tours was more promising: two good booksellers, including one (Vauquier Lambert) who was also a printer, and three "not good." More important, it was the headquarters of one of the three Letourmy brothers, the most enterprising dealers in the Loire Valley. They worked as a consortium, peddling books and selling them from three separate shops. A second brother operated out of Blois, and the third, who handled orders for all three, had a shop in Orléans, where Favarger planned to go to solicit their business. After Tours, he stopped briefly in Amboise, where he learned that the town's only bookseller, a certain Philippe, was nothing more than a peddler, "who does not merit much confidence." Then came Blois, which presented some interesting dilemmas.

Aside from the second Letourmy brother, who also operated as a peddler, Blois had no booksellers other than two printers, Pierre-Paul Charles and Philbert-Joseph Masson, who had merged their businesses and sold nothing except liturgical and devotional works.[3] Yet Blois had become a fairly important outlet for the STN, owing to the efforts of another entrepreneur who, like Malherbe, did business outside the official trade. In the same way as many individuals on the fringes of the market,[4] Constantin Lair saw an opportunity to make money by satisfying the demand for books, which he stocked and sold from his home without worrying about the *chambres syndicales* of distant Poitiers and Orléans. The book trade was only one of several sidelines that Lair pursued. He was also a teacher, vintner, and boarding house keeper, who struggled hard to maintain a position at the margins of Blois's bourgeoisie. By the time Favarger arrived on the scene in November 1778, the STN had come to know him well.

Lair first contacted the STN in 1773, writing at the recommendation of Malherbe. At that time Malherbe was attempting to ingratiate himself with the STN by suggesting retailers for its books. Lair was high on his list, because, as Malherbe explained in a letter to Ostervald, he could open up a lucrative market in Blois, where he had excellent contacts among the local notables. When he began corresponding with the STN, Lair presented himself as a schoolmaster (*maître de pension*) who also owned enough vineyards to profit from the demand for the renowned Loire Valley wines. He taught French to English students who boarded with him, and probably gave instruction in other subjects to other boarders (in one letter he offered to sell the STN a manuscript of a mathematical textbook). Having built "a large and beautiful house," he also took in travelers and people with business at the regional law court (*Conseil supérieur*) established at Blois in 1771 during the reorganization of the judicial system under Chancellor Maupeou. His letters, written in a fine hand, suggest a man of considerable culture. Lair had built up a superb library, he wrote with some pride to the STN. Gentlefolk came to consult it and to enjoy the company of "a society as amusing as it is gracious." To accommodate them, he had taken to ordering and selling books. He received catalogs from suppliers in Paris and elsewhere and planned to convert his collection, supplemented by subscriptions to Parisian journals, into a lending library (*cabinet littéraire*). This activity had aroused the hostility of the established bookseller-printers, but Lair planned to keep them at bay by acquiring a *brevet de libraire* in Paris, so that he could sell books outside the normal guild structure.

In Lair's early letters to the STN, he presented his tiny business as the avocation of a gentleman with a penchant for literature. He stressed his "inclination by taste for men of letters, whom I esteem and whose works, which are truly useful, I seek to acquire." He wrote knowingly about different editions of the *Encyclopédie* and expressed admiration for Voltaire: "It is supernatural that the inimitable M. de Voltaire should do so much work at such an advanced age." His orders to the STN included works by the most famous philosophes, along with those of more popular authors such as Simon-Nicolas-Henri Linguet, whose polemical pamphlets struck him as particularly attractive, owing to their trenchant style and fascinating subject matter. Not that Lair sounded radical himself. He deplored the decline in the quality of education in France brought about by the suppression of the Jesuit order, and he objected to the anti-Catholic bias of the Protestant *Encyclopédie* produced by Fortuné-Barthélemy de Félice in Yverdon.

From 1773 to 1775 Lair ordered an increasing number of books from the STN, and his correspondence took on an increasingly commercial tone. He desired more Voltaire and Rousseau, he wrote, for the "honest and lucrative sales" they would produce. He also requested *nouveautés* of all kinds—current works of topical interest, the latest novels, and scabrous books. He could open up a profitable market for the STN, he promised, if it could provide him with "bagatelles, with those little trifles written with art which conform to the frivolity of our century and are intimately linked to the genius of our nation—that lightness which is sought out so avidly by our stylish youth and little ladies (nos petits maîtres et nos femmelettes)." "Some have asked me for libertine novels," he added. "Do you deal in them?" His clients included "wealthy and inquisitive persons" who placed advance orders with him for the works of Molière, Bolingbroke, Voltaire, and Rousseau. One customer wanted them printed on superior Dutch paper and bound in straw-colored calfskin. Others looked for bargains, such as cheap editions of Diderot's *Encyclopédie* and Raynal's *Histoire philosophique*.

Lair's passing references to contacts and clients—a law professor, a canon from the cathedral, wine growers—suggest a milieu of provincial notables, though he may have emphasized their wealth and worldliness to impress the STN and to win its confidence. If the STN trusted his willingness and ability to pay, he wrote, it could send him fairly large shipments of books and accept in return promissory notes or bills of exchange due to mature in twelve months. By selling the books, Lair would accumulate enough cash to pay at the due date, or, more likely, he would endorse a note from one of his business contacts over to the STN, which it could negotiate for cash, assuming that the signature on the note also warranted confidence.

Lair's correspondence with the STN shows how these financial relations, so typical of early modern capitalism, operated in a concrete case. At first, judging from his payments, Lair seemed to be "solid." In December 1773 he paid for a shipment of the Yverdon edition of the *Encyclopédie* with a remittance on a Parisian source for 252 livres, and he accompanied the payment with a fairly large order of books, including several Enlightenment tracts, which, he said, he had arranged to sell to local "amateurs." When the next shipment arrived, he wrote that he was pleased with the quality of the editions but not with the shipping costs, which he considered excessive. He sent in another order nonetheless, offering to pay for it by endorsing over to the STN notes he had received from some cider and brandy merchants from Normandy, who had come through Blois buying wine to compensate for their poor harvest of apples. Lair's crop of grapes had been excellent, and he intended to expand his book business by purchasing a *brevet de libraire*.

At this point, in early 1774, Lair's letters began to contain troubling symptoms of insolvency. Grapes might help sell books, but harvests varied, and the local economy, as he remarked, depended entirely on wine and brandy, "the sole cause of the abundance or rareness of cash" in the region. Blois's great château and visits of the royal court had attracted many wealthy persons in the sixteenth century, but in the eighteenth century the city's population had stagnated at about 11,000 souls, and there was little more than a law court and a garrison. The STN refused to accept Lair's offer of notes signed by unknown Norman wine merchants, and his remittance for 252 livres was protested when presented for payment in Paris. He then replaced it with another note, assuring the STN that he had 20,000 livres at his disposal in case of need. His orders continued throughout 1774, growing larger and more varied, with a heavier emphasis on forbidden books, notably atheistic and erotic works like *Système de la nature* and *Histoire de Dom B ..., portier des Chartreux*, which were often favored by dealers who had fallen behind in their payments and then took up speculating on the riskier but more profitable sector of the trade. In November 1774 Lair traveled to Paris to negotiate the purchase of his certificate as a *marchand libraire*.[5] He arrived in time to witness the ceremonial installation of the old Parlement de Paris, which replaced the court established by the Maupeou reforms. Unfortunately for him, however, the reversion to the previous judicial system meant that Blois would lose its own Maupeou court and that he would therefore be deprived of the customers who came to do business with it while lodging in his boarding house.

Lair's affairs took a downward turn in 1775. One of his notes was protested in June, and in November the STN wrote a draft directly on him because his account had fallen badly into the red. (The draft was a *traite*, also known as a *billet à vue*—that is, a note that was supposed to be paid upon presentation to the debtor but that he could legally reject because, unlike a promissory note or a bill of exchange, it did not carry his signature.) Apparently he refused to acquit it (some of the correspondence may be missing at this point), and his deficit continued to grow in 1776 and 1777, when the STN sent two more drafts, which also went unpaid. In July 1777 it announced that it had run out of patience. It sent him an account statement with a draft on him for 873 livres and threatened prosecution if he failed to pay it. Lair tried to parry the blow with a remittance for 400 livres as a down payment, which the STN credited to his account while also insisting on its determination to recover the rest of his debt. He had abused its indulgence, the STN wrote. It would not accept any more of his notes, which invariably bounced, and it was ready to take him to court. Lair replied in February 1778 with a litany of excuses: credit was tight; his last harvest had been terrible; and he had been forced to devote all his cash to the dowry of his daughter, who was about to get married. Instead of paying the balance of his account, which the STN recalculated at 486 livres, 4 sous, he sent three notes for a total of 300 livres and whose maturity dates extended far into 1779.

The STN refused to be mollified, dismissing his constant lamentations about his harvests with the observation that the vineyards in Neuchâtel had also suffered and that the payment of debts should not be determined by the weather. It returned his notes and ordered Batilliot, the Parisian bill collector who specialized in bad debts in the book trade, to collect the balance or initiate a lawsuit. Lair pleaded for clemency in a letter of March 7, 1778. He had not meant to dupe the STN; he had simply run out of money. Reluctantly, the STN extended the debt for another two months, writing two drafts on him, each for 243 livres, 2 sous, which were to become due in May and June.

When May came round, sure enough, Lair failed to pay the first draft. The STN shot off a furious letter. "Have you sworn to vex us forever?" To justify his refusal, he had claimed that there were errors in the account statement and spoiled sheets in the books it had sent. The STN rejected those arguments out of hand as pretexts to avoid honoring his debt. It received a wounded reply. At great effort, he had managed to pay the second draft, he said, but could do no more until mid-September, after the grape harvest, which fortunately promised to be excellent this year. Still angry, the STN answered that it had a traveling agent who would soon arrive in Blois and force him to pay up.

It was at this point that Favarger appeared. He immediately went to the *poste restante* to see whether the home office had sent any information about the current state of Lair's account, but nothing had arrived. It was therefore impossible to reach a settlement. After bearding Lair in his boarding house-cum-school-cum book shop, however, Favarger sent his employers some good news. Lair's harvest had indeed been excellent, and he promised firmly to send a payment soon. He acknowledged that he had deserved to lose the STN's confidence. He also made a favorable impression on Favarger, who wrote that Lair "is reputed to be a respectable man who has some assets, but three or four bad affairs and as many bad harvests have made it impossible for him to honor part of his business affairs."

A few days later, Lair sent the STN a note for 180 livres, claiming that this should balance his account. The STN accepted the note, although it would not mature for another four months. But it continued to berate him about his refusal to pay what the STN considered to be the remnant of his debt so that it could finally close the account. It would not countenance any more excuses: "It's not the good or small harvests that should stand in the way of a settlement."

The STN did not hear from him again. On June 2, 1782, Lair's wife wrote that he had just died. The STN continued to try to settle the account, but widow Lair did not know what to make of its demands. According to one of its reports she owed 110 livres, 8 sous, and according to another she owed to 374 livres, 8 sous. In January 1785, she acknowledged a debt of 352 livres, 8 sous and sent a note for 109 livres, 6 sous as an installment, asking the STN to be indulgent about its far-off date of maturity: "I beg you to consider the situation of a widow with children from two marriages whose husband has left her with some very messy affairs." The STN replied that it would accept her note as a final settlement, "considering the circumstances in which you find yourself and which assuredly have a claim on our sympathy."

Hopes for striking it rich, overextended orders, bounced promissory notes, recriminations, excuses, negotiations, a settlement, and at the end a widow who takes over the business and tries to extract it from "messy affairs"—Lair's story, like many others in the papers of the STN, expressed the syndrome that Balzac later identified as "lost illusions."

Orléans

Unlike Blois, Orléans prospered in the eighteenth century. Thanks to its strategic position at the northernmost bend on the Loire, it dominated commerce both upstream and downstream and between central France and Paris. Its population had expanded from 30,000 in 1700 to 39,000 by 1780, including many workers employed in sugar refineries and textile manufacturing. It had an intendancy, a *bailliage* court, and an assortment of cultural institutions—an academy, a theater, a university with 240 law students—that favored consumption in its bookshops. There were a dozen of them when Favarger arrived on November 5, 1778.

He gave the booksellers, who appear only with their family names in his correspondence, fairly high marks as he made his rounds. Although he steered clear of the syndic of the local guild (Jacob), who was known for his hostility to pirated books, Favarger hit it off with the syndic's deputy (Mussot), who promised to help the STN's shipments pass inspection behind Jacob's back and also agreed to order a shipment of his own. Perdroux, who ran a *cabinet littéraire*, nibbled at Favarger's offerings but did not bite, because he restricted most of his trade to religious books. Widow Rouzeau and Chevillon l'aîné, both rated "excellent," traded mainly in classics rather than in the sort of contemporary literature that the STN sold. Several other booksellers listed in the *Almanach de la librairie* turned out upon closer inspection "not to merit much confidence." That left two, Louis-Pierre Couret de Villeneuve and the third of the Letourmy brothers, whom Favarger had been tracking ever since he entered the Loire Valley.

When at last he buttonholed the third brother, Jean-Baptiste Letourmy, Favarger hoped to conclude some lucrative business. He had learned from

Orléans, etching from *Nouveau voyage pittoresque de la France*, Paris, Ostervald, 1817 (BiCJ).

the other Letourmys in Tours and Blois that the brothers operated as a consortium, and that Jean-Baptiste placed orders for all of them. Unfortunately, however, Favarger timed his visit badly. Jean-Baptiste was to get married on the following day and could not take out time to negotiate over books. They only had a quick discussion about bills of exchange and mistakes the STN had made in a recent shipment (it had sent twenty-five copies of *Eloges de l'Hôpital* instead of some *Pensées de Pascal* that he had ordered). Therefore, Favarger left the shop—apparently a well-appointed establishment in the Place du Martroi in the center of town—without a new order but confirmed in the conviction that Letourmy, now that he was extending his family ties deeper into Orléans by marriage, could be trusted as a solid customer.

Solidity of this sort was hard won. The Letourmy brothers had begun as peddlers, hawking woodblock prints and chapbooks.[6] From this modest beginning, their trade grew to include all kinds of books, which they marketed jointly. Each kept his own stock and developed his own network of clients in the surrounding towns and villages. They divided the joint enterprise into three separate businesses in 1779, though Jean-Baptiste assured the STN that they continued to cooperate closely and asked that it extend its "confidence" to all three.

None of them had been mentioned in the survey of printing and the book trade conducted by the French government in 1764. At that time, according to the report on Orléans, the local trade seemed to be wide open. It was overrun by unauthorized dealers, the town officials had no idea what they sold, and the police never intervened unless someone sent in a denunciation. The government tried to gain control of the situation in 1778, when it created a *chambre syndicale* to inspect shipments and confiscate illegal books. As Favarger noted, Jacob, the head of the new *chambre syndicale*, was particularly severe in repressing pirated works. After readjustments in the system of smuggling, the trade revived, although it never reached the level it had attained before 1778, when pirated and prohibited books were easily available, especially outside the city's boundaries. That was where the Letourmy brothers had built up their business in the 1760s and 1770s, and they succeeded remarkably well.

Unfortunately, Jean-Baptiste Letourmy's dossier in the archives of the STN has many gaps, and the letters that survive reveal little about how the brothers peddled books throughout the countryside. But the record of Jean-Baptiste's orders and the STN's letters to him, which it copied into its ledger of *Copies de lettres*, indicate what the brothers sold. In contrast to Couret de Villeneuve, Orléans's most eminent bookseller, and the widow Rouzeau, who would not even stock editions of plays, the Letourmy brothers dealt heavily in illegal literature.

Jean-Baptiste Letourmy's first orders to the STN included several *livres philosophiques*, and the proportion of forbidden works increased as he piled order upon order. In its records of its shipments (*Livres de commission*) the STN noted that it topped off the bales it sent to him with "new philosophical works," even though he had not ordered them. Most shipments reached him without difficulty, but in December 1775 a bale was stopped at Frambourg on the Swiss-French border, because the customs officers, who normally permitted such shipments to pass without inspection, had received a special order to search shipments for a seditious pamphlet. Although they did not find the pamphlet among Letourmy's books, they confiscated twenty copies of *Recueil de comédies et de quelques chansons gaillardes* [Compendium of Plays and Some Bawdy Songs] and twenty-five *Mémoires de Louis XV*. Letourmy agreed to pay for half of that loss, but he suspended his orders until the STN guaranteed that it could get its bales to him as far as Lyon with no risk. By the end of 1776 it had repaired all the damage to its route, and on February 25, 1777, he sent a particularly large order. It contained fifty-one titles covering a wide variety of literature, from sentimental novels and philosophical treatises to pornography, along with a special request for anything the STN could procure about "the history of the last reign"—that is, scandalous accounts of politics and life at the court under Louis XV, which, as we've seen, were bestsellers after the king's death in 1774.

A month later Letourmy asked for more of the same, although he noted that the book trade had taken a turn for the worse. His main competitor, Couret de Villeneuve, was so desperate for cash that he had begun selling off his stock at ruinous prices, "hurting the trade a great deal." But Letourmy continued to send large orders, and he accompanied one of them with a proposal from an anonymous individual to sell a "Collection of manuscripts—libertine, comic, and burlesque poems," for the STN to print. The "Collection" contained twenty-one works, some of them running to hundreds of lines, such as "That Which Pleases Ladies, a tale in comic and burlesque verse, 458 lines" and poems adapted from notorious prose works, such as "An Abridged History of D... B.... (an allusion to the erotic bestseller, *Histoire de Dom B....., portier des Chartreux*) in comic and burlesque verse, 614 lines." The STN did not publish such things, but the proposition and other references in Letourmy's letters suggest that he knew his way around the literary underground.

By compiling Letourmy's orders, one can create a list of the works that sold best in his branch of the book trade, which combined peddling with retailing from a well-located shop. As a rule, he asked the STN to send him only a few copies of most works, presumably because he wanted to be sure to avoid overstocking. The book that stands out at the top of the list is *Les Incas, ou la destruction de l'empire du Pérou* [The Incas, or the Destruction of the Empire of Peru] by Jean-François Marmontel, which Letourmy ordered on six occasions, making a total of 118 copies. It condemned the cruelty of the conquistadores and missionaries of the Spanish Empire in America as seen from the perspective of an eminent philosophe, yet despite its anticlerical message, it was never forbidden by the French authorities. Letourmy purchased it on favorable terms, as he bought the relatively inexpensive pirated edition printed by the STN. The other works that he ordered most often came from the STN's general stock (*livres d'assortiment*). A large number of them could be called pornographic: *L'Ecole des filles*, *La Fille de joie*, and *Recueil de comédies et de quelques chansons gaillardes*. Sex, mixed liberally with politics, characterized other works near the top of the list: *Anecdotes sur Mme la comtesse du Barry*, *La Chandelle d'Arras*, and *Mémoires turcs avec l'histoire galante de leur séjour en France* [Turkish Memoirs with the Bawdy History of Their Stay in France]. The list also included three works by Voltaire and two perfectly legal (if pirated) books: *Essai sur les maladies des gens du monde* [Essay on the Illnesses of Society People] by Samuel-Auguste-André-David Tissot and *Le Bureau d'esprit* [The Department of Wit], a comedy by Jean-Jacques Rutledge. The entire list of all the books ordered by Letourmy includes a little of everything, from the atheistic works of the baron d'Holbach to collections of sermons and popular novels. Compared with lists of orders by other booksellers, it contains relatively little history, travel literature, and, surprisingly, not a single book by Rousseau. Of course, Letourmy may have ordered Rousseau's works and other kinds of books from other suppliers, but the general tenor of his trade seems clear: he concentrated on the most dangerous and most lucrative sector of the book business.

Unlike other booksellers who dealt heavily in illegal literature, Letourmy never got caught and never failed to pay his bills. By February 1778, nine months before Favarger's visit, he had paid for 1,180 livres' worth of books—a large sum for a provincial dealer. He had disagreements with the STN over shipments with *défets* or spoiled sheets and incomplete copies, and these sometimes developed into disputes over the balance in Letourmy's account. Relations also suffered from the irregular repressive measures taken by the French government. On October 5, 1778, after the new *chambre syndicale* had been established in Orléans, Letourmy wrote that he was worried about a serious interruption of his trade, not just in Orléans but also in the countryside, where he and his brothers peddled their wares. But the STN continued to get bales to him through the service of Jacques Revol in Lyon. Their trade tapered off in 1780 and ceased altogether in the following years, probably because financial difficulties forced the STN to withdraw from the riskier branches of its business but also owing to a dispute over a shipment worth 348 livres. Letourmy claimed that he had never received it and therefore refused to honor a note that the STN wrote on him. He seems to have been in the right, because a local merchant sent by the STN to collect on the note gave him a clean bill of health: "This individual, who at first had nearly nothing, has built up his fortune during approximately ten years to such an extent that he can afford some quite considerable enterprises. They have succeeded as well as could be wished, so that we now consider him to be very solid."[7] In short, Letourmy's career was a success story—a rare case of a peddler who rose into the upper ranks of the established booksellers.

Letourmy's career stands in contrast to his main competitor, Louis-Pierre Couret de Villeneuve, who began with every possible advantage and ended in virtual bankruptcy. Couret came from a family whose connection with printing and bookselling went back to 1582.[8] He succeeded his father as a master bookseller in 1772, having acquired the position of "printer of the king" the previous year, when he was only twenty-one. The printing shop with four presses and the bookshop at the sign of l'Immortalité in the rue des Minimes (later the rue Royale) at the heart of Orléans probably kept many family members busy. According to the royal survey conducted in 1764, Couret père had a good reputation, worked hard, and seemed to be wealthy. When Couret fils took over from him, an older brother, François, was associated in some way with the business. A printed circular and catalog dated May 14, 1772, carried the signature "frères Couret de Villeneuve," but François is not mentioned in any letters after that date. Their sister married Charles-Joseph Panckoucke, the wealthiest and most powerful publisher in Paris. Louis-Pierre referred to his brother-in-law several times in his letters to the STN and printed some of the volumes of Pancoucke's enormous *Encyclopédie méthodique* on his own presses. Few if any provincial booksellers had better connections in the publishing industry.

Two of Couret's printed catalogs appear in his dossier in the STN archives. They give a good idea of the books that were for sale in his shop. The first, which is dated May 14, 1772, and lists 169 titles, covers a wide variety of literature. Religious works—Bibles, devotional treatises, and especially sermons—predominate. The secular works consist mostly of dictionaries, history books, and serious nonfiction on subjects such as botany and medicine. Among the books in belles-lettres and fiction, the authors that stand out are the great figures from the seventeenth century: Corneille,

The Letourmy brothers began as peddlers of prints, mostly crude woodcuts that they commissioned themselves, and they continued to deal in prints such as the one above during the early years of the Revolution.

Musée d'Orléans.

Racine, La Fontaine, La Rochefoucauld, Fénelon, and Bossuet. The Enlightenment philosophes occupy only a minor place on the list, although it contains some moderate works by Voltaire (*La Henriade*), Montesquieu (*Lettres persanes*), and Rousseau (*La Nouvelle Héloïse*). Thirteen of the books were published by Couret himself. Of them, most were devotional works such as *Epîtres et évangiles avec des réflexions* [The Epistles and Gospels with Commentary], *Etrennes du chrétien* [A New Year's Gift for the Christian], and *La journée du chrétien* [The Christian's Day]. The second catalog, from May 1774, contains thirty-eight titles, most of them published by Couret and most of them religious. *Le Philosophe moderne, ou l'incrédule condamné au tribunal de la raison* [The Modern Philosopher, or the Unbeliever Condemned at the Court of Reason] exemplifies the orthodox tone of several of the works. Couret sent the catalogs through the mail to other booksellers and bookseller-printers. In a printed circular that accompanied the second catalog, he presented himself as someone of some standing in the world of publishing. He produced well-made books that were sure to sell, he claimed, and they could be had on reasonable terms or by exchange for books that he would choose from the stock of others.

Catalogs of this sort circulated constantly among booksellers. They provided useful information about the character of a publisher's trade, though to assess the soundness of any business, the professionals relied on information that reached them through the trade grapevine and on what they could surmise by corresponding directly with the firm in question. Couret's letters resembled those of other bookseller-printers, except in one respect: they were well written, even florid. He took great care with his phrasing. His concern for language—and the way he used it—stands out in a letter he sent to the STN in May 1774: "I would be extremely flattered if a few poetic fragments, the products of my leisure, could perhaps, if you deigned to be indulgent, find a place in your most agreeable periodical revue." In other words, Couret was not just a bookseller but also a poet, and he wanted the STN to publish his verse in its monthly journal.

The STN's *Journal helvétique* was a closely edited periodical that carried belletristic essays and light verse of the kind Couret submitted. He, too, published a periodical, although his *Affiches de l'Orléanais*, a continuation of his father's *Annonces de l'Orléanais*, was mainly a vehicle for local advertising. He offered to exchange journals and assured Ostervald that, for the sake of French literature, the *Journal helvétique* deserved to be better known in France. Although Couret adopted the tone of a fellow printer-bookseller–man of letters, his situation differed greatly from Ostervald's. In 1774, Ostervald was sixty-one; he enjoyed a reputation as a *littérateur* and civic leader in Neuchâtel; the STN produced books on a large scale, and it sold them throughout Europe. Couret, then twenty-five, was trying to expand the modest business he had inherited from his father, while making a name for himself in Orléans.

From what can be gleaned from local sources, Couret seems to have participated actively in the town's cultural life. He was a founding member of the Société royale de physique d'Orléans, which developed into the town's academy. He pursued an interest in botany as a supporter of the local *Jardin botanique*, became an enthusiastic member of a Masonic lodge, and churned out volumes of poems and essays, which he printed himself, probably after declaiming them in salons and literary circles. To read through his publications is to take the measure of a bookseller with literary pretensions and in doing so to raise a question about the role of booksellers as cultural intermediaries: to what extent did their personal tastes and convictions influence their choice of the books they made available to the public?

Couret published his first work, *Les Troglodites*, a five-act tragedy written in classical alexandrines, at age twenty-one. It appeared with a censor's approbation in 1770 "in Orléans at the printing shop of Couret de Villeneuve, printer of the king." As he explains in a preface, Couret took the basic idea from Montesquieu's *Lettres persanes* with the intention of demonstrating "that the gods protect virtue and that a corrupt nation sooner or later will be overcome by a people that has good morals." The theme of virtue appears in a more sentimental vein in an anthology, *Recueil pour servir de suite aux Lectures pour les enfants et les jeunes-gens, ou choix de petits contes, également propres à les amuser et à leur inspirer le goût de la vertu* [An Anthology to Serve as a Sequel to Readings for Children and Young People, or Selection of Short Stories Equally Suited to Amuse Them and to Inspire in Them the Taste for Virtue] (1782). In explaining the rationale for his choice of the texts, Couret stresses the themes of simplicity, naturalness, and the innate innocence of children. Another anthology, *L'Anacréon français, ou recueil de chansons, romances, ariettes, vaudevilles, et à propos de sociétés* [The French Anacreon, or Anthology of

Songs, Romances, Ariettas, Ballads, and Witticisms for Social Occasions]
(1780), features light verse of the sort that Couret wrote himself and that
he evidently recited at social gatherings. It begins with a poem that he addresses gallantly to "Mme de C ****," and it goes on for two volumes full
of frothy *vers de circonstance*, which, he claims, express the "frank gaiety"
of the French character.

The worldly side of Couret's writing recedes before a tide of Rousseauis-
tic sentiment in *Discours sur l'amitié, suivi de quelques poésies fugitives, par
M. Couret de Villeneuve, auxquelles on a réuni les Sentiments de reconnais-
sance d'une mère, addressés à l'ombre de Rousseau de Genève, par Madame
P**** [Discourse on Friendship, Followed by Some Casual Poems, by
M. Couret de Villeneuve, to Which are Attached the Sentiments of a
Mother's Gratitude Addressed to the Ghost of Rousseau of Geneva, by
Madame P***] (1782). The main part of this little volume is the text of a
speech that Couret had delivered at a meeting in his Masonic lodge.
Speaking as a "perfect Mason," he invokes the "Great Architect of the
Universe," without the slightest reference to Christianity, and proclaims
the principle of equality as the basis of all social virtues—"charity, benef-
icence, love of the fatherland and of one's neighbor." Far from being mere
abstractions, those concepts, as Couret expounds them, challenged the
hierarchical order of the Ancien Régime. The nobility was not entitled to
a superior rank in society, he insists, and any aristocrat who claimed special privileges deserved nothing but contempt: "If you have no personal
merit,… I will look upon you as perched upon your genealogical tree,
fearful of falling into the mud." The accompanying essay by Mme P***,
who turns out to be Couret's sister, the wife of the publisher Panckoucke,
reinforces this message. She celebrates Rousseau as the champion of natural sentiments and social relations, especially within the family. Yet the
volume ends incongruously with one of Couret's most worldly *vers de circonstance*: "To Madame de… upon giving her in a ball an orange on which
were written these words: to the most beautiful of all."

There was nothing original or unusual in these publications. They
show a young writer chasing disparate themes and trying to win some
recognition in his small corner of the republic of letters. What sets them
apart from the writing of other aspiring authors is the fact that they were
printed and sold by Couret himself. Although a few booksellers, including Ostervald, published an occasional volume, Couret was the only one

who tried to pursue a literary career while running a book business—at least, the only one in France. Samuel Richardson in England and Christoph Friedrich Nicolai in Germany combined both roles with great success. Couret never gained any recognition for his writing, but he wrote so much that it is possible to see where he stood amid the conflicting literary trends of his time. He aligned himself with the Enlightenment. His ideas derived explicitly from Montesquieu and Rousseau, and he expressed them in a way that sounded somewhat radical.

Did these personal convictions affect the choice of books Couret sold in his shop? Judging from his printed catalogs, the answer is no. As mentioned, his stock consisted primarily of orthodox religious books and serious nonfiction with an admixture of standard literary works, mainly by authors from the seventeenth century. Of course, Couret could have kept illegal works for sale under the counter, and he would not have included them in a printed catalog with his name on it. But they are not reflected in the pattern of his orders with the STN, which shows little that can be considered radical. The book at the top of the list of his "bestsellers"— that is, the statistics showing those he ordered most often—was Millot's popular and inoffensive *Eléments d'histoire ancienne et moderne*. Next came abbé Raynal's *Histoire philosophique et politique des établissements et du commerce des Européens dans les deux Indes*, which certainly represented a radical strain of Enlightenment thought, particularly in the passages contributed anonymously by Diderot. However, Couret ordered all his copies before the book was condemned in 1781 and none of them afterward, when it became a bestseller in the underground trade. Nearly all the other books on the list were utilitarian in character—tracts on treating ailments, caring for horses, and dressing hair. Couret ordered a comparatively large number of *Lectures pour les enfants*, which served as a model for his own anthology of stories for children. Aside from Raynal's *Histoire philosophique*, the only Enlightenment work on the list was the STN's edition of Voltaire's *Questions sur l'Encyclopédie*. Rousseau's writings are conspicuously absent.

Among the general list of all the books Couret ordered—in contrast to those on the list of his "bestsellers"—there are three works on freemasonry, which might indicate a personal interest. The general list also contains some Voltaire, one radical treatise, d'Holbach's *Système de la nature*, and two of the political libels about Louis XV and his ministers. Yet these illegal works look like exceptions to a rule: Couret dealt with literature that circulated openly and everywhere in the book trade. The Enlightenment had a place on the shelves of his shop, but a minor place. His personal convictions included some radical ideas, but they had little or no effect on the literature that he offered to the public.

Couret's business also looks unexceptional as a commercial operation. After establishing relations with the STN, he sought to develop a steady flow of provisions—and to build up its "confidence" in him as a regular customer—by placing a succession of small orders and paying for them on time. He had to overcome the obstacles encountered by all provincial booksellers who drew supplies from Switzerland: shipping costs, delays, difficulties with *chambres syndicales* at inspection points like Lyon, and what he deplored as the "vigilant interference of the booksellers of Paris to prevent the sale and circulation of pirated works." Couret dealt so heavily in pirated editions that when he learned of the government's intention to reorganize the administration of the book trade, he dreaded a catastrophe. Imports of books had not been subjected to inspection in Orléans, but the 1777 edicts created a new *chambre syndicale* in the city whose primary mission was to eliminate piracy. Couret informed the STN that rather than run any risks, he would cease importing books from abroad. In January 1778, he confirmed that the new *chambre syndicale* was as severe as he had feared, because it operated under close surveillance by the government. Five years later, however, he was serving as its deputy syndic (adjoint) and soon would become its syndic, a position that would make it possible, he promised, to favor shipments from the STN.

The greatest constraint on Couret's dealings with the STN was economical not political. In January 1775 he sent the first of a long series of letters that complained about hard times in the book trade, and he refused to pay a note that the STN had written on him. In its place, he sent a note of his own but set for a later date of maturity and with an order for more books. The succession of notes and orders continued over the next three years, accompanied by refusals of acceptance, squabbles over the dates of maturity, and disagreements about the balances due in Couret's account. The exchanges finally became so acrimonious that Couret announced in a letter of July 25, 1779, that he would settle his account and stop ordering books from the STN: "The meager credit that you allow, the inflexibility of your behavior in a trade as difficult as ours, have forced me to abandon this correspondence, which has been so unfruitful for me."

In fact, the correspondence continued intermittently until June 1787, when the last letter from the STN shows that it was still dunning Couret for an old debt of 233 livres. Although his last letters are missing, it is clear from the STN's responses that he disputed its version of his account. He may have been justified in protesting against its inflexibility, although the STN did not become involved in such quarrels with truly "solid" book-sellers, who protected their reputations—and, as they put it, the honor of their signatures—by paying their bills on time. When Favarger inspected Couret's business in 1778, he concluded, damningly, "Couret de Villeneuve, although he appears to be brilliant, must be relegated to the class of the mediocre." Couret managed to prop up his business until 1789; but it collapsed when the Revolution broke out in Orléans. He left for Paris and found employment in the revolutionary administration responsible for overseeing printing shops. Meanwhile, the Letourmy brothers continued in business, marketing some of the most popular prints favoring the cause of the Third Estate. In the general struggle for survival in the 1780s, the bookseller as author had been bested by the peddlers as booksellers.

Dijon

Favarger left Orléans on November 10 and arrived in Dijon late on November 15: nearly two hundred miles in five days, a quick pace considering that he stopped en route to inspect the bookshops of Auxerre. His horse continued to hold up, although some of its gear showed sign of wear. Favarger had to buy a new halter and to have the saddle repacked, while getting the horseshoes replaced. Auxerre had only two booksellers, both reputed to be "very difficult in making payments." But one of them, Pierre Bonnard, struck Favarger as an *honnête homme* with a well-stocked store, and he placed an order for a large and varied assortment of books.

Favarger entered Dijon through one of the four great gates in its massive, oval wall. Its broad streets were lined with elm and linden trees and led to the city center, where the bookshops were located. The grandest buildings, with polychrome tiles on their roofs, dated from the heyday of the dukes of Burgundy in the fifteenth century, and there were many

Dijon, etching from *Nouveau voyage pittoresque de la France*, Paris, Ostervald, 1817 (BiCJ).

townhouses in the latest, neoclassical style. Seen from a publisher's perspective, Dijon seemed to offer a happy balance of trade: kegs of wine out, bales of books in. That view, of course, did not do justice to a complex economy, which involved wheat, textiles, iron, and mirrors as well as wine. Dijon's function as a provincial capital made it a hub of the book trade, for it possessed a mix of institutions that were most likely to attract customers to bookshops: a *parlement*, tax and fiscal courts (a *Cour des aides* and a *Chambre des comptes*), an intendancy, a university with a large faculty of law, and an academy. The number of booksellers increased from seven in 1764 to ten in 1777 and twelve in 1781. They sold an unusually large number of subscriptions to the *Encyclopédie* (152, nearly twice as many as were sold in Grenoble, which had a population of the same size, about 20,000 inhabitants). The province as a whole had a relatively high rate of literacy—54 percent of adult males. Readers subscribed to the local *affiches* (advertising news-sheet) and joined the *cabinet littéraire*. All the signs suggested that Dijon had great potential as a market for the STN.

Yet Favarger did not tarry in Dijon's bookshops. The STN had ordered him to avoid delays, and he needed to reach the passes in the Jura before the snows would compound the difficulty of riding on mountain roads. Of the ten booksellers in the city, he considered only two, Jean-Baptiste Capel and Louis-Nicolas Frantin, as possible customers for the STN. He left a catalog with Frantin but seemed doubtful that it would lead to anything, and it did not; Frantin never sent a letter to Neuchâtel. The STN received a few letters from three other booksellers, François Desventes, Antoine Benoit, and Jean-Baptiste Mailly; but they, too, did not develop into customers. Capel, who ran a printing shop as well as a bookshop on the Place Saint Jean in the center of the city, remained the only possibility for the STN to gain access to a market that, on the face of it, had the capacity to absorb a great many books.

Favarger already knew Capel. He had called on him during a business trip two years earlier and had reported that despite his position as head of the local *chambre syndicale*—or, rather, because of it—Capel was eager to buy forbidden books and to help the STN diffuse them: "Dijon… M. Capel is one of the good ones. At least his shop is well assorted. He trades a great deal in philosophical books.… He is an inspector of the book trade. All the bales we sent via Jougne [a town along a route through the Jura Mountains] passed through his hands. He has no scruples about this, but warned me to be careful after he finishes his term as inspector. He may be replaced by someone who will be worse."

Despite its promise, this opening did not lead to a great deal of business during the next two years. The STN kept running into difficulties with its supply lines, both at the Swiss-French border and in Dijon itself, where it needed a trusty agent to expedite its shipments. As explained in chapter 2, Capel refused to act as its agent, although he was willing to cooperate from time to time. The most important *commissionnaire* in the city, Veuve Rameau et fils, were willing to handle the STN's bales—until they learned what was in them. In an indignant letter of March 18, 1777, they wrote: "Why is it then that you send forbidden books into the kingdom?… We do not want to receive any more of them; and if anyone ships some to us, we will be the first to demand their confiscation,… as we do not want to get involved in any operation against the orders of the sovereign.… It is astonishing that in violating the laws of the state you pretend to make us personally responsible for any mishap."[9]

The STN rarely received such forthright assertions of loyalty to the regime, except in the case of the *lettres ostensibles* that were designed to be intercepted in the mail by the police. Veuve Rameau's testimony apparently was sincere, and it disproves the notion that foreign publishers never had difficulty in finding accomplices among the middlemen of the transport system.

When Favarger tried again to arrange for shipping to Dijon in 1778, he steered clear of Veuve Rameau et fils and went to Jacques Nubla et fils, a *commissionnaire* who also did a small business manufacturing candles. Nubla agreed to receive the STN's shipments and to handle the delicate operation of getting the accompanying *acquits à caution* discharged, although the local *chambre syndicale* was not authorized to do so, as Dijon was not an official *ville d'entrée*. The *chambre syndicale* was a sloppy affair. Its officers held meetings in a miserable, third-floor room, and they did not have enough funds from local taxes to rent a storage space suitable for inspections.[10] Therefore, book shipments had their seals removed by local customs officials when they arrived in Dijon, and then they were sent to the market-hall (*halles*) along with all sorts of other merchandise. According to the arrangement worked out with Favarger, Nubla would retrieve them from the market-hall, bring them to his own office, remove all the forbidden books, which the STN packed separately at the top of the bale, and invite Capel to perform an inspection. Despite his responsibilities as a syndic, Capel was happy to accommodate the STN. Having found nothing illegal, he would discharge the *acquit à caution* so that Nubla could send it back to the customs officers at the Swiss border. Although the weight of the shipment was entered on the *acquit*, Capel would neglect to verify it, so there was no trace of the volumes that had been removed. If the shipment was intended for him, he would take it back to his bookshop. Otherwise, Nubla would forward it to another customer of the STN, and it would be safe from further inspection, because it would travel as a domestic shipment. The system worked well for the publisher-wholesalers in Lausanne and Geneva, Favarger learned. When he left town, everything seemed prepared to facilitate a bountiful trade between Neuchâtel and Dijon.

Things did not work out that way. In December 1778, a month after Favarger's visit, Nubla confirmed that he would play his part, but warned the STN that he would not assume responsibility for any mishaps and that the risks now looked serious, because new syndics had replaced Capel, and they had announced that they would be very rigorous in making inspections. A year and a half later, Nubla gave up his business as a shipping agent in order to devote himself entirely to making candles. His retirement left the STN without anyone to shepherd its shipments inside Dijon's imposing city walls.[11]

Meanwhile, the trade between the STN and Capel had faltered. It had looked promising in February 1777. En route to Paris on a business trip, Ostervald called on Capel during a stopover of the coach that he had taken from Besançon. He evidently made a persuasive case for the STN's excellence as a supplier, because a few days later Capel sent an order from the catalog that Ostervald had left with him. The order contained thirty-six titles from a wide variety of genres: travel literature, history, books for children, novels, and a few classics from the seventeenth century (Molière and La Fontaine). He also requested *Mémoires de l'abbé Terray*, a political libel, which he assumed the STN could supply, even though it did not appear in the catalog. This was a sample first order, Capel explained, which would serve as a way for him to assess the quality of the paper and printing of the works in the STN's stock. He hoped it would lead to mutually advantageous relations.

Writing as a fellow printer in June, he recruited some workers who were willing to take employment in the STN's shop. In September, he sent another order, although the first one had been delayed, owing to difficulties at the border crossing. In reply, the STN sounded him on his willingness to act as an insurer who would expedite shipments through his *chambre syndicale*. He refused, not on principle but because of the danger: the government had recently sent orders for the *chambre* to be especially strict in its inspections, he explained. The STN continued to ask Capel for help, but he ignored its requests, and by the end of the year he sounded irritated.

Although always polite and well written (he seemed better educated than many of the more marginal booksellers), his letters took on a frosty tone. None of the STN's books had reached him, he complained on November 27, 1777. He had received contradictory information about the shipments from the STN and its middlemen, and he was annoyed at having to pay postage (in the eighteenth century, letters traveled COD) to no effect: "The difficulties and delays have completely discouraged me.... When one receives several letters from Neuchâtel, some of them saying nothing and others announcing merchandise that fails to arrive, that makes everything seem like a comedy in which I am the actor who is being tricked and made a dupe."

Many of these difficulties resulted from the uncertainty produced by the edicts of August 30, 1777. Capel had not received a copy of them three months after their promulgation, even though he was the syndic of Dijon's guild. He finally got a chance to glance through their text in December, when a friend loaned him a copy. His first reaction was to predict that the Parisian booksellers, who had protested against some aspects of the legislation, would succeed in blocking its execution. Nonetheless, the booksellers in Dijon were supposed to send the government a report on their holdings of pirated books and to begin stamping them before the end of the year.

At last in January 1778, Capel received a shipment from the STN. But when he sorted through it, he found that it did not contain the books he had ordered. It later turned out that the bale had been intended for Chaboz, a bookseller in Dôle and sent to him by mistake. Despite the fact that this error made the STN's shipping system look increasingly dysfunctional, Capel asked it to send him a half dozen copies of *Eloge historique de Michel de L'Hospital, chancelier de France* [Historical Eulogy of Michel de L'Hospital, Chancellor of France] and said that he was also eager to buy subscriptions to the quarto edition of the *Encyclopédie*. In February, the main shipment for Capel finally arrived. He responded with a letter expressing hope that their commerce would continue thereafter on a sound footing.

In July 1778 Capel wrote that the edicts still had not gone into effect in Dijon. He expected to be replaced by two new syndics, as required by the edicts, and he could not say how the STN's shipments would be treated in the future. He would do what he could to help, but, he warned, "I have no desire to compromise myself." That was how things stood when Favarger arrived four months later. Thanks to his arrangement with Nubla, Favarger expected that trade with Dijon would pick up. It never did. In December 1778, Nubla reported that the new syndics had been installed and were determined to confiscate all illegal shipments. At that point, Capel ceased ordering books from Neuchâtel.

Because Capel's orders never resulted in large-scale shipments, the statistics drawn from them provide only a glimpse of the trade in Dijon around 1777. Capel sensed a demand for pedagogical works, ordering a dozen copies of Pierre Restaut's *Abrégé des principes de la grammaire française* and Nicolas-Antoine Viard's *Les Vrais principes de la lecture, de l'orthographe et de la prononciation française* [The True Principles of Reading, Spelling, and French Pronunciation], along with a half dozen *L'Arithmétique ou le livre facile pour apprendre l'arithmétique de soi-même et sans maître* [Arithmetic or an Easy Book for Learning Arithmetic by Oneself and Without a Teacher]. He also requested an anonymous anthology, *Lectures pour les enfants, ou choix de petits contes également propres à les amuser et à leur faire aimer la vertu*, and the popular *Magasin des enfants, ou Dialogues d'une sage gouvernante avec ses élèves de la première distinction* [Miscellany for Children, or Dialogues by a Wise Governess with Her Pupils of Great Social Distinction] by Jeanne-Marie Leprince de Beaumont. Among political works, he ordered the radical libel, *Mémoires de l'abbé Terray*, and the theoretical tract by the abbé Mably, *De la législation ou principes des lois* [On Legislation or the Principles of Laws].

One can imagine Dijon's lawyers and parliamentary officials thumbing through those works in Capel's bookstore, although he never identified any of his customers. He ordered the controversial pamphlet by Simon-Nicolas-Henri Linguet, *Lettre de M. Linguet à M. le comte de Vergennes*; but he later regretted it, as it did not arrive in time: "It's a work that has now passed out of vogue and that I would give away for less than ten sous." The other books that Capel requested came from a wide variety of genres. They were typical of what provincial dealers generally ordered, and they were not peculiar to what the STN supplied, because Capel noted that he received the same books from other houses, including some in Lyon and Paris. His dossier confirms impressions garnered from those of other booksellers: there was plenty of demand for all sorts of literature in the French provinces, though much of it remained unsatisfied, owing to difficulties in getting the books to the booksellers. The publisher-wholesalers from Geneva and Lausanne may have succeeded better than the STN, but its relations with Dijon amounted to little more than a story of missed opportunities. Although he had made some new contacts and had arranged for a few lucrative orders, Favarger's journey through France's heartland was a disappointment.

12

Besançon

Book Country at Its Best

ANYONE WHO HAS TRAVELED FROM DIJON TO BESANÇON (sixty miles) and other locations in the Franche-Comté knows how dramatically the landscape changes. Vineyards give way to meadows, hills turn into mountains, and valleys cut through cliffs, exposing rushing streams far below. We cannot know what Favarger made of it, not just because he wasn't given

Besançon, etching from *Nouveau voyage pittoresque de la France*, Paris, Ostervald, 1817 (BiCJ).

to description but because he stopped writing letters altogether after he left Dijon (he would arrive in Neuchâtel soon enough to give an oral report on the last stage of the journey). His diary shows that he passed through Dôle en route to Besançon and then followed the route across the Jura plateau from Besançon to Pontarlier (thirty-eight miles) and from Pontarlier down the Val de Travers to Neuchâtel (thirty-six miles). Favarger made it alone, on a horse, across rugged mountain passes, through the first storms of winter.

When he arrived in Besançon, he entered familiar territory. Not only had he been there before, but the city's booksellers had close ties to their suppliers in Neuchâtel, on the other side of the Jura. Besançon was good book territory. It had a high rate of literacy, a *parlement* and other law courts, an intendancy, numerous administrative offices, and a rich variety of cultural and educational institutions. Judging from the 1764 survey, selling books in Besançon was something of a free-for-all. There was no guild and no *chambre syndicale*, nor were there official requirements for entering the trade. Anyone could set up shop, even without having served an apprenticeship, simply by getting permission from the police. As a result, the survey noted, all sorts of undereducated and unqualified dealers sold all kinds of books, including illegal works, which they easily procured from Switzerland. By 1781 the *Almanach de la librairie* listed twelve booksellers and four bookseller-printers, a large number for a city of 25,000 inhabitants.

There is no better place to examine Besançon's book market than the correspondence of Charles-Antoine Charmet l'aîné and his wife, who worked actively with him and took over the business after his death in 1783. They kept up a steady stream of letters to the STN from 1769 to 1788—179 in all—so rich in detail that they offer an unusually intimate view of the life of a provincial bookseller.[1]

Charles-Antoine was born into a family of booksellers on December 18, 1735.[2] His father was a *marchand libraire*, and his younger brother, Jean-Félix, became a printer. According to the 1764 survey, Charles-Antoine, then twenty-nine, had run a bookshop that had recently gone bankrupt. Five years later, when he first appears in the archives of the STN, he was part of a family operation, "Charmet frères et soeurs," which supplied the STN's new printing shop with paper and other materials. The "brothers and sisters" also ran a small book business, and by the end of 1771 they began to place orders with the STN, starting with Mercier's *L'An deux mille quatre cent quarante*. By October 1773 Charles-Antoine was running his own bookshop in the center of the city on rue St. Pierre.

Charmet's letters occasionally refer to other suppliers, notably in Lausanne and Geneva, but they show that he always favored the STN in ordering books. On September 6, 1782, he wrote, "We would prefer to do all of our business with your house, to which we are attached by gratitude and esteem." The STN had earned Charmet's gratitude because it had agreed to postpone the settlement of his account at a time when a severe illness had confined him to his bed. By then he had got to know the STN's directors personally. He often traveled to Neuchâtel to negotiate purchases face-to-face and also to arrange supply lines, including smuggling operations at the border near Pontarlier. The visits led to something approaching friendship, as one can tell from the tone of the letters. Although they kept to the businesslike style that prevailed in commercial correspondence, they became increasingly cordial. On March 7, 1777, Charmet wrote to Ostervald and Bosset, who at that time were on a business trip in Paris, simply to assure them that all was well back in Neuchâtel. He had just visited the STN's office, and their wives, who were in good health, had received him with "great marks of affection, politeness, and warmth."

Thanks to these close ties, Charmet's letters have a dimension that is lacking in the commercial correspondence of most other booksellers. They reveal not only what books he ordered but also the strategy behind his orders—that is, the way he assessed the market and allowed for shifting circumstances as he built up his stock. The guiding principle of his trade was caution. Although he ordered some forbidden books, he never did so if he sensed the slightest danger, and the bulk of his trade was in inoffensive varieties of literature. He tried to read new books before ordering them so that he could calculate what would appeal to his customers. Whenever possible, he arranged for purchases among his own clients before purchasing them from the STN, and he rarely ordered large numbers of a particular book. "Sales serve as my compass," he explained, "and I cannot deviate from it without danger. That is why I do not want to take the slightest risk." In his early letters, he describes himself as a "small retailer," although when the French government created a *chambre syndicale* in 1778, he was chosen as its top official (syndic). He avoided risks, calculated demand conservatively, and never requested more copies than he thought he could sell. According to Mme Charmet, his strategy in ordering was "to take many items and a small number of each."

The statistics compiled from Charmet's orders bear out that remark. Although he sometimes requested a baker's dozen of a particular work in order to get the free thirteenth copy (a favor that the STN extended to its best customers), he usually ordered a half dozen or fewer copies and then came back for more if he found that it sold well. For example, in ordering Mme de Genlis's *Théâtre à l'usage des jeunes personnes*, a work that had great appeal for eighteenth-century readers but is forgotten today, he requested a total of 110 copies spread out in eight separate orders sent between December 1779 and April 1787. Like other booksellers, Charmet saved on transport costs by ordering enough individual works to make up a bale that weighed at least 50 pounds. A typical order, sent to the STN on May 29, 1775, contained twenty-seven titles, and the number of copies per title was usually two to six. Only on rare occasions, when he sensed great demand for a work, did Charmet risk a large initial order—and the repetition of the orders usually showed that he had calculated correctly. Thus his orders for a new work, which promised to be a bestseller, in 1781, Necker's *Mémoire donné au roi par M. N. en 1778 sur l'administration provinciale* [Memoire on Provincial Administration Given to the King by M. N. in 1778]. Charmet ordered one hundred copies of it on May 30, fifty more on June 29, and another seventeen at various dates between 1783 and 1785.

By compiling statistics from Charmet's orders, month after month, it is possible to have an unusually clear view of the demand for literature in a provincial capital. Necker's *Mémoire* (supplemented by *Collection complète de tous les ouvrages pour et contre M. Necker* [Complete Collection of All the Works for and Against M. Necker]) and Mme de Genlis's plays stood at the top of the list of the works that Charmet ordered most often. They were followed by some favorites from the scandalous literature about the court of Louis XV, although Charmet generally avoided ordering forbidden books. He favored moderate works by the philosophes: Voltaire's *Lettres philosophiques* and his *Eloge historique de la raison*, along with Rousseau's *Confessions*. He was even more eager to get Mercier's *Tableau de Paris* and Marmontel's *Les Incas*. The light verse, plays, and fables of Claude-Joseph Dorat also stood out among the orders, along with Raynal's *Histoire philosophique*.[3] And the full list of all Charmet's orders shows considerable demand for history, travel, a few novels, and some science.

This general pattern can be found in the orders of most important booksellers in other parts of France, although the demand for individual titles varied from shop to shop. What makes Charmet's case unusual is the running commentary on books and authors that accompanied his orders. Like many booksellers, he seized on opportunities to cash in on the reading public's fascination with the inner life of Versailles, though he would not take any risks and did not want to fill his shop with crude *libelles*. On September 30, 1775, he wrote: "I would be much obliged if you would send to me by mail... 2 *Mémoires de Louis XV* octavo so that I can see what it is. If this work is good and likely to bring in sales, I will take a hundred copies. But if it is in the same style as *Précis de Mme du Barry* (a scandalous life of Louis XV's mistress), 12 copies would be sufficient." He evidently decided the *Mémoires de Louis XV* good enough to be recommended to his customers, because he complained when the STN failed to get a shipment to him on time: "I am being tormented every day for the *Mémoires de Louis XV* by customers to whom unfortunately I mentioned them too soon." Charmet also spotted *Vie privée de Louis XV* as a potential bestseller. But the demand for it was so great at the level of the publisher-wholesalers that the STN could not supply him adequately. After a two-week delay, it got twenty-six copies to him; but he wanted twenty-six more, complaining that his competitors had already received shipments from other suppliers. Caught short, the STN explained that it had made a deal for two hundred cut-rate copies with another publisher, but that he had reneged on the agreement in order to make some quick cash by selling them himself.

The scramble to profit from the demand for scandalous literature began to taper off in late 1781, according to Charmet's calculation. He advised the STN to print a new edition of the four-volume *chronique scandaleuse* known as *L'Espion anglais*, even though it was no longer a hot item. "This book, which is good, is beginning to drop off in sales. 25 copies would suffice for me. 100 copies of it have been sold here. But *L'Observateur anglais*, the *Mémoires secrets*, *L'Espion français*, and this last book—all that amounts to many works about the same subject, and the public is already abundantly supplied."

Charmet detected a demand for serious political works, especially the polemical literature related to Jacques Necker and his measures as finance minister from 1776 to 1781. He acquired one hundred copies of *Compte rendu au roi*, Necker's extraordinary public report on the state's finances, which triggered the polemics in January 1781. (It does not show up in the statistics of Charmet's orders from the STN, because it came to him indirectly through a deal arranged by the STN with Lépagnez, another bookseller in Besançon.) Necker wrote the *Compte rendu* as part of a propaganda offensive to whip up support for his financial measures. He had it published as a handsome, officially authorized edition with two illuminated maps, and to promote it he kept the price down to 3 livres, while ordering strict repression of pirated editions. As anticipated, the pirates, including the STN, immediately began turning out competing editions, and they continued to reprint pamphlets for and against Necker during the polemics that followed his dismissal from the government on May 19, 1781. When the STN offered to supply a large number of *Mémoire de M. Necker au roi sur l'établissement des administrations provinciales* in May 1781, Charmet sent an immediate order for one hundred copies, and he kept a close watch on the pamphlet literature for the rest of the year. One anti-Neckerite pamphlet, *Lettre de M. le marquis de Carraccioli à M. d'Alembert*, circulated in manuscript and stirred up a great deal of interest in Besançon, he reported to the STN. He recommended that it print a quick edition, as "this is a favorable moment for selling it." The STN did so, and he snapped up one hundred copies. He encouraged it to reprint other pamphlets, including *Les Comments* and *Lettre d'un ami à M. Necker*, keeping to the same format as the *Compte rendu* so that they could be sold together. On October 9, 1781, the STN sounded him about the prospects of publishing a cheap reprint of a three-volume collection of works about Necker that Jean-François Bassompierre was then printing in Geneva. Charmet advised against it, because the market, at least in Besançon, seemed to be satiated. The STN eventually abandoned this project, but it supplied Charmet with nineteen copies of *Collection complète de tous les ouvrages pour et contre M. Necker*, which it apparently procured by means of an exchange with Bassompierre.

The STN relied on this kind of information from Charmet and a few of its most trusted customers in order to decide what books to pirate. In June 1781, for example, it asked Charmet's opinion about two works that it was considering: *Philosophie de la nature*, an anti-Christian tract by Delisle de Sales (the pen name of Jean-Baptiste-Claude Isoard) and

Raynal's *Histoire philosophique et politique des établissements et du commerce des Européens dans les deux Indes.* Both had been transformed into potential bestsellers by being condemned by the French authorities and were being reprinted in many places. Could the market support a new edition of each? the STN asked. Charmet advised against *Philosophie de la nature*: "I think the demand for this work has declined a great deal, as it has for all philosophical books in general. For a year now we have received very few requests for them." But Raynal's work was another matter: "As to the projected edition of the abbé Raynal, I find this enterprise excellent, according to your plan." As it happened, the STN did not produce its edition of Raynal until nearly two years later. In the meantime Charmet continued to supply his friends in Neuchâtel with reports about other reprints, notably the edition of the *Histoire philosophique* being produced in Lausanne in 1781. He also sent them copies of freshly published books so that they could begin work in their printing shop in time to beat their competitors to the market. In February and March 1777, he provided them with two potential bestsellers, *Les Incas* and a full set of Beaumarchais's enormously popular *Mémoires* from his legal battles with Louis-Valentin Goezman in the *parlement* installed by Chancellor Maupeou in place of the Parlement de Paris in 1771.

Thanks to messages transmitted through the professional grapevine, Charmet also helped the STN protect itself against the tricks of the trade. In April 1782, he warned the STN that a book it planned to reprint, *Recherches philosophiques et historiques sur le célibat* [Philosophical and Historical Inquiry on Celibacy] had been selling, and selling very well, for the last seven months under another title, *Les inconvénients du célibat des prêtres* [The Disadvantages of Celibacy Among Priests]. As the STN knew from its dealings with Mossy in Marseille, publishers sometimes manufactured misleading title pages in order to sell old material in new trappings; and to find out what was going on in other printing shops, they resorted to what today would be called industrial espionage. In July 1784 Mme Charmet warned the Neuchâtelois that one of their workers was secretly supplying a publisher in Lyon with sheets of Mercier's *Mon Bonnet de nuit* while they were printing the original edition.

The letters from Besançon also indicate what authors most attracted local readers and, to a certain extent, who those readers were. In addition to Voltaire and Rousseau, three writers stood out during the 1780s: the abbé Raynal, the comte de Mirabeau, and Simon-Nicolas-Henri Linguet. The condemnation of Raynal's *Histoire philosophique* in 1781 and his flight into exile made him a celebrity and his book a bestseller. Mirabeau's fiery denunciation of the abuses of state power, *Des Lettres de cachet et des prisons d'état*, printed in Neuchâtel by Fauche fils aîné et Cie., had special appeal in Besançon, where he had inflamed imaginations by escaping from the nearby prison in the Château de Joux with the wife of an elderly magistrate. When Mme Charmet took over the business in 1782, she implored the STN to get a shipment of *Des Lettres de cachet* to her (along with Mirabeau's pornographic *Ma Conversion*, later reprinted as *Le Libertin de qualité* [The Well-Born Libertine]) in time for the *parlement's* opening session in the fall. Linguet's *Mémoires sur la Bastille* struck a similar theme and had equal appeal for a city full of lawyers. As a lawyer turned polemical journalist, Linguet had many readers in Besançon. Charmet described his *Lettre de M. Linguet à M. le comte de Vergennes, ministre des affaires étrangères en France* as the hottest work on the market in June 1777: "Anyone would be lucky to snare a copy for 25 louis.... Some have been sold for 4 to 5 louis." Three years later, Mme Charmet was sure she could sell plenty of copies of the *Mémoires sur la Bastille*, if only the STN could get its shipment to her on time. In her view (and she seemed to be as astute an observer of the market as her late husband) the books that sold best were those written with "power" (*force*), at least in the field of politics and current events. She assured the STN that a posthumous edition of Turgot's works was in great demand in 1787, because, "this book is written with power and energy." For the same reason, the works of Louis-Sébastien Mercier sold well—but not all of them. His *Tableau de Paris* had attracted a great many customers, but not his *Réduction de Paris*: "The public found nothing new in this work and does not run after it, despite the power of the preface, which is composed of reworked material."

Neither Charmet nor his wife described in detail the nature of that public, but the remarks scattered throughout their letters indicate its general character. Readers connected with the law probably constituted the largest proportion of their customers. Charmet encouraged the STN to publish legal treatises in May 1777, and he estimated the number of copies that it could sell in every city with a *parlement*. (Paris and Besançon headed the list at one hundred copies each; Aix-en-Provence came last with forty.) In March 1785 Mme Charmet said her customers were clamoring for *Un Indépendant à l'ordre des avocats sur la décadence du bar-reau en France* [An Address to the Order of Lawyers on the Decadence of the Bar in France by an Independent Observer], an attack on the French bar by Jacques-Pierre Brissot, owing to "the current state of the bar in our city." The few references to individual customers in the letters from Besançon included a marquis, a magistrate, a canon from the cathedral, the provincial director of the Ferme générale, and four army officers. The garrison certainly accounted for many sales. In February 1780, Charmet wrote that he could not order any more copies of the memoirs of the war minister Claude-Louis de Saint-Germain, because the American war had depleted the number of soldiers stationed in Besançon. And in 1787, Mme Charmet said she would not know how many copies of the works of Frederick II to order until she knew how many soldiers would be in the garrison at the time of its publication. None of the letters mentioned sales among the lower ranks of the population, but, like many provincial booksellers, Charmet used his shop as the site of a *cabinet littéraire*, where members paid a small fee for access to the books in his stock. Anyone who crossed its threshold was likely to encounter persons from a variety of stations in the professional and upper classes but not artisans and workers.

The Charmet correspondence also abounds in details about another aspect of the book trade: communication and transportation. Before 1778, the bales of books that arrived from Switzerland were cleared at the office of the Ferme générale and then were inspected at the intendancy. In a letter of August 13, 1775, Charmet explained that he participated in the inspections and bribed the intendant's employees so that they merely took a cursory look at the sheets in the top of the bales. By packing its forbidden books in the bottom, the STN made sure they reached him safely. In fact, thanks to special "permissions of the intendancy," Charmet helped forward the STN's books to other customers inside France. Sometimes he could flash a falsified receipt provided by the STN to the officials, and they would let him collect a bale without any inspection at all. He could even intervene to get the release of forbidden books in cases where they had been confiscated along the route. In early September 1775, Charmet learned that three bales sent from Neuchâtel had recently been seized in Frambourg. He offered to rescue them even though they were only being sent to him for forwarding to others: "I will use my exceptional pull to get you out of this problem... but... it is necessary to keep protections in reserve so as to be able to use them for oneself in urgent cases."

The case of the three bales turned out to be difficult, because they contained copies of Mirabeau's *Essai sur le despotisme*, which the French government tried to suppress by means of special orders sent through the Ferme générale in Paris without informing the intendant in Besançon. Charmet worried that this incident would make it difficult for the STN to get future shipments to him, especially if the employees in Besançon's tax office, as opposed to his friends in the intendancy, intervened in the inspection process. "If they are ill-disposed, I might get bitten," he wrote on October 4, 1775. "I will judge from their looks if [a bale en route with some forbidden books] can get through easily and if I can get others through immediately afterwards.... I repeat my offers to do what I can within my small amount of power. But please understand that I must take the requisite precautions." The confidential tone of the letter indicated how closely Charmet had become linked to the STN, though its emphasis on caution expressed a key factor in his relations with the Neuchâtelois. He might sound like a veteran of the underground trade, but he never dealt heavily in forbidden books and he always avoided risks.

As the case of the three confiscated bales worked its way through the French bureaucracy, Charmet reported that it would have serious consequences. Some middlemen who had been compromised by the shipment would be fined as much as 2,000 livres compounded by symbolic measures—a "defamatory punishment" and a book burning, although some innocent works that did not sell would be substituted for the forbidden books. Fortunately, he had not been implicated, and above all he felt confident of the intendant's support: "He is the one who must give the definitive judgment.... As word has spread that they are bad books, it is certain that there will be a book burning in the middle of the court of the intendancy—and that merely to appease some idiots.... It would be better to replace them with the Dissertations [*Dissertation sur l'établissement de l'abbaye de St. Claude*, a book that had sold so badly that Charmet thought it should be pulped]." To clear the way for the resumption of their trade, he had had to resort to "palpable civilities"—that is, bribery, including two copies of Raynal's *Histoire philosophique*, bound in Morocco with gold tooling that he planned to present to the intendant.

The auto-da-fé with the substitute books, staged with the support of the intendant, indicates the extent to which the Enlightenment had penetrated the top levels of the French administration by 1775, though the intendant's protection did not extend to the toleration of radical political works. Charmet believed that the attempt to suppress the *Essai sur le despotisme* lay behind the unusual recent vigilance at the Swiss border. Because Mirabeau had had his tract printed by Fauche fils aîné et Cie. in Neuchâtel, everything coming from Neuchâtel was suspicious. "Do not try to get the *Essai sur le despotisme* through here," Charmet warned in a letter of December 7, 1775. "That could cause trouble for the author, who is known, and for the printer through the intervention of the [French] ambassador in Soleure. The ministry is determined to take firm action on this occasion.... There has been a great uproar about this at Pontarlier." Unfortunately, however, eight bales from the STN were seized in Frambourg in early December. By drawing on his influence with the intendant and more bribery, Charmet managed to pry seven of them loose from the customs officials, who had received secret orders to be vigilant from the ministry in Versailles. But this disaster put an end to Charmet's services as a shipping agent for the STN—until new possibilities arose in 1778, when he became the syndic of Besançon's new *chambre syndicale*.

The *chambre syndicale* was installed in Besançon in 1778 as required by the edicts of 1777, and Charmet was chosen as its syndic, charged with the responsibility of overseeing all book imports and seizing everything illegal. As soon as it heard this good news, the STN asked him to expedite its shipments everywhere in France. But he worried that a police inspector, who was to accompany him in clearing the bales, would make it impossible to cheat while discharging the *acquits à caution*, especially as he had heard that the French government wanted the new edicts enforced rigorously. Despite his close relations with the STN, he was determined to avoid all risks: "As to the philosophical side, I will not handle anything more in that genre. The new book trade administration will make it impossible for us," he announced in a letter of February 20, 1778. Undeterred by entreaties from the STN, he refused to forward anything suspicious to booksellers located elsewhere. The STN kept asking him nonetheless. Couldn't he help them open a direct route to the Paris market by leaning on his contacts in Dijon? Wouldn't he consider slipping shipments through Besançon at the going rate charged by smugglers at the border,

15 livres per hundredweight? The answer was always no. Charmet continued to include a few illegal works in his own trade, but as always he refused to take any chances, and by 1783 he had ceased to do much business with the STN.

By this time, too, the personal element in the correspondence had become more pronounced. Like many provincial booksellers, Charmet frequently went on the road, selling books to retailers in small towns, inspecting supply lines, and negotiating with publisher-wholesalers. And like many booksellers' wives, Mme Charmet took over the correspondence in his absence. As a rule, when the wives did the writing, the quality of the letters declined, both in spelling and in grammar, because girls normally received a poorer education than boys. But Mme Charmet had an excellent hand, a perfect mastery of syntax, and no hesitation to use complex phrasing, even in the past subjunctive tense. In reading through the Charmet dossier, one has a vivid impression of a husband-and-wife team struggling to cope with shifting political and economic circumstances—and also with personal disaster. Mixed with the running account of commercial affairs are scattered references to Charmet's health, parenthetical at first and then increasingly urgent.

Mme Charmet first mentioned her husband's illness on September 25, 1781, when he had returned from one of his many business trips to his suppliers in Switzerland and his clients in the Franche-Comté. He recovered well enough to resume the correspondence and the trips during the next twelve months. But on September 6, 1782, Mme Charmet reported that he had arrived a week ago, "very ill," from another journey: "The onset of his illness struck him during his trip. He wanted to defeat it, and it defeated him. His lack of care for himself and some ineffective remedies made the illness longer and more resistant. I hope that he will pull out of it, but that will certainly take a long time." The STN sent its sympathy, and in a letter dated October 2 Mme Charmet replied that things looked better: "We are all very happy to have escaped with nothing more than a fright and a loss of time." By November 3, however, her husband had suffered a relapse. He could not get out of bed or pay any attention to the business, which had taken a turn for the worse. The STN helped by agreeing to delay the payment of a debt. It also recommended some kind of medication, which was provided by a mutual friend in Besançon. Mme Charmet sent a letter of thanks on November 15, saying that she had not given up hope, although Charmet had remained bedridden for three months and the doctors gave contradictory prognoses. The STN's generosity, she wrote, "made him weep tears of gratitude toward you and all of yours.... At this time he can barely sign his name." Six weeks later, on January 2, 1783, he was dead.[4]

By January 9, Mme Charmet had settled the estate and resumed the correspondence. She would continue the business by herself, she wrote to the STN, and by hard work would clear off the accumulation of debt. Not only did the STN send its sympathy, it also formally renewed its "confidence" in the business, beginning with a further extension of the payments she owed. From this point on, her letters showed her plunged back in the affairs of the shop, sounding the preferences of her customers, ordering books, intervening to get shipments cleared through inspections, and providing confidential information about the hazards of shipping books across the border.

In the first months of 1783, widow Charmet was especially eager to profit from the demand for two of the scandalous works by Mirabeau, *Des Lettres de cachet et des prisons d'état* and *Ma Conversion*. She knew all about the circumstances of their publication, a complex story involving disputes within the Fauche family of Neuchâtel, where they were originally published, and piracy in Lausanne, where a cheap reprint of *Des Lettres de cachet* was produced. She ordered all of her copies from the STN, which, as she assured it, would always have her "preference" in buying supplies, but it had difficulty in extricating its own supply from the embroiled Swiss publishers. Other booksellers in Besançon managed to stock their shops with these hot-selling items before they reached Mme Charmet; so she had to watch helplessly while they creamed off the demand. She hoped to have better luck with an equally sensational work, Linguet's *Mémoires sur la Bastille*. Genevan sources said an edition was being produced in Lausanne, she wrote; and it was sure to sell well, if only the STN could get a shipment to her on time.

Widow Charmet kept attuned to the latest news, and like her husband before her, she passed on to the STN inside information that was reserved for correspondents tied by the closest bonds of "confidence." In July 1783, she warned the STN that the French authorities were planning to crack down on the trade from Neuchâtel, because they had arrested Jacques Mallet, the distributor of Mirabeau's works in France, who had confessed everything about their publication during his interrogation in the Bastille.[5] As explained in chapter 2, the publisher, Fauche fils aîné et Cie., was a fly-by-night enterprise, which had been founded in Neuchâtel by Jonas Fauche, the son of Samuel Fauche, a founding partner of the STN. Samuel had set up shop on his own after a dispute with the other STN partners, and Jonas did the same after quarreling with him. The feuding among the Neuchâtel publishers played into the hands of the French authorities and disrupted the supply lines, because the Neuchâtelois all used the same route through the Jura Mountains in trying to get books to Besançon. If a shipment from one publisher was confiscated, all the others were endangered.

Quarrels among publishers and the loss of occasional bales were acceptable hazards, but the basic conditions of the trade were transformed by the 1783 order requiring that all book imports be cleared by the *chambre syndicale* of Paris. A shipment from Neuchâtel to Besançon therefore had to make a ruinously expensive detour, unless the STN could find an effective smuggling route. It never did, although it managed to get a few shipments to widow Charmet. She complained that it had failed to do as well as other suppliers, who somehow had succeeded, at least occasionally, in circumventing the regulation. For her part, she refused to take any risks. She reported that demand had held up for some kinds of literature, such as books on administrative affairs, which would interest the lawyers and magistrates connected with Besançon's *parlement*. Turgot's *Oeuvres posthumes* would sell well, she reported, and she had high hopes for the works of Frederick II and for a mathematical treatise, which ought to appeal to the artillery officers in the garrison. But there was no getting around it: business was bad. "For some time now our trade has been in a miserable state," she lamented in a letter of July 17, 1785.

The STN did not need to be told. The downturn in the book trade had affected its finances so severely that it had to suspend the payments on its outstanding bills of exchange at the end of 1783. A group of local investors came to its rescue, and it continued under new management for the rest of the decade—but on a reduced scale while concentrating on selling off the enormous stock that it had accumulated in its warehouse. When widow Charmet learned of its difficulties, she sent a sympathetic letter, reaffirming her "confidence" in the STN just as it had done to her during her crisis: "It was almost impossible for you to escape being included in the general revolution of the trade. The lack of liquidity, your [overextension of] confidence, the hindrances to our commerce, all these things together cannot but inflict terrible damage on you."

The cooperative but cautious tone of widow Charmet's letters confirmed the character of the business her husband had established. He ordered what his customers wanted, primarily steady sellers of the most familiar kinds. He carried a small proportion of *livres philosophiques* as long as he perceived a demand for them and ran no risk. The local authorities protected him, delighted to receive their own copies of the occasional bestseller. But by the time Charmet had become a syndic of Besançon's new guild, the risk factor had increased. After the crisis of 1783, he had maintained his cautious course, and after his death, his widow followed the same strategy. She proved to be astute enough to keep the business going, despite what she diagnosed as a general decline in the book trade, and she was still tending the shop when Besançon was swept up in the Revolution.

Lépagnez cadet[6] was the second most important bookseller in Besançon, and he occupied a secondary place in the STN's trade, which always favored Charmet, its long-standing ally and the city's foremost bookseller. Yet Besançon was such a good market for books and its supply lines bound it so closely to Neuchâtel that Lépagnez's business warrants study on its own, particularly because of his skirmishes with the French authorities. He was an aggressive entrepreneur who played according to the rules of the game but also bent them as far as they would go.

Lépagnez first appeared in the STN's correspondence in 1777 at the height of the speculation on the quarto edition of the *Encyclopédie*. Booksellers everywhere scrambled to collect subscriptions to it and Lépagnez outdid them all. He printed his own subscription forms, circulated prospectuses, beat the bushes throughout the Franche-Comté, and in the end sold 390 subscriptions, a remarkable number for a sparsely populated province. In December 1779, he wrote with some pride that he had drained the demand down to the vanishing point. "As I have larded my small province with 390 copies of your quarto Encyclopédie, not including those sold by the peddlers, it is no longer possible to find a place for any more."

Lépagnez's success opened the way to extensive trade with the STN. By 1777 Charmet, though still the STN's preferred bookseller, was slowing down, and he had refused to participate in the chase after *Encyclopédie* subscriptions, because, he explained, he preferred to avoid the difficulties that plagued subscription publishing—problems collecting money, delays in delivery, complaints of all kinds, many of them justified, from unsatisfied customers. The quarto *Encyclopédie* did indeed turn out to be one of the most contentious enterprises that any bookseller had ever encountered—and also the most profitable. As the greatest *Encyclopédie* salesman in the kingdom, Lépagnez looked like the rising star among the thirteen booksellers of Besançon. In fact, Charmet acknowledged that he had made a mistake in neglecting the demand for *Encyclopédies*, and Lépagnez's success worried him so much that in June 1777 he asked the STN to formally renew its "confidence" in him. Although Charmet remained its primary customer in Besançon, the STN opened up a line of credit with Lépagnez in 1778.

Lépagnez's first letters to the STN concentrated almost entirely on the *Encyclopédie*, but by 1778 he was helping to expedite the STN's shipments and reporting on the government's plans to reorganize the book trade according to the 1777 edicts. During a business trip to Paris in the spring of 1778, he tried to discover how the edicts would be implemented in Besançon. In a letter to the STN of May 11, he reported that Le Camus de Néville, the official in charge of the book trade, had summoned him to discuss the situation: "Ever since this interview, I have been in the good graces of this magistrate, and his door is always open to me. That is why I know about everything." One should allow for a good deal of self-promotion behind this remark, but it seems possible that Néville intended to use Lépagnez as his instrument in setting up the new *chambre syndicale*. Lépagnez, in turn, used the information from Néville as a way to ingratiate himself with the STN. According to his version of their understanding, Néville had granted him, as a personal favor, a delay of twenty to thirty days in the establishment of the *chambre syndicale*, so that he would have time to return to Besançon and get his own stock of pirated books stamped.

Lépagnez did not send this inside information simply to satisfy the curiosity of the Neuchâtelois. He urged them to ship him as many of their pirated books as possible so that they could be stamped before the end of the grace period—"and don't lose any time." By working fast and then pretending that he had accumulated those books in his own storerooms, he could absorb a huge infusion of illegal works into his business under the cover of the law and without running any risk. This would only be a one-off operation, but it could make him a favored client of a key Swiss supplier; and after the establishment of the *chambre syndicale*, he could use his influence in it to keep the supplies coming by means of other maneuvers.

The STN failed to take advantage of this window of opportunity, perhaps because it was too occupied with the *Encyclopédie* at that moment, but in July 1778 it asked whether it still was possible to send off shipments for stamping in the new *chambre syndicale*. Too late, Lépagnez replied. The new book inspector had recently arrived with orders about setting up the *chambre syndicale*, and the *parlement* of Besançon was expected to complete the formalities by registering those orders in the near future. Lépagnez himself had decided to avoid all risks at this critical juncture, though by the end of 1779 he had begun ordering books regularly from the STN. He was also being supplied by other Swiss houses, notably the new Société typographique de Genève, which had sold him a large number of its monumental, posthumous edition of Rousseau's works.

As his relations with the STN settled into a pattern of mutual trust as well as trade, Lépagnez intervened whenever it needed help in getting its shipments through Besançon. He joined Charmet as an adjoint or subordinarte officer in the *chambre syndicale* in January 1780. Although he and Charmet competed, they also cooperated, and generally got along quite well, judging from Lépagnez's letters. For the most part, the letters dealt with orders and payments. Occasionally Lépagnez commented on the demand for particular books, such as *Introduction aux observations sur la physique, sur l'histoire naturelle, et sur les arts* [Introduction to Observations on Physics, Natural History, and the Arts] by the abbé Rozier: "It's a good book, which will sell well." His remarks took on a tone of increasing pessimism in the last months of 1780. In July, he complained that the book market had gone into a slump, which he attributed to a general economic downturn produced by the American war. He sounded even unhappier in August: "Please don't think that I do a large trade in books here. I swear to you that apart from *L'Histoire universelle* [by abbé Raynal and others], *L'Histoire ecclésiastique* [by Johann Lorenz von Mosheim], the history of the Gallican church, the Vence edition of the Bible, the *Encyclopédie*, and the Rousseau, nothing has been selling for the past two years."

Relief from the slump came with a few bestsellers related to current events such as Necker's controversial ministry. When the STN offered to provide Lépagnez with one thousand copies of the *Comte rendu*, which it was printing in March 1781, he jumped at the chance: "The quarto that you mention is sure to sell very well if it can be produced quickly, because we cannot get any copies from Paris, where people have snatched it up.... But we have received strict orders against pirated versions." The STN did its best to disguise its piracy by copying the Paris edition exactly, but it failed to produce an accurate reproduction of the maps, and its shipment arrived late. Lépagnez complained bitterly about the delay in delivery and the inaccuracies, which, he claimed, would expose him to the accusation of fraud. "We will be considered here as charlatans and deceivers.... You are cruel." He therefore refused to accept the shipment. In the end, he sold a few copies, though only on commission as a distributor of the STN edition; and it did not object, because the demand remained strong and it easily marketed the rest of its edition to other customers.

Lépagnez was even more disappointed in his attempt to make a killing with Necker's *Mémoire donné au roi par M. N. en 1778 sur l'administration provinciale*. On May 29, the STN offered to provide four hundred copies of the *Mémoire* as a joint sale to him and Charmet. When the STN's letter arrived in Besançon, however, Lépagnez was on a trip to Paris. The clerk in charge of the shop assumed that the deal for the two hundred copies had been settled and sent Lépagnez a letter saying they soon would be shipped. Lépagnez then arranged to sell them from Paris; but when he returned to Besançon, he learned that the STN had supplied Charmet with all four hundred copies. Assuming that he had been cut out of the market by an arrangement made behind his back by the STN and Charmet, he protested in an angry letter to Neuchâtel. The STN defended itself by insisting that it had never received confirmation of his intention to order two hundred copies; and the recriminations flew back and forth between Besançon and Neuchâtel for several weeks, leaving unhappy feelings on both sides.

But, as the French saying puts it, *Les affaires sont les affaires*. Trade resumed, and Lépagnez, along with Charmet, continued to help seeing the STN's bales through the *chambre syndicale*. In November 1781, the STN requested assistance in getting the release of a shipment of a Protestant edition of the Bible, which the inspector of the *chambre syndicale* had confiscated. In December, it asked Lépagnez to forward a shipment of Mercier's *Le Philosophe du Port-au-bled*, and he complied. But in January

1782, he wrote that he could no longer provide such service, because his term as an officer of the *chambre syndicale* had expired. He added, however, that Charmet would continue as syndic for two more years. "I am sure that he will do everything he can to be of service to you, provided that he does not compromise himself, because we have received some new edicts that make it harder than ever to fulfill our good intentions." Lépagnez and Charmet had remained allies, despite their commercial rivalry, in the efforts of Besançon's booksellers to protect themselves against the new *chambre syndicale* by taking it over.

A year later, on January 5, 1783, Lépagnez wrote that he had just attended Charmet's funeral. Although he put the message diplomatically, he clearly hoped to succeed Charmet as the STN's most favored retailer in Besançon. In fact, as explained, Charmet's widow continued the business, and the STN supported her by delaying the payment of some bills. But it maintained good relations with Lépagnez, and he obliged by offering again to get its shipments to other booksellers through the *chambre syndicale*. He could make sure they escaped detection by the inspector, he wrote, and once they cleared inspection he would forward them to Adolphe Veny, the STN's shipping agent in Besançon, who operated out of an inn called Aux trois rois. Veny claimed to have seventy horses at his disposal and to be able to get books to Versailles (the palace and outlying buildings served as a great entrepôt for illegal literature destined for Paris) without passing through Dijon and Troyes, two dangerous outposts of the police.[7]

Many of Lépagnez's letters in 1783 concerned these shipping arrangements. Once they went into effect, the STN began to funnel a great deal of its trade through Besançon, hoping to use the Lépagnez-Veny combination to unlock markets throughout northern France. Favarger traveled to Besançon in February and agreed to pay Lépagnez 7 livres, 10 sous per bale for his services. By March 16, Lépagnez had cleared five bales through the *chambre syndicale*, but Veny had failed to find wagon drivers for them. Despite his bragging about horses, Veny got on badly with the drivers. Sometimes he refused to reimburse their costs, because, according to Lépagnez, his own finances were shaky. "He is a man who is not worthy of trust." Following Lépagnez's advice, the STN shifted its business from Veny to one of his competitors, a shipping agent named Péchey, who promised to reimburse the drivers for all costs from Neuchâtel and to forward the bales at fixed rates to destinations in northern France.[8]

After this adjustment, the system worked quite well—until disaster struck in June 1783.

As soon as he heard "the sad news" of the order that required all book imports to be sent for inspection in the *chambre syndicale* of Paris, Lépagnez fired off a letter to Neuchâtel. As a special favor to him, he explained, the director of the Ferme générale in the Franche-Comté had granted a short delay in putting the order into effect. That would give the STN time to get several bales through Pontarlier to Besançon, where he could shepherd them through the *chambre syndicale*. As with the 1777 edicts, Lépagnez was using inside information to gain a short-term advantage and ingratiate himself further with the STN. He was a hustler who seized every opportunity he could get, and he usually got away with it.

Not this time. Seven bales made it to Besançon in mid-June, but another shipment ran into serious difficulties. A clerk of the STN named Fenouillet accompanied it from Neuchâtel, while Lépagnez rushed to meet him in Pontarlier in order to be sure that everything was in order. It was not. In his haste to get the bales to safety, Fenouillet had hired a wagon driver from Pontarlier to haul them to Besançon at night without going through the usual customs formalities. According to standard procedures, Fenouillet was supposed to submit the bales on the following morning to customs officers, who would have them sealed and furnished with an *acquit à caution*, which would be discharged, with Lépagnez's help, after inspection at the *chambre syndicale* in Besançon. Unfortunately for Lépagnez, the shipment also could be identified by its bill of lading, which the original wagon driver had submitted to the custom officers before returning to Neuchâtel, and the bill of lading showed that the books were being sent to Lépagnez. Once they discovered that the shipment had been forwarded illegally under the cover of night, the customs officers sent a squadron of men to capture it. To his horror, Lépagnez then realized that he was in danger of being exposed as a collaborator in a smuggling operation. As it happened, the bales did not contain any forbidden books, but the fraudulent maneuver might be enough to ruin him in the eyes of the authorities.

Seized by panic, he wrote three desperate letters to the STN from Pontarlier, one after the other. Word about the illegal nighttime shipment had spread everywhere, he complained. People were pointing at him in the street. The head of the customs at Pontarlier had sent a circular letter to six other offices of the Ferme générale, describing Lépagnez not only as the intended recipient of the shipment but as an accomplice in an egregious fraud. The STN's idiotic clerk had destroyed his reputation. Even worse, Lépagnez wrote in a later letter, he had not dared return to Besançon for several weeks, because he feared a *lettre de cachet* would be issued for his arrest. At the very least, he had expected the government to forbid him to continue in business as a bookseller.

In its reply, the STN wrote that the situation could not be as desperate as he had imagined; he must have overreacted. He shot back a letter saying that it had not understood; the crisis could put an end to his commercial existence; and their exchange of letters made him feel as if "I was talking about the pope, while in your reply you talked about the harem of the grand vizir." Fortunately, widow Charmet and one of Lépagnez's clerks had managed to substitute legal works for two pirated books that the bale contained. Lépagnez resumed his trade, but he emphasized in his later letters that he would never again help the STN with its shipments. "I cannot make any commitments or compromise myself in any way. I had a close brush with disaster and cannot for any reason expose myself again. For the same reason, I cannot send you any more orders for as long as the cruel order [of June 12, 1783] lasts." The order was never revoked, and Lépagnez never acquired any more books from the STN.

The general pattern of Lépagnez's trade, drawn from the compilation of his orders, corresponds to the main themes of his correspondence. The *Mémoire de M. Necker au roi sur l'établissement des administrations provinciales* dominates the list of books in greatest demand, reflecting Lépagnez's efforts to acquire works related to Necker's ministry at a time when interest in it was at its peak. He also sent two orders for *Collection complète de tous les ouvrages pour et contre M. Necker.* His purchase of ninety-nine subscriptions to the quarto *Encyclopédie* was a similar effort to strike while the iron was hot. (In fact, those ninety-nine subscriptions, the first of the 390 that Lépagnez collected, were eventually credited to the quarto consortium and therefore do not represent his unilateral commerce with the STN and do not appear on his "bestseller list.") Aside from those special cases, his orders resembled those of many provincial booksellers. He seems not to have dealt extensively in forbidden books, even though he willingly helped the STN smuggle them through the *chambre syndicale.* He ordered a number of dictionaries, travel books, and tracts about subjects such as freemasonry and black magic. The names of Enlightenment philosophers—Rousseau, Voltaire, and Condillac—figure in his orders, although he did not ask for their works in large quantities. Instead, he favored current fiction and belles-lettres such as the plays of Mercier and Madame de Genlis, the poetry of Delille, and *Les Liaisons dangereuses* by Choderlos de Laclos.

Lépagnez's orders provide only a glimpse of his trade during a relatively brief period. But the information from his dossier supplements the more extensive material in the dossier of Charmet. Taken together, the orders of the two booksellers and their comments on the trade give a full view of the demand for literature in a provincial capital during the last decades of the Ancien Régime. The chain of letters extends to October 1788. By then, however, the circuit between Neuchâtel and Besançon had ceased to function effectively, the Revolution had begun to gather momentum, and the history of books had entered a new phase.

13

Neuchâtel

An Overview of the Demand for Literature

JEAN-FRANÇOIS FAVARGER'S TOUR DE FRANCE had no formal finish line. His arrival back in Neuchâtel sometime in late November or early December 1778 probably was undramatic—no ceremony or celebration, except perhaps a reunion with the staff of the STN and later with his family over some bottles of wine. After following him day by day for five months and more than 1,200 miles, it is difficult to leave him at this point. But this is where the documentation gives out, except for a few references scattered through disparate sources.

In all likelihood, Favarger gave a full report to the directors of the STN. His three-year contract came to an end a year later, on December 1, 1779. At that time, he probably received the bonus of 6 louis (144 livres), which it had held out as a reward for satisfactory behavior. As noted in the first chapter, he made two short business trips for the STN in 1782 and 1783, and by 1784 his letters disappear from the STN archives. Research in the notarial archives of the Canton of Neuchâtel has turned up some additional information. On December 6, 1779, Favarger married Marie-Elisabeth Affolter from the village of Aarberg twenty or so miles east of Neuchâtel in the canton of Bern. Jean-François's brother Samuel was married on the same occasion. After this double wedding, the brothers probably remained close, because on December 13, 1782, they bought a small vineyard together, and a year later they cooperated to cover the debts of another brother, Louis, a master watchmaker. The notarial documents identified Samuel as a "master baker" in 1782, though he later appears as a "grocery merchant" (*négociant en épiceries*). He and Jean-François jointly founded a business in grocery supplies, on July 13, 1776, while Jean-François was employed by the STN. To support it, they borrowed funds at various times in 1776 and 1777, amounting to 840 livres. It therefore seems likely that after investing in the business, Jean-François continued to work for the STN until sometime in 1783, and then became a full-time partner of his brother. On September 28, 1784, the STN wrote to its former shipping agent in Lyon, Claudet frères, "M. Favarger is no longer in our house. He now does business in groceries [*épicerie*] under the name [S?] & J. F. Favarger." Jean-François appears in the early documents without an occupation attached to his name as a "*marchand et bourgeois*"—that is, a tradesman with civil rights as a member of the bourgeoisie or municipality of Neuchâtel. In 1795 he bought a fairly large vineyard for 72 louis d'or (1,728 French livres), and his status sounded somewhat grander: "négociant, aussi bourgeois de cette ville" (merchant as well as bourgeois of this city). On November 30, 1796, the last time he is mentioned in the archives, he owned a house in the handsome rue de l'hôpital worth 6,000 livres. He had a son, also named Jean-François, who was born on September 26, 1780. The archives do not mention his death. From what little they reveal, it seems likely that Favarger used the commercial savvy he had acquired as a clerk for the STN to build a successful business career somewhere in the middle of Neuchâtel's middle class.[1]

Favarger's trip, now that it's over, allows us to return to the question raised when we saw him off at the beginning of his tour de France: what was the demand for literature in France on the eve of the Revolution? As indicated along the way, an answer can be found by close study of the businesses of the booksellers he encountered. Yet before those case studies can be integrated in a general conclusion, it is crucial to ask a further question: can the archives of the STN be taken to represent the book trade in general? Nothing like them exists anywhere else. And yet, extensive as they are, they provide only a small keyhole through which to see a large phenomenon. And there is little help to be provided by other studies, because incomplete and unreliable sources make it devilishly difficult to compile statistics about the production and diffusion of books anywhere in Europe before the nineteenth century.

In England, only a minority of newly published books were entered in the registry of the London Stationers' Company. In Germany, the catalogs of the book fairs of Leipzig and Frankfurt exclude a great deal of popular literature along with a large proportion of works from southern and Catholic regions. And in France, the official records are misleading in several ways. The registers of requests for book privileges exclude

Another view of Neuchâtel.

"View of the lake and the city of Neuchâtel," by Niklaus Sprunglin, colored engraving, circa 1780.

everything that was not submitted for formal approval by the censors, and records of books submitted for other kinds of permissions—*permissions tacites* (books approved by a censor but without a formal privilege and usually published with a false address to suggest that they had been printed outside France) and *permissions de sceau* (books that were permitted but without any guarantee of an exclusive right to sales)—do not indicate what books were actually published and how many copies were printed, to say nothing of sales. Moreover, the enormous production of books that were printed outside France and marketed inside the kingdom cannot be estimated. I would guess that it constituted at least half the books in circulation between 1769 and 1789.[2]

Why such a high proportion? The approbation of a censor and the conferral of a privilege did not merely certify that a book contained nothing that would offend religion, the state, morals, or the reputation of an important personage; they also served as a royal stamp of approval for the quality of the book—its style and content as well as its ideological correctness. Censorship became less rigorous during the last years of the Ancien Régime. But it took money, time, and trouble to obtain even a *permission tacite*. The members of the Parisian booksellers guild owned the great majority of all the privileges in existence, and the state reinforced their monopoly by police action, not only in Paris but also in faraway cities like Marseille, where Favarger found the *inspecteur de la librairie* to be a merciless tyrant. A few provincial booksellers, including some of those we've met, such as Mossy in Marseille, Gaude in Nîmes, Bergeret in Bordeaux, and Couret in Orléans, published original editions. Some even speculated secretly in pirating, especially in Lyon, where the intrepid Joseph Duplain outdid everyone in raiding the Parisians' markets. The reforms of 1777 were meant to redress the balance of the trade in favor of the provincial booksellers, and they did make it possible for the provincials to reprint books whose privileges had expired; but they did not transform the publishing industry, and they were not applied effectively, not even in the new *chambre syndicale* of Besançon, where Charmet and Lépagnez did everything possible to help the STN market its books. Within France, the Parisian guild remained the dominant power in publishing right up to the Revolution.[3]

In the face of these constraints and costs, many authors like Louis-Sébastien Mercier, whose works sold like hotcakes all along Favarger's route, preferred to have their books produced outside France. Their publishers developed an elaborate system to market them inside the kingdom, using agents like Faivre and Revol to get them past the customs officials at the border and the *chambres syndicales* in key distribution centers like Lyon, Nîmes, and Bordeaux. These foreign publishing houses, which had sprung up like mushrooms around France's borders, produced nearly all the works of the Enlightenment along with everything else that could not pass the censorship. But they made most of their money from piracy and therefore aroused the fury of the owners of the original privileges, who were nearly always booksellers in the Parisian guild. (Authors could not sell books themselves before the reforms of 1777 and rarely did so afterward.)

The provincial booksellers, by contrast, were natural allies of the foreign publishers, primarily because of economic factors. They could procure pirated books at lower prices than the originals, which had to be produced according to the quality standards set by royal regulations. Paper, which represented half or more of production costs depending on the size of the press run, was cheaper outside France, and the pirate publishers could churn out inexpensive editions without purchasing the original manuscripts from the authors. Of course, they had to cope with the problem of getting their books smuggled into France, as illustrated by the STN's relations with the Meuron brothers in Saint-Sulpice and Faivre in Pontarlier. But they could count on allies among the booksellers in most *chambres syndicales*, from Lépagnez in Besançon to Pavie in La Rochelle. Despite occasional breakdowns, the illegal distribution system supplied relatively inexpensive books to a broad public everywhere in provincial France. This kind of publishing, based on pirated and uncensored editions, had developed into a major industry by 1750, much to the chagrin of royal officials, who deplored the flight of capital to foreign manufacturers. It outdid the upscale, Paris-centered, and guild-based system in linking supply to demand.[4]

How to measure demand? That is the problem I have addressed by compiling information from the papers of the STN, the only publishing house from this era whose archives have survived almost completely intact. The STN documents reveal literary demand in two ways: first, by letters with orders for books sent by booksellers in nearly all the cities of France from 1769 to 1789; and second, from various account books, in which the STN's clerks recorded the orders and the shipments sent in response to them. With the help of research assistants over the last fifteen years, I have chosen a sample of the most important customers of the STN, transcribed their letters, compiled statistics from their orders, added transcriptions of dossiers from the middlemen of the book trade, mapped trade routes, furnished information about the social and economic conditions in each of the cities, and digitized all of the original manuscripts. This material can be studied in detail on the website robertdarnton.org.

Rich as it is, however, the material comes almost entirely from one source—the archives of the STN—so there is no getting around the basic question of whether one publisher's trade can adequately represent the demand for virtually all of contemporary French literature. The way toward an answer leads through two further questions: how did publishers publish books, and how did booksellers order them? Both concern crucial aspects of the book business in early modern Europe that distinguish it from publishing today.

The STN rarely published original editions, unless it was commissioned to do so by authors who covered the costs. It reprinted—or "pirated," as the original publishers would put it—books that were already selling well. In choosing them, it studied the market carefully and culled through information that it received every day from its vast network of correspondents. It also received advice about what to reprint from retail booksellers who gauged demand from their contact with individual consumers. Favarger passed on many recommendations about bestsellers, favorite genres, and the most popular authors after talking shop with the booksellers along his route. But the record of the STN's reprints provides only a small part of the information about demand that can be gleaned from its archives, because the full panoply of the works it marketed exceeded by far the output of its presses. When it printed an edition, usually at a run of about one thousand copies, it commonly traded a large proportion—one hundred or more copies—for an assortment of an equal number of books in the stock of one or more allied publishers. As explained in chapter 7, exchanges were usually calculated according to the total number of sheets involved in the trade; and when the STN selected an assortment from a partner in an exchange, it chose the books that it thought would sell best. The STN's dealings with Garrigan in Avignon and Mossy in Marseille illustrate the way the system worked, and those exchanges were small in scale compared with the regular swapping that went on between the STN and other Swiss houses, who cooperated as much as they competed, because each had a distribution network of its own. By carefully building up exchanges, the STN maximized the value and variety of its stock, and at the same time it minimized risk, because it could not be sure that an edition it printed would sell out or would sell rapidly enough to cover the investment of its capital. When a bookseller ordered a work that it did not have in stock, the STN often procured it by an ad hoc trade or a discount purchase with an allied publisher in Lausanne, Geneva, Bern, or Basel. Publishing as practiced by the major Swiss houses was therefore inseparable from wholesaling, and cooperation among the publisher-wholesalers meant that they could draw on a large corpus of literature, a virtual, floating stock, which was available to all of their allies. The catalogs of the Société typographique de Lausanne and the Société typographique de Berne were similar to those of the STN, and the STN's customers often remarked that they could procure the same books from many different suppliers, not only in Switzerland but also from *sociétés typographiques* as far away as Bouillon and Liège.[5]

The importance of exchanges in this publishing system has never been appreciated by historians except in the case of Germany, where it functioned as the primary means of marketing books until the late eighteenth century.[6] In Switzerland, it continued to be a vital force until the French Revolution, and it spilled over into Swiss relations with certain houses in Lyon, Avignon, Nîmes, Montpellier, Marseille, and several other cities, despite the transport costs. Of course, the Swiss wholesalers often competed for the business of the same retailers. Favarger crossed paths with sales reps of other publishers following the same circuit, and he learned in cities like Bourg-en-Bresse, Poitiers, and Orléans that only a few booksellers in each town could order books in large enough quantities to cover the shipping expenses. Nonetheless, most provincial markets usually could absorb the shipments of several suppliers, and the ubiquity of the exchanges favored the development of alliances among the Swiss houses. Sometimes they published books together, sharing costs and risks. Joint publications were especially effective in speculations on pirated editions, when it was crucial to beat other pirates to the market before the demand dried up. At various times the STN concluded formal treaties with the Société typographique de Lausanne and the Société typographique de Berne so that all three houses combined forces to pirate books systematically and on a large scale.[7]

The swapping and pirating arrangements meant that the STN built up a large and varied stock of books, although some were more important than others in the general pattern of its trade. It sold more copies of the books that it had printed than it did of the books that it procured by exchanges. In describing its business in its commercial correspondence, it distinguished between *livres de fonds* (its own editions) and *livres d'assortiment* (general stock), and it separated them in its account books, where each of its own editions had a separate account, in contrast to the exchanged books, which were grouped together in a *compte d'échanges* (also called *compte de changes*). In compiling the orders of the booksellers, it is important to keep this distinction in mind so as not to give too much weight to the STN's editions.[8] The statistical base will then be strong enough to support general conclusions, because the overall stock of the STN grew to be enormous by the mid-1770s. In 1773 it claimed, "There is no book of any importance that appears in France that we are not capable of supplying."[9] Its catalog of 1785 contained seven hundred titles, and an inventory of its warehouses in 1787 included fifteen hundred titles.

The broad range of the books supplied by the STN was in part a response to the way booksellers placed orders for them. Practices varied, of course, but close study of the STN's correspondence shows that the wholesale trade involved two distinct kinds of transactions: hit-or-miss orders from transitory customers and steady orders from regular customers. Just as Favarger carried catalogs and prospectuses in his saddlebags, the STN sent information about its offerings to hundreds of dealers. Most of them, attracted by a particular title or curious to try out the services of a new supplier, ordered only a few works and never developed regular commercial relations. They drew the bulk of their stock from other wholesalers, who offered better conditions or quicker shipping or had won a retailer's goodwill by years of reliable service. While dealing with these transitory customers as occasions arose, the STN built up its own network of regular clients, those featured in Favarger's list of his most important contacts. Their correspondence reveals a common tendency in the ordinary flow of the STN's business: when placing orders, retailers were cautious. They often arranged sales in advance with their own customers before committing themselves to purchase books from a foreign supplier; and rather than scattering orders among many suppliers, they usually restricted their trade to a few reliable houses. They tended to wait until they had accumulated enough items to group them in a single order. And they did not speculate on large shipments of one work unless they detected an unusual surge of demand. Instead, they ordered small numbers of many different books and later sent in new orders for those that continued to sell. As the widow of Charles-Antoine Charmet explained soon after his death when she took over their business in Besançon, "My husband's principle [in ordering] was to take many items and small numbers of each."[10] Returns did not exist in the eighteenth-century book trade. (In very rare cases, such as the liquidation of stock after a bankruptcy, books might be sold en commission, but those arrangements had no resemblance to the modern practice of returns.) Therefore, booksellers rarely ordered more than a dozen copies of a single title (by ordering a dozen they sometimes got a free thirteenth) and ordered enough titles to form a shipment large enough for them to take advantage of cheaper rates.

As mentioned everywhere in the STN's correspondence with its shipping agents, books were shipped unbound in bundles of sheets packed into bales; binding was normally arranged by individual customers and sometimes by retail booksellers. In accordance with state regulations, wagon drivers would not accept bales that weighed less than 50 pounds, and they often gave discounts for bulk shipments. Small shipments, sent in packages (*ballots* as opposed to *balles*) weighing less than 50 pounds, had to go by coach at a much higher price. The distinction between the wagon (*voiture*) and the coach (*carrosse*) was crucial in the book trade, because books had relatively low intrinsic value in relation to shipping costs. Also, the recipient normally had to pay for the shipping charges in cash upon delivery. The letters of booksellers—especially garrulous southerners like Mossy in Marseille and Boisserand in Avignon—read like an endless wail about the cost of shipping.

Booksellers sometimes played suppliers off against one another in order to extract the most favorable terms, but they also developed special relationships with particular publisher-wholesalers, who could be flexible about payments, give their orders priority, and offer occasional discounts. Instead of dispersing their business among many suppliers, therefore, they concentrated it among a few whom they could trust. Trust (*confiance*) was a key term in the book trade (and probably in early capitalism everywhere), owing to the need to avoid cheating. The tricks of the trade could be exploited endlessly by entrepreneurs who operated far away from the home territory of their victims. Some publishers announced that they were reprinting a book merely in order to see whether the demand was sufficient to justify an edition, while at the same time deterring a competitor from publishing it. Others put fabricated title pages on old texts and sold them as if they were new. And they often played favorites with their shipments so that some booksellers creamed off the demand before others in the same area received their copies.

Yet the publisher-wholesalers suffered more from abuses of confidence than the retailers, especially in the shadier branches of the trade. Once they had won the trust of the STN, marginal dealers like Malherbe of Loudun piled order upon order, until they drew most of their stock from Neuchâtel, always finding an excuse to avoid paying bills of exchange on the date of maturity.[11] On the other hand, some scrupulously honest retailers, such as Charmet of Besançon, also sent the bulk of their orders to the STN, because they preferred to draw large numbers of books from a single supplier whom they had known for many years and who had proved to be both reliable and flexible if difficulties arose. Either way, the accumulation of orders makes it possible to form a general idea of the business of a bookseller who traded regularly with the STN.

I emphasize this point because it bears on a critical decision about the best method for compiling statistics. It would be possible to work through all the accounts of the STN (beautifully kept registers called *journaux*, *brouillards*, and *mains courantes*) and to record the sale of every book to every customer. I considered this strategy when I began to study the STN's accounts along with its correspondence in 1965. It raised the prospect of tracing the diffusion of French literature everywhere in Europe. But closer examination showed that the results would be misleading. Although the STN corresponded with hundreds of booksellers located everywhere from Moscow to Naples and from Budapest to Dublin, most of its correspondents belonged to the class of transitory customers. They placed very few orders—often only one, "par essai," as they put it. A prospectus or a few titles in the STN's catalog would catch their eye, and they would make a trial purchase in order to assess the quality of the editions, the cost of transportation, and the time it took for the books to reach them. The great majority did not renew their orders, because they found that they could get better terms or quicker service from another supplier, usually one closer to home or one more firmly connected by ties of trust. Therefore, the STN often sold only a few copies of a particular book in a large area or an entire country, and the small number of copies that it managed to sell cannot be taken to typify the diffusion of that book or the trade of the bookseller who bought it. The irregular, hit-and-miss quality of the sales records makes it misleading to lump all of the sales together in an attempt to generalize about the dissemination of literature. Also, unfortunately, the data is too thin for one to reach conclusions about the general character of large markets such as Spain, Portugal, Denmark, Sweden, England, and Germany.

Consider the example of a great bestseller, Voltaire's *Candide*, reprinted many times after its first publication in 1759. The STN's accounts make it possible to plot every copy sold by the STN on a map of Europe, but the statistics are so trivial as to make the map useless.[12] Fourteen copies were sold to booksellers in Moscow and Saint Petersburg, and none at all were sold in Spain, Portugal, the Low Countries, Britain, and all of Scandinavia. Can one conclude that the demand for *Candide* was greater in Russia than in all those other countries combined and that it had ceased to exist in most of Western Europe during the years 1769–1789? Certainly not, because booksellers in those countries drew supplies from other publishers and wholesalers. Gabriel Cramer, Voltaire's publisher in Geneva, did a large trade in the Iberian Peninsula and probably sold many copies of *Candide* there, but one cannot know for sure, because all that survives from his papers is his *Grand livre*, or general account book, which mentions his customers but not the books they bought.[13] Voltaire exerted great influence on the cultural life of Berlin, thanks in large part to his relations with Frederick II; yet the STN did not sell a single copy of *Candide* there. By 1769, the book market in Berlin and all of northern Germany had fallen under the dominance of Philipp Erasmus Reich, the publisher who transformed the German trade,[14] but Reich never had any contact with the STN. In fact, it is very difficult to follow the STN's sales in Germany because most of them took place in the book fairs of Leipzig and Frankfurt from which they went to unknown destinations.[15] Moreover, the STN did not sell books at the fairs by itself but worked through middlemen such as Johann Jacob Flick and C. A. Serini of Basel and the Société typographique de Berne and Emmanuel Haller of Bern. The diffusion of the books left no trace in the STN's accounts. What the accounts do reveal is an extensive trade, especially by exchanges, between the STN and other Swiss houses, who then sold its books within their own commercial networks. The ultimate destination of those books, which represent at least a quarter of the STN's business, cannot be determined.

Many of the same problems apply to the study of the STN's sales in France, its largest market. Despite its efforts to open up a northwest passage to the Parisian area (explained in chapter 2), it never did much business in Paris, where the booksellers' guild, reinforced by the police, did everything possible to eliminate competition from foreign publishers who specialized in pirated editions. Provincial dealers were attracted by the STN's relatively cheap prices, but they often made a trial order to test the quality of the STN's editions or the effectiveness of its supply lines and never came back. A delay in the shipment or a large number of spoiled sheets (*défets*) was enough to dissuade them from establishing regular relations. Their names show up once or twice in the STN's account books and then disappear. The STN gradually built up a network of its own, of course, but the process was irregular and uneven, making it difficult to compare sales in one city with those in another. In fact, most of the STN's contacts with retailers did not lead to enough sales for one to sketch even a tentative profile of their trade. Only in exceptional cases, such as the sales of the quarto edition of the *Encyclopédie*, can one draw on the STN archives to follow the diffusion of a book geographically and sociologically.[16] And one cannot trace a large proportion of the STN's sales beyond its dealings with the middlemen in Geneva, Lausanne, Bern, and Basel. I see no way around a disappointing conclusion: any attempt to compile statistics by indiscriminately counting every sale recorded by the STN is bound to be fatally flawed. One attempt to follow this procedure, an online work titled *The French Book Trade in Enlightenment Europe, 1769–1794*, commits these and other errors. Although it contains some useful maps and bibliographical information, it does not succeed in studying diffusion.[17]

Instead of lumping all of the STN's transactions together, I have opted for a strategy of sampling, and I have combined qualitative with quantitative analysis. To gauge the extent to which the orders of a bookseller can be taken to represent his business, I found it necessary to compile an adequate number of them and also to read the letters in which they appear. Only by careful study of the correspondence can one reconstruct the context of the sales, the conditions that determined their limits, and the nature of the rapport between customer and supplier. Booksellers usually wrote terse, businesslike letters; but after they developed a trusted relationship (one based on reciprocal *confiance*) with the STN, they often interspersed their orders with personal remarks and reflections on the trade, as in the case of Charmet and his widow. Far from restricting themselves to business, their commercial correspondence then opens up a fresh view of life in provincial France, because in many cases one can follow booksellers at different stages of their careers—when they set up shop, fight off competitors, confront economic crises, and in some cases succumb to disease and death. Letters from neighbors and other merchants complete the picture. For all their homeliness—in fact, because of it—the letters make fascinating reading. Hundreds of them can be sampled on the website. If studied along with the statistics, one can get the feel of the book trade as it was embedded deep in the social order of the Ancien Régime.

Only a small minority of the dossiers in the STN archives offer such a rich view. I have selected eighteen of them and, with help from research assistants, have transcribed all of the booksellers' letters, identified the books they ordered, and tabulated the number of copies ordered for each title along with the number of orders and the dates of their occurrence. Whether a modest operation in a private home as in the case of Lair in Blois or a large enterprise with a printing shop such as Mossy's establishment in the arsenal of Marseille, each bookseller's business had its own character; yet the eighteen case studies conform to a general pattern. They provide a reliable indication of the demand for books over a large area of provincial France from the eastern provinces, down the Rhône Valley, across Provence and Languedoc, up the west coast to the Loire, along the Loire Valley to Burgundy, and back through the Franche-Comté to Neuchâtel. That was the itinerary followed by Favarger, and his reports, both in his correspondence and his diary, can be supplemented by the correspondence of the booksellers themselves. Therefore, it is possible to compare a horizontal view of the trade in 1778 with a vertical perspective derived from letters that extend from 1769 to 1789. I studied all the dossiers of all the STN's customers in the rest of France (and everywhere in Europe), but instead of attempting to extend the statistical sampling beyond Favarger's itinerary, I decided to concentrate on the parts of the archives where the documentation was densest.

By combining quantitative analysis with a critical reading of the correspondence, it is possible to make inferences about the sale as well as the demand for books. The orders of the eighteen booksellers correspond fairly well with the books they actually received, although the STN sometimes failed to supply some of the books ordered by a customer, because it did not have them in stock.[18] In those cases, however, the booksellers could procure copies of the missing books from other Swiss publisher-wholesalers, who sold the same works as those sold by the STN, owing to the frequency of exchanges. Therefore, the statistics drawn from the orders of the eighteen booksellers can be taken as a measure of the diffusion of books as well as a more accurate picture of the demand for them.

This argument may be convincing as far as it goes, but does it go far enough to support sound conclusions? In advancing it, I am aware of the deficiencies in the strategy I have just described, and I need to answer some potential objections.

In some cases, the statistical base may be dangerously thin. Among the eighteen booksellers in the sample, Constantin Lair of Blois ordered the smallest number of books—only thirty-four titles in all. He was a schoolmaster and small-time vintner who sold books as a sideline, but his letters indicate that he depended on the STN for all or most of his supplies. Despite the modest size of his orders, I have therefore included him in the sample to illustrate the business of a marginal dealer in the capillary sector of the book trade. Veteran professionals in large cities—Rigaud in Montpellier, for example, and Mossy in Marseille—placed regular, carefully calculated orders with the STN, but they also drew supplies from other publisher-wholesalers such as the Société typographique de Lausanne and the Société typographique de Berne. In order to form a general idea of the business of these other Swiss houses, I have studied their correspondence with the STN. Some of their dossiers are enormous,[19] and the constant flow of correspondence as well as exchanges among the publishers shows that they sold the same kinds of books and many of the same titles. Their catalogs, which are included in the letters, are also essentially the same. Retailers like Rigaud, Gaude, and Mossy often ordered the same book from two or three of the Swiss houses in order to be sure of receiving an adequate supply on time and to minimize the risk of confiscation by spreading the orders among several suppliers.

It would be incorrect, however, to claim that the STN archives are rich enough—rich as they are—to represent the trade of all the publishing houses in Switzerland. They contain only three letters from the important Genevan publisher Gabriel Cramer. Unlike the Neuchâtelois, he printed a great many original editions, especially of Voltaire's works. He never developed close contacts with the STN because he resented its pirating, notably when it reprinted his edition of Voltaire's *Questions sur l'Encyclopédie* behind his back (and with the complicity of Voltaire). Similarly, the STN did not trade extensively with Barthélémy de Felice in nearby Yverdon, probably because he built his business around his expurgated and expanded edition of the *Encyclopédie*, which competed with the STN's speculation on the quarto reprint produced in Geneva, Neuchâtel, and Lyon. The secondary literature on Swiss publishing contains a great deal of valuable information, but not enough to make systematic comparisons.[20]

It is therefore possible, although unlikely, that the business of other Swiss publishers differed substantially from that of the STN or that the Swiss trade as a whole had a different character from that of the Low Countries. But I have not found any indication of fundamental differences in studying the correspondence of Pierre Gosse Junior of The Hague, J. L. Boubers of Brussels, Clément Plomteux of Liège, and other publishers to the north of France.[21] When the directors of the STN made business trips through the Low Countries, they got a cool reception from most of the publishers they visited, because they were treated as rivals in the general struggle to sell the same kinds of books. The prevalence of piracy everywhere around France's borders meant that dozens of publisher-wholesalers competed to satisfy the demand on the same French markets. The flow of pirated works that reached France from the Netherlands via Rouen was probably very similar to the current that passed from Switzerland through Lyon.

I must hedge that assertion with a "probably," because I have no solid proof. But to support it, I would insist on another key characteristic that distinguished early modern publishing from publishing today. Today's bestsellers are produced by one publisher who sells many copies of the same work, usually by large reprints and sometimes by selling off the paperback rights. In the eighteenth century, bestsellers were produced by many publishers in many small editions (usually about one thousand copies) and sold on the same markets at the same time. That is why libraries now contain so many different versions of the same eighteenth-century works.

I have therefore concluded that my statistics provide an accurate measure of the STN's trade in France, though they represent only a sample of all the orders that it received. They cover 1,145 titles—that is, books ordered by the eighteen French booksellers between 1769 and 1789. Whether the sample serves as an indication of the French trade in general is a different matter. It is difficult to estimate the number of new works produced each year in France; but if one relies on the record of requests both for privileges and for tacit permissions (unsatisfactory sources, as they say nothing about print runs and sales, and do not even indicate whether the demand for a privilege was followed up with an actual edition), the total number of titles for the forty years from 1750 to 1789 comes to about 30,000. The annual output of new books, which did not vary greatly after 1767, came to about 750.[22] Therefore, one could estimate that the 1,145 titles in the STN sample were the equivalent of about 8 percent of the new legal works that appeared in France during the twenty years of the STN's existence. But the disparity of the sources—orders by booksellers on the one hand and requests for permissions to publish on the other—vitiates any attempt to calculate exact percentages and proportions. I think it preferable to rely on calculations made by the book professionals as they went about their business. In deciding which books to reprint, the STN judged what would sell best on the market as a whole; and in ordering books from the STN, the booksellers indicated what they thought would sell best in their local territory. The numbers attached to the 1,145 titles in the statistical tables are not meant to be precise, but they are also not random. They represent the judgment of experts who made it their business to satisfy demand as well as it could be perceived in the conditions of the eighteenth century.

The statistics show the demand for each of the 1,145 works, and they provide a rough profile of the trade of each of the eighteen booksellers. By aggregating them, it is possible to establish "bestseller" lists—that is, an indication of the books that were most in demand in the business of each bookseller and among all of them taken together. Of course, bestseller lists are often flawed today, owing to difficulties and deficiencies in sampling orders;[23] and one should not expect a great deal of precision in lists of books that circulated two and a half centuries ago. I can claim only that the lists and tables I have compiled provide the best available guide to the preferences among the French for the literature that was available to them in bookshops between 1769 and 1789.

Before offering an overview of the statistics, it is important to take account of three additional difficulties. First, the unevenness in the STN's business during those twenty years means that the volume of orders it received was not consistent. It did not develop an extensive trade in France until 1771; and after its shipments began reaching booksellers everywhere in the kingdom, it had to cope with the shifting measures of the French state: the temporary tax on book imports levied in 1772, the campaign against piracy decreed in the edicts of August 30, 1777, and the attempt to control book imports by subjecting them to inspection in the Paris *chambre syndicale* as required by Vergennes's order to the Ferme générale of June 12, 1783. The STN's correspondence with its smugglers—from Guillon in 1772 to Revol in 1778 and Faivre in 1783—shows that it found ways around the first two of these obstacles. But Vergennes's order caused permanent damage to its supply lines. Moreover, a general decline of the trade set in during the late 1770s, according to the testimony of the STN's most trustworthy correspondents—"solid" dealers like Gaude, Rigaud, Mossy, Bergeret, and Charmet. The theme of bankruptcy, present in so

many of the stories connected with Favarger's stops, suggests the serious-
ness of the situation. By the end of 1783, the STN itself faced bankruptcy.
It raised an emergency fund of capital, cut back on its expenses, and concentrated on selling off its stock rather than expanding its business with
new publications and exchanges. Therefore, the most revealing statistics
come from the period 1771–1784. Those covering the last five years of the
Ancien Régime are less reliable.

Second, some titles weigh more heavily than others in the statistics
based on the orders that the STN received. As mentioned, booksellers
often ordered what their customers had requested, and they also followed
their own instinct about what would sell, particularly when they learned
of new publications from their commercial correspondence and from advertisements in periodicals. But in placing orders, they commonly chose
from the works that appeared in the STN's catalogs, which it sent out
frequently to booksellers everywhere in France. A title from the STN
catalog tended to attract more orders than a title that did not appear in it,
just as the STN's own publications outweighed its *livres d'assortiment* in
the pattern of its trade. An analysis of the statistics should take account of
such factors, and it also may run into difficulties in interpreting the geographical distribution of the orders. If a bookseller in Marseille asked for
nearly the same books as one in Besançon, did the similarity derive from
the common character of the sources they consulted when they sent in
their orders—not only the STN's catalogs but also the prospectuses and
circular letters that it sent through the mail and the advertisements that
appeared in periodicals—or did the relatively wealthy and well-educated
elite who bought books have the same preferences in both cities, perhaps
even everywhere in France? I do not know, but I am struck by the lack of
a local flavor in most of the orders. One must allow for special cases, such
as the high demand for Protestant books in Nîmes, for medical treatises
in Montpellier, and for works on viticulture in Bordeaux. But it seems
likely that the same tastes, at least in the realm of contemporary literature,
prevailed everywhere in the upper ranks of society, despite the great
diversity in regional cultures.

Finally, I should point out that the statistics express a few characteristics that were peculiar to the trade of the STN. Although it did not specialize in any particular genre, it dealt heavily in Protestant works, and it
drew on networks of Huguenots to market them in France, especially in

cities like Nîmes and La Rochelle. It did not include many Catholic books in its stock (although at one point it offered to print a breviary for the Cistercians in Cîteaux). Therefore, the statistics give a rich picture of the demand for religious books among French Protestants, but not for religious literature in general. The STN did not carry some other kinds of literature—chapbooks, almanacs, various sorts of ephemera, professional manuals, and most varieties of textbooks. It sold a great many travel books and works aimed at children, although it did not specialize in those genres. Highly forbidden books, such as atheistic tracts, pornographic novels, and political libels, made up a fairly important portion of its business. But they, too, did not constitute a specialty of its trade. In response to the demand from booksellers, it procured them by arranging exchanges with marginal publishers like Jacques-Benjamin Téron and Gabriel Grasset of Geneva, who speculated in the most dangerous (and usually the most profitable) sector of the trade. Despite some of its own publications, such as d'Holbach's *Système de la nature* and Voltaire's *Questions sur l'Encyclopédie*, the STN did not particularly favor works of the Enlightenment philosophers. It carried a large assortment of ordinary books—"mid-list" works, as they are known today—and it invested heavily in bestsellers, or whatever it thought would sell best.

The diffusion of Enlightenment is an important theme in studies of the book trade, and it raises the question of whether personal outlook, taste, or ideological engagement determined the decisions of booksellers when they ordered books and of publishers when they chose what to print and what to exchange.[24] The case studies of the booksellers in the preceding pages demonstrate that their primary concern was to satisfy the demand of their customers. Favarger encountered only one bookseller, Gaudion of Arles, who refused to sell Protestant and Enlightenment works because he disapproved of them. Although booksellers often avoided ordering *livres philosophiques* because of the risk, they did not favor one variety of literature over another because of their personal preferences. The case of Couret de Villeneuve is especially revealing in this respect. His own publications demonstrate a strong attachment to Enlightenment ideals, yet his orders show that he did not request a large proportion of works by the philosophes. In the case of the STN's directors, the conclusion is even clearer. Nothing indicates that their principles, values, and attitudes differed substantially from those of their contemporaries. After reading thousands of their letters and studying their own writings (two of the founding partners of the STN, Frédéric-Samuel Ostervald and his son-in-law, Jean-Elie Bertrand, did not merely publish books; they also wrote them), one gets the impression that they were cultivated and rather conservative gentlemen, fairly typical of the elite in the Swiss principality of Neuchâtel and Valangin, which had governed itself under Prussian suzerainty since 1707. Everything I can discover about them suggests that their views corresponded in a general way to enlightened ideas but that they did not use their business to promote the Enlightenment or any other cause. Their primary goal was to make money, "the moving force of everything" (*le grand mobile de tout*), as they put it in their correspondence.[25]

They did not always succeed. In fact, their brush with bankruptcy in 1783 could be taken as evidence that they had a poor record in linking supply with demand. But their financial difficulties resulted from other factors, notably Vergennes's order of June 12, 1783. Therefore, even when it failed to fill them, the orders that the STN received from its customers constitute the best source for discovering what the demand for French literature actually was on the eve of the Revolution. By pointing out its deficiencies, I do not mean to discourage the study of the statistics. On the contrary, I want to make them available for others to analyze and criticize. There is, after all, a great deal at stake in this kind of research, not only for the understanding of pre-revolutionary France but also for the study of literature and of history in general.

This discussion of the conceptual and methodological problems is meant to clear the way for a presentation of the statistics. The following "bestseller" list—if this is not too anachronistic a term—shows the books that were most in demand. It excludes works that were published by the STN, because they weigh more heavily in the statistics than the books that came from the STN's general stock, which it built up by means of exchanges. (Of course, demand was the main consideration of the STN when it decided to reprint a book in the first place, and therefore a second "bestseller" list with the STN's publications as well as its *livres d'assortiment* can be consulted on the website.) The list favors Protestant works, which are set off by square brackets, because they represent a specialty of the STN rather than the demand of French readers as a whole. Aside from that exception, the list indicates the kinds of books that sold best on the literary marketplace. Each title is followed by a number representing the total copies from all the orders in the sample; that number can be taken to indicate the relative importance of the demand for the books, although, of course, it does not correspond to the total number of copies that actually existed.

[*Psaumes (Les) de David*, 2036]

Anecdotes sur Mme la comtesse du Barry by Mathieu-François Pidansat de Mairobert, 1001

An (L') deux mille quatre cent quarante: Rêve s'il en fût jamais by Louis-Sébastien Mercier, 691

Mémoire donné au roi par M. N. en 1778 sur l'administration provinciale by Jacques Necker, 367

Mémoires de l'abbé Terray: Contrôleur général: contenant sa vie, son administration, ses intrigues et sa chute by Jean-Baptiste-Louis Coquereau, 324

Journal historique de la révolution opérée dans la constitution de la monarchie française par M. de Maupeou by Mathieu-François Pidansat de Mairobert and Barthélémy-François-Joseph Mouffle d'Angerville, 294

Histoire philosophique et politique des établissements et du commerce des Européens dans les deux Indes by Guillaume-Thomas-François Raynal, 236

Abrégé des principes de la grammaire françoise, par Monsieur Restaut by Pierre Restaut, 231

Lectures pour les enfants, ou Choix de petits contes également propres à les amuser et à leur faire aimer la vertu, anonymous, 213

Apparat royal, ou nouveau dictionnaire françois et latin: Enrichi des façons de parler les plus élégantes en l'une et en l'autre langues: recueilli des meilleurs auteurs, et mis dans un ordre très-facile et très-méthodique pour la composition du françois en latin by Laurent-Etienne Rondet, 203

[*Abrégé de l'histoire sainte, et du catéchisme, retouché & augmenté pour l'usage des écoles de charité de Lausanne* by Jean-Frédéric Ostervald, 200]

Comédiens (Les) ou Le foyer, comédie en un acte et en prose by Jean-Jacques Rutledge, 200

Pucelle (La) d'Orléans, poème héroï-comique, en dix-huit chants by François-Marie Arouet dit Voltaire, 200

Recueil de comédies et de quelques chansons gaillardes, anonymous, 196

[*Prières pour tous les jours de la semaine, et sur divers sujets* by Bénédict Pictet, 182]

[*L'antiquité et perpétuité de la religion protestante* by Jean-Baptiste Renoult, 168]

Vie privée de Louis XV, ou Principaux événements, particularités et anecdotes de son règne by Barthélémy-François-Joseph Mouffle d'Angerville, 154

Paysan (Le) perverti ou les dangers de la ville: Histoire récente by Nicolas-Edme Restif de la Bretonne, 149

Homme (De l'), de ses facultés intellectuelles, et de son éducation: Ouvrage posthume d'Helvétius, Claude-Adrien Helvétius, 144

[*Sermons pour les fêtes de l'Eglise chrétienne, pour servir de suite aux Discours sur la morale Evangélique* by Elie Bertrand, 143]

Lettre d'un théologien à l'auteur du dictionnaire des Trois siècles littéraires by Jean Antoine Nicolas de Caritat, marquis de Condorcet, 143

[*Nourriture (La) de l'âme, ou Recueil de prières pour tous les jours de la semaine pour les principales fêtes de l'année et sur différents sujets intéressants* by Jean-Rodolphe Ostervald, 137]

Collection complète des oeuvres de Jean-Jacques Rousseau by Jean-Jacques Rousseau, 136

Lettres philosophiques by François-Marie Arouet de Voltaire, 130

[*Vrai (Le) communiant ou Traité de la Sainte Cène et des moyens d'y bien participer* by Daniel de Superville, 130]

Christianisme (Le) dévoilé, ou Examen des principes et des effets de la religion chrétienne by Paul-Henri-Dietrich Thiry, baron d'Holbach, 128

Voyage sentimental, par M. Sterne sous le nom d'Yorick, traduit de l'anglois by Laurence Sterne, 127

Amants (Les) républicains, ou Lettres de Nicias et Cynire by Jean-Pierre Bérenger, 127

Compère (Le) Mathieu ou les bigarrures de l'esprit humain by Henri-Joseph du Laurens, 124

Avis au peuple sur sa santé by Samuel-Auguste-André-David Tissot, 119

This list can be supplemented by the top books on the list of orders for works published by the STN or by the STN in collaboration with allied publishers. They include 161 copies, in addition to the 236 sold from its general stock, of Raynal's *Histoire philosophique*, which demonstrates that it certainly was one of the books most in demand—particularly when one takes into account that the STN's edition, printed in collaboration with Jean Abram Nouffer of Geneva, ran to ten volumes. Among the other STN editions most frequently ordered by booksellers were two of the most popular works by Louis-Sébastien Mercier, *Tableau de Paris* in four volumes (300 copies, of which the STN printed 274; editions by other publishers contained up to twelve volumes) and *Mon bonnet de nuit* (233 copies); the complete works of Claude-Joseph Dorat in nine volumes (320 copies); *Système de la nature* by Paul-Henri-Dietrich Thiry, baron d'Holbach (306 copies); *Les Incas* by Jean-François Marmontel (288 copies); and *Eléments d'histoire générale ancienne et moderne* in nine volumes by Claude-François Xavier Millot (218 copies).

Lists of titles can produce a dizzying effect, as if one were being drawn into a vortex of unmanageable data. How is it possible to keep one's bearings amid hundreds of orders for 1,145 titles, books that cover the entire range of contemporary literature? To cite a few dozen of the books that were ordered most often by the STN's most regular clients is hardly adequate. Aside from the obvious bias toward Protestant works, which appealed only to the minority of Huguenots in the French reading public and therefore have been eliminated from this analysis, the compilation of bestsellers can give misleading impressions in several ways. In order to arrive at a more nuanced view of literary demand, it is important to study the entire corpus of 1,145 titles, order by order and bookseller by bookseller. Having worked through this material many times, I have organized it schematically according to the following headings, which are intended to bring out its dominant characteristics—and anyone can challenge these conclusions by consulting the master list on the website robertdarnton.org.[26]

Scandalous Libels

The most surprising element in the bestseller list—or at least the cluster of titles that are most unfamiliar to readers today—is the prevalence of works that attacked Louis XV, his mistresses, and his ministers. As explained in the preceding chapters, which often mentioned the eagerness of booksellers to order them, they were published soon after the death of the king on May 10, 1774, and they were gobbled up by a public curious to learn the supposedly inside story about life in the secret corridors of

Versailles. Aside from their keyhole-peeping appeal, they had political implications, because they exposed corruption and abuses of power, which ran through the entire reign from 1715 to 1774, and they concentrated on the political crisis during the Maupeou ministry from 1771 to 1774, which broke the political power of the *parlements* and made the monarchy look like a despotism in the eyes of many contemporary observers. Many of these "*libelles*," as they were known, drew material from clandestine news-sheets, songs, and gossip written on scraps of paper, which circulated "under the cloak" before 1774 and then were recycled into pseudo-historical narratives afterward.[27]

When I first encountered this literature, which had been largely for-gotten, I concluded that it was a powerful ideological force during the pre-revolutionary years.[28] Having studied it more closely in the context of all the other orders, I must nuance that conclusion. One problem derives from the peculiar character of the orders placed by Malherbe of Loudun who specialized in forbidden books more heavily than any of the STN's other customers, and ordered a great many of them—far more than did well-established booksellers who rarely took risks on such highly illegal literature. In fact, the pattern of Malherbe's business looks so out-of-line when compared with that of the other booksellers that I was tempted to eliminate it from my sample. I retained it, because it represents the kind of literature diffused by a great many peddlers, and their trade must be taken into consideration if one wants to study the capillary system as well as the main channels of diffusion. But the excessive tendency in Malherbe's orders distorts the picture of the demand for libels.[29] His orders account for 278 of the total of 1,001 copies ordered for *Anecdotes sur Mme la comtesse du Barry*, the leading title on the "bestseller" list (except for various editions of the psalms, which were aimed at Huguenot readers). He also ordered 268 of the 324 copies of *Mémoires de l'abbé Terray* and 110 of the 294 copies of *Journal historique de la révolution opérée dans la constitution de la monarchie française par M. de Maupeou*. Of course, those books were much in demand among the more conventional and "solid" booksellers such as Rigaud in Montpellier, Mossy in Marseille, Bergeret in Bordeaux, and Charmet in Besançon. But another factor deserves to be taken into consideration: the dates of the orders. All of the libels related to Louis XV were ordered between November 8, 1774, and December 3, 1777, except for a large order for *Vie privée de Louis XV* by Charmet in 1781. Most of the orders for them were placed in 1775 and 1776. According to Charmet, the demand for this kind of literature had declined greatly by 1780. In light of this information, I would retreat from my earlier interpretation and would advance a more moderate conclusion: scandalous libels had a great shock appeal for French readers during the mid-1770s, but they did not dominate the demand for literature throughout the period 1769 to 1789, and they are somewhat overrepresented in my list of bestsellers.

Enlightenment Works

Books by the philosophes figure prominently on the bestseller list, and they look even more important if one studies the entire corpus of 1,145 titles. So many strains ran through the French Enlightenment that no selection of titles does it justice. But two philosophic works certainly deserve a place at the top of the bestseller list. Mercier's utopian novel, *L'An deux mille quatre cent quarante*, popularized the ideas of the philosophes, especially Rousseau, so effectively that booksellers constantly renewed their orders for it. Raynal's *Histoire philosophique*, which included important contributions by Diderot, offered readers an enormous compendium of Enlightenment themes, and to judge by the booksellers' orders as well as the large number of its editions, readers kept clamoring for it, especially after it was condemned by the *parlement* of Paris and burned by the public hangman on May 29, 1781.

Voltaire and Rousseau had well-earned places on the bestseller list—Voltaire for his scabrous and anticlerical *La Pucelle d'Orléans* and his famous *Lettres philosophiques*, Rousseau for various editions of his complete works. If one looks further into the master list of all the orders, the Voltairean strain turns out to be especially strong. The STN easily sold out its nine-volume edition of the *Questions sur l'Encyclopédie*, and it received orders for more than two dozen of his other works, so many orders for such a wide variety of publications—novels, histories, poems, plays, essays, miscellanies, and polemical tracts—that their combined effect demonstrated a large demand for the moderate kind of Enlightenment that Voltaire embodied. Taken together, they represent a coherent set of themes: a commitment to toleration, rationalism, anticlericalism, deism, and principles of justice and liberty that deviated from the dominant values of the Ancien Régime but did not challenge the hierarchical order of society or the authority of the king.

The STN threw itself into the struggle to acquire the manuscript of Rousseau's *Confessions* and his other unpublished works after his death in 1778, but it failed. Still, it managed to procure them from other publishers, and its clients clamored for them. It received orders for ninety-eight copies of Rousseau's *Oeuvres posthumes*, 129 copies of the *Confessions*, and 136 copies of various editions of his complete works. It received orders for only four separate copies of *Du Contrat social* and for six of *Emile*, although both books were included in the editions of the collected works that sold so briskly. Furthermore, the Rousseauistic strain in the orders showed through other publications, such as the writings of Mercier and Antoine Servan's *Réflexions sur les Confessions de J.-J. Rousseau.*

The more radical, atheistic strain in the Enlightenment occupied a subordinate but significant place in the pattern of the orders. Here, too, however, one must allow for the distortion created from the books requested by Malherbe. He invested heavily in the most extreme *livres philosophiques*. In the case of *De l'homme*, the materialist treatise by Helvétius, his orders account for all but six of the 144 copies ordered, and therefore I would not consider it a true bestseller. Malherbe also ordered fifty of the total of 128 copies of d'Holbach's *Le Christianisme dévoilé*, another work on the bestseller list. And in the case of d'Holbach's *Systéme de la nature*, the only atheistic work published by the STN, Malherbe's orders made up 230 of the 306 copies in the total orders of the sample. Prominent booksellers such as Rigaud, Pavie, Robert et Gauthier, and Charmet placed many orders for these last two books, but not enough to suggest that outright atheism had a strong appeal for French readers.

Among the radically anti-Christian works, the most outspoken, sixteen in all and all of them anonymous, came from the circle of the baron d'Holbach.[30] The total number of orders looks impressive, but as in the case of *Le Christianisme dévoilé*, a large proportion of them were sent by Malherbe, who made a specialty of selling such literature. If one subtracts his orders from each title, the total number of copies of the Holbachean works that were ordered comes to 179, far less than for the works of Voltaire and Rousseau.[31] Malherbe also ordered most of the copies of books by Helvétius: *De l'Esprit* and *Le Bonheur* in addition to *De l'homme*. His share was somewhat smaller in the orders for one of the most notorious of the irreligious tracts, *Traité des trois imposteurs*: sixteen of the total of fifty-one copies. All in all, this extreme variety of anti-Christian philosophy was much less pervasive than the anticlericalism that permeated a great deal of fiction as well as the works of Voltaire.

Books by other philosophes, such as Montesquieu, Diderot, and Condorcet, appear scattered among the orders but not in large numbers. Condillac's *Cours d'études pour l'instruction du prince de Parme* deserves special mention, because it covered such a wide range of Enlightenment ideas on such a large scale: thirteen volumes, which were ordered by many booksellers in small quantities, amounting to twenty-eight copies in all. The *Encyclopédie*, which came to be considered as the bible of the Enlightenment, brought together a much greater fund of material compiled into thirty-six volumes in its quarto edition. It was a spectacular bestseller, but it does not have a place on the above list, because the orders for it went to an international consortium of publishers. As a member of the consortium, the STN collected a great many subscriptions for the quarto edition, but it forwarded them to the headquarters of the enterprise in Lyon.[32]

Multivolume works such as the *Encyclopédie*, Condillac's *Cours d'etudes*, and Raynal's *Histoire philosophique* represented a much greater investment than a relatively slim volume like Mercier's *L'An deux mille quatre cent quarante*. It is important to take disparities in size and cost into account when making comparisons. Therefore, the demand for Enlightenment literature looks quite impressive when one considers orders for the complete works of individual philosophes. As already mentioned, the total number of copies in orders for the works of Rousseau came to 236, including ninety-eight orders for the *Oeuvres posthumes* published after his death in 1778. For Montesquieu's works the total was thirty-three; for Diderot's works, twenty-five; and for the works of Jean-François Marmontel, fifty-six. Marmontel belonged to the later generation of philosophes, and he had gained a reputation as a prominent man of letters during the time of the STN's activity, whereas Montesquieu had been dead for fourteen years before the STN was founded. The market for many important books probably had been sated by the time it went into business, and its business favored current literature. An analysis of all the orders for complete works[33] shows one case of strong demand for the works of an author who had long been dead: Molière, whose continued popularity is indicated by orders for a total of seventy-four copies. Yet they were dwarfed by orders for the complete works of popular contemporary writers: a total of 331 copies for

Collection complète des oeuvres de M. Dorat and 121 copies of *Collection complète des oeuvres de Madame Riccoboni*. Claude-Joseph Dorat and Marie-Jeanne Laboras de Mézières, known as Madame Riccoboni, along with François-Thomas-Marie de Baculard d'Arnaud, were authors of books that sold best in the 1770s and 1780s, although they have been almost completely forgotten today. That consideration also applies to the following category.

General Fiction

The bestseller list includes a few novels that have survived the erosion of taste over the centuries and still occupy a place in histories of French literature: *Le Paysan perverti ou les dangers de la ville* by Nicolas-Edme Restif de la Bretonne and *Voyage sentimental* by Laurence Sterne, whose writing, in various translations, did well on the French market. If the STN's own editions are taken into consideration, the bestsellers include two other well-known novels, *Les Incas, ou la destruction de l'empire du Pérou* by Marmontel and *Les Liaisons dangereuses* by Pierre Choderlos de Laclos. With the exception of Laclos, these authors also wrote other novels that were much in demand. Marmontel's *Bélisaire*, Rétif's *Le Nouvel Abelard*, and Sterne's *La Vie et les opinions de Tristram Shandy* as well as his *Lettres de Yorick à Eliza* have quite strong numbers on the master list of all the orders. Yet the orders for them were small in comparison with sentimental novels whose popularity can be gauged, in a very approximate manner, according to the total number of copies ordered:

Les Epreuves du sentiment by Baculard d'Arnaud: 150 copies
Cécilia, ou Mémoire d'une héritière by Fanny Burney: 145 copies
Les Malheurs de l'inconstance by Dorat: 115 copies
Adèle et Théodore by Mme de Genlis: 95 copies
La Fille naturelle by Restif de la Bretonne: 88 copies
Les Sacrifices de l'amour by Dorat: 82 copies
Mémoires de Fanny Spingler by Madame Beccary (pseudonym): 57 copies

These statistics provide only a rough indication of the demand, because the numbers, compiled from orders of eighteen booksellers, compose a small sample of all the literature in circulation. Taken together, however, they indicate a preference in the reading public for sentimental and moralistic narratives, featuring romantic intrigues, suffering heroines, and various shades of pathos. They summon up the novels of Samuel Richardson (and to a lesser extent Rousseau) rather than the *contes* of Voltaire, whose works figured most strongly in the nonfiction sectors of the market. Several of these novels were set in England or adopted a tone of *sensiblerie* with an English accent. The STN's customers did not order a great deal of Richardson in translation,[34] although they often requested Goldsmith's *Histoire de François Wills*. But they particularly favored the epistolary novels of Mme Riccoboni, which featured English heroines—*Lettres de mistriss Fanni Butler*, *Lettres de Milady Juliette Catesby*, and *Histoire de Miss Jenny*—in various editions of her collected works. Sentiment and moralizing also characterized the novellas or *contes* that booksellers frequently ordered: Marmontel's *Contes moraux* and *Contes moraux et nouvelles idylles* by Salomon Gessner and Diderot, who was a great admirer of Richardson.

Among other genres of fiction, the STN sold a large number of plays, almost entirely by contemporary authors, except for Molière and, in smaller number, Racine. The largest demand came for its editions of the works of Caroline-Stéphanie-Félicité du Crest de Saint-Aubin, comtesse de Genlis—her *Théâtre de société* and especially her *Théâtre à l'usage des jeunes personnes*. The demand for the *Théâtre complet de Voltaire* was paltry in comparison, although readers had access to his plays in the numerous editions of his complete works. Beaumarchais's *Le Barbier de Séville* had a prominent place among the orders (the STN had cut back on its business before the publication in 1785 of *Le Mariage de Figaro*), as did two plays by Mercier, *La Mort de Louis XI* and *La Brouette du vinaigrier*. But Mercier's other plays, many published by the STN, did not attract a large number of orders, particularly if compared with his novel *Jezzenemours*, which he described in its subtitle as a "*roman dramatique.*" The STN marketed relatively little poetry, but it received substantial orders for Voltaire's epic, *La Henriade*, and for its edition of *Les Jardins* by Jacques Delille. Also, its literary offerings included a few classics and works from the seventeenth century. Those most in demand were the *Fables* and *Contes of La Fontaine*, *Sentences et maximes de morale* by la Rochefoucauld, Bayle's *Dictionnaire historique et critique*, and *L'Eloge de la folie* by Erasmus. Because the STN's trade concentrated so heavily in contemporary literature, one should not be surprised that it received few orders for

Montaigne's *Essais* and Pascal's *Les Provinciales*, or for French editions of Cervantes and Shakespeare.

Finally, one should take note of what today would be called pornography. That term did not exist in the eighteenth century, although Restif de la Bretonne titled one of his books *Le Pornographe, ou Idées d'un honnête homme sur un projet de règlement pour les prostituées*.[35] Eighteenth-century narratives often interspersed erotic motifs with philosophical, political, and especially anticlerical themes in a way that now would seem peculiar. Eroticism runs through many of the greatest works of the Enlightenment such as *Lettres persanes*, *Candide*, and *Le Rêve de d'Alembert*. Bawdy verse appeared in popular compilations like *Recueil de comédies et de quelques chansons gaillardes* and *La Lyre gaillarde*. And scandalous libels often included bedroom scenes in their attempts to provide inside views of the lives of the great. In contrast to such incidental use of sexual material, a subset of the *livres philosophiques* stood out by their obvious appeal to prurience. Those most ordered were the following:[36] *La Putain errante, ou dialogue de Madeleine et Julie* usually attributed to Niccolò Franco, *L'Ecole des filles* by Michel Milot; *Vénus dans le cloître* by Jean Barrin; *La Fille de joie*, a translation of John Cleland's *Fanny Hill: Memoirs of a Woman of Pleasure*; and *Histoire de la tourière des Carmélites* by Anne-Gabriel Meusnier de Querlon. The numbers are too small to provide a precise index to demand, and they may under-represent the staying power of older favorites such as *Histoire de Dom B . . . ., portier des Chartreux*, usually attributed to Jean-Charles Gervaise de Latouche, and *L'Académie des dames* by Nicolas Chorier. Pornography, or something approximating it, occupied a special sector on the marketplace for books, but it was relatively unimportant, especially if compared with the genres of nonfiction that made up the bulk of the STN's business.

Travel Literature

Accounts of journeys to remote destinations constituted a genre that had particular appeal to readers in the eighteenth century and that has since receded in importance. Travel literature played on the public's fascination with exotic parts of the globe at a time when global connections began to determine the course of political and economic affairs in Europe. The discovery of peoples and parts of the world that had been entirely unknown made the adventures of James Cook, Louis Antoine, comte Bougainville, and Jean-François de Galaup, comte de La Peyrouse at least as gripping as reports of missions in outer space today—far more, in all likelihood, because each voyage was a series of adventures with a strong human component. All the explorers faced extraordinary dangers. The greatest of them, Cook, died heroically at the hands of strange creatures, described as cannibals and savages in the accounts of his travels. La Peyrouse disappeared mysteriously somewhere in the vast reaches of the Pacific and Indian oceans while on a round-the-world trip packed with colorful episodes. On an earlier voyage around the world, Bougainville encountered an extraordinary civilization of Tahitians, whose casual practices of sex made great reading, especially when worked into fiction by Diderot in *Supplément au Voyage de Bougainville*. There was an important scientific element in travel narratives: information about botany, geography, astronomy, and navigation, including technological details about subjects such as the problem of determining longitude. Accounts of travels in Europe, several derived from the grand tours of Englishmen, often featured discussions of art and architecture. Journeys to the mid-East and Far East tended to dwell on the exotic mores of the natives, feeding into what would eventually emerge as anthropology. Something of everything could be found in this literature, and the STN received a great many orders for it.

In the STN's large offerings on travel literature, Bougainville's *Voyage autour du monde* attracted the most orders. Different versions of Cook's travels sold well, although the STN failed to capitalize on the first wave of enthusiasm for them. The travel book ordered most often was the STN's edition of *Voyage en Sicile et à Malte*, a grand tour narrative by Patrick Brydone. The other translations of English travel books that had the most appeal were *Lettres d'un voyageur anglais sur la France, la Suisse, l'Allemagne et l'Italie* by John Moore and *Lettres d'un voyageur anglais* by Martin Sherlock. Next among the most ordered accounts of travels were *Voyages dans les Indes orientales* by John Nicolas Niecamp; *Voyage à l'Isle de France, à l'Isle de Bourbon, au Cap de Bonne Espérance, etc.* by Jacques-Henri Bernardin de Saint-Pierre; *Voyage pittoresque aux glacières de Savoye* by André-César Bordier; and *Voyage dans les mers de l'Inde* by G.-J.-H.-J.-B. Legentil de la Galaisière, which contained an account of his failed attempts to observe the transit of Venus in order to measure the distance between the sun and the earth. Among the other specifically scientific travel books, one should mention *Voyage minéralogique et physique, de Bruxelles à Lausanne* by the Russian geologist and botanist Grégoire de Razoumowsky, and among the more strictly aesthetic works, *Voyage d'Italie, ou recueil de notes sur les ouvrages de peinture et de sculpture qu'on voit dans les principales villes d'Italie* by the great engraver Charles-Nicolas Cochin.

History and Geography

Travel books shaded off into history and geography, as in *Histoire des découvertes faites par divers savants voyageurs dans plusieurs contrées de la Russie et de la Perse* by Pierre-Simon Pallas, which was much in demand. Standard geographical treatises like Anton Friedrich Büsching's *Introduction à la connaissance géographique et politique des états de l'Europe* were also wide-ranging and attracted many orders, and a similar emphasis on broad themes characterized the best-selling history books. One of the top bestsellers, Raynal's *Histoire philosophique et politique des établissements et du commerce des Européens dans les deux Indes*, incorporated history in a "philosophical" survey of so many subjects that it rivaled the *Encyclopédie* as a vehicle for the ideas of the Enlightenment.

The STN published several more strictly historical works, especially those of Claude-François-Xavier Millot, a prolific popularizer, who rose through the ranks of the clergy and enjoyed some eminence as a member of the Académie française. Although he admired Montesquieu, Millot did not infuse much philosophy into his straightforward surveys. Among his works, the book that received the most orders by far was his nine-volume *Eléments d'histoire générale ancienne et moderne*, which the STN printed in 1775 and then reprinted in 1778 in association with the Société typographique de Lausanne. It received few orders for its editions of Millot's other books, *Eléments de l'histoire de l'Angleterre* and *Eléments de l'histoire de France depuis Clovis jusqu'à Louis XV*. Two general histories that were more in demand and that the STN sold from its general stock were *Histoire de France* by Paul-François Velly and *Abrégé de l'histoire ancienne de Monsieur Rollin*, an abridged version of Charles Rollin's *Histoire romaine*, which it also sold, though not in large number, as a separate publication. Taken together with the works of Millot, they represent a fairly orthodox view of the past. But another STN publication, William Robertson's four-volume *Histoire de l'Amérique*, belonged to the mainstream of the Scottish Enlightenment. It capitalized on the French fascination with the new American republic and sold very well. David Hume's *Histoire d'Angleterre* did not attract many orders, nor did the historical writings of Voltaire—not *Le Siècle de Louis XIV*, nor *Essai sur les moeurs*, nor *Histoire de Charles XII*. Only his polemical *Histoire du parlement de Paris* attracted a good many orders. The STN also received fairly substantial orders for histories of individual cities such as Bordeaux and La Rochelle and a few for countries like Poland that figured prominently in current affairs. Historical works certainly had a great appeal for the STN's customers, especially if they are considered in connection with the related subjects of travel and geography. Those subjects along with general fiction and Enlightenment tracts formed the core of the works most in demand. But the STN sold a wide variety of other books, which also should be taken into consideration if one wants to get an adequate view of the marketplace for literature.

Science and Medicine

With some exceptions such as physics, the natural sciences did not occupy a clearly demarcated position in the world of learning during the eighteenth century. Fields such as botany and zoology belonged to the vague general category of natural history. Although chemistry was emerging as a rigorous discipline, geology remained in a formative stage, and a large body of writing about agronomy and enology often took the form of self-help manuals rather than systematic theory. Above all, the enormous literature on medicine often utilized concepts such as humors and elements that went back to the Middle Ages and antiquity. Nowhere is the danger of anachronism greater than in considering works that belong to the history of science yet lacked the logic and experimental rigor that prevails today in scientific writing.

Some of the scientific works expressed a conviction at the heart of Enlightenment thought—namely, that prejudice could be dispelled by the sheer force of reason; thus *Réflexions d'un homme de bon sens sur les comètes et sur leur retour, ou Préservatif contre la peur* by the Swiss pastor and naturalist Jonas de Gélieu, which derived from Pierre Bayle's *Pensées diverses sur l'occasion de la comète* of 1682. The writings of Lazzaro Spallanzani communicated a respect for experimental methodology, although they did not attract many orders in comparison with the *Dictionnaire de chimie* by Pierre-Joseph Macquer, who is known for advocating the notion of chemical affinity in opposition to the more rigorous theories of Antoine Lavoisier. The scientific work that received the most orders was the twelve-volume *Dictionnaire raisonné universel d'histoire naturelle* by Jacques-Christophe Valmont de Bomare, an eminent naturalist who had close ties with the *Encyclopédistes*.[37]

Among the works on applied science, the demand was greatest for tracts on viticulture, especially those by "Agronome" Maupin (his first name is unknown), who wrote dozens of short books and pamphlets.[38] They outdid the demand for the more serious treatise, *Les Principes de l'agriculture et de la végétation*, by Francis Home, an important figure in the Scottish Enlightenment. Medicine attracted more orders than any other branch of science, and within the medical literature the most orders by far came for the popular works of Samuel-Auguste-André-David Tissot, particularly his *Avis au people sur sa santé*. Bleeding and purging remained standard treatments of disease, as Favarger testified in discussing his case of scabies. But the traditional approaches to medicine, enshrined in the medical faculty of the University of Paris, underwent many attacks, especially from the vitalistic school in the faculty of Montpellier, and the STN tried to make the most of the polemics in its edition of Jean-Emmanuel Gilibert's *L'Anarchie médicinale ou la médecine considérée comme nuisible à la société*, which, however, did not attract a particularly large number of orders. Gynecology and venereal disease stood out among the other medical works that were most in demand,[39] and veterinary science accounted for a modest number of orders.[40]

Dictionaries, Reference Works, and Self-Help Manuals

Popular science overlapped with the heterogeneous category of reference works and related literature. Booksellers ordered several primers on mathematics,[41] and they favored guidebooks on subjects as varied as horsemanship, German, and letter writing.[42] Self-help manuals on reading and writing offered down-to-earth instruction on spelling and grammar, while the more advanced variety added advice about manners and how to behave in high society.[43] The orders for dictionaries included the *Dictionnaire de l'Académie française*, which the STN acquired in large number by exchanges with the publishers that Favarger met in Avignon and Nîmes. It also received a steady stream of orders for dictionaries of Latin, German, and Italian. Of course, Diderot's *Encyclopédie* was first and foremost a reference work. And by adopting an alphabetical order, many of Voltaire's tracts gave the impression of compendia that readers could consult for information. Information, instruction, and self-improvement all belonged to this general variety of literature, which was high in demand.

Children's Literature

The STN offered what may seem to be a surprisingly large assortment of books for children, and its clients avidly ordered them. Following in the wake of *Emile*—which did not sell well as a separate work, perhaps because the market was already sated—they adopted a moralistic tone. The book most in demand was an anonymous anthology, which attached moral lessons to simple tales, *Lectures pour les enfants, ou choix de petits contes également propres à les amuser et à leur faire aimer la vertu*. Two authors stood out among the specialists in this genre, lending a somewhat aristocratic flavor to the all-pervasive sentimentality: Stéphanie Félicité du Crest de Saint-Aubin, comtesse de Genlis and Jeanne-Marie Leprince de Beaumont. The STN published two of Mme de Genlis's best-selling works, *Théâtre à l'usage des jeunes personnes* in four volumes and *Théâtre de société* in two volumes, and it did a brisk trade in two others, *Adèle et Théodore, ou Lettres sur l'éducation* and *Annales de la vertu, ou Cours d'histoire à l'usage des jeunes personnes*. It published an edition of Mme Leprince de Beaumont's *Magasin des enfants* and received many orders for four of her other works.[44] Similar books by less well-known authors such as Abraham Tremblay were also much in demand.[45] If considered together with the STN's small stock of schoolbooks,[46] they indicate a vogue for children's literature, which may have corresponded to a new attitude toward childhood in general.[47]

Law and Political Theory

Although the STN did not deal in what we would call professional textbooks, it received many orders for works on political theory and law. It published three editions of Emer de Vattel's *Le Droit des gens, ou Principes de la loi naturelle*, a standard work on natural law and international relations, which was much in demand. Two other well-known treatises on natural law also attracted orders but in smaller numbers: Jean-Jacques Burlamaqui's *Eléments du droit naturel*, a straightforward and widely used account of the normative principles behind statecraft, and *Le Droit de la nature et des gens* by Samuel von Pufendorf, the seventeenth-century German philosopher who became the leading exponent of the natural law theory developed earlier by Hugo Grotius. Although these treatises are rarely read today, they had a great impact on political thinkers and statesmen during the eighteenth century, notably Jean-Jacques Rousseau and the Founding Fathers of the American republic. Although Favarger encountered interest in the American Revolution nearly everywhere he went, he did not detect a great demand for books about it, and the STN received only two dozen orders for *Recueil des lois constitutives des colonies anglaises, confédérées sous la domination d'Etats-Unis de l'Amérique septentrionale.*[48] But booksellers sent in many orders for Adam Smith's *Fragments sur les colonies en général et sur celles des Anglais en particulier.*

Among treatises on politics, the STN received a surprisingly large number of orders for quite radical works, including some by d'Holbach: *La Politique naturelle, ou discours sur les vrais principes du gouvernement* and *Système social, ou principes naturels de la morale et de la politique.*[49] The orders showed a great demand for *De la Législation, ou principes des lois*, by Gabriel Bonnot de Mably, a friend of Rousseau, whose theoretical antagonism to private property has earned him a place among the forerunners of modern socialism. A small demand also existed for *Code de la nature*, a proto-socialist utopia commonly attributed to Etienne-Gabriel Morelly. Mirabeau's denunciation of arbitrary government, *Essai sur le despotisme*, attracted many orders, as did the treatise on criminology by César Beccaria, *Des Délits et des peines*, a favorite work of the philosophes. Criminal law lent itself to enlightened philosophizing and attracted a fair amount of orders, particularly for the reformist tracts of Joseph-Michel-Antoine Servan, the prominent attorney general in the *parlement* of Grenoble.[50]

Politics and Current Events

The STN did not carry many works directly connected with political affairs, except in one case: the polemics by and about Jacques Necker, director-general of Finances in the French government from 1777 to 1781. As recounted in chapter 12, the STN scrambled to meet the demand for the pamphlets stirred up by Necker's measures, although it did not print any of them. Necker stoked the debate by his own writings, especially *Compte rendu au roi* and *Mémoire donné au roi par M. N. en 1778 sur l'administration provinciale.* The STN received a great many orders for them and, in smaller number, for the popular anthology, *Collection complète de tous les ouvrages pour et contre M. Necker.* It also tapped the demand in another pamphlet war, which had political implications. When Beaumarchais became entangled in a legal case against Louis Valentin de Goezman, a judge in the *parlement* created by Chancellor Maupeou, he defended himself in a series of judicial memoirs, which were masterpieces of polemical writing. By ridiculing Goezman, they helped turn public opinion against Maupeou's ministry and its attempt to destroy the old Parlement of Paris as a break on the power of the king. They sold very well among the topical works in the STN's stock.[51] So did the writings of another master polemicist, Simon-Nicolas-Henri Linguet, including his powerful *Mémoires sur la Bastille.*[52]

The only other works that had political implications were journalistic compilations that were printed in book form and contained a little of everything related to current events. Some included enough defamatory material about courtiers and ministers to rank with libels among the most dangerous of the *livres philosophiques*—and the ones ordered most often by marginal dealers like Caldesaigues and Malherbe. *L'Espion anglais, ou Correspondance secrète entre mylord All'eye et mylord All'ear* and *Le Gazetier cuirassé* stood out in the demand for these works. They, too, concentrated on abuses of power under the Maupeou ministry, whereas other chronicles strayed into other kinds of scandal, particularly sex. Thus the work that epitomized the genre but did not figure in many orders: *La Chronique scandaleuse.* Naughty miscellanies, full of gossip; anticlerical anecdotes; the wicked ways of actresses; revelations about the private lives of public figures; and occasional protests about the abuse of governmental power were more in demand, among them *L'Arrétin moderne* and *La Chandelle d'Arras* by Henri-Joseph Du Laurens and supposed reports of spies and foreign observers such as *L'Espion chinois* by Ange Goudar and *Mémoires turcs* by Claude Godard d'Aucourt. *Mémoires secrets pour servir à l'histoire de la république des lettres en France*, the longest such compilation and the one that has attracted the most attention from historians, did not elicit a great many orders from the booksellers.[53]

Freemasonry and Magic

A final category of publications includes works at the furthest remove from the interests of readers today: revelations about the activities of freemasons and recipes for performing magic. Although the masonic orders went back to the seventeenth century, they spread everywhere in the eighteenth century and fascinated a public eager to learn about their secret rituals and organization. They were not severely repressed by the authorities in charge of the book trade, but they did not circulate legally, and they had some of the attraction of the taboo. The books ordered most were *Les plus secrets mystères des hauts grades de la maçonnerie dévoilés* by Carl Friedrich Koeppen, *Abrégé de l'histoire de la franche-maçonnerie* by Joseph-Jérôme le François de Lalande, and *L'Adoption, ou la maçonnerie des femmes* by Guillaume de Saint-Victor.[54]

Sensational revelations and secrets about magic had a similar appeal. Several of them were attributed to the supposed alchemical writings of the medieval philosopher and theologian Albertus Magnus, brought up to date and vulgarized under titles like *Le Grand Albert* and *Le Petit Albert*, and to the sixteenth-century polymath Cornelius Agrippa. The most popular among the orders received by the STN were *L'Albert moderne* by Pons-Augustin Alletz, *Secrets merveilleux de la magie naturelle et cabalistique du Petit Albert* by Alberti Parvi, and the anonymous *Le Grand Oeuvre dévoilé*.

Such, in broad outline, was the demand for literature in the last years of the Ancien Régime. Pick up the novels by Mme Riccoboni, the accounts of Bougainville's travels, the *Histoire philosophique* of abbé Raynal, or the dictionary of natural history by Valmont de Bomare, and you will be transported into another world: the world of books that existed more than two centuries ago.

Conclusion

Lived Literature

BY FOLLOWING A SALES REP AROUND THE KINGDOM in 1778, I have tried to show how books reached readers; and by studying the correspondence of booksellers between 1769 and 1789, I have attempted to demonstrate what those books were—that is, to delineate the general character of the literature that circulated in France during the last decades of the Ancien Régime. Far from being exhaustive, this approach to literature leaves out what could be considered its most important aspects: creation and reception. I would not contest the importance of studying those subjects, far from it. But I have limited this investigation to an aspect of literature that can be examined from an unfamiliar viewpoint—at street level, where wagonloads of books rumbled across the country, and from within bookshops, where booksellers provided the link between production and consumption. By concentrating on such subjects, it is possible to come up with solid conclusions about the diffusion of literature, although not to answer a crucial question: what was it to "consume" books more than two centuries ago? The lived experience of literature—*la littérature vécue*—is essentially a matter of reading, and readers, alas, do not figure prominently in this story.

They appear here and there, often enough for one to form a general idea of the reading public. Judging from references in the booksellers' letters and from exceptional documents like the bankruptcy papers of Robert et Gauthier, it was composed of mixed groups in the upper and middle ranges of society: noblemen, magistrates, administrative officials, military officers, clergymen, lawyers, doctors, merchants, well-off landowners in the country, and perhaps some relatively wealthy tradesmen in towns and cities. What went on in those people's heads when they read books remains a mystery. Recent attempts to reconstruct the history of reading have made important advances, but they keep stumbling into great gaps in the available information.[1] Despite suggestive margin notes, commonplace books, diary entries, and other documents scattered through archives, they do not draw on enough evidence to sustain a general interpretation. We are reduced to case studies, many of them masterful but none aligned in such a way as to provide a clear path through the past.

Although we have not solved the problem of how people read, we can know what they read. Close study of the business of booksellers shows what books fared best on particular markets, city by city. The results can be combined in a panoramic view of the literary marketplace—and even in a retrospective bestseller list. Of course, the list should not be taken literally. It provides a general guide to the books that were most in demand, not a precise measure of the rank of individual works, and it concerns publications currently on the marketplace, not books that had been accumulated over the years in libraries. The preference of readers for the latest novel by Madame Riccoboni does not mean that they had lost interest in the novels of Mme de La Fayette published a century earlier, to say nothing of all the classics going back to antiquity, which formed the basis of the culture inherited by the educated elite. Religious books, from breviaries to theological tracts, also were a staple in many readers' diets. While concentrating on Protestant works, the STN marketed relatively few books that appealed to Catholics, yet at one time or another most of the consumers it supplied probably had come across *L'Imitation de Jésus-Christ*, which had gone through more than two thousand editions since its publication in the fifteenth century.

However approximate, the quantitative information can be supplemented by a close reading of the booksellers' correspondence. While ordering supplies, they engaged in a constant dialogue with the STN about the state of the market, prospective editions, competing *nouveautés*, favorite authors, gossip about colleagues, and everything else that belonged to the shoptalk of the trade. The flow of information was an important factor in their business—crucial, in fact, for their basic task of connecting supply and demand. Other intermediaries also operated at the connecting points. Literary history should make room for smugglers like Faivre, wagon drivers like Pion, *commissionnaires* like Revol, and sales reps like Favarger. All of them made their living in the most obscure sectors of the distribution system; all deserve a place in an account of *la littérature vécue*.

The place of booksellers deserves special attention. Despite great variations in the size and character of their businesses, they can be described by a general typology. A few wealthy wholesaler-retailers dominated the trade in regions around large cities. They often belonged to family dynasties, got on well with local authorities, and rarely took risks on strictly illegal books, although they relied heavily on pirated editions, which were widely tolerated in the provinces, even after the execution of the edicts of 1777. Around them, smaller booksellers struggled to survive in the retail trade and often went under as economic conditions took a turn for the worse during the late 1770s and 1780s. On the outer margins, individual entrepreneurs speculated on anything they thought would sell, and beyond the limits of legality peddlers or *"marchands forains"* hawked a little of everything, especially *livres philosophiques*. This general pattern corresponded to the observations of Favarger as he graded the degrees of solidarity among booksellers in town after town. It was also the view of the booksellers themselves when they described their lot in petitions to the state, carefully omitting, of course, any mention of illegal books.[2]

A great many, perhaps even most, of the books on the market passed through the hands of the marginal dealers; for the demand for literature existed everywhere, and it could not be satisfied from within the guilds, which lacked the capacity to enforce royal edicts and often cooperated with the trade in pirated books instead of suppressing it. Except in a few large cities such as Marseille and Bordeaux, the provincial book trade was not effectively policed. Illegal booksellers like Malherbe in Loudun and Lair in Blois conducted business without interference from the authorities.[3] They suffered primarily from inadequate resources, which exposed them to downturns in the economy, and also from a tendency to extend their speculations beyond their capacity to pay their debts. Most of them teetered on the edge of bankruptcy, and many went under, although they sometimes resurfaced, especially if they plied their trade from a horse and wagon as in the case of Noël Gille known as *"la Pistole," "roulant par la*

France." More often when disaster hit, they simply disappeared like Caldesaigues in Marseille, abandoning their families or, as the phrase went, "leaving the keys under the door."

The world of books in pre-revolutionary France was a world in motion. Even official booksellers like Robert et Gauthier occasionally took to the road with a horse and cart in order to satisfy the demand for literature in small towns and villages. The demand kept expanding until the last decade of the Ancien Régime. It could not be contained within the structure of guilds inherited from the seventeenth century. A large population of entrepreneurs and middlemen grew up to satisfy it, operating at the periphery of the official institutions and often outside the law. By 1770 the circulation of books had overflown the barriers that had once kept it in check.

The professionals who tried to manage the flow, and were sometimes swept away in it, occupied an important place in the culture of eighteenth-century France. Their story belongs to literary history in its widest sense. Balzac captured much of it, as it existed in the early nineteenth century, in *Les Illusions perdues*, but before Balzac, a whole human comedy had to be set in motion for books to arrive on the marketplace of ideas. How the characters played their parts and how the world of books operated as a system of communication is the main focus of this study. The story turns on the problem of identifying literary demand, an empirical question, which can be answered. Of course, it raises larger questions about the relation of literature to revolution, questions that concern public opinion and collective action, which could be debated endlessly. Important as they are, I have not pursued them in this book, because I decided to restrict the argument to concrete issues resolvable within the range of the history of books as it has developed as a discipline.

By way of speculation, however, I can indicate how this research has implications for understanding the ideological origins of the French Revolution. The statistics on literary demand demonstrate that Enlightenment ideas penetrated deeply into the culture of the Ancien Régime. Of course, many different strains of thought were expressed in the books written by the Enlightenment philosophers, but if I had to choose one work that best exemplified the popularization of the Enlightenment, it would be Mercier's *L'An deux mille quatre cent quarante*, a supreme bestseller that offered a vision of a society governed by Rousseauistic principles in contrast to Mercier's *Tableau de Paris*, another bestseller, which exposed the cruelty and injustices of the current social order. I also would stress the popularity of three other authors mentioned constantly in the correspondence of the booksellers: Raynal, Mirabeau, and Linguet. After the deaths of Voltaire and Rousseau, they exerted the greatest appeal to the public, and each of them, in his own way, personified the threat of arbitrary power to the liberty of ordinary Frenchmen. Political libels, represented best by *Anecdotes sur Mme la comtesse du Barry*, reinforced the theme of despotism and associated it with a picture of decadence at the summit of society. But this kind of slander probably resonated less than sentiment among readers who favored novels like *Les Epreuves du sentiment* and books intended for children such as *Lectures pour les enfants, ou choix de petits contes également propres à les amuser et à leur faire aimer la vertu*. Some of the most popular books held the established order up to ridicule in the manner of Voltaire, whose works appear everywhere in the booksellers' orders. Yet the dominant tone that runs through the corpus as a whole was an appeal to *sensiblerie* and virtue. Few of the books made direct connections with contemporary politics, except for the polemical works related to Necker's ministry. Rather than explicit political messages, the books most in demand communicated a general outlook that was at odds with the established order. This perspective was expressed most forcefully in Raynal's *Histoire philosophique des établissements et du commerce des Européens dans les deux Indes*, a vast, disordered work, full of fault lines and contradictions, yet pulsating with energy, much of it in the form of moral indignation. Despite their variety, these books conveyed a view of the world imbued with an implicit message: the world as it is is not the world that has to be. An alternate reality was thinkable. In 1789, in the wake of the books that had circulated through the channels of commerce since 1769, thought would turn into action.

None of the professionals who made it their business to satisfy the demand for literature had any idea that they were preparing the way for a revolution. They concentrated on the tasks at hand, and when they reflected on their experience, they sounded disabused. Speaking as a publisher, Ostervald observed, "You can only believe what you see with your own eyes and what you can hold with four fingers and the thumb."[4] Speaking as a bookseller, Jean-François Billaut of Tours wrote to the STN,

"You surely know the proverb or epithet of our city… 99 rich rotisserie chefs and one bookseller dying of hunger."[5] The world of books as they experienced it was unforgiving in its harshness and too deeply embedded in the Ancien Régime to survive the Revolution. In the end, therefore, it was a world of lost illusions.

ACKNOWLEDGMENTS

HAVING WORKED IN THE ARCHIVES OF THE SOCIÉTÉ typographique de Neuchâtel since 1965, I owe a special debt of gratitude to the staff and directors of the Bibliothèque publique et universitaire de Neuchâtel. From Eric Berthoud to Jacques Rychner, Michel Schlup, and Thierry Chatelain, the directors of the library provided generous help, first by offering unrestricted access to the archives of the STN, then by microfilming, photocopying, and digitizing many hundreds of documents. I would particularly like to thank Michel Schlup for providing most of the illustrations in this book and for inviting me to collaborate in the production of two large volumes published by the library, *L'édition neuchâteloise au siècle des Lumiéres: La Société typographique de Neuchâtel (1769–1789)* (Neuchâtel: Bibliothèque publique et universitaire de Neuchâtel, État 2002) and *Le rayonnement d'une maison d'édition dans l'Europe des Lumières: La Société typographique de Neuchâtel 1769–1789* (Neuchâtel: Éditions Attinger, 2005). Maurice de Tribolet guided me through the labyrinthine collections of the notarial papers in the Archives de l'État de Neuchâtel, and other Neuchâtel friends helped in many other ways, including housing, a big problem for a large family with a small budget. Aside from many short visits, we spent fourteen summers and one winter in Neuchâtel and the surrounding villages. My gratitude goes out to the late Charly and Liliane Guyot, who loaned their apartment to my wife, Susan, and me in

1966 and 1967; Jacques Rychner, who found rooms for us in several of the villages along the lake; Rémy Scheurer, who introduced us to the late Annie Gutknecht, our beloved landlady in le Landeron; Maurice and Nicolas de Tribolet, who shared with us their family's château in Môtiers, full of eighteenth-century furniture and memories of Rousseau; Philippe and Marie-Anne Marguerat, who put us up many times in their home high above the vineyards; and Alain and Ann Robert, who served us endless meals from their own perch on the mountainside. Our friends took us on hikes along the *crête du Jura* with stops at *alpages* for meals of country ham and, in the autumn, *civet de chevreuil*. For many summers Jacques and Ingrid Rychner picknicked with us outside the library on the bank of the lake. We would top off our *tartes au fromage* with a swim, and then Jacques and I would repair to the archives, working side by side, he on the records of the printing shop, I on the papers related to the book trade. Michel Schlup and Caroline Calame initiated us in the ways of the "*gens du haut*" and the delights of the *fermes-restaurants* in the mountain country around La Chaux-de-Fonds. Philippe Marguerat helped me find my way through the university, where I taught for one semester as a visiting professor and often returned for lectures and conferences. Other friends offered other kinds of help. How to thank them adequately? They took my wife and me into their lives, and they became part of ours. While I worked through the archives, dossier after dossier, year after year, our children grew up with theirs, and we adults grew, too, sharing sorrows as well as joys, for more than fifty years. This book—and a companion volume, which I hope to complete in the near future—represents the culmination of that experience, and I dedicate it to my Neuchâtel friends, in memory of the dead and in solidarity with the living. My thoughts go out particularly to Jacques Rychner, who died just as I was putting the finishing touches on the final draft.

I supplemented the research in Neuchâtel with many years of work in Parisian archives, especially the Collection Anisson-Duperron and the papers of the Chambre syndicale de la Communauté des libraires et des imprimeurs de Paris in the Bibliothèque nationale de France, but also the papers of the Bastille in the Bibliothèque de l'Arsenal and various other archives. The directors of the BnF, from Emmanuel Le Roy Ladurie to Jean-Noël Jeanneney and Bruno Racine were unfailingly friendly, and

I was especially helped by their staff, above all Jean-Dominique Mellot and Jacqueline Sanson.

The sources in Neuchâtel and Paris are so rich and extensive that one cannot do justice to them in one book. Therefore, I decided to include the most important documents, along with maps, illustrations, essays, and a selection of my earlier publications on an open-access website, www .robertdarnton.org, which I launched in the spring of 2013. Readers of this book can consult the website for further information and documentation. No individual could have transcribed all the digitized manuscripts, identified all the books, and compiled all the statistics that appear on the website. I was aided at different stages of this work during the last twenty years by graduate students and research assistants, and I want to extend my warm thanks to them for their long, hard labor. They are Elissa Bell, Sarah Benharrech, Martine Benjamin, Andrew Clark, Brigid Dorsey, Nathaniel Hay, Frédéric Inderwildi, Miriam Nicoli, Thierry Rigogne, Madeleine Schwartz, Jennifer Tsien, and Catherine Witt. The website was designed and engineered by Robert Levers and Aristos Koyanis, who received a great deal of help from my excellent assistant, Arlene Navarro. Scott Walker in the cartography section of the Harvard Library provided the maps, which benefited greatly from his expertise in handling historical material.

I would like to thank the Princeton University Committee on Research in the Humanities and Social Sciences and the Florence A. Gould Foundation for supporting this project over many years. I am especially grateful to John R. Young, president of the Florence A. Gould Foundation, and to his late wife, Mary. They generously renewed their grant several times while I had to interrupt work on this project in order to meet deadlines and fulfill responsibilities, especially in my capacity as university librarian at Harvard from 2007 until 2015. I completed the final draft of this book while a fellow at the Institut d'Etudes Avancées de Paris, with the financial support of the French State managed by the Agence Nationale de la Recherche, programme "Investissements d'avenir" (ANR-11-LABX-0027-01 Labex RFIEA+).

Finally my thanks go to Timothy Bent, my editor at Oxford University Press, and to Jean-François Sené, the translator for the French edition published by Gallimard, who worked long and hard to improve the text.

NOTES

Introduction

1. The most important sources, which I have consulted heavily for this book, are the archives of the Bastille in the Bibliothèque de l'Arsenal and two great collections in the Bibliothèque nationale de France: the Collection Anisson-Duperron and the papers of the Chambre syndicale de la Communauté des imprimeurs et des libraires de Paris.

Chapter 1

1. One livre was worth 20 sous, 1 sou was worth 12 deniers. These were abstract units used in bills of exchange and accounts, and they did not correspond to actual coins. Favarger probably carried in his purse liards (1 liard was worth 3 deniers) and écus (1 écu was worth 3 livres). It seems unlikely that he traveled with coins as valuable as the louis d'or, which was worth 24 livres, owing to the danger of highwaymen. When he needed large sums, he could procure them in cities where the STN had trusted relations with bankers or merchants. The purchasing power of the livre varied. In 1789 the daily wages of a common laborer in Paris amounted to 20–30 sous, and a journeyman mason made about 40 sous. The cost of a standard, 4-pound loaf of bread usually came to 8 or 9 sous, but it could double in times of scarcity. See George Rudé, *The Crowd in the French Revolution* (Oxford: Oxford University Press, 1967), 21–22.
2. Favarger's diary with the expense account appears in the website created to accompany this book: www.robertdarnton.org. It can be consulted in a French transcription of the manuscript, in a digitized reproduction of the manuscript, and in an English translation. All quotations in the following

chapters come from documents reproduced, both as transcriptions and as digitized versions of the manuscripts, in the website, where they can be located easily by searching for the names of the relevant persons. Because the website contains so much documentation, which is so easy to consult, I have kept the endnotes of this book to a minimum.

3. Ranson to STN, November 7, 1778, archives of the Société typographique de Neuchâtel, Bibliothèque publique et universitaire de Neuchâtel, Neuchâtel, Switzerland. Quotations from documents that do not appear on the website will be identified in notes. They come from the archives of the STN, unless indicated otherwise.

4. The rebuilding of the main routes from the provinces to Paris, thanks to the forced labor of the *corvée des chemins*, had cut the traveling time by half between 1738 and 1780, but Favarger had to follow transversal roads, which often remained in very bad condition. See Guy Arbellot, "La grande mutation des routes de France au milieu du XVIIIe siècle," *Annales. Histoire, Sciences Sociales* 28 (1973): 765–791; and J. Letaconnoux, "Les transports en France au XVIIIe siècle," *Revue d'histoire moderne et contemporaine* 11 (1908/1909): 97–114.

5. Quoted in Henri Sée, "Les auberges françaises à la fin de l'Ancien Régime d'après Arthur Young," *Revue d'histoire économique et sociale* 18 (1930): 446, 447, and 450.

6. Bornand to STN, April 12, 1784.

7. Bornand to STN, March 2, 1785.

8. The only reference to sales reps or commercial travelers in the eighteenth century that I have found in the secondary literature is George V. Taylor, "Notes on Commercial Travelers in Eighteenth-Century France," *The Business History Review* 3 (1964): 346–353. However, they could be found everywhere in inns and around tables d'hôte under the Ancien Régime, according to the memoirs of a contemporary commercial traveler named Marlin: "What are *commis voyageurs*? They are usually young men who travel every year in all the cities of the kingdom soliciting orders for commercial houses" (quoted in Albert Babeau, *Les Voyageurs en France depuis la Renaissance jusqu'à la Révolution* [Paris, 1885; reprint, Geneva: Slatkine, 1970], 309). For the later period, see Bill Bell, "'Pioneers of Literature': The Commercial Traveller in the Early Nineteenth Century," *The Reach of Print: Making, Selling, and Using Books*, ed. Peter Isaac and Barry McKay (Winchester and New Castle, Del.: St. Paul's Bibliographies, 1998), 121–154.

9. Ostervald and Bosset from Paris to STN, April 4, 1777.

10. Favarger to STN, August 16, 1776.

11. Jean-François Favarger was born in Saint-Blaise, a town 5 kilometers north of Neuchâtel, on June 28, 1749 (Archives de l'État de Neuchâtel, État Civil de Neuchâtel, EC158). His father was Jean-Frédéric Favarger, and his mother's maiden name was Anne Barbe Chatelain. Notarial archives refer to his father as a "bourgeois," meaning he enjoyed full civic rights in the municipality of Neuchâtel, and they indicate that, like many Neuchâtelois, he owned

vineyards in the surrounding countryside, but they do not mention his profession (Archives de l'État, F9, register of the notary Jean-Jacques Favarger, entry for January 28, 1780). Jean-Frédéric Favarger knew Ostervald, because he served as a witness for one of Ostervald's financial transactions in 1786 (Archives de l'État, B656, register of the notary Claude-François Bovet, entry for June 24, 1786). It could be, therefore, that he had intervened in some way to persuade the STN to hire his son a decade earlier.

12. See chapter 13 for information about Favarger's later life and references to the sources.

13. The contract follows Favarger's diary from his trip of 1776 in his dossier, ms. 1150.

14. Favarger may well have worked behind a plow at some point in his youth, but he was no peasant. As mentioned above, his father owned vineyards and enjoyed full civic rights as a "bourgeois"—a distinction that excluded the lower classes.

15. Bornand to STN, August 20, 1769.

16. The contract and other relevant documents appear at the end of Bornand's dossier in the STN archives, ms. 1124.

Chapter 2

1. Royal edicts governing transport required that packets in shipments by wagon (roulage) weigh at least 50 pounds. The common French pound (*livre, poids de marc*) then was the equivalent of 489.5 grams or about a half a kilogram. Shipping agents charged by the hundredweight or quintal, about 45.4 kilograms. Wagons usually were solid structures with four wheels pulled by two or more horses, and they often carried loads of 5,000 pounds. See J. Letaconnoux, "Les transports en France au XVIIIe siècle," *Revue d'histoire moderne et contemporaine* (1899–1914), 11; (1908–1909), 97–114. Letaconnoux's information can be confirmed by hundreds of letters sent to the STN by shipping agents, who hired the wagon drivers and bargained hard over charges.

2. The marque was not an address but rather an abbreviated formula that was not only painted on the bale but also used in notifying shipping agents and booksellers by *lettres d'avis* and *lettres de voiture* and in keeping accounts. For example, the bale marked "RP 85" was shipped by the STN on March 29, 1779, to Rigaud Pons, booksellers in Montpellier; it weighed 200 pounds and it was the eighty-fifth bale shipped by the STN that year: "Livre de commission," STN archives, ms. 1019. I have published photographs of the accounts and accompanying documents in an essay on the STN archives, "Entre l'éditeur et le libraire: Les étapes des ventes," in *La Société typographique de Neuchâtel 1769–1789. Actes du colloque Neuchâtel 31 octobre au 2 novembre 2002*, ed. Robert Darnton and Michel Schlup (Neuchâtel: Éditions Attinger, 2005), 365–369.

3. Printers allowed for *défets* by supplementing the print run with additional sheets known as the *chaperon*. The size of the *chaperons* varied, although

printers' manuals said it was customary to include one main de passe (twenty-five sheets) for every two reams or every ream (one thousand or five hundred sheets) being printed: S. Boulard, *Le manuel de l'imprimeur* (Paris: Boulard, 1791), 72. The extra sheets were mainly meant to cover spoilage produced in printing, but they also were used when customers complained about *défets*, which often resulted from mishandling during shipping.

4. For a full account of this affair, see my monograph, *The Business of Enlightenment: A Publishing History of the Encyclopédie, 1775–1800* (Cambridge, Mass.: Harvard University Press, 1979); or, for a brief version, see "The Encyclopédie Wars of Prerevolutionary France" on the website robertdarnton.org.

5. The procedure involving *acquits à caution* is mentioned in several of the manuscripts concerning the book trade in the Bibliothèque nationale de France, notably Fonds français 22079, no. 140, "Mémoire. Renseignements sur les chambres syndicales et les moyens d'en établir une à Besançon," June 11, 1773; and Fonds français 22081, no. 165, "Mémoire donné à M. de Sartine le 10 novembre 1763." To reconstruct its actual functioning, however, I have relied on the correspondence of *commissionnaires* in the STN archives.

6. The cultural complexity of boundaries, long a favorite subject among anthropologists, has attracted the attention of some historians. See, for example, Greg Dening, *Islands and Beaches: Discourse on a Silent Land: Marquesas, 1774–1880* (Melbourne: Melbourne University Press, 1980); and Peter Sahlins, *Boundaries: The Making of France and Spain in the Pyrenees* (Berkeley: University of California Press, 1989).

7. Lamoignon de Malesherbes, *Voyages des montagnes neuchâteloises en été 1778* (Geneva: Editions Slatkine, 2011), 80.

8. See the documents and essays under "Middlemen and Smugglers" on the website for a more detailed account. An economic analysis of "insurance," along with a detailed study of smuggling at another border crossing, can be found in the essay on Guillon under "Middlemen and Smugglers" on the website. Some of my early publications on book smuggling have found their way into popularized literature, including one book that made me one of the smugglers: "A circuit of smugglers and middlemen supplied this flux [of illegal books], which wound up in cafés and reading groups. One of the principal propagators of the seditious works was a certain Robert Darnton, a publisher in Thionville. He worked with the Société typographique de Neuchâtel, which printed gazettes and scandalous pamphlets. To cover this illegal activity, Darnton also published legal works such as almanacs, pious tracts, and school books" (André Besson, *Contrebandiers et gabelous* [Paris: France-Empire, 1989], 207, quoted in Dominique Varry, "Pour de nouvelles approches des archives de la Société typographique de Neuchâtel," in *The Darnton Debate. Books and Revolution in the Eighteenth Century*, ed. Haydn T. Mason [Oxford: Voltaire Foundation, 1998], 235).

9. Meuron frères, Philippin et Favre to STN, February 13, 1781, in the STN archives. This discussion is based on the voluminous dossiers of Meuron

frères, Jean-François Pion, François Michaut, Henry Rosselet, and Ignace Faivre in the STN archives. Faivre's letters can be consulted on the website.

10. Of the many *chambres syndicales* in France, only the following could discharge *acquits à caution* before 1777, when the regulations were modified: Paris, Lyon, Rouen, Strasbourg, Nantes, Marseille, Bordeaux, Metz, Reims, Amiens, Lille, and Calais.

11. The Franche-Comté, like most of southern France, belonged to the "*provinces réputées étrangères,*" and therefore shipments sent through it had to pay transit duties to reach central and northern markets. But Alsace and Lorraine paid much heavier duties as "*provinces traitées à l'instar de l'étranger effectif.*" By special arrangement, Lyon did not pay duties for goods shipped to the north within the area known as the "Cinq Grosses Fermes." See J. F. Bosher, *The Single Duty Project: A Study of the Movement for a French Customs Union in the Eighteenth Century* (London: Athlone, 1964); and P. M. Jones, *Reform and Revolution in France: The Politics of Transition, 1774–1791* (Cambridge: Cambridge University Press, 1995).

12. See my essay on an "insurance" operation at Clairvaux-les-lacs, "Books and Border Crossings in the Age of Enlightenment," forthcoming in a festschrift in honor of Roland Mortier and Raymond Trousson and available on my website, robertdarnton.org.

13. Meuron to STN, June 26, 1783.

14. Meuron to STN, September 28, 1778.

15. Meuron to STN, April 22, 1780.

16. Montandon to STN, July 16, 1779.

17. Montandon to STN, August 28, 1771.

18. Montandon to STN, September 3, 1771.

19. Meuron to STN, June 25, 1770.

20. STN to Meuron, April 9, 1776.

21. Michaut to STN, October 30, 1783, and December 22, 1783.

22. STN to Saillant et Nyon, January 17, 1771.

23. Faivre to STN, July 27, 1772. Most of the following account is based on Faivre's dossier in the STN archives, which can be consulted on the website.

24. Faivre to STN, October 4, 1783.

Chapter 3

1. Of course, there are a few fine-grained studies of printing and the book trade in particular towns and regions, some of them published long ago yet not outdated: for example Jean Quéniart, *L'imprimerie et la librairie à Rouen au XVIIIe siècle* (Paris: Presses Universitaires de France, 1969); and René Moulinas, *L'imprimerie, la librairie et la presse à Avignon au XVIIIe siècle* (Grenoble: Presses Universitaires de Grenoble, 1974). Among more recent studies, see especially Jean-Dominique Mellot, *L'édition rouennaise et ses marchés (vers 1600–vers 1730)* (Paris: École des chartes, 1998); and

Claudine Adam, *Les imprimeurs-libraires Toulousains et leur production au XVIIIe siècle* (Toulouse: Presses Universitaires du Mirail, 2015). Other secondary sources are listed in the website robertdarnton.org. Research on so-called popular literature such as almanacs and chapbooks has flourished since the publication of Robert Mandrou's *De la culture populaire aux 17e et 18e siècles. La bibliothèque bleue de Troyes* (Paris: Stock, 1964). For a fairly recent example of this work, see Lise Andries and Geneviève Bollème, *La Bibliothèque bleue: Littérature de colportage* (Paris: Robert Laffont, 2003). For the trade in religious books in general, see Philippe Martin, *Une religion des livres (1640–1850)* (Paris: Éditions du Cerf, 2003).

2. The 1764 survey can be consulted in the Bibliothèque nationale de France, fond français 22184–85. Passages from it and other relevant documents are reproduced on the website robertdarnton.org under the sections devoted to the towns that Favarger visited. For a general discussion of the survey and the administration of the book trade, see Thierry Rigogne, *Between State and Market: Printing and Bookselling in Eighteenth-century France* (Oxford: Voltaire Foundation, 2007). A similar work, which concentrates on printing shops, is Jane McLeod, *Licensing Loyalty: Printers, Patrons, and the State in Early Modern France* (University Park: Pennsylvania State University Press, 2011).

3. "Literature" in the modern sense of the word was only beginning to come into common use at the time of Favarger's tour de France. The *Dictionnaire de l'Académie française* in its standard edition of 1762 defined "littérature" as "Erudition, doctrine" and as an example of usage, it noted, "He is a man of great literature." But it added, "This word concerns more strictly Belles-Lettres." On the distinction between the traditional concept of "letters" and the romantic notion of "literature," see Alvin Kernan, *Printing Technology, Letters and Samuel Johnson* (Princeton: Princeton University Press, 1987), 7. Another example of the term's use in the book trade occurs in a report on Besson of Bourg-en-Bresse, which Favarger sent to the STN on September 4, 1776: "Besson only deals in prayer books [*des usages*] that he prints himself. When I offered a catalogue to him, he said that he did not carry any books of literature [*livres de littérature*]."

4. A great deal of research remains to be done before we have a clear view of the markets for books in France and the rest of Europe from the time of Gutenberg to the present. The best general account of the French trade remains Henri-Jean Martin and Roger Chartier, eds., *Histoire de l'édition française*, 4 vols. (Paris: Promodis, 1983–1986).

5. Favarger referred to these categories throughout his diary and correspondence. For example, in his report on Béziers he wrote, "Barbut is dead. Boussquet isn't worth anything. L'Allemand is away in Marseille. That leaves widow Odezenes and son and Morbillon who are said to be fairly good. But I think one must put them in the class of the mediocre."

6. In a letter of August 11, 1776, the STN instructed Favarger, who was then in Lyon, to calibrate the credit he would extend to potential customers according to their degree of "solidity." He was to give the "*solides*" twelve months to pay their bills and the "*médiocres*" six months, but the "*peu solides*" would have to pay immediately, either in cash or in an equivalent amount in kind. In its general "*bilans*" or balance sheets (ms. 1042), the STN divided its debtors into three classes: "débiteurs réputés bons," "débiteurs réputés douteux," and "débiteurs réputés mauvais." In a personal notebook from 1774 (ms. 1056), Ostervald wrote observations on eighty booksellers and ranked them in three numbered classes, number 1 being the most credit-worthy. Thus, for example: "3 Le Francois... Argentan; 1 Le Roy... Caen; 2 Le May l'aîné... Bruxelles." This was the ranking system used by Favarger when he assessed the businesses of booksellers.

7. Bill Bell, " 'Pioneers of Literature': The Commercial Traveller in the Early Nineteenth Century," in *The Reach of Print*, ed. Peter Isaac and Barry McKay (New Castle, Del.: Oak Knoll, 1998), 125–126.

8. See the reprint of the 1781 edition with an introduction about the earlier editions by Jeroom Vercruysse in Antoine Perrin, *Almanach de la librairie* (Aubel: P. M. Gason, 1984).

9. For example, in his report on Castelnaudary, Favarger wrote, "At Castelnaudary I saw the supposed booksellers Annat and Sérié, who are wrongly indicated in the almanac, because Annat is a goldsmith who never sold a book and Sérié is a cloth merchant who sells a few prayer books but nothing more."

10. Favarger to STN from Dijon, September 4, 1776.

Chapter 4

1. Favarger reported that Gaude, père et fils of Nîmes "are enchanted with the taste, the correction and the general manner with which our editions are printed."

2. Favarger to STN, September 4, 1776. Neither Vernarel nor Robert et Gauthier was mentioned in the survey of 1764.

3. Letters of the firm are scattered through five dossiers in the archives of the STN. Its partners are difficult to identify, as the letters did not mention first names; but at various times the partnership included Jacques Robert and probably one of his brothers, Pierre Gauthier and one of his brothers, and Vernarel, who left the firm in order to continue business on his own in 1773. In a letter of July 3, 1773, Vernarel informed the STN of "the dissolution of my company with MM. Robert and Gauthier.... MM. Robert and Gauthier are no longer in Bourg. M. Robert is in Lons-le-Saulnier, and M. Gauthier is in Belley en Bugey." The *Almanach de la librairie* of 1781 lists Vernarel under Bourg and "Robert et Gauthier" under Belley without reference to any other locations. In fact, Robert et Gauthier continued to do most of their

business in Bourg-en-Bresse, while ordering books from many other places. The Belfort branch also dealt in the paper trade. In 1784 it sold its stock of books, valued at 3,000 livres, to André Faure, identified both as a clerk and an "associé" of the company; and he continued as an independent bookseller in Belfort until at least 1788 (he has a separate dossier in the STN archives). For a detailed discussion of Robert et Gauthier and a selection of documents from the archives of the STN, see the section concerning Bourg-en-Bresse on the website robertdarnton.org.

4. For a detailed discussion and documents concerning Guillon's operation, see the section "Middlemen and Smugglers" on the website robertdarnton.org.

5. Reydelet, *procureur au bailliage de Bourg-en-Bresse*, to STN, July 31, 1778.

6. Archives du Département de la Seine, now Département de Paris, Fonds de faillites, D.4B6.

7. The full set of statistics for every book and every order can be consulted on the website robertdarnton.org.

Chapter 5

1. On piracy in general, see François Moureau, ed., *Les presses grises: La contrefaçon du livre, XVIe–XIXe siècles* (Paris: Aux amateurs de livres, 1988). The state was fully informed about the prevalence of piracy in Lyon. See, for example, the letter of Claude Bourgelat, the inspector of the book trade in Lyon, to Joseph d'Hémery, the inspector in Paris, January 1760 in Bibliothèque nationale de France, fonds français, 22080, no. 101. Among the studies of Lyon and its booksellers and printers, see especially the publications of Dominique Varry, who has made good use of the STN archives along with Lyonnais sources; for example, "La diffusion sous le manteau: La Société typographique de Neuchâtel et les Lyonnais," in *L'Europe et le livre: Réseaux et pratiques du négoce de librairie XVIe–XIXe siècles*, ed. Frédéric Barbier, Sabine Juratic, and Dominique Varry (Paris: Klincksieck, 1996), 309–332; "Les échanges Lyon-Neuchâtel," in *La Société typographique de Neuchâtel 1769–1789: Actes du colloque organisé par la Bibliothèque publique et universitaire de Neuchâtel et la Faculté des lettres de l'Université de Neuchâtel, Neuchâtel, 31 octobre–2 novembre 2002*, ed. Robert Darnton and Michel Schlup (Neuchâtel: Éditions Attinger, 2005), 491–518; "Les gens du livre à Lyon au XVIIIe siècle: Quand de 'loyaux sujets' sont aussi des 'maronneurs,'" in *Le peuple des villes dans l'Europe du Nord-Ouest de la fin du Moyen-Age à 1945*, ed. Philippe Guignet (Lille: Centre de recherche sur l'histoire de l'Europe du Nord-Ouest, Université Charles-de-Gaulle, 2003), 2: 229–242; and "Pour de nouvelles approches des archives de la Société typographique de Neuchâtel," in *The Darnton Debate: Books and Revolution in the Eighteenth Century*, ed. Haydn T. Mason (Oxford: Voltaire Foundation, 1988), 235–249. See also Louis Trenard, *Commerce et culture: Le livre à Lyon au XVIIIe siècle* (Lyon: Imp. réunies, 1953); and Roger Chartier, "Livre et espace: Circuits commerciaux et géographie culturelle de la librairie," *Revue française d'histoire du livre* 1 (1971): 77–103.

2. See Henri-Jean Martin, *Livres, pouvoirs et société à Paris au XVIIe siècle (1598–1701)* (Geneva: Librairie Droz, 1969), especially 3:678–756; Henri-Jean Martin, "L'édition parisienne au XVIIe siècle," in Martin, *Le Livre français sous l'Ancien Régime* (Paris: Promodis, 1987); and Jean Quéniart, "L'Anémie provinciale," in *Histoire de l'édition française*, ed. Henri-Jean Martin and Roger Chartier (Paris: Promodis, 1984), 2:282–293.

3. On the edicts of August 30, 1777, see Raymond Birn, "The Profits of Ideas: Privilèges en librairie in Eighteenth-Century France," *Eighteenth-Century Studies* 4 (1971): 131–168; Anne Boës and Robert L. Dawson, "The Legitimation of Contrefaçons and the Police Stamp of 1777," *Studies on Voltaire and the Eighteenth Century* 230 (1985): 461–484; and Jeanne Veyrin-Forrer, "Livres arrêtés, livres estampillés: Traces parisiennes de la contrefaçon," in Moureau, *Les presses grises: La contrefaçon du livre (XVIe–XIXe siècles)*, 101–112.

4. The fullest expression of the opposition of the provincial booksellers, led by the Lyonnais, to the monopoly of privileges by the Parisians is "Mémoire à consulter pour les libraires et imprimeurs de Lyon, Rouen, Toulouse, Marseille et Nîmes concernant les privilèges de librairie et continuations d'iceux," October 15, 1776, in Bibliothèque nationale de France, Fonds français 22073, no. 144. See also "Au Roi et à nosseigneurs de son Conseil," an undated petition by the Lyonnais booksellers protesting against the continuation of the Parisians' privileges in ibid, Fonds français, 22073, no. 141.

5. Bertrand, "Carnet de voyage," 1773, ms. 1058.

6. The instructions and the text of the diary, in French and in English, can be consulted on the website robertdarnton.org.

7. The following paragraphs summarize the research I have discussed at length in *The Business of Enlightenment: A Publishing History of the Encyclopédie, 1775–1800* (Cambridge, Mass.: Harvard University Press, 1979).

Chapter 6

1. Revol's correspondence with the STN along with background material can be consulted on the website robertdarnton.org under "Lyon" and under "Middlemen and Smugglers."

2. Pion to STN, May 29, 1779.

Chapter 7

1. The exchange trade has attracted little attention from book historians concerned with early modern France, England, and Italy, but it has been thoroughly studied in research on the German book trade. See Johann Goldfriedrich, *Geschichte des deutschen Buchhandels: Im Auftrag des Börsenvereins der Deutschen Buchhändler* (Leipzig: Börsenverein für den deutschen Buchhandel, 1908–1909), vols. 2–3; and Reinhard Wittmann, *Geschichte des deutschen Buchhandels: Ein Überblick* (Munich: C. H. Beck, 1991). In the early modern period, printer-booksellers often arrived at the spring and autumn book fairs of Frankfurt and Leipzig with a

wagon full of the books they had recently produced, exchanged them for selections of books produced by other printer-booksellers, and returned with a wagonload varied enough to constitute the bulk of the stock in their shops until they sought new provisions at the next fair. In the late eighteenth century, booksellers such as Philipp Erasmus Reich in Leipzig transformed the retail trade by shifting to cash transactions conducted independently of the fairs. France did not have book fairs comparable to those of Frankfurt and Leipzig, although the fair at Beaucaire attracted a great many booksellers. But I believe that swapping—especially among publishers in Switzerland and Avignon and wholesalers in centers like Lyon—constituted a fundamental aspect of the trade until the nineteenth century.

2. I have discussed Favarger's tour of 1776 at length in "The Travels of a Publisher's Sales Rep, 1775–1776," *Book History* 20 (2017): 111–125.

3. René Moulinas, *L'Imprimerie, la librairie, et la presse à Avignon au XVIIIe siècle* (Grenoble: Presses Universitaires de Grenoble, 1974). The French authorities were fully informed about the pirating in Avignon and even received some of their information from the Lyonnais booksellers, such as Pierre Bruyset-Ponthus, who sent a "Mémoire sur les contrefaçons" to the police inspector Joseph d'Hémery on September 16, 1769. See Bibliothèque nationale de France, Fonds français, 22075, no. 117. For further information about Avignon and its publishers, see the website robertdarnton.org.

4. See Pierre Joseph Roberty to STN, January 16, 1775; and Veuve Joly & fils to STN, November 22, 1780.

5. The following are close paraphrases of Favarger's notes, although not exact quotations: "Chambeau: Good but difficult to deal with; Offray: Mediocre and insists on cheaper prices; Dubier: Mediocre, might buy some Bibles; Fabre: Very good, liked some of the works in the catalog and might make a trial order; Mérande: Very good, but would not even look at the catalog; Aubanel: Mediocre, his proposals for an exchange are not worth pursuing; Niel: A good printer but absent from his shop; Seguin: Also very good and willing to do an exchange, but few outstanding books listed in his catalog."

6. The full details of the exchanges can be followed from Garrigan's correspondence, which is available, along with other material about Avignon, on the website robertdarnton.org.

7. Roberty to STN, February 8, 1775.

8. Moulinas, *L'Imprimerie, la librairie, et la presse à Avignon*, 259–260.

Chapter 8

1. Jacques Antoine Hippolyte comte de Guibert, *Voyage de Guibert dans diverses parties de la France et en Suisse, faits en 1775, 1778, 1784 et 1785: Ouvrage posthume, publié par sa veuve* (Paris, 1806), 177–178.

2. In general, Favarger's references conform to the names of the booksellers and printers listed in the *Almanach de la librairie* of 1778, although he often found that it was inaccurate, and the spelling of the names was inconsistent. The

Almanach was originally published in 1777 under the title *Almanach de l'auteur et du libraire*. It was expanded and reprinted in 1778 as *Almanach du libraire*, and a third edition appeared under the same title in 1781. For detailed information about each of these towns and their booksellers, see the website robertdarnton.org. The best general study of printing and the book trade in this area is still Madeleine Ventre, *L'Imprimerie et la librairie en Languedoc au dernier siècle de l'Ancien Régime* (Paris: Mouton, 1958).

3. *Almanach général des marchands, négociants, armateurs et fabricants de la France et de l'Europe et des autres parties du monde* (Paris, 1779), 353.

4. Gaude may have been more adventuresome in his relations with other suppliers, notably François Grasset, who dealt heavily in forbidden literature. In July 1766, Joseph d'Hémery, the inspector of the book trade in Paris, was sent on a mission to investigate the trade in pirated books produced in Avignon and sold at the fair in Beaucaire. In a series of raids at the fair, he confiscated forty-seven bales of books. They included two bales that had been sent to Gaude by Grasset that contained a selection of erotic and anti-Catholic works such as *Les Délices du cloître*, *Margot la ravaudeuse*, and *La Chandelle d'Arras* (Bibliothèque nationale de France, Fonds français, 22098, nos. 30–48). That is the only time that Gaude's name appears in the archives of the police. (The Beaucaire fair, and particularly the raid of 1766, warrant further study.)

5. Buchet supplied details about this episode in a letter to the STN of May 4, 1778.

6. André to STN, February 21, 1785.

7. Batilliot l'aîné to STN, March 18, 1781.

8. Bibliothèque nationale de France, Fonds français, 22185, f. 22.

9. This account is based on the dossiers in the STN archives of Cézary, ms. 1132, ff. 267–273; Vialars, ms. 1228, ff. 42–76; and the attorney Chiraud, ms. 1135, ff. 219–220.

10. All of Rigaud's orders along with those of the other seventeen booksellers studied in this work can be studied on the website robertdarnton.org.

11. The quotations are from Vialars's letters to the STN of August 30, 1784; November 3, 1784; and May 1, 1785.

12. Jacques-Antoine Dulaure, *Description des principaux lieux de France* (Paris, 1789), 1:96–97.

13. Bibliothèque nationale de France, mss. Fr. 22185, f.8.

14. Favarger's judgment, picked up from many booksellers and *commissionnaires*, was confirmed by several of the letters they sent to the STN. See Allemand to STN, June 4, 1777; and Guibert to STN, June 9, 1777.

15. Mossy's letters, like those of all of the eighteen booksellers studied here, can be read on the website robertdarnton.org. I have taken a few liberties in translating them in order to make their meaning clear, and I have quoted them at some length, because they provide unusual examples of a bookseller's testimony about his trade.

16. Archives municipales de Marseille, FF 208–209.

17. The information about Mossy comes from the Archives de la ville de Marseille, liasses FF 208 and 209, kindly supplied by the archivist, Isabelle

Bonnot, in a letter of January 29, 1986. I also received information about the Mossy family and the politics of Marseille from James K. Pringle, who completed a dissertation at Johns Hopkins University in 1984: "The Quiet Conflict: Landlord and Merchant in the Planning of Marseille, 1750–1820."

18. Bibliothèque nationale de France, mss. Fr 22185, f. 8.

19. See my study of the diffusion of *Encyclopédies* in *The Business of Enlightenment: A Publishing History of the Encyclopédie (1775–1800)* (Cambridge, Mass.: Belknap, 1979), chap. 6.

20. Claudet to STN, April 4, 1777.

21. Claudet to STN, June 27, 1777.

22. De Veer, Bugnot et Cie. to STN, February 19, 1779. See also Claudet to STN, March 5, 1779, and Isoard to STN, July 15, 1779.

23. De Veer, Bugnot et Cie. to STN, December 22, 1779.

Chapter 9

1. Bibliothèque nationale de France, mss. fr. 22185, f. 176. On Toulouse, see Claudine Adam, *Les imprimeurs-libraires Toulousains et leur production au XVIIIe siècle* (Toulouse: Presses Universitaires du Mirail, 2015).

2. For a contemporary view of veterinary science related to horses, see Claude Bourgelat, *Eléments d'hippiatrique ou nouveaux principes sur la connaissance et sur la médecine des chevaux* (Lyon, 1750–1953), 3 vols.; and for a panoramic view of the place of horses in history, see Daniel Roche, *La Culture équestre de l'Occident, XVIe–XIXe siècle* (Paris: Fayard, 2008–2015), 3 vols.

3. Chappuis frères to STN, January 22, 1774.

4. The secondary literature about books in Bordeaux is listed on the website robertdarnton.org, and I would like to acknowledge the help of Jane McLeod, who provided some information about Bergeret in a letter of June 30, 1982. She discusses him and other Bordelais in *Licensing Loyalty: Printers, Patrons, and the State in Early Modern France* (University Park: Penn State University Press, 2011), although her research focuses on printers rather than booksellers.

5. Bibliothèque nationale de France, mss. fr. 22185, f. 100.

6. M. Dumoulin, *La Géographie, ou description générale du royaume de France divisé en ses généralités* (Paris: Leclerc, 1767), 5:73.

7. Jacques-Antoine Dulaure, *Description des principaux lieux de France* (Paris: Lejay, 1789), 4148.

8. For a detailed account of the exchanges, which illustrate the calculations and negotiations involved in eighteenth-century business deals, see the essay on Chevrier and the accompanying correspondence on the website robertdarnton.org.

Chapter 10

1. *Almanach général des marchands, négociants, armateurs, et fabricants* (Paris: l'Auteur, 1779), 4:174.

2. Among the studies of this still quite obscure subject, see Laurence Fontaine, *Le voyage et la mémoire: Colporteurs de l'Oisans au XIXe siècle* (Lyon: Presses universitaires de Lyon, 1984); Anne Sauvy, "Noël Gille dit la Pistole 'marchand foirain libraire roulant par la France'," *Bulletin des bibliothèques de France* (May 1967): 177–190; Jean-Dominique Mellot, "Rouen et les 'libraires forains' à la fin du XVIIIe siècle: La Veuve Machuel et ses correspondants (1768–1773)," *Bibliothèque de l'Ecole des chartes* 147 (1989): 503–538; and Jean-Dominique Mellot, "Libraires en campagne: Les forains normands du livre à la fin du XVIIIe siècle," *Le livre voyageur (1450–1830): Actes du colloque international tenu à l'ENSSIB du 23 et 24 mai 1997* (Paris, 2000), 153–175.

3. Batilliot l'aîné to STN, February 18, 1778.

4. Information kindly sent in a letter of January 16, 1987, by the Mairie de Loudun from the registers of the État Civil de la Mairie de Loudun.

5. Laurence to STN, March 18, 1787, and June 17, 1787.

6. Luca to STN, July 26, 1787.

7. Bibliothèque nationale de France, Fonds français 22081, ff. 357–368.

8. The following account is based on the collection of bankruptcy papers in the Archives du Département de la Seine (now Département de Paris), D.4B6, carton 59, dossier 3773.

9. Ibid., memoir dated August 14, 1776.

10. The titles of the following books in the order provide examples of Gilles's spelling: "*lette a un genit*" (*Lettres à Eugénie, ou préservatif contre les préjugés* by d'Holbach), "*citemme delanaturre*" (*Système de la nature* by d'Holbach), "*bibes de volterre*" (*La Bible enfin expliquée* by Voltaire), "*an faires detrui*" (*L'Enfer détruit ou examen raisonné du dogme de l'éternité des peines* by d'Holbach), "*teraise philosf*" (*Thérèse philosophe*, attributed to the marquis d'Argens and others), and "*heuvre de janjacle rousau*" (*Oeuvres de J.-J. Rousseau*).

11. Bibliothèque nationale de France, Fonds français 22096, f. 493: note by Joseph d'Hémery, December 15, 1764.

12. Bibliothèque nationale de France, Fonds français 22099, ff. 43 and 45: undated note addressed to d'Hémery by a spy.

13. Archives du Département de la Seine, D.4B6, carton 59, dossier 3773.

14. Ibid.

15. Archives du Département de la Seine, D.4B6, carton 62, dossier 3980, memoir dated March 18, 1777, for Claude René Sabine, "*marchand forain libraire roulant par la France*."

Chapter 11

1. On this theme, see the works of Norbert Elias, notably *The Civilizing Process*, rev. ed. (Oxford: Basil Blackwell, 1994); and *The Court Society* (New York: Pantheon, 1983).

2. Unlike Favarger, eighteenth-century travelers often commented on the beauty of the landscape. While traveling through the Loire near Blois, for example, an Englishwoman wrote in her diary, which was later published in French:

"I could not weary of admiring the countryside of this area, and for a long time I shall not forget the spectacle I observed: to the left, curved the Loire with houses in the midst of clumps of greenery scattered along its border; to the right, rich slopes of vineyards" (*La vie française à la veille de la Révolution [1783–1786]: Journal inédit de Madame Cradock* (Paris: Perrin, 1911), 298. During a trip that took him along the route that Favarger followed between Saumur and Tours, François duc de La Rochefoucauld wrote in his diary: "I cannot but repeat the pleasure afforded me by the route along the Loire; it is impossible to see anything more beautiful and varied" (*Voyages en France de François de La Rochefoucauld [1781–1783]*, ed. Jean Marchand [Paris, 1928], 196). A similar appreciation of landscape and architecture along the route that Favarger took in the south of France can be studied in the diary of an anonymous curate: *Journal d'un voyage aux environs de la Loire et de la Saône jusqu'à la Mer Méditerrannée et sur les côtes du Languedoc et de la Provence*, ed. Henri Duranton and Christiane Lauvergnet-Gagnière (Saint-Etienne: Publications de l'Université de Saint-Etienne, 1993), 95–119.

3. See Patrick Daubignard, *Imprimeurs et libraires blésois (1554–1790)* (Blois: Les amis de la bibliothèque de Blois, 1988).

4. As an example of a similar entrepreneur, see my monograph on Bruzard de Mauvelain of Troyes: "Trade in the Taboo: The Life of a Clandestine Book Dealer in Prerevolutionary France," in *The Widening Circle: Essays on the Circulation of Literature in Eighteenth-Century Europe*, ed. Paul J. Korshin (Philadelphia: University of Pennsylvania Press, 1976), 11–83.

5. He probably succeeded in acquiring his brevet because he is listed as a "*libraire*" under Blois in the *Almanach de la librairie* of 1781.

6. Henri Herluison, *Recherches sur les imprimeurs et libraires d'Orléans* (Orléans, 1868), 142.

7. Veuve Chassaing et Paupaille le jeune to STN, July 12, 1784.

8. See Herluison, *Recherches sur les imprimeurs et libraires d'Orléans*, 126–134; the article on Couret by an anonymous contemporary who apparently knew him well in J. F. Michaud and L. G. Michaud, *Biographie universelle ancienne et moderne* (Paris: Michaud frères, 1811–1862); and an undated manuscript "Bio-Bibliographie du Loiret" by a certain Cuissard kindly provided to me by the Archives du Loiret.

9. Veuve Rameau et fils to STN, March 18, 1777.

10. Archives départementales de la Côte d'Or, mss. C381–383.

11. Nubla et fils to STN, December 29, 1778; January 13, 1780; and May 2, 1780.

Chapter 12

1. Charmet's dossier in the STN archives refers to him as "l'aîné" (the elder), without giving his first name. When I first published an account of his business, I wrongly assumed that he was Jean-Félix Charmet, who appears in the *Almanach de la librairie*, as an "*imprimeur-libraire*," rather than Charles-Antoine Charmet, who was listed only as a "*libraire*." See my *The*

Forbidden Best-Sellers of Pre-revolutionary France (New York: Norton, 1996), 32–39. Information from the municipal archives of Besançon kindly provided to me by Hervé Le Corre proves that the elder Charmet was Charles-Antoine. The younger brother, Jean-Félix, was a printer, who produced liturgical works, almanacs, and legal briefs for Besançon's lawyers, according to the 1764 survey of printers and booksellers (for details, see the material on Besançon on the website robertdarnton.org). Jean-Félix sold his own productions and other material, mainly devotional tracts, from his printing shop. As explained above in chapter 3, provincial printers often developed a small business in retailing works of this kind, which were suited for the local market but did not circulate in the general book trade. Although book historians have usually concentrated on books related to the Enlightenment and other varieties of current literature, they have never doubted the widespread diffusion of breviaries, devotional works, almanacs, calendars, chapbooks, and other kinds of so-called popular literature. See, for example, Robert Mandrou, *De la culture populaire aux 17e et 18e siècles* (Paris: Stock, 1964); Lise Andriès, *La bibliothèque bleue: Littérature de colportage* (Paris: Robert Laffont, 2003); François Furet et al., eds., *Livre et société dans la France du XVIIIe siècle*, 2 vols. (Paris: Mouton, 1965, 1970); and Philippe Martin, *Une religion des livres (1640–1850)* (Paris: Éditions du Cerf, 2003). Simon Burrows emphasizes this religious literature in an article on Charmet: "Culture and the Book Police: Clandestinity, Illegality and Popular Reading in Late *Ancien Régime* France," published online by H-France, May 12, 2015, www.h-france.net/rude/rudevolvi/BurrowsVol6.pdf. For some reason, Burrows takes my earlier work on Charmet to be "a highly misleading" account of an adventurous specialist in forbidden books, although my essay on Charmet published several years ago on my website, robertdarnton.org, stresses Charmet's caution and the relatively small proportion of forbidden books in his trade. Burrows's own interpretation makes Charmet out to be a bookseller who specialized overwhelmingly in religious literature. Unfortunately, however, he studied the wrong Charmet—the printer, Jean-Félix, rather than the bookseller, Charles-Antoine—and therefore reached a conclusion that is the opposite of what the evidence indicates. By drawing on records of inspections of bookshops at the time when dealers were having their pirated editions stamped in conformity with the edicts of August 30, 1777, Burrows came up with the unsurprising conclusion that Jean-Félix carried a large proportion of religious works. He found that Charles-Antoine Charmet, the subject of my study, had none at all in his stamped stock. Moreover, religious books accounted for only 5 percent of the stamped stock of the only other important bookseller in Besançon, Lépagnez cadet, who also traded heavily with the STN. As elsewhere in France, the small-scale, local dealers restricted their trade largely to devotional and ephemeral literature, leaving the sale of current fiction and nonfiction (the rough equivalent of what are known today as "trade books") to the one or two booksellers in their town who ordered books on a large scale. For a detailed discussion of these issues, see my essay, "Diffusion and Confusion in the Study of Enlightenment," forthcoming by H-France.

2. Archives municipals de Besançon, GG 189, f. 28. I am grateful to Hervé Le Corre for supplying this information to me.

3. In fact, as the STN's "*Livres des commissions*" (a register of orders and shipments) show, Charmet ordered many more copies of the *Histoire philosophique* during his visits to the STN. Such orders, made in person by booksellers located near Neuchâtel, were exceptional, and they do not appear in the booksellers' correspondence. Unfortunately, the "*Livres des commissions*" only cover the period 1774–1784; and for reasons of consistency, I have compiled statistics only from the letters of the booksellers. Therefore, the results do not correspond perfectly with all the books that Charmet purchased from the STN.

4. Archives municipals de Besançon, GG 237, f. 2, information supplied by Hervé Le Corre.

5. For a transcription of Mallet's confession and background on this affair, see the section on Mallet on the website robertdarnton.org.

6. Lépagnez signed his letters as "Lépagnez cadet" without giving his first name. The *Almanach de la librairie* of 1781 lists two booksellers named Lépagnez, Claude-Joseph and Dominique, but it does not indicate which one was the younger.

7. Veny to STN, December 31, 1781, and the contract between Veny and the STN dated February 4, 1782, which contains details about the route the shipments would take, in Veny's dossier in the STN archives.

8. Péchey to STN, March 14, 1783.

Chapter 13

1. Archives de l'État: État civil de Neuchâtel, mariages, EC158. Archives de l'État, notarial registry F9 and F10 (registry of Jean-Jacques Favarger), transactions recorded on August 26, 1779; January 28, 1780; November 20, 1782; December 10, 1783; June 24, 1795; and November 30, 1796. Also registry B654 (registry of Claude-François Bovet), transactions recorded on July 13, 1776; May 13, 1777; and October 21, 1777. Favarger is a common name in the Neuchâtel area, and it is difficult to identify documents concerning Jean-François, the STN's clerk and *commis voyageur*. Some additional information might turn up, but I consulted the registers of the most important notaries during the years 1769–1789—namely, Simon-Pierre Andrié, Jean-Henri Berthoud, François Bonhôte, Jean-Frédéric Bosset, Abram Bourgeois, Claude-François Bovet, Henri Breguet, Jacques Clottu, David Colin, Samuel Monvert, Pierre-David Courvoisier, Louis-Frédéric Duplan, Jean-Jacques Favarger, Guillaume-Pierre d'Ivernois, and Guillaume Jeannin. In a letter to the STN of March 15, 1780, Ostervald and Bosset, who were then on a business trip to Paris, warned that Favarger should not let his interests in his business interfere with his work for the STN.

2. For a survey of the literature and a discussion of the problems of measuring French book production before the nineteenth century, see my essay originally published as "Reading, Writing, and Publishing in Eighteenth-Century France: A Case Study in the Sociology of Literature," *Daedalus* (Winter 1971): 214–256, and reprinted in my *Literary Underground of the Old Regime* (Cambridge, Mass.: Harvard University Press, 1982), 167–208. Further information is available in the section "Literary Demand: Sources and Methods" on the website robertdarnton.org. On the inadequacy of the registers of the Stationers' Company, see D. F. McKenzie, *Making Meaning: "Printers of the Mind" and Other Essays* (Amherst: University of Massachusetts Press, 2002), chapters 4 and 5. On the unrepresentative aspects of the Frankfurt and Leipzig book fair catalogs, see Reinhard Wittmann, "Die frühen Buchhändlerzeitschriften als Spiegel des literarischen Lebens," *Archiv für Geschichte des Buchwesens* 13 (1973): 614–932; and Reinhard Wittmann, *Geschichte des Deutschen Buchhandels* (Munich: C. H. Beck, 1991), 111.

3. I have developed this argument at length in *Censors at Work: How States Shaped Literature* (New York: Norton, 2014). See also the excellent study by Raymond Birn, *Royal Censorship of Books in Eighteenth-Century France* (Stanford: Stanford University Press, 2012). The edicts of August 30, 1777, were an attempt, among other things, to reform earlier legislation that favored the Parisian booksellers guild, and they did indeed stimulate the reprinting of books whose privileges had expired; but I have found little evidence of a revival of publishing in the provinces between 1777 and 1789.

4. As an example of the economic concerns of the French administrators of the book trade, see Chrétien-Guillaume de Lamoignon de Malesherbes, *Mémoires sur la librairie*, ed. Roger Chartier (Paris: Imprimerie nationale, 1994; text composed in 1759), 85–86.

5. The archives of the STN contain a large number of the catalogs of other Swiss publishers, and still more catalogs can be consulted in the Bibliothèque nationale de France, the Newberry Library in Chicago, and other libraries. Although I have consulted these catalogs often, I have not mined them for statistics. A systematic study would be very revealing.

6. See Wittmann, *Geschichte des Deutschen Buchhandels*, chapters 3 and 4; and Johann Adolf Goldfriedrich, *Geschichte des deutschen buchhandels vom beginn der fremdherrschaft bis zur reform des Börsenvereins im neuen Deutschen Reiche* (Leipzig, 1886–1909), vol. 3.

7. I have developed this argument more fully in "The Science of Piracy: A Crucial Ingredient in Eighteenth-Century Publishing," *Studies on Voltaire and the Eighteenth Century* 12 (2003): 3–29.

8. Detailed statistics can be consulted on the website robertdarnton.org. In order to avoid misleading comparisons, the titles of the STN editions are set off in the statistical tables by colored fonts, and the lists of books most in demand are given in two forms: a list that includes books published by the STN along with those in its general stock and a list that excludes the STN editions.

9. STN to Astori of Lugano, April 15, 1775, archives of the STN.

10. Widow Charmet to STN, August 16, 1784, archives of the STN.

11. I have published a detailed study of one such bookseller, Bruzard de Mauvelain in "Trade in the Taboo: The Life of a Clandestine Book Dealer in Prerevolutionary France," in *The Widening Circle: Essays on the Circulation of Literature in Eighteenth-Century Europe*, ed. Paul J. Korshin (Philadelphia: University of Pennsylvania Press, 1976), 11–83.

12. These criticisms apply especially to *The French Book Trade in Enlightenment Europe, 1769–1794*, ed. Simon Burrows (2012), online at http://fbtee.uws.edu.au.

13. See Giles Barber, "The Cramers of Geneva and Their Trade in Europe Between 1755 and 1766," *Studies on Voltaire and the Eighteenth Century* 30 (1964): 377–413; and Georges Bonnant, "La librairie genevoise dans la péninsule ibérique au XVIIIe siècle," *Genava* 9 (1961): 104–124.

14. See Goldfriedrich, *Geschichte des deutschen buchhandels*, vol. 3; and Wittmann, *Geschichte des deutschen buchhandels*.

15. See Jeffrey Freedman, *Books Without Borders in Enlightenment Europe: French Cosmopolitanism and German Literary Markets* (Philadelphia: University of Pennsylvania Press, 2012), chapter 1.

16. See Robert Darnton, *The Business of Enlightenment: A Publishing History of the Encyclopédie, 1775–1800* (Cambridge, Mass.: Harvard University Press, 1979).

17. For a detailed critique of this study, see my review essay, "The French Book Trade in Enlightenment Europe, 1769–1794," *Reviews in History* (December 2012), http://www.history.ac.uk/reviews/review/1355.

18. In account books known as *livres de commission*, the STN's clerks recorded the orders on the left (verso) page of the register and the shipments on the right (recto) page. The disparities between the two facing pages demonstrate that the STN often failed to fill an entire order. In the records of the eighteen booksellers, however, the match between the orders and the sales was usually quite close. Charmet presents a particular problem, because he sometimes traveled to Neuchâtel and placed his orders in person. Therefore, they do not show up in his correspondence and in the statistics compiled from his letters.

19. The dossiers of the other Swiss publishers include 631 letters from the Société typographique de Berne; 223 from the Société typographique de Lausanne in addition to 151 separate letters from its astute director, Jean-Pierre Heubach, and 83 from his associate, Jean-Pierre Bérenger; 421 from François Grasset of Lausanne; 207 from Barthélémy Chirol of Geneva; 130 from Jean Abram Nouffer of Geneva; and 75 from C. A. Serini of Basel.

20. This is not the place to include a bibliography of this large subject, but the reader can follow up the numerous references in two collective works: *Cinq siècles d'imprimerie genevoise*, ed. Jean-Daniel Candaux and Bernard Lescaze (Geneva: Société d'histoire et d'archéologie, 1981); and *Aspects du livre neuchâtelois*, ed. Jacques Rychner and Michel Schlup (Neuchâtel: Bibliothèque publique et universitaire, 1986).

21. Gosse's dossier contains fifty-nine letters, Boubers's thirty-five, and Plomteux's fifteen.

22. See François Furet, "La 'librairie' du royaume de France au 18e siècle," in *Livre et société dans la France du XVIIIe siècle*, vol. 1 (Paris: La Hay, Mouton & Co., 1965), 7–14; and Robert Estivals, *La Statistique bibliographique de la France sous la monarchie au XVIIIe siècle* (Paris: La Hay, Mouton & Co., 1965), 213–291. The estimate of thirty thousand new titles for the forty years before 1790 is probably high, because many requests for *privilèges*, *permissions du Sceau* (an authorization like a privilege but one that did not convey the exclusive right to sell a book), and *permissions tacites* did not result in actual publications. Also, many of the requests concerned proposals to reprint works whose *privilèges* had expired. There are no records for casual authorizations such as *simples tolérances* and *permissions de police*, but they mainly concerned ephemera. Of course, all of the official records exclude illegal literature. The STN sold a great many books that would not have been submitted for any kind of authorization by the state, but it pirated an even larger number of legal and quasi-legal works. It also sold works published before it went into business, but it concentrated heavily in the trade in recent literature.

23. *The New York Times* bases its list on reorders of selected booksellers, not on actual sales, and Bookscan relies on barcode sales at selected retailers.

24. For the view that intellectual engagement was a decisive factor in publishing and the book trade during the eighteenth century, see Elizabeth Eisenstein, *Grub Street Abroad: Aspects of the French Cosmopolitan Press from the Age of Louis XIV to the French Revolution* (Oxford: Clarendon, 1992). I find little evidence for that view, although I agree that there were a few publishers that specialized in works of the Enlightenment. See Raymond Birn, *Pierre Rousseau and the Philosophes of Bouillon* (Geneva: Institut et Musée Voltaire, 1964).

25. Bosset to STN, April 1, 1780, in the dossier of Bosset de Luze, archives of the STN. For biographical sketches of the STN's partners, see *Biographies neuchâteloises*, ed. Michel Schlup, vol. 1 (1996), 197–201; and *L'Edition neuchâteloise au siècle des Lumières: La Société typographique de Neuchâtel (1769–1789)*, ed. Robert Darnton, Jacques Rychner, and Michel Schlup (Neuchâtel: Bibliothéque publique et universitaire, 2002), 67–70.

26. Although I have tallied the number of copies in the orders for all of the books discussed below, I decided not to include the numbers in my discussion of them. To do so would be to give a specious impression of precision, particularly as the numbers are relatively small. Therefore, I have limited my remarks to general indications of the extent of the demand. Any reader can consult the exact numbers on the website.

27. I have described the process of cobbling books out of fragments of information in "Blogging, Now and Then (250 Years Ago)," *European Romantic Review* 24 (2013): 255–270.

28. I developed this argument most fully in *The Forbidden Best-Sellers of Prerevolutionary France* (New York: Norton, 1995), a book that was limited to

strictly illegal literature and that did not pretend to characterize the book trade in general.

29. As explained in chapter 10, Malherbe and the STN agreed on an enormous order of "philosophical books" at a large discount when the STN was clearing its stock of such literature. Because that order did not represent demand in the normal course of Malherbe's affairs, it has been excluded from the statistics.

30. Because the publications of d'Holbach and his friends were shrouded in secrecy, it is difficult to identify all the books and authors associated with the group, whose members did not all embrace the outright materialism and atheism of d'Holbach himself. See Alan Kors, *D'Holbach's Coterie: An Enlightenment in Paris* (Princeton: Princeton University Press, 1976).

31. After discounting Malherbe's orders and excluding the STN's edition of *Système de la nature*, the demand for the Holbachean works can be ranked as follows: *Le Christianisme dévoilé* (orders for a total of seventy-seven copies), *La Politique naturelle* (forty-four copies), *La Contagion sacrée* (thirty-two copies), *De la Cruauté religieuse* (thirty-one copies), and *Le Bon sens* (twenty-three copies). The other Holbachean works were ordered for fewer than twenty copies each.

32. The subscriptions sold by the STN appear on the master list, but they belonged to the business of the quarto enterprise as a whole, as I have recounted in *The Business of Enlightenment: A Publishing History of the Encyclopédie, 1775–1800* (Cambridge, Mass.: Harvard University Press, 1979).

33. Unfortunately, the orders do not consistently contain information on the editions of individual works, including the number of volumes they contained, which often varied from edition to edition. In some cases, that information can be supplied by standard biographies, but the identification of editions involves too much guesswork to be included in the statistics compiled from the orders.

34. The main exception was a fairly substantial number of orders for *Nouvelles lettres anglaises, ou Histoire du chevalier Grandisson*.

35. See Lynn Hunt, ed., *The Invention of Pornography: Obscenity and the Origins of Modernity, 1500–1800* (New York: Zone, 1993). In an earlier work, *The Forbidden Best-Sellers of Pre-Revolutionary France* (New York: Norton, 1996) and its companion volume, *The Corpus of Clandestine Literature in France, 1769–1789* (New York: Norton, 1995), I tried to identify the corpus of books that were most illegal in the eyes of French officials and in the practices of booksellers. These books included large numbers of bawdy libels and obscene works that sometimes contained radical philosophical and irreligious themes. In concentrating on this largely unknown literature, I did not pretend to characterize eighteenth-century literature in general. But some of my critics have misconstrued my argument and have even made absurd claims that I have advocated a " 'pornographic' interpretation of the French Revolution" (Vivian Gruder, "The Question of Marie-Antoinette: The Queen and Public Opinion Before the French Revolution," *French History* 16 [2002]: 270).

36. Because Malherbe's orders had such a large and disproportionate number of salacious works, they would give a misleading impression about the general demand and therefore have been omitted from these calculations, just as they were in the earlier discussion on libels and atheistic books.

37. The STN published this work in association with the Société typographique de Lausanne and the Société typographique de Berne. Because it was an STN publication, it has greater weight in the statistics than do books from the STN's general stock. But there was also considerable demand for *Supplément au Dictionnaire raisonné universel d'histoire naturelle de M. Valmont de Bomare* by Philippe-Rodolphe Vicat.

38. Among the four works by Maupin that appear in the orders, the one most in demand was his *L'Art de faire le vin.*

39. *Essai sur la santé et sur l'éducation médicinale des filles destinées au mariage* by Jean-André Venel and *Traité des maladies vénériennes* by Pierre Fabre attracted substantial orders.

40. For example, *Recettes pour les maladies des chevaux* by "Chevalier" Harpur (his first name is unknown).

41. For example, *Cours de mathématiques* by Christian Wolff; *Traité d'arithmétique* by Pierre Senebier; and *L'Arithmétique, ou le livre facile pour apprendre l'arithmétique de soi-même et sans maître* by François Barrême.

42. For example, *La Science et l'art de l'équitation* by Louis-Charles Mercier du Paty de Clam; *Le Maître de la langue allemande* by Johann Christoph Gottsched, a work much in demand; and *Le Nouveau secrétaire de la Cour, contenant une instruction pour se former dans le style épistolaire* by René Milleran.

43. See the modest manual by Nicolas-Antoine Viard, *Les Vrais principes de la lecture, de l'orthographe et de la prononciation française*; the more advanced *Abrégé des principes de la grammaire française* by Pierre Restaut; and the guide to manners as well as the art of writing by René Milleran, *Le Nouveau secrétaire du cabinet, contenant des lettres sur différents sujets, avec la manière de les bien dresser; les compliments de la langue française, les maximes et conseils pour plaire et se conduire dans le monde.*

44. *Magasin des adolescents, Le Mentor modern, Nouveau magasin des jeunes demoiselles*, and *Oeuvres mêlées de Mme Leprince de Beaumont.*

45. There was large demand for Tremblay's *Instructions d'un père à ses enfants.* Other works ordered fairly often were *Les Enfants élevés dans l'ordre de la nature* by Jean-Louis de Fourcroy, *Les Hochets moraux, ou contes pour la première enfance* by Monget (first name not identified), and *L'Ami des enfants à l'usage des écoles de la campagne* by Friedrich Eberhard von Rochow.

46. For example, *Abrégé d'histoire universelle: Pour la direction des jeunes gens qui commencent cette étude* by Jacob Vernet.

47. The most important work on this much-discussed subject is Philippe Ariès, *Centuries of Childhood: A Social History of Family Life* (New York: Vintage, 1962; first French edition, 1960).

48. There was little demand for *Recherches philosophiques sur les Américains*, a speculative work on the supposed inferiority of native Americans by Cornelius de Pauw.

49. However, a large proportion of the orders for these works came from Malherbe, who catered to the market for *livres philosophiques*.

50. The STN received many orders for Servan's much-admired *Discours sur l'administration de la justice criminelle* and a fair number for his *Oeuvres diverses*. One of Servan's admirers was the future revolutionary Jacques-Pierre Brissot, who hired the STN to publish his *Théorie des lois criminelles*, which the STN marketed for him but without great success. It did not do better with *Observations sur des matières de jurisprudence criminelle* by Paolo Risi.

51. The editions marketed by the STN were collections titled *Mémoires de M. Caron de Beaumarchais, Mémoires de M. Pierre-Augustin Caron de Beaumarchais, suivis de ses oeuvres de théâtre,* and *Suite des Mémoires de M. Pierre-Augustin Caron de Beaumarchais*. The STN archives contain a great deal of information about Goezman and his writing, which deserves to be studied by some future researcher.

52. There was also large demand for Linguet's *Lettre de M. Linguet à M. le comte de Vergennes* and for his *Essai philosophique sur le monachisme*.

53. See Christophe Cave, ed., *Le règne de la critique: L'imaginaire culturel des Mémoires secrets* (Paris: Éditions Honoré Champion, 2010).

54. Other works in this large literature that also received quite a large number of orders were *Les Devoirs, statuts, ou règlements généraux des francs-maçons*, commonly attributed to a certain La Tierce; *L'Ordre des Francs-Maçons trahi* by Gabriel-Louis-Calabre Pérau; and Pérau's *Les secrets de l'ordre des francs-maçons dévoilés*. Small orders also arrived for supplementary writings such as the anonymous compilation *Recueil des chansons des francs-maçons*.

Conclusion

1. See Roger Chartier and Guglielmo Cavallo, eds., *A History of Reading in the West* (Amherst, Mass.: University of Massachusetts Press, 2003), a collection of excellent essays, which contain references to many other publications in this growing field of research. My own attempt to sketch the contours of the field is "First Steps Toward a History of Reading," first published in the *Australian Journal of French Studies* 23 (1986): 5–30, and reprinted in *The Kiss of Lamourette: Reflections in Cultural History* (New York: Norton, 1991), chap. 9.

2. Bibliothèque nationale de France, Fonds français 22073, "Mémoire à consulter pour les libraires et imprimeurs de Lyon, Rouen, Toulouse, Marseille et Nîmes concernant les privilèges en librairie," October 15, 1776: "One can divide them [provincial booksellers] into two classes. The first includes those who print [books] or have them printed and deal in the wholesale trade—that is, between bookseller and bookseller. By means of mutual exchanges of their editions, they build up a varied stock from which the retail booksellers draw

their supplies. The second [class] is composed of those who do not produce [books] and limit their trade to those they buy. Some of these live in small cities and market towns from which they fan out into the countryside.... One could also subdivide this last class by distinguishing those who, aside from their retail sales to the public, also resell [books] to booksellers in the smallest towns.... The latter in turn resell part of their purchases to peddlers who travel about the countryside selling their wares at fairs and missionary houses."

3. Lair eventually emerged as a legal dealer by purchasing a "*brevet de libraire*." I believe there were many unofficial entrepreneurs like him, although it is impossible to calculate their number, because they do not appear in administrative archives or the *Almanach de la librairie*, which as Favarger discovered was an inaccurate guide to the population of booksellers. As a case study of one of the illegal entrepreneurs, see my monograph, "Trade in the Taboo: The Life of a Clandestine Bookseller in Provincial France," in *The Widening Circle: Essays on the Circulation of Literature in Eighteenth-Century Europe*, ed. Paul J. Korshin (Philadelphia: University of Pennsylvania Press, 1976), 11–83.

4. Ostervald to STN from Paris, February 20, 1780.

5. Billaut to STN, September 29, 1776, STN archives ms. 1122.

INDEX

Illustrations and notes are indicated by f and n following the page number.